ENTREPRENEURIAL FINANCE

ENTREPRENEURIAL FINANCE

SIMON HULME • CHRIS DREW

First published 2020 by
RED GLOBE PRESS

Red Globe Press in the UK is an imprint of Macmillan Education Limited, registered in England, company number 01755588, of 4 Crinan Street, London, N1 9XW.

Red Globe Press® is a registered trademark in the United States, the United Kingdom, Europe and other countries.

ISBN 978-1-352-00981-1 (paperback)

This book is printed on paper suitable for recycling and made from fully managed and sustained forest sources. Logging, pulping and manufacturing processes are expected to conform to the environmental regulations of the country of origin.

A catalogue record for this book is available from the British Library.

A catalog record for this book is available from the Library of Congress.

CONTENTS

Part 5 FINANCIAL CAPITAL

PREFACE

Whether you are an entrepreneur, a director, or a manager; if accounting and finance are subjects you find confusing or daunting, this book has been specifically written for you. I have had the pleasure of teaching Entrepreneurial Finance to students at UCL and other institutions for nearly a decade, and the majority of these students have had no prior knowledge of accounting, finance or any significant commercial experience.

The approach I took when teaching, and have followed in this book, is to break the topic down into small components and to deliver them in a progressive and logical manner. The structure of this book reflects that approach – a gentle spoon-feeding of the information in a fun and light-hearted way. But do not be mistaken in thinking the content is light-weight: we have explained some complex areas of accounting, and also introduced a bundle of other useful commercial knowledge. The latter not only makes the book more interesting, but also sets the context for why accounting information and good financial management is so powerful when applied correctly.

The final section of the book draws all the knowledge together, and sets out how it is possible to drive the profitability higher in a number of very practical ways.

A few points to help you navigate the book:

- We have progressively introduced you to the many powerful financial ratios, inserting these where appropriate throughout the book. However, Appendix 2 contains a highly comprehensive list of them all in one place for easy reference.
- As new terms are introduced, we have put these in **bold**. A full definition of their meaning is included in a comprehensive glossary.
- We have made reference to numerous small and large companies and offer our thanks to those who have provided information to us. In the case of our former business, the greeting card publisher Card Connection Limited, we have made an adaptation of some of the original accounts. Where we have done this, we refer to the business as Tulip Greeting Cards, rather than the company's actual name.
- In many cases we give examples from spreadsheets we have created. These, along with additional lecture resources for teachers, are available for readers to download from www.macmillanihe.com/Hulme-EntrepreneurialFinance.

This book has been primarily written by myself, with the invaluable support of my friend, former business partner, and co-author Chris Drew. For simplicity we have used the term 'we' in most situations, but these experiences or comments may have come from just one of us, or both of us.

Please feel free to get in touch should you have any comments or ideas concerning entrepreneurial finance, and in particular this book. We would be delighted to hear from you and to answer any questions you may have. You can contact us at efbook@simonhulme.co.uk.

I would like to express my sincere thanks to the many people who have made this book possible and are listed in our acknowledgements. In addition, a special thanks the many hundreds of students I have taught over the years, who have been a pleasure to teach and get to know, and have inspired me to create this book.

Simon Hulme
January 2020

ACKNOWLEDGEMENTS

We would like to express our sincere thanks to the numerous individuals who have helped with the journey of creating this book.

From UCL: Nick Bertalan, Dave Chapman, Bert De Reyck, Itxaso Del Palacio Aguirre, Gillian Lacey-Solimar, Barry McCarthy, Alan Parkinson, and Amy Valentine.

From companies featured in this book: Richard Canterbury, Tim Evans, Joyce de Haas, Raissa de Haas, Darren Hall, Zain Jaffer, Edward Perry, James Perry, and James Wilkinson.

Other help and guidance: Nicki Dann, Ruth Davis, Greg Gillespie, Miruna Girtu, Michael Johnson, James Laslett, Martha Mador, Dwain Reid, Luke Smith, Janja Song, and David Stokes.

From Red Globe Press: Jon Finch, Verity Rimmer, Amy Brownbridge, and Krishna Kumar.

And finally, our families: Our wives Gill Hulme and Margaret Drew; and children Katherine Hulme, Annabel Hulme, and Florence Hulme.

PART 1

INTRODUCTION

1.1 THE PURPOSE OF ACCOUNTS AND FINANCIAL MANAGEMENT

'But I'm an entrepreneur – I don't need to know about accounting and finance!'

Oh dear! If you feel your head nodding even slightly in agreement with this statement, then our first job is to disavow you of this notion – completely! That said, it is shocking how commonplace this idea, or something like it, is among those wishing to start a business. Here are some other ill-advised thoughts that budding entrepreneurs might harbour:

'Balance sheets aren't important, are they?'
'Only accountants need concern themselves with accounts.'

Even the old adage, *cash is king*, should be taken with a large helping of salt. *Cash* is, of course, important. However, if we are really going to crown it *king*, then we must consider *profit* to be queen – and, arguably, more powerful.

The good news is that the fact you have picked up this book suggests you are at least halfway to scrapping such ideas as these – if you ever had them in the first place.

The other good bit of news is that this book is not just about financial statements and raising capital. Throughout the book, we will bring you a healthy dose of commercial knowledge and useful insights based on direct experiences, demonstrating in *highly practical ways* how you can use financial information to drive profitability and create wealth. In the final chapter, we describe what we think a *Five-Star Financially Intelligent* business looks like. Our goal with this book is to take you on a fun, illuminating journey to this, hopefully fruitful, destination.

Business Survival Rates

But, first, some sobering thoughts: you may be shocked to learn that fewer than half of all businesses survive beyond their fifth year from launch, and only about a third of businesses make it beyond their tenth anniversary.

The actual survival rates may vary over time, and between different sample groups, but the pattern remains essentially the same, as illustrated in the chart below. In all three datasets illustrated, the survival rate is below 50% after 5 years and below one-third after 10 years.

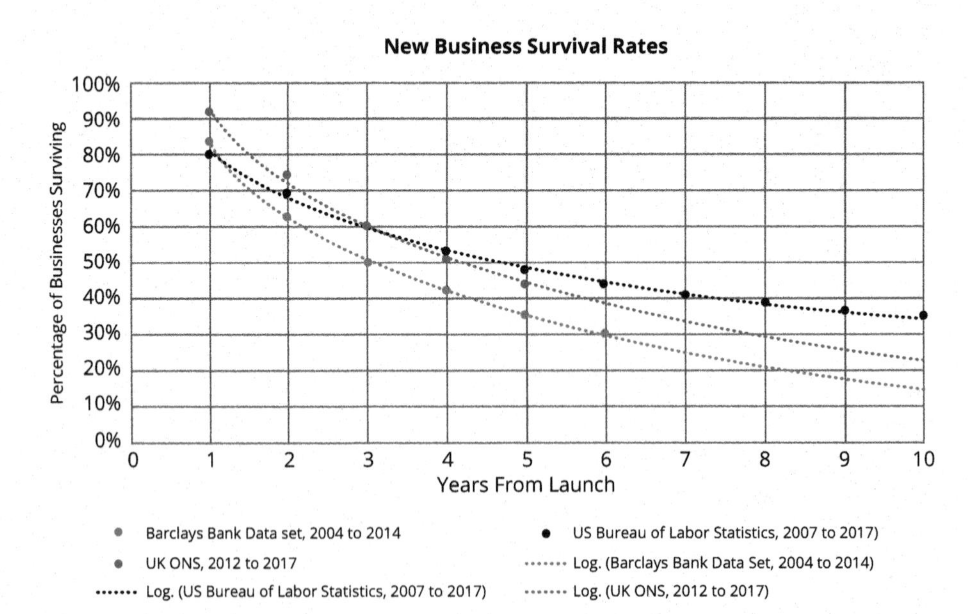

Please do NOT let these statistics put you off, though! As most true entrepreneurs will tell you, failure, and the ability to handle it, are part and parcel of the life of an entrepreneur – there are whole books written on the subject. What we are concerned about in this book is helping you to steer clear of those causes of failure that can be avoided for want of a sound understanding of your business's accounts and finances.

Reasons That Businesses Fail

Many studies have been done on why businesses fail, and many reasons have been identified. However, the key reasons that concern us in this book are:

- **Inadequate planning:** You will find lack of planning or inadequate planning at, or near, the top of most lists of reasons given for business failure. This can encompass shortcomings in any or all aspects of business planning – from marketing planning to resource planning to staffing planning – but the key area of planning that is relevant to this book, and which is all too often neglected, is, of course, financial planning.

'If you fail to plan, you are planning to fail' – Benjamin Franklin. As he got a prime spot on the US $100 bill, he may be worth listening to!

- **Over-trading:** This is where a business expands faster than its ability to manage that rate of growth. It is closely related to the next item on the list.
- **Under-capitalisation:** This is where a business fails to secure sufficient funding to allow the business to establish and grow properly. It is often a result of inadequate planning.
- **Inadequate stock control:** In some businesses, **stock** (inventory) can represent the most significant use of capital. If it is not managed properly the result can be a fatal drain on financial resources (i.e. cash), and low margins. It is, therefore, linked to the next item.
- **Inadequate understanding/control of gross margins:** As will be discussed in Chapter 2.2, a healthy gross margin is essential to business success. To help achieve this, it is important for the management of the business to have a good, detailed handle on what is driving its margins.
- **Inadequate control of expenses:** It is all too easy for expenses to be allowed to rise to unsustainable levels – especially in those vulnerable early years of a business's life – often with calamitous consequences.

All of the above potential contributors to business failure can be avoided (or, at least, the risks mitigated) by the early implementation of comprehensive financial planning and timely, good-quality accounts.

Accounting and Finance: What Is It All About?

The words *accounting* and *finance* are so often strung together as one phrase that it is easy to think of them as describing a single concept. Although they are clearly closely linked, they have, in fact, two quite distinct meanings – although it is arguably fair to say that accounting is a subset of finance, but not vice versa.

Accounting refers to the processes and techniques involved in recording, categorising, organising, reporting on and analysing the monetary transactions and economic events conducted by a business. Its purpose is to inform:

- **Who:** management, investors (potential or actual) and other stakeholders such as lenders, creditors, debtors, suppliers and employees
- **Why:** to allow them to make informed decisions
- **When:** at regular intervals and in a timely manner
- **About what:** the business's trading and financial performance, and financial status (including solvency and liquidity)

The methods applied, and the reporting formats used, in accounting will conform to a set of consistent and widely accepted practices and principles.

A distinction should be drawn between **management accounts** and **statutory accounts**. Although they will be based on the same underlying pool of accounting data, there may be considerable differences between them, especially in format. Management accounts are prepared, usually monthly, for the exclusive benefit of the management in performing its duties of running the business (and, possibly, a select circle of other stakeholders). Statutory accounts are prepared, usually annually (though could be quarterly for larger companies), for a wider set of stakeholders, including shareholders, lenders, tax authorities, creditors, etc. This type is subject to far more stringent rules, set by an external regulatory body and governing methodology and presentational format.

Finance relates to the wider aspects of the financial management of a business, encompassing the above but also involving:

- The efficient management of financial resources
- The procurement and deployment of capital
- Financial planning and forecasting
- Assessment and management of risk
- Budgeting
- Cash management

The ability to manage the financial aspects of the business – even if delegated – is a vital part of a good entrepreneur's armoury of skills, and a sound understanding of the practices and outputs of the accounting function are a necessary part of this.

A final – perhaps, galvanising – thought: we have met and mentored *hundreds* of entrepreneurs over the years. All the successful ones had one thing in common: *they possessed, or quickly acquired, a good level of financial intelligence*, i.e. a profound understanding of at least the profit & loss and cash flow statements. Whilst there will be some entrepreneurs who *have* been successful despite not having this knowledge... we genuinely can't recall having met any!

Accounting and Finance

- Financial control and planning are essential features of every business, and, if done properly, will greatly reduce the risk of failure.
- Accounting predominantly relates to the collection of the financial data of the business (sales, costs, etc.) and turning it into meaningful financial reports (i.e. accounting statements).
- Finance predominately relates to the sourcing and application of capital within the business.

1.2 SETTING THE SCENE

The Concept of Double Entry

It all began with an Italian monk called Friar Luca Pacioli, over 500 years ago. This was no ordinary monk, though – he was a mathematics genius. He even taught Leonardo da Vinci, so he must have been good. Incredibly, the method he developed and codified all that time ago is exactly the same as that used by businesses, large and small, all over the world to this day – quite an achievement!

At the heart of this system is a simple idea: that the total of funds *used* must always be equal to the total of funds *sourced*. Any difference between the two indicates a discrepancy – the bane of every accountant's life. Incidentally, we use the word 'funds' here in its widest possible meaning – i.e. not just money, but any measure of value. We also use the word 'used' in the widest possible sense – for instance, not just used as in spent, but used as in deployed but still available as a resource to the business.

The logical extension of this idea is that any transaction must inevitably be recorded by *two* entries: first, what happened to the money; and, second, where did it come from. Hence, we call the system, **double entry**.

This simple idea also leads us to the fundamental equation that lies at the heart of all accounting processes:

Funds Used = Funds Sourced

Accountants use special words for each side of this equation. Entries on the left-hand side, funds used, are called **debits**, and entries on the right-hand side, funds sourced, are called **credits**. So, we can reconsider the equation as, simply:

Debits = Credits

Historic Images / Alamy Stock Photo
Image: Jacopo de' Barbari – Portrait of Fra Luca Pacioli and an Unknown Young Man

'A person should not go to sleep at night until the debits equal the credits' – Friar Luca Pacioli (clearly not much of a party-animal, but he knew how to keep good accounts).

Why these particular words have come to refer to the two sides of this equation, we will not speculate about here – even accountancy historians (yes, apparently there are such people) cannot agree on this – but, once you have got this concept firmly embedded in your mind, you will be well equipped to navigate the tricky notion that sometimes debits are negative and credits are positive, but at other times it is the exact opposite, depending on the circumstances.

You will learn more about the practical application of debits and credits as we explore other aspects of accouting and finance. In the meantime, though, have a go at identifying which of the following items might represent *use of funds*, debits, or *source of funds*, credits:

- The total value of items sold in a given period of time
- Costs incurred in running the business
- Machinery used in making the product
- Stock waiting to be sold
- Money owed by customers
- Money owed to suppliers
- Money owed to the bank
- Shareholders' money invested in the business

How did you do? Remember to ask yourself in each case, *is this a use of funds, or a source of funds?* The answers should become clear below.

Types of Accounts

One of Friar Luca's brilliant insights was to divide the accounts into five broad categories, each of which can be considered to be either funds used (debits) or funds sourced (credits). Here they are listed accordingly:

Funds Used (Debits)

- **Expenses** – funds *used* in the sense that they are spent
- **Assets** – funds *used* in the sense that they are deployed for ongoing use

Funds Sourced (Credits)

- **Revenue** – funds *sourced* from the sale of goods and services, or other revenue
- **Liabilities** – funds *sourced* from third parties who have loaned money or provided goods or services on credit
- **Share capital** (also known as equity or shareholders' funds) – funds *sourced* from shareholders, either by injecting new share capital or by the retention of past profits

Hopefully, the answers to the challenge posed above now become clearer!

Financial Statements

The key outputs of the accounting process are the 'holy trinity' of financial statements:

- **The balance sheet** shows the residual balances of all the debits and credits at a particular *moment* in time, itemised by the various categories of assets, liabilities and equity. It represents a snapshot of a company's financial affairs at that moment.

- **The profit & loss statement** shows all accrued revenues and expenses during the course of a defined *period* of time. It describes the trading and profit-generating performance of a company in that particular period.
- **The cash flow statement** accounts for how cash has moved through the company, also over a defined period of time. There are two methods that can be used – **direct** or **indirect** – which we shall explore in more detail in Chapter 4.1.

While each of these has a distinct purpose in its own right, they all form part of a unified and integrated whole. Focus on one, or even just two, of these and you will fall short of a comprehensive picture of the business's finances and operating performance. Think of them as the legs on a three-legged stool: take one away and it will fall over!

Their individual and collective importance is such that we have dedicated a separate chapter to each. If you have struggled to understand the above, please don't worry. We will take you through each statement in a slow and progressive fashion and we will do our very best to ensure you understand it all in due course.

The Accounting Equation

Now we can see that each of the five types of account listed earlier can be assigned to either the balance sheet or the profit and loss statement, and, combining this with our new-found understanding of which is a debit and which is a credit, we can summarise the entire system in the following table:

	Debits	Credits
Balance Sheet	• Assets	• Liabilities • Equity
Profit & Loss	• Expenses	• Revenue

Remember that the total of the debit column must always equal the total of the credit column. So, basic algebra tells us that if we move, say, the liabilities to the left-hand column, we must change its sign from positive to negative in order for the equation to hold true. Likewise, if we move the expenses to the right-hand column, we must also change its sign from positive to negative.

Let's do that! Let's move expenses over to the right-hand column, so now the table is as follows:

	Debits	Credits
Balance Sheet	• Assets	• Liabilities • Equity
Profit & Loss		• Revenue • *minus* Expenses

You might now spot that revenue minus expenses is, in fact, profit for the period. And profit for the period belongs to the shareholders, so it's part of their equity. That means we can simplify the whole equation to:

$$\text{Assets} = \text{Liabilities} + \text{Equity}$$

This is known as the **accounting equation**, the significance of which we will explore in Chapter 3.2.

Cash Versus Accrual Accounting

You might think that a simple way to keep a tally on our day-to-day transactions is just to add up what we have received (cash in), and deduct what we have paid out (cash out). This method, known as **cash accounting**, might have a place in some basic situations but, unfortunately, for most accounting purposes it is too simplistic. The result would be a poor guide to what is really going on in the business because it makes no allowance for the fact that value (whether debit or credit) can increase, or accrue, even if there is no actual exchange of money at that particular moment in time.

To deal with this issue, we need to turn to the method known as **accrual accounting**, and it is this approach to accounting that we address throughout this book.

It is best explained by a simple example. Imagine we have just sold a widget for £10. If the widget had been sold for cash, the cash accounting method would accurately reflect what has happened. However, what if we have allowed our customer 30 days in which to pay? We know we have made the sale, because we have delivered the goods and the customer has undertaken to pay £10 for them, but we have not yet actually received that money so we cannot post the transaction as cash in. The answer is that we need to make what is known as an *accrual* posting. We register the sale as a *source* of funds (i.e. a credit, as described above), and we also register that this money is yet to be received, so we register that as a *use* of funds (i.e. a debit) to the balance of the amounts that we are owed – i.e. an asset.

In short, under accrual accounting events are recorded when they become economically significant to the business – not necessarily when cash changes hands. For sales, this is when the goods are delivered or a service is completed. For expenses, this is essentially when they are incurred. We explore this in more detail in Chapter 2.4.

The Basic Principles of Accounting

As described above, the fundamental purpose of preparing accounts and financial statements is to *inform*, which means that those accounts and statements must represent a *true and fair view* of the financial affairs of the business. In order to achieve this, companies must adhere to a widely-recognised set of standards that govern the way accounts are prepared and presented. These standards are set by the particular regulatory body or regime in each country, and will define a set of principles and practices that must be adopted to ensure compliance. They are commonly referred to as **Generally Accepted Accounting Principles**, or **GAAP** for short (pronounced 'gap').

Generally Accepted Accounting Principles

Please mind the GAAP! The principles dictate how we produce our accounts.

Generally speaking, the larger the company, and the more stakeholders that are involved, the more rigorous the standards are, and the more diligently applied. Publicly quoted companies face the most rigorous standards.

Different countries may have slight variations in the particular standards adopted, but, by and large, the most important principles are universal. In fact, many countries, including the United Kingdom, have adopted a common framework, known as International Financial Reporting Standards (IFRS).

The six key accounting principles are:

1. **The Accrual Principle** is concerned with the idea that value (whether debit or credit) can increase (or accrue) without there necessarily being an exchange of money. It goes to the heart of accrual accounting and can be divided into two subsidiary principles: revenue recognition and matching. **The Revenue Recognition Principle** defines when a sale should be recognised and recorded in the accounts, typically at the point when value is delivered to the customer. **The Matching Principle** specifies that all costs arising directly from sales must be recorded in the same period as the corresponding sale, and that all other expenses (i.e. not necessarily directly linked to sales) should be recorded in the period in which the good or service in question is consumed by the business.

2. **The Prudence Principle** demands that, when making a judgement call between two or more otherwise legitimate values or methodologies, the company should choose the more cautious (or prudent) option, such that profit or balance sheet values would be lower as a result.

3. **The Materiality Principle** allows that, if the result of recording or tracking a transaction or correcting a discrepancy is likely to be insignificant (or immaterial) to decision-making (whether by management or other stakeholders), or the cost of gathering the information outweighs the benefit, then it can be overlooked.

4. **The Consistency Principle** specifies that accounting principles, assumptions and methodologies must remain consistent across a set of accounts and between accounting periods.

5. **The Going Concern Principle** states that a company's accounts should be prepared on the assumption that it will continue as an active trading concern for the foreseeable future. For instance, stock can be valued in the balance sheet on the basis that it will be sold in the normal course of the business rather than in a 'fire sale'.

6. **The Objectivity Principle** states that, as far as possible, the financial records and statements of a business should be free of bias (i.e. objective), reliable and verifiable.

Setting the Scene

- The basis of accounting comes from Friar Luca Pacioli, who invented the concept of double entry book-keeping over 500 years ago. And we still use it today!
- Debits and credits can be horribly confusing, but it will help if you can master the notion that debits are the *application* of funds, whilst credits are the *source* of funds, and that debits and credits must always add up to the same number.
- Cash accounting is dangerously simplistic, and will not give a true and fair picture of the profitability of a business in any given accounting period. To achieve this properly, we need to adopt accrual accounting principles.
- Internationally, there are Generally Accepted Accounting Principles (GAAP), and the United Kingdom has adopted the International Financial Reporting Standards (IFRS) framework, which follows these principles.
- There are 6 key principles that must be followed to ensure that accounts give a 'true and fair view' of the financial status of a business.

PART 2

PROFIT & LOSS

2.1 THE PROFIT & LOSS STATEMENT

The Vital Importance of the Profit & Loss Statement

When it comes to operating a business, understanding the **profit & loss statement** is nothing short of critical. It will tell you whether you are generating profit or consuming wealth. If you are generating profit, ultimately this should become cash, whilst if you are losing money cash will disappear (and/or debts will rise).

By having a clear understanding of what is happening, you are then able to make better decisions about how the business is operated. But not having this information – or not understanding it – is like driving in the dark without headlights. An accident is likely to quickly follow.

The profit & loss statement may also be referred to as the profit & loss *account*, or the P&L account or, simply, the P&L. In the United States, it is called the *income statement*.

The Profit & Loss Statement Is for a Period of Time

It is important to understand that a statement is always for a specific period of time. In this respect, it is like a video – a recording of what has happened from one point in time to another. The time period can be for a month, quarter, or year.

Most companies produce monthly management accounts – as the name suggests these are just for the management to understand what is happening in the business. Management accounts may be produced by either an internal or an external accountant.

Companies are required by law to produce annual accounts. These are produced by external accountants (e.g. KPMG, PwC, etc.) and filed with the UK Government at Companies House. For larger businesses, these have to be audited, i.e. an external firm of accountants has checked a sample of the accounting data to ensure that it is true and fair.

Companies listed on stock markets will typically report interim results every quarter or every six months and produce a full audited report annually.

A profit & loss statement is like a video – it is a recording of what has happened over a period of time.

Simple Profit & Loss Statement

Imagine a business that had managed to sell 100 iPhone cases at £15 each on the web. The only costs the business faced were the cost of the cases, which was £5 each, and the fees for promoting them were £400.

This is how the profit & loss statement would look for the example described above:

Profit & Loss Statement	£	Gross Margin
Sales	1,500	
Cost of sales	(500)	
Gross profit	**1,000**	*67%*
Advertising	(400)	
Profit before tax	**600**	*40%*

Just two levels of profit are shown here – the **gross profit**, which is the profit made after deducting the cost of the products sold, and the **profit before tax**, which is the profit made after all other trading costs.

This is, of course, an extremely simplistic example but once you have understood this you are well on your way to grasping the profit & loss statement.

Note something else. On the right-hand side, you can see two percentage margins. The first one is the gross profit margin and is calculated by dividing the gross profit in £'s by the sales in £'s:

$$\frac{£1{,}000}{£1{,}500} = 67\%$$

This number is saying: *'For every £1 of sales I make, 67p is a profit contribution towards my operating expenses and profit before tax.'* It is *not* saying: *'This is my final profit figure'* – it is just the profit made *after subtracting the cost of the goods sold.*

The profit before tax *margin* is calculated by dividing the profit before tax in £'s by the sales in £'s:

$$\frac{£600}{£1{,}500} = 40\%$$

This number is saying: *'After all my operating expenses have been taken into account, for every £1 of sales, I made a 40p final profit.'*

Finally, make a mental note that when you calculate any form of margin, the denominator (the number on the bottom of the equation) is always sales. You are continuously looking at profit levels, or cost levels, *relative to sales*.

We will look at all this in more detail in the next chapter and also explore how to calculate gross profit in service businesses.

The Profit & Loss Statement

- The profit & loss statement is a bit like a video – it is a recording of what has happened over a specified period of time.
- Management accounts are produced for internal use by the management of the business. These will typically be produced each month.
- Statutory accounts are produced by external firms of accountants (e.g. KPMG, PwC, etc.). Only larger companies are required to have an audit.
- Companies quoted on the stock market have to provide extensive information to shareholders, and they may provide interim statements (every six months or quarterly) in addition to their annual report.

The Five Levels of Profit

Above we saw two levels of profit. There are, however, five levels to understand and each offers the opportunity to look at the performance of the business in different ways. You will not necessarily see all of them at once – usually only one or two more levels are shown after gross profit, depending on the scope and purpose of the profit & loss statement.

These five levels of profit, along with two levels of revenue, are set out in the table below, with an explanation of how each line might differ from the line above.

	Name	Deducted from Line Above
Revenue	**Gross sales**	
	Net sales	• Refunds to customers • Rebates to customers • Returns, etc.
Profit	1. **Gross profit**	• Cost of sales
	2. **EBITDA**	• Operating expenses excluding depreciation, amortisation and, sometimes, other one-off or extraordinary business costs
	3. **Operating profit**	• Depreciation • Amortisation
	4. **Profit before tax**	• Interest receivable • Interest payable • Other non-operating expenses • And, *added*, other income (e.g. investment income, grants, etc.)
	5. **Profit after tax**	• Corporation tax

And here is an example of the five levels in a statement:

Profit & Loss Statement	£ '000	
Sales	8,500	
Cost of sales	(3,900)	
Gross profit	**4,600**	LEVEL 1
Operating expenses	(2,700)	
EBITDA	**1,900**	LEVEL 2
Depreciation	(350)	
Operating profit	**1,550**	LEVEL 3
Interest	(150)	
Profit before tax	**1,400**	LEVEL 4
Corporation tax	(250)	
Profit after tax	**1,150**	LEVEL 5

Again, this is a simplified statement. You can see that **operating expenses** have been shown as just one line – normally there would be several items or headings listed here. You can also see that five levels of profit are shown. The first is gross profit, and then, as items are progressively deducted, we get down to the last and final level, profit after tax.

It is worth mentioning that not all profit & loss statements will go right down to profit after tax. Management or divisional accounts[1] are likely to stop at the **operating profit** level, or profit before tax.

Confusing Terminology

As in many other situations with accounting terminology, the same thing can be described in different ways. Generally 'net profit' will mean 'net profit before tax' or 'profit before tax'. For the purposes of simplicity and clarity, we have used just one set of consistent terms throughout the book.

Note that in the United States, profit before tax can be described as *income before income taxes*. What we call **corporation tax** is called *income tax* and profit after tax can be called *net income*. This is extremely unhelpful because, in the United Kingdom, Income Tax is what employees pay from their salary in taxation!

The contrasting UK and US terms are listed in the Glossary on page 321. But do not take these as being definitive – you may well come across variances to these too.

Taxation and the Profit & Loss Statement

The very first line of the statement, **sales**, highlights an important difference between this statement and a cash flow statement. This difference centres around a type of sales tax known as **value added tax (VAT).**

The second key tax is corporation tax, which is applied to the profits the business has made. We will address this tax when we get to the end of the statement. The important thing to recognise now is that these two taxes are entirely different.

Value Added Tax (VAT)

VAT is a sales tax and is applied in a relatively uniform manner throughout the European Union. In the United Kingdom at the time of going to press, the standard rate of VAT was 20%. Prices to the consumer are quoted *including* this tax. In the United States, for example, prices are quoted excluding their sales tax, but their sales taxes are lower and vary from state to state.

So, if you buy a designer shirt in the United Kingdom for £60, the real sales price is £50. The rest is the sales tax called VAT.

Price including VAT	**£60**	
VAT (20%)	£10	
Price excluding VAT	**£50**	P&L figure

VAT does not feature in the profit & loss statement. Quite simply it is not the company's money – it belongs to Her Majesty's Revenue & Customs (**HMRC**), who collect it on behalf of the UK Government. Whilst the VAT collected does not count as revenue, and does not affect the company's profit & loss, it most definitely affects the cash flow statement. This is cash coming in ... but it will be going out again within a short period of time, when it is paid over to HMRC or offset against VAT on purchases (see below).

By the same token, suppliers to the business will add VAT to their invoices. This might seem like an additional cost, but, like VAT on sales, does not feature in the profit & loss statement and is deducted from the amount owed by the business to HMRC.

Treating VAT as if it is your own revenue is a terrible mistake. It may seem tempting to use this cash flow to help fund the business in the very short term. For example, delaying payment of VAT to HMRC may allow a business to meet its monthly payroll expenses. But this type of cash management is indicative of far worse problems in the business and is probably only delaying an inevitable subsequent collapse.

There is a worse misdemeanour than delaying VAT payments, and that is deliberately evading paying VAT. HMRC have significant legal powers – messing with them is a fast track way of landing in jail.

Taxation and the Profit & Loss Statement

- Value added tax (VAT) is a sales tax collected by companies on behalf of Her Majesty's Revenue & Customs (HMRC) in the United Kingdom. It does not feature in the company's profit & loss statement, as it is not the company's money.
- VAT does feature in the company's cash flow statement (as both cash coming in and going out). It also appears in the balance sheet if it has not yet been paid out to HMRC.
- Funding your business by delaying payment of VAT is likely to lead to financial failure in the long term.
- Corporation tax is the tax on a company's final profits and should not be confused with VAT.

Now let's get a good understanding of each of the five levels of profit …

Level 1 – Gross Profit

Gross profit is, conceptually at least, quite simple to understand. It is the profit made *specifically on the product or service* after deduction of costs arising *directly* from the purchase, manufacture, processing and delivery of the product or service, but before any other costs, known as overheads, fixed costs,[2] or operating expenses.

These operating costs would be items like marketing, warehousing, and distribution costs.

Profit & Loss Statement	£ '000	
Sales	8,500	
Cost of sales	(3,900)	
Gross profit	**4,600**	LEVEL 1
Operating expenses	(2,700)	
EBITDA	**1,900**	
Depreciation	(350)	
Operating profit	**1,550**	
Interest	(150)	
Profit before tax	**1,400**	
Corporation tax	(250)	
Profit after tax	**1,150**	

Let's go back to the designer shirt example to understand this further. We will assume that the £60 shirt is manufactured in China, and is imported to the United Kingdom as a completed item for £25 (and there are no further costs directly connected to the purchase). This amount is called the **unit cost**, or how much the product has cost. And, if we multiply that unit cost by the number of shirts we end up selling in a given period of time, we get our total **cost of sales** for that period.

So, what is the gross profit per shirt sold (unit gross profit)? Is it:

$$£60 - £25 = £35$$

or

$$£50 - £25 = £25$$

If you think it is £35, then you need to go back to the start of this chapter and really understand VAT properly. Although the sales price to the consumer is £60, from the company's viewpoint it is a £50 sale. The VAT element is *not relevant to the profit & loss statement*, and hence is not relevant to the gross profit calculation.[3]

So, as the cost of the shirt is £25, we can express the gross profit in the form of a percentage:

$$\frac{\textit{Gross Profit}}{\textit{Sales Value}} = \frac{£25}{£50} = 50\%$$

The gross profit, when expressed as a percentage, is known as the **gross margin**. Whilst there are no hard and fast rules, generally a gross margin refers to a *percentage*, and a gross profit refers to a *monetary value*.

The gross margin percentage is an *absolutely critical* **key performance indicator (KPI).** If for some reason this starts to decline, then the management of the business needs to be aware of it as early as possible, and to take appropriate action.

Gross profit may appear to be incredibly simple – it is the profit made after deducting all costs that can be directly assigned to making the product ready for sale – but what if the shirt in the example above was packaged in the United Kingdom after it was brought in from China? Would that be included in the cost of sales calculation? And what about the cost of postage if it was sent out to the consumer? *What do you think?*

Whilst there are no strict rules, generally the costs of the packaging *would* be included in the cost of sales calculation regardless of the fact it was done after the product was imported. The cost of sales can, of course, be made up of numerous costs, providing they are relevant. In this case, the packaging *would* be relevant.

With regard to the postage cost, this is less clear-cut. We would suggest it should be treated separately so the gross margin is not distorted by varying amounts of postage. Postage may also be charged on to the customer, so may be recovered.

Another complication to consider is: what if the shirts had arrived in two batches and, in the second batch, the cost of each shirt had gone up to £28? Even if you are still selling shirts from the first batch, should you continue to count your gross profit as £25 per shirt even though you know each shirt sold will cost £3 extra to replace in stock? Food for thought! This introduces the significance of the relationship between gross profit and stock valuation, which is covered in more detail later in the book.

In the next chapter, we will explore gross profit further and look at how it is calculated for a service business.

Gross Profit

- Gross profit is the profit made *directly* from the sale of the product or service. At the per-unit level, it is the selling price (excluding VAT) less the unit cost.
- When calculating gross profit, always use the sales price excluding VAT.
- What constitutes the cost of sale is not always clear-cut and is very much up to the individual company to decide.
- Gross profit is generally expressed as a monetary value, whilst gross margin is generally expressed as a *percentage*.
- The gross margin percentage is a critical key performance indicator.

Level 2 – EBITDA

EBITDA is *earnings before interest, tax, depreciation & amortisation.* That's quite a mouthful, hence shortening to EBITDA, pronounced 'ee-bit-dah'! Let's try and understand the meaning.

Profit & Loss Statement	£ '000	
Sales	8,500	
Cost of sales	(3,900)	
Gross profit	**4,600**	
Operating expenses	(2,700)	
EBITDA	**1,900**	LEVEL 2
Depreciation	(350)	
Operating profit	**1,550**	
Interest	(150)	
Profit before tax	**1,400**	
Corporation tax	(250)	
Profit after tax	**1,150**	

In essence, EBITDA is a high-level measure of the operational profitability of the business. It is looking at the profit after operating expenses, but before the specific items of depreciation/amortisation, interest and corporation tax. Or, looked at another way, it is operating profit before non-cash items such as depreciation and amortisation.

This choice of definition has become widely used since the 1980s and 1990s, particularly within the venture capital community. Its attraction is that it removes the potential distortion of non-cash accounting adjustments such as depreciation and amortisation, and excludes interest which is affected by funding choices rather than actual trading performance. However, it is a controversial measure of profit for a number of reasons, which we shall explore later in this chapter.

Operating Expenses

Firstly, let's try and understand what is meant by operating expenses, which can also be called overheads or fixed costs. These would include items such as wages, rent, advertising, vehicles, fuel, accountancy fees, legal fees, IT services, etc. Generally speaking, they are the fixed costs of operating the business, and the list will vary from business to business.

The term 'overheads' can also be used to include depreciation and interest, but in a situation where EBITDA is shown, these two particular items would be shown separately.

In determining how to treat operating expenses, we need to adhere to the **matching principle** – one of the six key principles of accounting that we outlined briefly in Chapter 1.2. We will discuss this in more detail later.

Why Exclude Depreciation/Amortisation?

Depreciation is the accounting method of allocating to a specific trading period the cost of an item that has a useful economic life of more than one year. Expenditure on items like this is known as capital expenditure (sometimes shortened to capex). The amount of the total cost that is not written off in the trading period is put on the balance sheet as an asset. So, if a manufacturer buys a machine for £10,000 that has an expected economic life of five years, it will typically divide the cost by five and charge the resulting amount, £2,000, to the profit & loss statement every year. The balance of £8,000 after the first year will appear in the balance sheet as an asset. This balance will diminish to zero over the course of the five-year expected life.

Amortisation follows the exact same principle, except in this case the asset is an intangible one (such as a patent, or goodwill).

Depreciation does not affect the ongoing cash flow of the business, as the asset has already been purchased. The purchase may, of course be financed by debt, which *does* have a cash flow implication, but that is a separate matter. However, EBITDA is getting closer to the cash generated by the business, and hence is a very real number.[4]

Let's Commit Some Fraud!

Depreciation can also be manipulated. If the depreciation rate is too low (i.e. spread over too many years), then it will artificially inflate profit before tax in the short term. Let's look at an example.

Profit & Loss Statements	£'000	£'000
	BEFORE CHANGE	***AFTER CHANGE***
Sales	18,000	18,000
Cost of sales	(9,000)	(9,000)
Gross profit	**9,000**	**9,000**
Operating expenses	(5,000)	(5,000)
EBITDA	**4,000**	**4,000**
Depreciation	(2,000)	(1,000)
Profit before tax	**2,000**	**3,000**

Here the company is making £4m at the EBITDA profit level, and with a £2m depreciation charge that leads to a £2m profit before tax. Let us imagine that the depreciation is based on £10m of capital equipment being depreciated over 5 years, i.e. £2m a year.

However, if we decided to change our depreciation period to 10 years, then the amount charged would drop to £1m a year. This has the effect of lifting our profit before tax by 50%, making us excellent business managers deserving enormous bonuses! But the truth is somewhat different – *all we've done is manipulate the figures.*

Clearly the issue here is determining what is the actual life of the capital assets. If it is 10 years, and we could justify it, then there is nothing wrong with what we've done. In fact, we're actually making it a *truer and fairer view* of the trading performance of the business. If, however, we know the life of the assets is far short of 10 years, but this method allows us to put a gloss over poor trading results, then we are committing fraud.

In the above example, such a dramatic change in our depreciation policy would be rather unsubtle and if the motivation was to manipulate performance it would be somewhat obvious. But a gradual change in our depreciation policy over a number of years, and a number of different asset types, might go unnoticed by our shareholders, with the background information lost in the formal accounting notes.

So, you can see why proponents of the EBITDA concept are so keen on it. If you were buying a company, EBITDA eliminates the potential for being deceived by the manipulation of depreciation rates. However, as we shall examine in the next section, this approach carries its own set of issues. Arguably, it is like a doctor claiming that she can eliminate the risk of heart disease – by removing your heart! That is a rather extreme analogy, but you get the idea!

Controversies and Weakness of EBITDA

The rise in the popularity of EBITDA can be traced back to the leveraged buyout mania of the 1980s, and later boosted in the dotcom bubble of the late 1990s. A nice fat EBITDA is more likely to justify a generous valuation than a skinny (or, worse still, negative) operating profit (EBIT). And therein lies its main weakness.

The greater the capital intensity of a business, the more meaningless EBITDA becomes as a measure of profitability. We were at a small networking dinner a few years ago, and the chief executive officer (CEO) of a large privately-owned premium hotel group was telling the other guests about the EBITDA performance of the company. We politely asked him what it cost to refurbish a hotel bedroom, and how many years they expected it to last. He replied that a premium bedroom cost around £80,000 to refurbish and had a life of around 12 years (we assume it would have a midlife redecoration in between as well). In addition, a hotel has enormous refurbishment costs of reception areas, corridors, dining rooms,

EBITDA is a fashionable, but imperfect, definition of profit.

bars, plus spas, gyms … the list goes on. *How could they possibly look at their performance ignoring depreciation?* Quite simply they can't.

When we pointed this out everyone around the table fell silent for a moment. They agreed – the business world has fallen in love with EBITDA, but it is most certainly not the best definition of profit.

Also, remember that the elimination of depreciation – which can easily be manipulated – does not resolve the issue of false accounting. *Almost every figure in a set of accounts can be manipulated*, either by adopting inappropriate accounting policies or by plain fraud.

Another issue with EBITDA is that it is not recognised under Generally Accepted Accounting Principles (GAAP), either in the United Kingdom or elsewhere. This means that individuals are free to play fast and loose with what it means and how it is calculated – not a good basis for a reliable measure of profit.

To conclude, EBITDA is a useful analytical tool for comparing the operating performance of a group of similar businesses or for monitoring one aspect of a single business's operating performance over time, but, otherwise, handle with care!

Level 3 – Operating Profit

Operating profit or **EBIT**, i.e. *earnings before interest and tax,* or *trading profit.* It is a useful definition of profit as it shows us the profit arising purely from the trading activities of the business.

Profit & Loss Statement	£ '000	
Sales	8,500	
Cost of sales	(3,900)	
Gross profit	**4,600**	
Operating expenses	(2,700)	
EBITDA	**1,900**	
Depreciation	(350)	
Operating profit	**1,550**	LEVEL 3
Interest	(150)	
Profit before tax	**1,400**	
Corporation tax	(250)	
Profit after tax	**1,150**	

It would be perfectly normal and acceptable to go straight from EBITDA to profit before tax, thus skipping operating profit as a separate line. In this situation, depreciation and interest would be listed as two items one after the other, without operating profit shown in between.

However, it can be argued that operating profit is perhaps the most meaningful measure of profit from a management viewpoint. It takes into account the impact of depreciation, but eliminates the cost of interest. Interest is a function of financing choices, and, therefore, a non-operating item which can have a severely distorting effect on profitability. The term operating profit (or, indeed trading profit) is a good descriptive name for a measure of profit arising purely from the operating (or trading) activities of the business.

Consider the following two companies (A and B). Take a look at their profit & loss statements, and ask yourself which is the better business? *Which one would you prefer to buy if you had the opportunity?*

Profit & Loss Statements	£'000	£'000
	Company A	***Company B***
Sales	18,000	18,000
Cost of sales	(4,000)	(4,000)
Gross Profit	**14,000**	**14,000**
Operating expenses	(12,000)	(10,000)
EBITDA	**2,000**	**4,000**
Depreciation	(1,000)	(1,000)
Operating profit	**1,000**	**3,000**
Interest	0	(4,000)
Profit before tax	**1,000**	**(1,000)**

We can see that company A is making £1m profit a year, and Company B is losing £1m a year. This is very clear-cut ... Company A is much better. There is nothing more to discuss. *Or is there...?*

Take a closer look. We can see that Company B is actually making *three times* the operating profit of Company A, but that its interest costs are so high as to cause it to make a loss. So, at an *operating level* it is very profitable relative to sales – and possibly a more attractive proposition, stripped of its debt burden, than Company A. But at a profit before tax level it looks far worse.

What Question Might You Now Want to Ask?

The key question now is why Company B has such high interest costs. *Is it related to the operation of the business, or is it a result of past mismanagement, which has left it with a legacy of debt?*

If it is the latter, then this business is in good shape but needs to reduce the debt burden. This could be done a number of ways, for example by issuing new shares or renegotiating the interest rate with the bank.

However, if the business is highly capital intensive, the enormous interest costs might result from a prior management decision to fund this capital requirement with debt. In this situation, the business may be inappropriately funded, i.e. rather than debt funding, equity funding may be more suitable. Or is it possible that the level of capital employed is unnecessarily high? Perhaps it is carrying too much stock? Or has it been slack in extending too much credit to customers? If so, these are priority issues for the management to address to improve cash flow and hence reduce debt.

Excessive debt can result in high interest charges to the profit & loss statement. This can distort the apparent profitability of a business.

Keeping the issue of capital employed in mind, let's go back to the example for a minute. We have already determined that Company B is more profitable at the operating profit level, though less profitable at the profit before tax level. But what would you think about their relative attractiveness as businesses if you then discovered that company B required £100 million of capital to generate its £3 million profit (which might explain its obvious debt problem), but Company A only required £5 million in capital? Suddenly, Company A is the favourite again!

This introduces us to another way of thinking about profitability: how much capital does the business require to generate the profits it makes. Or, put another way, how much profit does it make for every pound of capital employed? This is known as **return on capital employed** (**ROCE**).

Introducing Return on Capital Employed

Return on capital employed is an absolutely fundamental KPI ratio, and is expressed as a percentage. If, for example, the ROCE was 35% for a business, what this figure is saying to you is *'for each £1 of capital you have tied up in the business, it is giving you back 35p each year'.* As you can imagine, you can grow a business much faster (without resorting to external funding) the higher this number is, or you can take out substantially higher dividends.

Why mention this now? It's because operating profit is the profit definition used to calculate ROCE:

$$ROCE = \frac{Operating\ Profit}{Capital\ Employed}$$

So even if operating profit is not shown in some accounts, you need to be able to work backwards to create it. We will come back to return on capital employed several times during the course of this book.

Operating Profit

- Operating profit – sometimes referred to as EBIT – is an extremely good measure of the underlying trading profitability of a business, as it takes into account depreciation but eliminates the distortion of interest costs. This is particularly helpful when comparing the performance of two businesses where their debt situations are very different.
- However, it falls short of being a definitive measure of profit as far as shareholders are concerned because there are still more costs (notably interest) to be deducted.
- Despite being a very good definition of profit, it is not always shown in accounts as a separate line.
- The relationship of operating profit to capital employed is a fundamentally important KPI known as return on capital employed (ROCE).

Level 4 – Profit Before Tax

Profit before tax, also known as *PBT*, *net profit before tax,* or *earnings* is by far the most widely used profit definition. It is also, arguably, the most comprehensive and is often described as 'the bottom line figure'.

Profit & Loss Statement	£ '000
Sales	8,500
Cost of sales	(3,900)
Gross profit	**4,600**
Operating expenses	(2,700)
EBITDA	**1,900**
Depreciation	(350)
Operating profit	**1,550**
Interest	(150)
Profit before tax	**1,400** ← LEVEL 4
Corporation tax	(250)
Profit after tax	**1,150**

Why Is It the Most Comprehensive Profit Definition?

Quite simply, it is leaving nothing out other than corporation tax – it includes all operating expenses, depreciation, plus interest costs. If all these items are accounted for correctly this is a very true picture of the performance of the business. The only remaining deduction is the corporation tax incurred as a result of making this level of profit.

Profit and Loss

> **Profit Before Tax**
>
> - Profit before tax is the most widely used definition of overall profit.
> - Assuming the figures are correctly calculated, it is generally the most meaningful profit definition from a shareholder perspective as everything is taken into account.

Level 5 – Profit After Tax

Profit after tax, also known as *net profit after tax*, or *net earnings*, is the final profit level after taking into account any corporation tax liabilities. It is a measure of the increase (or decrease!) in shareholder wealth in the year, and is the pot of money left over either for retention within the business (perhaps for reinvestment), or to be paid out to shareholders in the form of a **dividend** or other method of distribution.

Profit & Loss Statement	£ '000
Sales	8,500
Cost of sales	(3,900)
Gross profit	**4,600**
Operating expenses	(2,700)
EBITDA	**1,900**
Depreciation	(350)
Operating profit	**1,550**
Interest	(150)
Profit before tax	**1,400**
Corporation tax	(250)
Profit after tax	**1,150** ◀ LEVEL 5

Corporation Tax

Corporation tax is paid on a company's **taxable profit**. If a company has not made a profit, no corporation tax will be payable. In fact, any losses incurred can be carried forward to be offset against profits in the future.

The profit before tax figure is adjusted as appropriate (in accordance with tax legislation) to arrive at the taxable profit. Broadly speaking, the main adjustment would be to add back depreciation, but to deduct capital expenditure (subject to a host of rules!).

The current rate of corporation tax in the United Kingdom is 19%[5] for nearly all businesses. If a company had a taxable profit of £100,000 (and no losses brought forward), it could expect a corporation tax liability of around £19,000. Calculations of corporation tax can be complicated and for larger companies would be done by specialist accountants.

Corporation tax is something quite different to VAT and should not be confused with it. One key point of difference is that the company's profits are very much the company's money, but a proportion has to be paid in tax. VAT, however, is never the company's money in the first place.

Corporation tax will feature near the *end* of the profit & loss statement as the final deduction to give you your profit after tax figure. If you think about it, this is the logical place for it. Until you have determined whether the company has made a profit before tax, you cannot determine whether there is a corporation tax liability or not.

Note, if a company has made losses in the past, these will be carried forward and offset against future profits. This means the company can make a profit and still not pay any corporation tax until all the losses have been fully offset.

Profit after tax is the figure used to calculate **earnings per share (EPS).** EPS is one of the primary drivers of a company's share price.

Profit After Tax

- Profit after tax comes at the very end of the profit & loss statement after corporation tax has been deducted.
- Corporation tax is the tax on a company's final profits. The profit before tax figure is adjusted to create the taxable profit. If the company does not make a profit, there will be no tax to pay.
- As always, terminology can be confusing. Note in the United States, what we call corporation tax is referred to as *income taxes*. See Glossary for more details.
- Profit after tax shows what is left over for re-investment in the business or possible distribution to shareholders.
- Dividends are the main method of distribution to shareholders. Another method is share buy back whereby the company purchases its own shares off the shareholders.

Examples of Profit & Loss Statements

You have now effectively seen the basic structure of every set of accounts, both in the United Kingdom and internationally. Whilst there will always be variations to layouts and terminology, in essence you should be able to navigate your way through most profit & loss statements.

Let's look at examples of profit & loss statements from two substantial companies.

Burberry Group Plc

Burberry is one of the world's most iconic fashion brands and a major UK company. Take a look at the statement below, which is an extract from their 2019 Annual Report. What can you observe about the layout, and deduce concerning their performance? We have added some margin percentages and changes between the two years to guide you.

Here is a summary of observations on the layout:

- We can see all the levels of profit except EBITDA. This suggests they have chosen to include depreciation & amortisation in the operating expenses. These numbers will be set out in more detail in the notes to the accounts (not shown here).
- In all other respects the format is very straightforward.

Here are some observations on the performance of the business. These are not intended to be comprehensive, but rather just to get you thinking about what you are being shown:

- We can see sales were £2.7bn for 2019, which are 0.5% down on the previous year.
- Gross margin is a healthy 68.4% and again slightly lower the previous year.

Burberry Group Plc

Group Profit & Loss Statement	**52 weeks to 30 March 2019**	**52 weeks to 31 March 2018**	**Change between years**
	£m	£m	
Sales revenue	2,720	2,733	*-0.5%*
Cost of sales	(859)	(835)	
Gross profit	**1,861**	**1,897**	*-1.9%*
Gross margin	*68.4%*	*69.4%*	
Net operating expenses	(1,424)	(1,487)	*-4.3%*
Operating profit	**437**	**410**	*6.6%*
Interest	3	2	
Profit before tax	**441**	**413**	*6.8%*
Profit before tax margin	*16.2%*	*15.1%*	
Corporation tax	(102)	(119)	
Profit after tax	**339**	**294**	*15.5%*
Earnings per share (£)	0.82	0.69	*19.4%*

- Operating expenses have been reduced by 4.3%, which have more than made up for the slight decline in gross profit. As a result, operating profit has risen by 6.6% to £437m.
- Net interest is £3.4m. Burberry has a strong balance sheet (not shown here) and is sitting on £875m of cash or cash equivalent assets. Hence it earns more in interest on these assets than it pays out on its smaller borrowings.
- Profit before tax has grown to £441m and at 16.2% of sales, can be regarded as a strong performance.
- Earnings per share, which is profit after tax divided by the number of shares in issue, has grown by 19.4% which should, in theory, have pushed their share price higher.

Netflix, Inc.

Let's now look at one of the world's most successful companies, Netflix. For the year 2019, the company had sales revenues of $20bn. Can you still understand their accounts despite their scale? Of course you can! The underlying format is the same. The biggest difference is the sheer scale of the numbers. Again, we have added some margin percentages and changes between the two years to guide you as well as used the terminology adopted in this book (which varies slightly from the actual published accounts).

Here is a summary of observations on the layout:

- Once again can see all the levels of profit except EBITDA.

Netflix, Inc.

Profit & Loss Statement	**Year to 31 December 2019**	**Year to 31 December 2018**	**Change between years**
	$m	$m	
Sales revenue	20,156	15,794	*27.6%*
Cost of sales	(12,440)	(9,968)	
Gross profit	**7,716**	**5,827**	*32.4%*
Gross margin	*38.3%*	*36.9%*	
Operating expenses			
Marketing	(2,652)	(2,369)	
Technology and development	(1,545)	(1,222)	
General and administrative	(914)	(630)	
	(5,112)	**(4,222)**	*21.1%*
	25.4%	*26.7%*	
Operating profit	**2,604**	**1,605**	*62.2%*
Interest paid	(626)	(420)	
Interest received and other income	84	42	
Profit before tax	**2,062**	**1,226**	*68.1%*
Profit before tax margin	*10.2%*	*7.8%*	
US corporate taxes	(195)	(15)	
Profit after tax	**1,867**	**1,211**	*54.1%*
Earnings per share ($)	4.26	2.78	*53.2%*

- The cost of sales will be made up of the production, or licensing, costs of their films and TV shows.
- They have simplified the reporting of their operating expenses (or overheads) into three distinct categories. These categories will include any depreciation charges.

Here are some observations on the performance of the business. Once again, these comments are not intended to be comprehensive:

- Overall sales are up by 27.6%. Given the scale of the numbers in the first place, this is an impressive performance.
- We can see the gross margin is 38.3%, which has slightly improved from the previous year.
- Their operating expenses have risen from the previous year by $890m to $5.1bn. But when looked at as a *percentage* of sales, they have actually fallen slightly in the year 2019. This suggests they have marginally improved efficiency relative to their volume of sales.

- Given the large rise in sales, and good control of gross margin and expenses, operating profit has risen sharply by 62% to £2.6bn.
- Unlike Burberry, Netflix has a substantial interest charge of $626m. But in the context of its operating profit, which covers this by over four times, it does not represent a problem to the company at the moment.
- Profits before, and after, corporation tax have also risen strongly.
- Finally, earnings per share have risen 53% to $4.26. As with Burberry, this is likely to have driven the share price higher.
- Taking an overall view of Netflix's figures, if we were shareholders, we would be delighted with the continued growth. But can you think of any statistics we might also want to be watching closely relating to the *future* performance of the business? After all, strong share price performance will be driven by *expectations* of performance as well as past performance. We would suggest keeping an eye on the growth in the number of subscribers and monitoring the subscription price. If either of these stall or decline, then the future growth in earnings per share could be undermined.

Profit & Loss Statements of Major Companies

- Have the confidence that you can understand these! The only real difference from a smaller company is the scale of the figures themselves.
- The terminology varies from business to business, and from country to country. But in essence the principles and formats are broadly the same.
- The numbered notes, if provided, give useful information in helping to understand how the figures are derived.

The Five Levels of Profit Summary

Here is a brief summary of the five levels of profit:

Level	Name	Significance	Issues
1	**Gross profit**	Provides critical information on how much profit is made *directly* from the sale of products or services. It may be that the business's management will want to drill down so they have figures for gross profit by product line, job or customer.	What constitutes the cost of sale is not always clear-cut. Hence gross profit can be calculated in several different ways.

Level	Name	Significance	Issues
2	**EBITDA** Earnings Before Interest, Tax, Depreciation & Amortisation	A fashionable measure of profitability particularly favoured by the venture capital community. It has the advantage of being the closest profit figure to the actual cash flow of a business. In addition, it eliminates any distortions from incorrect levels of depreciation.	If the business is capital intensive, leaving out depreciation makes the profit figure somewhat misleading.
3	**Operating profit**	Also known as EBIT. It is an extremely good measure of profitability as it eliminates the distortion of interest costs. It is the level of profit that reflects the overall *trading* performance of the company. This is particularly helpful when comparing the performance of two businesses where their debt situations are very different.	Where a business is extremely capital intensive and requires a large amount of debt in order to operate, ignoring the interest costs associated with this is clearly misleading.
4	**Profit before tax**	The most common definition of profit. It is generally the most meaningful as everything is taken into account.	Assuming the figures are correctly calculated, there is nothing 'bad' about this figure!
5	**Profit after tax**	Shows what is left over for re-investment in the business or possible distribution to shareholders.	Assuming the figures are correctly calculated, there is nothing 'bad' about this figure!

Notes

1. By divisional accounts we mean a subsidiary or subset of a larger company.
2. Note, though, that a proportion of fixed or overhead costs can sometimes be included as a cost of sale, especially in manufacturing businesses (e.g. factory overheads). For simplicity, we are showing them as a separate item.

3. The exception to this would be if the VAT cost could not be recovered. We will cover this eventuality later.
4. Although EBITDA is getting closer to the actual cash generated by the business, it is certainly not necessarily that figure. It does not, for example, take into account the capital expenditure that may be required to maintain the operations of the business. This is an argument for saying operating profit (EBIT) may represent a better *longer-term* indicator of the cash generated by a business.
5. For up-to-date rates and further details consult HMRC website (https://www.gov.uk/government/organisations/hm-revenue-customs).

2.2 THE IMPORTANCE OF GROSS PROFIT

Gross Profit and the Cost of Sales Calculation

Gross profit is the profit made specifically on the sale of goods or services after deduction of costs directly associated with those sales – known as the **cost of sales** (or, sometimes, **cost of goods sold**) – but before any other costs.

The cost of sales would include costs arising directly from the purchase, manufacture, processing and delivery of the goods or services sold.

The other costs to be deducted after this are known as overheads, fixed costs, or, simply, expenses. Operating expenses would include items such as marketing, warehousing, and distribution costs.

So, gross profit can be calculated by deducting the total cost of sales from total sales:

$$Sales - Cost\ of\ Sales = Gross\ Profit$$

In per-unit terms (i.e. for each product sold), this can be expressed as:

$$Selling\ Price - Unit\ Cost = Unit\ Gross\ Profit$$

In Chapter 2.1, we looked at an example of an imported designer shirt and speculated what would be included in the cost of the product. These would include all of the following:

- The cost of the shirt itself delivered into the United Kingdom
- The cost of the packaging for the end customer
- The cost of the delivery to the customer

The total cost of sales arising from these unit costs will vary according to how many shirts we actually sell to our customers, and consequently should be included in the gross profit calculation. However, as pointed out, we would also want to see the gross profit before any delivery costs to customers, so it could be advisable to consider having two levels of gross profit analysis.

Café Example

We can all understand the concept of a café business; hence we will use this for the purposes of an example. Let's consider what would be included as a cost of sales.

Cost Item	Should It Be in Cost of Sales?	Comments
Food, tea, coffee	Yes	These costs are directly related to the cost of supplying the product/service.
Rent of premises	No	This is a fixed cost that will not change regardless of how busy the café is on a particular day.
Heat & lighting	No	Although it is possible that these may vary according to how much product is sold, they would also be regarded as fixed costs.
Cost of wages	Debatable!	This is where some judgement is required. The cost of the staff who specifically prepare the food and make the tea and coffee could be included. But the cost of the wages to serve at the tables, wash up, and clean the floors would probably be regarded as a fixed cost. Given that the staff employed may carry out a variety of all these tasks, a simpler solution would be to treat *all labour costs as fixed costs*, and only the food element as a cost of sales.

So we can see that even with the simplest of businesses there will be an element of judgement in deciding what to include in the cost of sales calculation.

Service Businesses

What if we are looking at a service business instead of a product-based one?

The same principles will apply – the cost of sales is the cost of providing the service. But, again, we have to ask what is included in working out the cost of providing a service? And this is where it can get difficult and confusing.

What is included in the cost of sales calculation for a service-based business like carpet cleaning?

Let's take a further example of a carpet cleaning business. Here the company will have employees who travel to customers' premises to clean their carpets. They arrive at a customer's house in a van and clean the carpets using their own shampoos and cleaning equipment. Clearly the biggest single cost is likely to be wages.

Let's look at the different cost items and see which ones should be in the cost of sales calculation in order to determine the gross profit.

Cost Item	Should It Be in Cost of Sales?	Comments
Wages of employee who cleans the carpets	Yes	This cost is directly related to the cost of supplying the service.
Shampoo and other consumables to carry out the work	Yes	This cost is directly related to the cost of supplying the service.
Cost of the cleaning equipment	No, unless it was hired specifically for this customer.	Assuming the cleaning equipment was owned by the company, it will be depreciated over a number of years (relating to its expected life). This charge in the profit & loss statement will not vary according to each customer and would not be in the cost of sales figure. However, if it was hired specifically for this customer only, then that would be charged as a cost of sale.
Cost of van	No	Same issue as cleaning equipment.
Fuel costs to get to the specific customer	Debatable!	This is an example of a cost that could be charged as a cost of sales, or shown as an operating expense. Normally, mainly because of simplicity, all fuel costs would be shown as a single overhead sum each month and not be allocated to a specific customer. But there are no fixed rules here.
Wages of the administrator who took the booking over the phone	No	This cost would be treated as an administrative overhead. After all, if the specific customer's job had not happened, the member of staff who answered the phone would still have to be paid.
Web marketing that generated the sales enquiry	No	This cost would be treated as an administrative overhead. After all, if the specific customer's job had not happened, the member of staff who answered the phone would still have to be paid.

As a very general rule, if the cost directly correlates or occurs with the provision of the service, then it should be included. The **materiality principle** of accounting will also be relevant in making this decision. We need to ask whether the cost is significant enough to be counted and allocated to that specific job/customer. So clearly in this example, the largest item will be the wages cost, hence this has to be included. However, the cost of a single piece of paper that the customer signs to say they accept the work has been finished satisfactorily, would be ludicrous to account for in the cost of sales. It is simply immaterial. (It would, however, be included within a general operating expense relating to stationery items.)

There are other challenges though! Let us assume that during a 40-hour week the employees typically spend 20 hours cleaning carpets, 10 hours driving, 5 hours having breaks, and 5 hours doing administration or other duties. Only 50% of his/her time is directly productive. If the 20 productive hours are charged to a revenue-generating customer (i.e. a specific sale), what happens to the cost of the other 20 hours? Try and think of a solution yourself. Two suggestions are shown in Appendix 1.

Software as a Service (SaaS) Businesses

How should we treat a SaaS business model with respect to calculating their gross profit? What would be included in their cost of sales calculation?

The usual approach is to identify what activity *directly* supports the revenue. If there is a service support team, they could reasonably be treated as a cost of sales. Let's explore the logic of this: the customer is paying a monthly fee to rent the software for their usage. In order for them to do this satisfactorily, they may need support from a service desk, otherwise their ability to make it function correctly for their needs could be compromised. If the service desk was removed, then the rental of the software would not be sustainable in the long term.

What about the software development team? This is a product development function, and would not normally be treated as a cost of sales. The cost of this development team would normally be treated as an operating expense. In some circumstances it may even be capitalised and treated as an asset, which is then depreciated over time.

Other items that could be included in the cost of sales for a SaaS business model could be hosting costs and credit card processing fees (if applicable). These costs vary with the volume the business is doing.

Allocating Some Fixed Costs to Cost of Sales

In the above examples, we have made clear our views that the fixed cost elements would *not* be included in the cost of sales calculation. In the case of the carpet cleaning business we suggested the wear and tear on the van and carpet cleaning equipment would be treated as a separate fixed cost (i.e. depreciation). However, for manufacturing businesses, some elements of the factory costs could be included in the cost of sales calculation in addition to materials and direct labour costs. A charge may be made per item; for example, to cover the cost of maintaining the machinery.

The Gross Profit Calculation

- Gross profit is the profit made *directly* from the sale of the product or service. At the per-unit level, it is the selling price (excluding VAT) less the unit cost.
- What constitutes the cost of sale is not always clear-cut. As a general rule, the cost element will vary if the sale takes place, and not occur if it does not. They are known as 'variable' costs. But what makes up the cost of sale is very much up to the individual company to decide.
- Items that are counted in the cost of sale should be of material importance. The inclusion of the cost of an extra piece of paper or a paperclip would be pointless.
- The most important thing is to create a gross profit calculation that gives the company and its shareholders meaningful performance data.

Calculating Cost of Sales for the Profit & Loss Statement

So far in this chapter, we have tended to focus on determining the total cost of sales – and hence gross profit – from the unit cost of each item that we sell multiplied by the quantity sold. This is certainly a valid way of calculating cost of sales, but it requires a lot of information about the cost of each individual item of stock at any point in time.

Another way would be to consider how much stock in total we have *purchased* in the period. However, when calculating the cost of sales for the profit & loss statement in this situation, we cannot simply use the total value of goods purchased during the trading period without making an adjustment for changes in stock levels. For example, the sales during the month may be from items already held in stock. Under these circumstances *the purchases during the month could be zero.*

When calculating the cost of sales, we have to take into account stock levels at the beginning and end of the month.

Likewise, during a trading month everything that has been purchased by the business may end up in stock, and none of these particular items may have been sold. *Again, what has been purchased will not, in itself, be relevant in the context of calculating profit.*

The reality is that during most trading months the sales will be made up of *both* goods purchased during the month *and* items taken from stock. We need a formula to take all this into account:

Cost of Sales = Opening Stock + Purchases – Closing Stock

This formula is eminently logical. This is what it is saying: *'At the beginning of the month I had some stock. I added to this by buying some more items. I have not sold all these items as I had some left over. So, by deducting what was left over from the total I can see what I have actually consumed during the month.'*

Computerised stock management systems are widely used to track stock, purchases and cost of sales on a continuous, individual product line basis. In addition, periodic physical stock-takes will be needed to verify that the stock figures on the computer system match what is actually in existence in the warehouse.

Valuation of Stock

When using the above equation, how do we value the stock? Which of the following do you think is correct?

1. What it cost us to buy or produce
2. What we will sell it for to our customer
3. What it is actually worth on the open market if neither of the above two are achievable

Under normal circumstances it would be the first, but if this is not achievable then it would be the third. The second one is not relevant to the stock valuation, but is of course highly relevant to our profitability!

Stock is valued at the *lower* of cost or net realisable value (i.e. what we can sell it for). We do not value it at what we plan to sell it for – we value it at what it cost us. However, if we believe we will sell it at *less than* what it cost us, then we would value it at this *lower* figure. We always take a prudent view and this may mean valuing old/obsolete stock at zero, even though there may be a slim chance of selling it for something in the future.

This is in accordance with the **prudence principle** first mentioned in Chapter 1.2, which is one of the six key principles of accounting. It is not just with stock that we take a prudent view, of course – it is with all our accounting judgements. More on this later!

Gross Profit Calculation and Stock

- When calculating the cost of sales (also known as cost of goods sold) for the profit & loss statement, we use this formula:

  Cost of Sales = Opening Stock + Purchases – Closing Stock

- When valuing stock, we always take a *prudent view*, and value it at the *lower* of what it cost us to buy or make, or its realisable value.

Gross Profit by Product Line

The gross profit (in monetary value) is the foundation stone of a company's profitability. It is the product of the following equation:

$$Sales(£) \times Gross\ Margin(\%) = Gross\ Profit(£)$$

Unless we are generating sufficient gross profit to cover our expenses, we will not be able to make a profit overall. Conversely, the more this gross profit exceeds our expenses, the larger our final profit will become. It is therefore a *critical* starting point for us to understand.

Building sales volume is achieved by offering customers the right product or service; and that topic is outside the scope of this book. *What we need to focus on, for the purposes of financial analysis, is to ensure that the sales we generate are profitable to the business.*

Let us consider the following example of a company's monthly sales:

Product	Sales	Gross Margin	Gross Profit
	£		£
Product A	10,000	*80%*	8,000
Product B	10,000	*60%*	6,000
Product C	10,000	*25%*	2,500
Product D	10,000	*5%*	500
	40,000	*43%*	17,000

Above we can see the business has four products, each bringing in a sales revenue of £10,000 each month. Whilst the revenue is identical, the profitability of each product line is wildly different. Product A has a gross margin of 80%, whilst Product D has one of just 5%. As a result, Product A brings in *16 times* the gross profit of Product D.

Overall we appear to be making a satisfactory gross margin of 43%, but hidden behind this figure is the fact that some products are extremely profitable, whilst others (such as Product D) are not. Product C may, or may not, be worthwhile – without understanding the operating expenses of achieving these sales it is hard to judge.

Warning: low gross margins can seriously damage your wealth.

If we decide to take decisive action to improve the profitability of the business, the following scenario may emerge:

- We delete Product D entirely and the sales revenue now goes to zero.
- For Product C, we substantially raise the price as well as procure at a better cost price. Consequently our gross margin improves to 50%, but because of the price rise, sales revenue declines to £8,000 a month.
- For Products A & B, we put in additional sales effort. This has come from reallocating the time spent on promoting Product D. As a result sales rise by 10% a month on each product.

We can now see the result of these changes:

Product	Sales	Gross Margin	Gross Profit
	£		£
Product A	11,000	*80%*	8,800
Product B	11,000	*60%*	6,600
Product C	8,000	*50%*	4,000
Product D	-	-	-
	30,000	*65%*	19,400

Although overall our sales have *fallen* to £30,000, our gross margin has *risen* to 65% and the gross profit has actually grown to £19,400. Assuming our operating expenses remained the same, our profit before tax would have grown by the £2,400 difference, despite having seen a significant drop in sales. Whilst this is a simplistic example, it does nicely illustrate how we need to dig deeper into an overall gross margin figure to determine how it is made up. Later in the book we will look at the real life example of Moody Sewage, and see how such actions transformed their business.

Gross Profit Analysis

- The gross profit (£) is the product of the following equation:

$$Sales(£) \times Gross\ Margin(\%) = Gross\ Profit(£)$$

- The gross margin % on each product line may vary considerably and will consequently significantly impact our overall profitability.
- We need to look closely at the gross margin on each product line in order to improve the overall performance of a business.

Tracking Gross Margin

Gross margin is one of the most critical KPIs to measure in a business. If you are watching your gross margin on a monthly basis by individual product or customer (as applicable), you will be able to immediately identify when a problem occurs. You can then take *immediate action*, such as adjusting your own prices to reflect any increase in the costs from your suppliers.

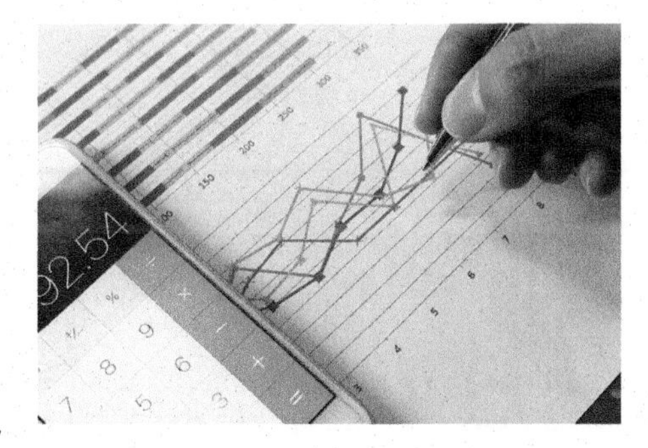

If you want to become obsessive about something, tracking your gross margin over time is a great place to start.

What Could Cause the Gross Margin to Decline?

If your business suddenly experienced a decline in its gross margin – which, to recap, is the profit *percentage* on each £1 of sales value – what could be happening? Give this some thought before reading on.

In fact, there are numerous reasons that could cause this to happen, summarised in the table below. Note that this list is not exhaustive, but it should stimulate your thoughts as to what could be happening.

Cause of Decline in Gross Margin	Further Explanation
Suppliers have put their prices up	This is the most obvious one. If you do not raise your prices after your suppliers have raised theirs, then your gross margin % will inevitably fall.
Wastage of product	If the business is throwing product in the dustbin, rather than selling it to customers, then this cost is present but the sales element is missing. Consequently the gross margin will fall. A café would be a good example of such a business, where wastage of food could be high.
Product theft	If product is being stolen, then as above, the cost is being absorbed by the business but there is no corresponding revenue. In a retail business, this could be customers shoplifting or employees stealing product.
Discounting of prices	If employees are giving customers too many discounts, then they are inevitably getting less revenue for each product sold and the gross margin percentage will be lower. Offsetting this may, of course, be an increase in sales and hence a higher gross profit in terms of monetary value. So as long as the management understands what is going on, this is not necessarily a bad thing.
Staff theft of cash	In a retail business, if an employee failed to ring the sale into the cash register, and instead stole the cash, we again have a situation when the revenue is not appearing for the company, but the cost is of course present. Note that the common way staff would do this is to *pretend* to ring up the sale by pressing the 'No Sale' key which just opens the till. The cash is then placed into the till, but later removed by the member of staff. Clearly sophisticated systems, such as barcodes etc, reduce or eliminate this risk to retailers.
Declining labour productivity	If labour costs are included in the gross profit calculation, such as in the carpet cleaning and SaaS business examples above, then should employee productivity decline it will negatively affect the gross margin. This is because more labour resouces will be required to achieve the given sales.
Shifting product mix	A shift in the mix of sales toward lower margin items could be a subtler, but equally damaging hit to overall profitability.

Note that 'falling sales' is not on the above list as this will *not* impact your gross margin *percentage*.[1] If you sell fewer products, you will have purchased fewer products, hence the percentage margin should remain constant. If you sell fewer products your actual gross profit in terms of *monetary value* will be lower. Remember we are talking about *margins* above, not values.

Tracking Gross Profit

- The gross margin % is a critical key performance indicator (KPI). Tracking this by individual product line or customer, as well as overall, is an extremely powerful way to drive profitability.
- There are numerous reasons why the gross margin % could be declining. Understanding how this can happen is of great value to a management team.
- Falling total sales (without a change to product mix) will not in itself result in a change to the gross margin % (although the gross profit in monetary value would fall).

Note

1. It is, however, possible that falling sales could alter the product mix and therefore the overall gross margin percentage. But on an individual product line basis, falling sales will not affect the gross margin percentage.

2.3 PRODUCT PRICING STRUCTURES

Pricing Structures

We have already highlighted that **gross profit** is a foundation stone of a business's profitability. We have also looked at how changing the **gross margin** percentage can have a significant impact on the gross profit generated in monetary terms, and consequently the final profit outcome. Quite simply, getting passionate about gross margins is a great starting point for building a highly profitable enterprise.

As described in the last chapter, gross profit arises from the difference between our sales revenue and the cost of the goods or services that we sell – or, in unit terms, the difference between the price of each item sold and its unit cost.

Note this chapter is not about deciding on whether a price is right or not in the context of marketing a product. That is outside the scope of this book. We are interested in understanding how profitable a product is once that price has been chosen, and also how the chosen price affects other parties in the supply chain, particularly our customers.

Simple Margin Structure

Let's look at a simple example of the pricing of a clock. In this example, let us assume that you source the clock at a cost price of £4. You then sell it to a retail store for £10, who in turn sells it to the final customer for £24.

VAT Rate: 20%		*Gross Margins*
Retail price (incl VAT)	**£24.00**	
VAT	£4.00	
Retail price (excl VAT)	**£20.00**	
Retailer's gross profit	£10.00	*50%*
Your selling price	**£10.00**	
Your gross profit	£6.00	*60%*
Your cost	**£4.00**	

Don't be selfish: when pricing a product, we may need to consider the gross margins of other parties in the forward supply chain, not just our own.

Note the following:

- Firstly, the price to the consumer is £24, but £4 of this is **VAT**, so the retailer's actual selling price is £20. This is the value that will be used in the profit & loss statement as the retailer's revenue.
- The retailer has a 50% gross margin and consequently has a gross profit of £10 over their £10 purchase price (i.e. they have doubled the price, or have *marked it up* 100%).
- You sell to the retailer at £10, having paid £4 yourself, and consequently have a gross margin of 60% and a gross profit of £6.

When calculating gross margin, we also relate it to the relevant selling price, *not the final consumer price*. So, in this example your gross margin is calculated as follows:

$$\text{Your Gross Margin} = \frac{\text{Your Gross Profit}}{\text{Your Selling Price}} = \frac{£6}{£10} = 60\%$$

A final important note about VAT: whilst you will have paid it on your purchase price, and you would have charged it to the retailer, under normal trading circumstances both you and the retailer will have recovered it in full.[1] Consequently, from a profitability viewpoint, VAT does not feature in the price structure. It does, however, appear for the *end consumer* who cannot recover any VAT.[2]

More Complex Pricing Structure

How would the pricing structure look if we had to sell through a distributor? It may be that we manufacture the clock and then sell it to other companies who manage the supply to the various retailers. These distributors also need to make a gross margin.

VAT Rate: 20%		*Gross Margins*
Retail price (incl VAT)	**£24.00**	
VAT	£4.00	
Retail price (excl VAT)	**£20.00**	
Retailer's gross profit	£10.00	*50%*
Distributor's selling price	**£10.00**	
Distributor's gross profit	£3.50	*35%*
Your selling price	**£6.50**	
Your gross profit	£2.50	*38%*
Your cost	**£4.00**	

In the above scenario the retail price is the same, and the retailer buys at the same price. But we have to allow a profit for the distributor. In this hypothetical example, the distributor buys at £6.50; their gross profit is £3.50; and gross margin 35%.

Both of the above pricing models are available to download from our website, www.macmillanihe.com/Hulme-EntrepreneurialFinance, and can be easily customised to your own needs.

Raising Prices to Customers

When it comes to raising prices, if we are considering the entire forward pricing chain, the process may become easier. Rather than simply presenting a customer with a cost increase, if it is shown with the final retail price rising too, then both retailer and distributor both have the opportunity to maintain their percentage gross margins and increase their gross profit in monetary terms.

> **Pricing Structures**
>
> - Become passionate about gross margins! They are one of the foundation stones of ultimate profitability.
> - When calculating the gross margin, we always divide the unit gross profit by the immediate selling price, which is not necessarily the final selling price to the final consumer.
> - When considering our profit margins, we may also have to consider the margins of our distributors and customers. This approach can also make raising prices an easier process.

Margins and Mark-ups

If you are ever talking to someone in the retail sector, you had better be clear about the difference between margins and mark-ups. These terms are part of their everyday language. A product may, for example, have a 67% gross margin but have a 200% (i.e. 3 times) mark-up. They are different ways of looking at how the profit on the item is quantified.

Product Mark-up Definition

The mark-up on a product is the amount by which the cost of a product (or service) is increased in order to derive the selling price. We can look at this either in terms of *monetary value*, or *percentage*, or a *multiple*.

	A	B	C
Retail price (excl. VAT)	£3.00	£4.50	£10.50
Cost price	£1.50	£1.50	£1.50
Gross profit	£1.50	£3.00	£9.00
Gross margin	*50%*	*67%*	*86%*
Mark-up by value	**£1.50**	**£3.00**	**£9.00**
Mark-up percentage	**100%**	**200%**	**600%**
Mark-up times	x 2	x 3	x 7

In the above table, we can see three different pricing scenarios A, B, and C. In each case the product costs us the same, i.e. £1.50. The selling prices vary considerably from £3.00 to £10.50.

You are now familiar with the calculation of gross margin, which for scenario B is as follows:

$$Gross\ Margin = \frac{Gross\ Profit}{Selling\ Price} = \frac{£3.00}{£4.50} = 67\%$$

The mark-up *by value* is exactly the same as the gross profit, i.e. the amount we are adding to the cost price:

$$Mark\text{-}up\ by\ Value = Selling\ Price - Cost\ Price = £4.50 - £1.50 = £3.00$$

To work out the mark-up *percent*, we use the following formula:

$$Mark\text{-}up\ \% = \frac{Gross\ Profit}{Cost\ Price} \times 100 = \frac{£3.00}{£1.50} = 200\%$$

In this situation, we are using the cost price as the denominator, and the resulting number indicates how many times bigger our gross profit is when compared with the cost price.

To calculate the mark-up *multiple*, we use the following simple formula:

$$Mark\text{-}up\ Multiple = \frac{Selling\ Price}{Cost\ Price} = \frac{£4.50}{£1.50} = 3\,times$$

It is worth noting that retailers nearly always express their selling price with VAT included. For this reason, the addition of VAT is often rolled up into the mark-up multiple. So, for instance, the multiple of ×3 would become ×3.6 to give the retailer the displayed selling price.

Margins and Mark-ups

- Margins and mark-ups are different and should not be confused.
- The mark-up on a product is the amount by which the cost of a product (or service) is increased in order to derive the selling price.
- We can look at this either in terms of monetary value, percentage, or multiple.

Notes

1. There can be situations where VAT is not recoverable, in which case the cost price would include the unrecovered VAT.
2. We are assuming the consumer is not purchasing it as a business expense. Under such circumstances they may be able to recover the VAT.

2.4 ACCRUAL ACCOUNTING

Accrual accounting is governed by the **accrual principle** whereby we produce accounts that reflect the trading activities of the company at the *time* these activities occurred, and not when the cash came in or out of the business. For example, if we buy an item of stock for the business in January and also sell it to our customer in January; pay our supplier in February; and get paid for it by the customer in March, how do we account for all this? On a *cash basis* all the activity happened in February and March, yet all the trading activity itself took place *solely in January*.

There are two accounting sub-principles to the accrual principle that we use here: the **revenue recognition principle** and the **matching principle**. We will look at each in turn and once you have grasped these you will be well on your way to understanding what is under the bonnet of the profit & loss statement.

We will also start to see how some of these events impact the balance sheet as well as the profit & loss statement. If the balance sheet implications are confusing at this stage, please do not worry. We will look at the balance sheet in detail later in the next section.

The Revenue Recognition Principle

We use the **revenue recognition principle** to help us determine how to treat sales revenues when preparing our management accounts each month or year. Sometimes the cash we have collected from our sales revenue during the month may relate to items that have been delivered in the past, or may yet be delivered in the future. How do we treat these situations? *Do we count them in our accounts in the period when the cash comes in, or do we allocate them in some other way?*

Deferred Income

If an airline sold you a ticket *today* to fly to Barcelona in two months' time, when should the sale be counted in their profit & loss statement?

A: Now: the sale has clearly been made and the cash has been collected by credit card from you.
B: In two months' time when you have actually taken the flight.

The answer is B. The sale is not counted as a sale for profit & loss purposes until the goods or services are *delivered to the customer*. Although the airline has collected the cash from you, it is technically not yet a sale. It is treated as **deferred income** and does not yet feature in the profit & loss until the month in which you take your flight.

Balance Sheet Implications

It will, however, feature in the balance sheet as a **current liability** to match the corresponding increase in cash. In other words, instead of crediting the transaction to sales – which would give the false impression that **shareholders' equity** had increased – it is credited to a special liability account called deferred income. If this was not done it would not be a *true and fair view* of the situation.

Accounting statements are about trying to help you gain *a true and fair view* of the trading situation.

Signing a contract or receiving a deposit also do *not* constitute the sale – unless the goods or services are *delivered* at the same time. Likewise, when an invoice is raised, or paid by the customer, these do not count as the date of sale, although in most cases an invoice is raised almost simultaneously with delivery of goods or services. The invoice may be paid some months after the goods or service has been delivered. This fact is *not relevant* to the profit & loss, but would of course be relevant to the cash flow statement.

Accrued Income

How about the reverse of the above situation where a company has delivered the goods or service but not yet raised an invoice? *Could this be treated as a sale?*

The answer is *yes*. For example, a legal firm may have done weeks of work for a client but not yet billed them. The work has been completed and the client is contractually liable to pay for the services received. This could, therefore, be treated as a sale and *included* in the profit & loss for the appropriate month.

Balance Sheet Implications

In this example, the transaction has been credited to the profit & loss statement in the form of sales, and therefore increased shareholders' equity accordingly. However, the corresponding debit in the form of cash and/or trade debtors will be 'missing' from current assets. Hence **accrued income** would be listed as a current asset in its place – it is an asset of the business just waiting to be converted to trade debtors and, eventually, cash.

The Revenue Recognition Principle

- A sale is only treated as a sale in the profit & loss when the goods or services are delivered. It is not when the invoice is raised, nor when the invoice is paid (although both could of course occur at the same time as delivery).
- A sale made but not yet delivered does not feature in the profit & loss statement, but if the payment has been received it does feature in the balance sheet as a current liability called deferred income.
- A sale made and delivered, but not yet invoiced can be included in the profit & loss statement. In the balance sheet, it is shown as a current asset called accrued income.

The Matching Principle

By applying the revenue recognition principle, we have tried to give a *true and fair view* of our sales revenue. Likewise, we need to do the same for all our costs. Let's begin again by looking at an example and posing a question.

A company pays £30,000 every quarter in rent at the beginning of this three-month period. Let us assume it has paid this on 1 January for the months of January, February and March. The entire cash sum of £30,000 left the business on 1 January. *How do we treat the payment in the profit & loss statement for each of the three monthly periods?*

A: We treat the £30,000 rent as an expense in January only, and as zero for February and March's accounts. The money, after all, left in January and therefore there was no rent to pay in February and March.

B: We divide the £30,000 by 3, for the 3 months to which it applies. This means we create a rental expense in the profit & loss of £10,000 for each of months January, February and March regardless of when it was actually paid.

The answer is B. We 'match' the costs to the periods in which they are incurred.

But the money went out in January... how can this be right? Yes, it's true that the money did go out in January, but be careful not to get confused between cash flow and the profit & loss. The profit & loss is not trying to be a cash flow statement. The profit & loss statement is attempting to give you a true and fair view of the *trading performance* (i.e. profitability) of the business in a defined period.

If we had said the business had an overhead of £30,000 in January it may have made the business show a trading loss. And as a result, it would have also inflated the profits in February and March. None of this would have been a true reflection of the actual trading of the business – it would have been badly distorted by allocating the costs in just one month, when in fact the business enjoyed the benefit of the property it rents for the full three-month period *on a consistent basis.*

Prepayments & Accruals

The example of the rental paid in advance by the business is called a **prepayment**. In the balance sheet this is treated as an asset, since until it has been 'consumed' it is an item that is of value to the company.

Something that has been consumed, *but not yet been paid for or even invoiced by a supplier*, also needs to be considered in the profit & loss statement. For example, the company may use the services of an accountant each month, but only be billed every six months. This is the reverse of the rent example, where cash has gone out in advance of the goods or service being consumed. Here we have a *liability* to pay the accountant for services that have already been used.

For the profit & loss statement, we simply estimate what we think the amount should be each month based on past experience, then charge this to the profit & loss as an expense item. This is known as an **accrual** – we are making an allowance for the cost in advance of payment.

What if our estimate for the amount each month was wrong?

Good question! When the invoice from the accountant finally arrives, we simply debit this to the profit & loss as per normal, but we also *reverse* the accrual posting – i.e. by posting a credit to the profit & loss statement. If the invoice is slightly different to the amount we accrued, then it doesn't matter because we have posted the actual invoice as normal. So the profit & loss for this latest month may be slightly lower, or slightly higher, than we had originally expected. But the point is the figures now have been adjusted to reflect reality.

In the balance sheet, any accruals are treated as a liability. We have used something but not been charged yet for it, but we know we will have to pay for it in the future. If our accounts are to be a *true and fair view* of the trading situation, we have to account for it in the balance sheet as well as the profit & loss statements.

The Matching Principle

- The matching principle means we match up costs to the period in which they are incurred. In this respect, the outward cash flow from these expenditures is not relevant to the profit & loss statement.
- An item paid for in advance, but not yet consumed does not feature in the profit & loss until the appropriate time it is used. In the balance sheet, it is treated as a current asset and called a prepayment.
- An item that has been consumed by the business must feature in the profit & loss in the appropriate month, even if an invoice for the services has yet to be received. This is known as an accrued expense in the profit & loss and as an accrual liability in the balance sheet.

2.5 DEPRECIATION

Depreciation and the Profit & Loss Statement

In Chapter 2.1 we were introduced to **depreciation** and learned that it is a key component of the profit & loss statement. To refresh, depreciation is the accounting method of allocating the cost of an item that has a useful economic life of more than one year to specific trading periods over the economic life of the item. Expenditure on items like this is known as **capital expenditure**, and the element of the cost of such tangible items that remains undepreciated is known as **fixed assets**. Examples might include plant and machinery, office equipment, fixtures and fittings, motor vehicles, etc.

Because this type of expenditure has a longer life than the single year's trading period, and the fact that we are trying to give a *true and fair view* of the company's profitability, we need to devise a way of allocating the cost of these assets over the years of its assumed life. There are two main methods of allocating the cost of the assets over time: **straight line depreciation** and **reducing balance depreciation**. We will look at each in turn, and discuss the merits of each. There are other methods, but they are less commonly used so we will concentrate on these two.

How Depreciation Impacts the Different Financial Statements

Before we move on to look at particular depreciation methods, it is important to understand that depreciation impacts *both* the profit & loss and the balance sheet statements. In this chapter, we will primarily look at the impact on the profit & loss, and return to depreciation again when we look at the balance sheet.

To keep track of each asset (or group of assets), and by how much they have depreciated, a business should keep a detailed list, probably in electronic form. This is known as a **fixed asset register**, which we will explore further in Part 3 on the balance sheet.

What about the third statement – the cash flow statement? How does depreciation affect this statement? Quite simply it does not. Depreciation is entirely an accounting adjustment and does not exist as a cash flow item. This is why, when you see a cash flow statement, you may notice a line that states, 'Add back depreciation', or similar words. This is because depreciation, being a non-cash item, needs to be *added back* to profit to calculate net cash flow.

When an asset is purchased, the purchase amount leaves the bank account *at the time of purchase* (or shortly afterwards) and the subsequent depreciation in the years ahead is not a payment out of the bank account – *the item has already been paid for.* Even if the asset is purchased by a loan, the loan repayments are independent of the depreciation charge in the accounts. The loan repayments will be a cash flow item, but this is not the same as a depreciation charge in the profit & loss. Also, note an asset with a life of ten years could theoretically be purchased using a bank loan repayable over three years – so recognise they are not directly connected.[1]

Depreciation and Corporation Tax

Depreciation is specifically excluded as an allowable expense for the purposes of **corporation tax**, and is *added back* to the profit before tax figure when calculating the **taxable profit**. However, the good news is that **capital allowances** are given instead on certain assets purchased (e.g. machinery and research & development). These allowances are generous, and up to 100% of the purchase of the asset may be offset against the taxable profit in their year of purchase/expense. This is done in order to incentivise businesses to investment.

The proper calculation of corporation tax can be complex and will generally require the assistance of a professional accountant. All the entrepreneur needs to know is the broad principle of adding back depreciation and deducting any capital allowances in order to arrive at the taxable profit.

Amortisation

We have already learned about EBITDA, and that it stands for earnings before interest, tax, depreciation and **amortisation**. We know what interest and tax are, and we've just learned more about depreciation, but what, you might ask, is this mysterious thing called 'amortisation' stuck on the end there? The answer is that it is the exact same concept as depreciation but applied to *intangible* (i.e. non-physical) assets, rather than tangible ones (i.e. things you can touch).

An example would be that you have spent £1 million developing a particular technology and registering its world-wide patent. You know the patent will last 20 years (in law), and that the intellectual property (IP) it covers has a real economic value. It is, therefore, clearly an asset – just not one that you can touch. So, the proper accounting treatment would be to amortise the £1 million cost over the 20-year life of the patent – i.e. £50,000 per year.

Straight Line Depreciation

Straight line depreciation is very simple. We ask how long we would expect the asset to last, taking a prudent or cautious expectation of this length of time, and then divide the cost of the asset by this period of time.

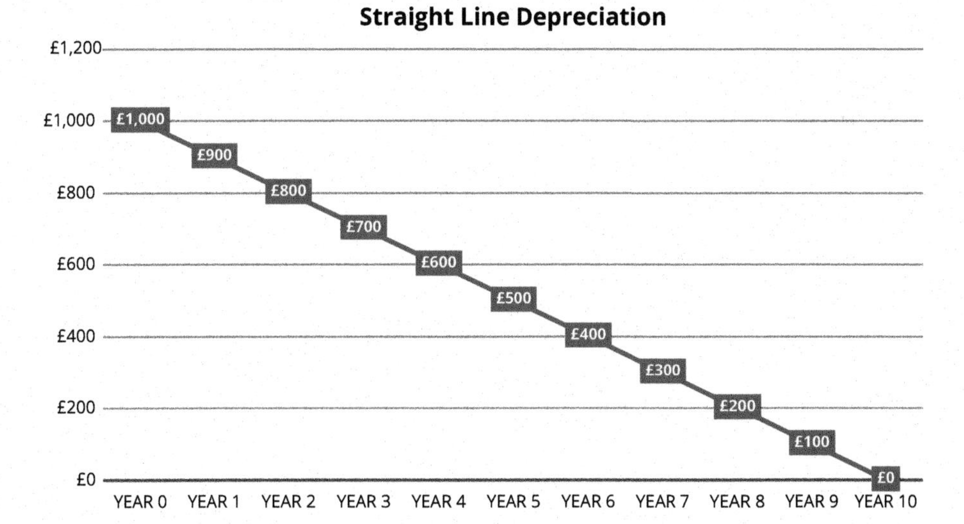

In the graphical example above, we have an asset that was purchased for £1,000 and has an expected life of 10 years. From the accounting viewpoint, we give it a zero value by the end of Year 10, and draw a straight line between today's value of £1,000 and the final value of zero.

In the balance sheet, we will value the asset at £900 after a year, then £800 after two years, £700 after three years, etc., until we reach zero at the tenth year. This £100 decline in value each year is the depreciation charge, and we will charge it to the profit & loss statement.

$$\textit{Annual Depreciation} = \frac{\textit{Cost}}{\textit{Expected Economic Life}} = \frac{£1{,}000}{10} = £100$$

If we were producing monthly accounts, we would divide the £100 by 12, thus always making a consistent charge for each accounting period.

In some circumstances, it might be deemed appropriate to apply a residual (or salvage) value to the calculation. In this case, instead of simply dividing cost by expected life to get the annual charge, you would subtract the estimated residual value first:

$$\textit{Annual Depreciation} = \frac{(\textit{Cost} - \textit{Estimated Residual Value})}{\textit{Expected Economic Life}}$$

Reducing Balance Depreciation

Reducing balance depreciation is a little more complex. Instead of applying a uniform *monetary* value consistently throughout the years, a consistent *percentage* value is applied.

In the second graphical example above, the same £1,000 asset is depreciated at a rate of 25% per annum. We can see that after a year the asset is worth £750, after two years £563, and three years £422. In each case the 25% depreciation rate is applied to the *previous year's* closing value. For calculation of the depreciation in Year 3, we apply the 25% to the closing value at the end of Year 2:

$$\textit{Year 3 Depreciation} = £563 \times 25\% = £141$$

$$\textit{End of Year 3 Asset Value} = £563 - £141 = £422$$

The *monetary amount* charged to the profit & loss slowly reduces each year. This methodology is superior should an asset tend to depreciate faster in the early years of its life. A car is a good example of such an asset – anyone who has purchased a brand-new shiny car from a showroom can be in for an unpleasant surprise should they decide to sell it soon afterwards! Under these circumstances, **reducing balance** seems to be a more appropriate method. At the opposite end of the scale, an old car may maintain its value well, and hardly decline in value towards the end of its life – the reducing balance methodology again works well here.

The reducing balance method of depreciation is more applicable for a vehicle, which suffers higher depreciation in the earlier years of its life as an asset.

Excel models illustrating both the straight line and reducing methods of depreciation are available for you to download.

Other Methods of Depreciation

As mentioned earlier there are some other methods. Although these are generally less common in practice, one at least merits a brief mention. That is the **unit of production** method. Here the rate of depreciation is not calculated as a function of time (as in straight line and reducing balance), but as a function of throughput.

A possible example might be a printing press. In this case, it could be argued that its depreciation in value will be linked more to the rate of throughput (and a machine like this would typically have a production counter) than time. Here the formula for depreciation in any particular period would be:

$$Depn.\ for\ Period = \frac{(Cost - Residual\ Value)}{Est.\ Total\ Production\ Capacity} \times Actual\ Production\ in\ Period$$

Depreciation Is Only an Estimate

If you are questioning whether any of these depreciation methods accurately reflect the open market value of the assets at each point along the line or curve, then you are thinking along the right lines. Quite simply, it is *unlikely* to represent open market value in any particular month or year. But it does allocate the cost of the asset in a uniform way over a period of time.

Besides, another principle of accounting comes into play here called **going concern.** In depreciating the asset, we are assuming we will be carrying on trading as a business (i.e. the business is a viable 'going concern') and that we will be retaining the asset for either its entire life, or certainly a substantial part of its life. *Consequently, the open market value at any one point is of less significance than the need to allocate the cost of the asset in a consistent manner.*

Regardless of which method of depreciation is applied, accounting principles expect us to be both *prudent* and *consistent.* Being *prudent* means choosing a rate of depreciation that is cautious and likely to understate the value of the asset, rather than overstate it. Being *consistent* means avoiding changing the rate or method of depreciation on each asset from year to year. For example, if the profits were looking a little disappointing one year, a quick way to apparently improve them would be to suddenly slow down the rate of depreciation of assets. This would reduce the charge to the profit & loss statement, and hence inflate the reported profit before tax.

It is, of course, acceptable to change policies of depreciation providing there is a justifiable and logical reason. However, changes should not be made for the purposes of manipulating financial results.

Disposal of Assets

When assets are sold, if we have applied our depreciation in a prudent manner, it may achieve a price above the book value we have in our accounts. Under such circumstances, we would make an exceptional profit (i.e. not expected to be recurring).

Likewise, if the sale price did not reach the book value, then we would make an exceptional loss. Both of these will impact the profit & loss statement in the month that the sale of the asset occurs. This would appear as 'Profit/(loss) on the sale of assets' in the profit & loss statement.

A similar approach would happen in the event of a write-off of an asset. Should, for example, an employee lose their new company laptop and, if it was not insured, the full book value would be immediately taken as a cost in the profit & loss. This might also happen if new technology or commercial developments had rendered a machine obsolete, even though it might otherwise have useful life left in it.

Effect of Extending Depreciation Periods Beyond Useful Life

In Chapter 2.1 we saw how extending the life of assets can reduce the depreciation charge each year, and as a direct result improve the *apparent* profitability of a business. *So, if this is the 'gain', where is the 'pain'?*

The pain comes when the asset physically falls to bits and needs replacing, long before its accounting life has expired. Two things then happen: as described above the value has to be written down to zero (or disposal value) immediately, causing an exceptional loss. Secondly, the business now has to fund any replacement to the capital asset.

Overstating profitability will eventually catch up with a business. Done on a major scale, this can cause financial collapse when the truth is discovered. The moral of the story is to always produce accounts that provide a *true and fair view* of the actual trading and financial situation. And choosing a suitable rate of depreciation is an important component of this process.

Depreciation

- Depreciation is the method by which we allocate the cost of a tangible asset to the profit & loss statement over a number of trading years.
- Amortisation is essentially the same as depreciation, but applied to an intangible asset.
- Depreciation is added back to profit before calculating corporation tax due and instead capital allowances are deducted.
- There are two main methods of depreciation: straight line and reducing balance.
- Straight line depreciation applies a consistent *monetary* value each trading period, whilst reducing balance applies a consistent *percentage* value to each trading period.
- The book value of an asset is unlikely to be the same as its open market value at any given time. But in applying depreciation, we are assuming we will be keeping the asset for a number of years and need to apply the charge in a *consistent manner.*

- Disposal of an asset can result in an exceptional profit or loss.
- Artificially lowering rates of depreciation can improve *apparent* short-term profitability, but in the long run can cause business failure.

Note

1. Although they are not connected in terms of the accounting statements, it is likely that a bank would consider the life of the asset when determining the time period of the loan. This would be particularly important should the asset itself be the security on the loan. For example, if purchasing a car, the length of the loan would not exceed the likely life of the car.

2.6 BREAK-EVEN ANALYSIS

What Is the Break-Even Point?

The **break-even point** (BEP) is the point at which a company is neither making a profit nor making a loss from its trading activity. In other words, it is the level of trading activity where revenue is equal to total costs (both fixed and variable). This point can be expressed as either a sales value (e.g. £) or in terms of volume (e.g. number of units).

Why Knowing the Break-Even Point Is Useful

Knowing the BEP of a business is extremely important to both an entrepreneur just starting a new business, as well as a CEO of a large business.

For an entrepreneur, it shows the sales level that has to be reached in order to start making money. For example, *'I need to be selling £500,000 of my products before I will make a profit.'* This realisation may make the entrepreneur reconsider his strategy, since it may be unrealistic to reach this level within the expected timeframe. The knowledge that £500,000 is too great a hurdle could lead to changes to the cost structure and pricing of his business, making it perhaps become profitable at a lower sales level.

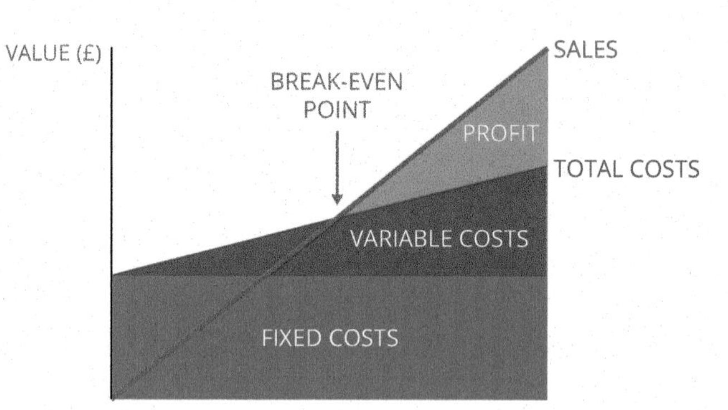

Knowing the break-even point is fundamentally important for any business.

A large, successful trading company that is profitable might wish to know the BEP of a new project to determine its viability. It will also be wise to know, should sales fall, at what point the business or project would start to lose money.

The Different Types of Costs in a Business

Every company's cost structure will be different, but there will tend to be common themes and elements. In most situations, it is possible to divide them up between **fixed costs** and **variable costs**.

Fixed Costs

Fixed costs are the costs a business incurs which tend *not to change* with the sales volume level. To illustrate this, let us return to a café as an example.

The fixed costs of a café will tend to be items such as rent, wages, heating, lighting, etc. Whether the café is busy or quiet on a particular day, these costs will have to be covered. Theoretically, should nobody come in the café at all and sales were zero, the basic cost structure of the business will still be there. And if the café had a record number of customers on that particular day instead, and the staff are 'rushed off their feet' trying to meet the demand, the basic cost structure will remain the same as if it had been empty. Clearly this simple example assumes there was no flexibility to the wages; i.e. no less and no more staff will be employed that day.

Fixed costs can also be described as overheads or operating expenses.

Variable Costs

As the name suggests, variable costs are the *costs that vary directly with the volume of goods or services sold*. For a café, these would be the tea, coffee and food used to supply the customers. Should the sales be zero for a particular day (and if we ignore any potential wastage issues) there would be no cost of products (i.e. no **cost of sales**).[1]

If, however, sales were high, these costs would also be high, and be *directly in proportion* with the sales level. A busy day in our café would see a high consumption of tea, coffee and food!

Importance of Break-Even Point

- The break-even point (BEP) is the point at which a company is neither making a profit nor a loss from its trading activity.
- All businesses should know their BEP, either as a sales level to reach, or as a sales level not to fall below, in order to make a profit.

Drawing Break-Even Charts

Break-even analysis would usually be done using a spreadsheet tool such as Excel, but can also be done graphically. We will discuss the use of spreadsheets later. In the meantime, the visual approach of using graphs is extremely helpful to us in understanding the concepts. It's also quite good fun drawing them!

To draw a break-even chart, we start by drawing the sales line, at approximately 45 degrees to the x and y axes. It does not have to be at 45 degrees, but obviously the scales on each axis will be slightly different if they are not.

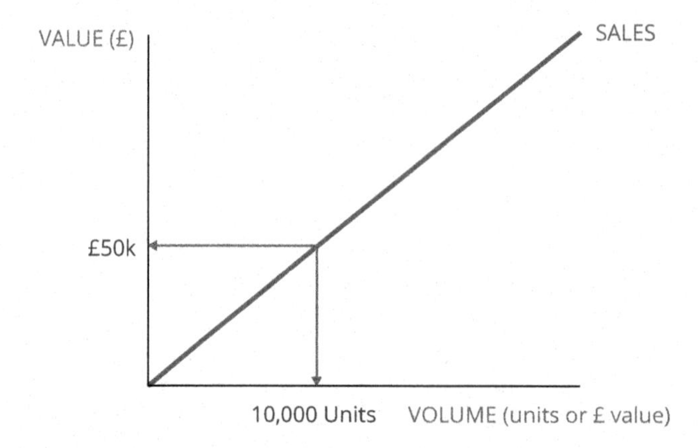

Traditionally the y-axis is in value (e.g. £) and the x-axis is in volume (e.g. units), although the x-axis can also be in a value as an alternative.

At any point along the sales line we can read off the values in terms of sales and volume. In the example above, we are showing a sales value of £50,000 which is equivalent to 10,000 units. This particular model assumes that the relationship between the sales volume and sales value is linear; i.e. sales value always goes up or down by the same amount for any given increase or decrease in volume. Clearly, in the example, the selling price of each unit is £5.

Let's now add two more lines:

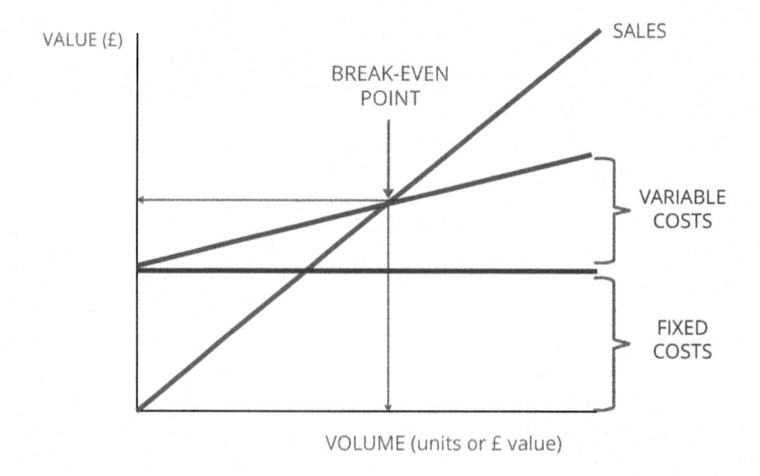

The position of the fixed costs line up or down the y-axis will be determined by the scale of these costs. The lower these are relative to the size of the business, the lower the line would be drawn. Likewise, the higher these are relative to the size of the business, the higher this line would be drawn.

The variable cost line is then placed *on top of* the fixed cost line so that its position represents the sum of all costs. To try and understand how this works, look at the chart at the point where the volume will be zero on the x-axis. You can see that at this point the only costs in the business are the fixed costs. But as the volume rises, and we progress along the x-axis, the sales start to rise. Now the variable costs start to appear.

The total costs of operating the business are shown by the very top of the variable costs line, as these include not just the variable costs but also the fixed costs as well. Where the variable costs line and the sales line intersect will be the break-even point (BEP).

At this BEP we can see visually the following formula:

$$Sales = Variable\ Costs + Fixed\ Costs$$

Another way of looking at this point is to see that the gross profit from the sales is just sufficient to cover the fixed costs. This can be illustrated by adjusting the formula:

$$Sales - Variable\ Costs = Fixed\ Costs$$

Which is the same as:

$$Gross\ Profit = Fixed\ Costs$$

The amount of gross profit generated from the sales is sufficient to cover the fixed costs *only*. The business is trading at neither a profit nor a loss – it is at the BEP.

Examples of Profit- and Loss-Making Businesses

Business Making a Profit

In the example below, at the sales volume indicated we can read off the total revenue from the y-axis, as well as the total costs of the business. Remember, the total costs are made up of the sum of the fixed costs and the variable costs.

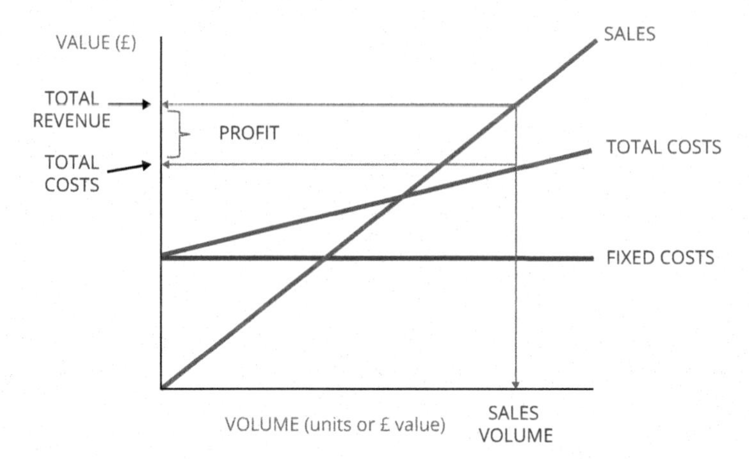

The difference between the total revenue and the total cost (shown on the y-axis) is the amount of profit the business is making at the sales volume specified on the x-axis.

Business Making a Loss

If the sales volume was lower, as indicated in the chart below, we can see that the total costs on the y-axis are greater than the total revenue. Consequently, a loss is made and illustrated by the gap between the two figures.

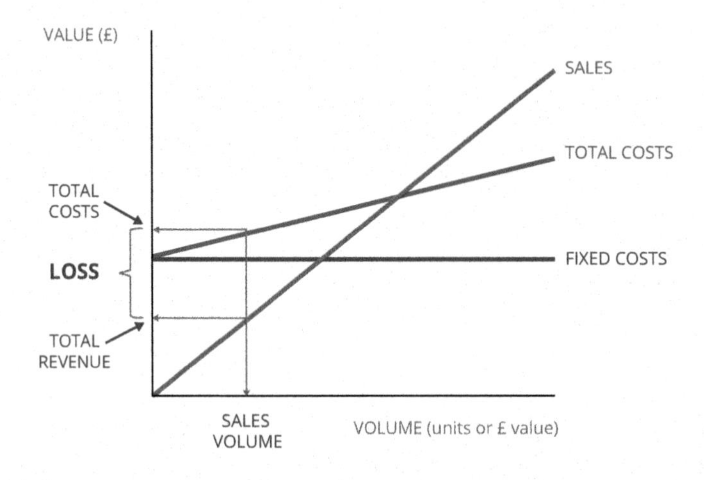

Business with a High Gross Margin

If the business has a high gross margin percentage, the variable costs will rise at a slower rate and will give the total cost line a shallow gradient, directly in proportion to the actual gross margin percentage figure.

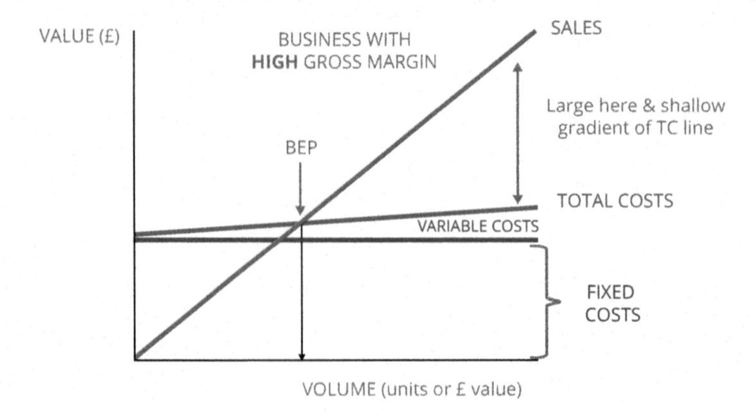

Business with a Low Gross Margin

If the business has a low gross margin percentage, the variable costs will rise at a faster rate and will give the total cost line a steeper gradient, directly in proportion to the actual gross margin percentage figure.

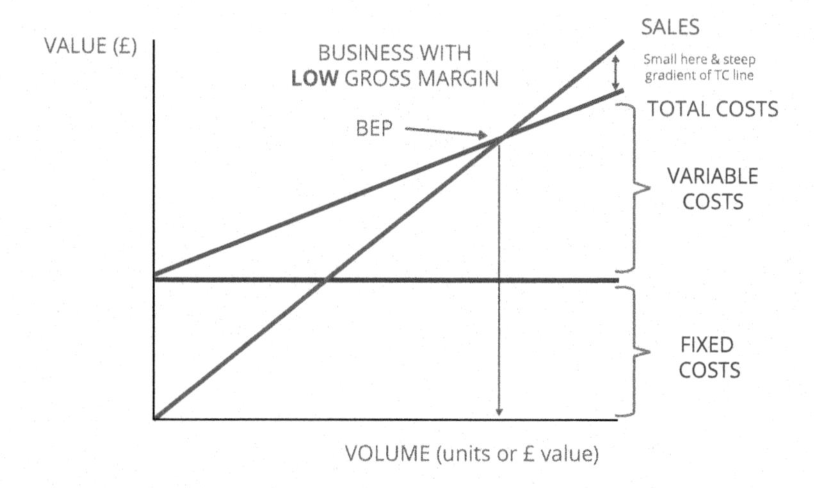

When comparing the two charts above, note how in the second scenario the business requires a far greater volume before it can reach its BEP.

> **Break-Even Charts**
>
> - Sales, fixed costs, and variable costs are all represented by a series of straight lines on the chart. Total costs are illustrated by placing variable costs on top of fixed costs. Where this intersects the sales line is the BEP.
> - The fixed cost line will be higher or lower corresponding to high or low overhead structures.
> - The gradient of the total cost line will depend on the gross margin percentage of the business. The higher the gross margin percentage, the shallower the line will be.

The Break-Even Point Formula

The break-even point is the point at which the gross profit generated from sales is equal to the fixed costs. In other words, the amount of profit the business is making on the actual products it has sold is just covering the costs of operating the business – no more and no less. *It is breaking-even.*

As a formula, we can express it as:

$$BE\ Sales\ Level \times Gross\ Margin\% = Fixed\ Costs$$

We can then express it as follows:

$$BE\ Sales\ Level = \frac{Fixed\ Costs}{Gross\ Margin\%}$$

Example Calculation

Profit & Loss	£	Margins
Sales	500,000	
Cost of sales	(100,000)	
Gross profit	**400,000**	*80%*
Fixed costs	(250,000)	
Profit before tax	**150,000**	*30%*

If we take the figures from the abbreviated profit & loss statement above, we can work out the BEP as follows:

$$BE\ Sales\ Level = \frac{Fixed\ Costs}{Gross\ Margin\%} = \frac{£250{,}000}{80\%} = \frac{£250{,}000}{0.8} = £312{,}500$$

Note we are taking the *gross* profit margin, not the profit before tax margin, for our calculation.

What this is saying: *'If I sell £312,500 of products, and I make 80p for every £1 of these sales, then I will make a gross profit of £250,000 (£312,500 x 0.8). This figure is the same as my fixed costs, and hence I am breaking-even at this point.'*

Break-Even Point in Terms of Number of Customers

If each customer spent £50 on average, then what would the BEP be in terms of the number of customers we would need? We would perform this calculation:

$$BE\ No.\ of\ Customers = \frac{BE\ Sales\ Level}{Average\ Customer\ Spend} = \frac{£312{,}500}{£50} = 6{,}250$$

If these were yearly sales, it would tell us that we have to gain 6,250 customers spending an average of £50 each, before we could start to make a profit. Again, this is extremely valuable information to an entrepreneur. We can also look at it on a daily basis:

$$No.\ of\ Customers\ per\ Day = \frac{6{,}250}{365} = 17.2 = 17$$

We would need approximately 17 customers each day in order to start making money. Again, potentially significant information. We can ask: *'How realistic is this for my business?'*

Inclusion of Depreciation and Interest Costs in Fixed Costs

As previously advised, many accounting terms can be interpreted in different ways under different circumstances. For fixed costs we could also use the terms overheads or operating expenses. Generally, we expect fixed costs to be the cost items *excluding* depreciation and interest costs. However, when it comes to calculating the BEP we need to take into account *all types of costs*. In the context of the BEP, if we ignored depreciation and interest, we would not be working out the true BEP. We would be working out a BEP that had cost elements missing – hence it would be incorrect.

Example with Depreciation and Interest Costs

Profit & Loss	£	Margins
Sales	500,000	
Cost of sales	(100,000)	
Gross profit	**400,000**	*80%*
Fixed costs	(250,000)	
EBITDA	**150,000**	*30%*
Depreciation	(30,000)	
Interest	(5,000)	
Profit before tax	**115,000**	*23%*

If we are presented with a set of figures such as those above, we would have to adapt our calculation:

$$\textit{BE Sales Level} = \frac{(£250{,}000 + £30{,}000 + £5{,}000)}{80\%} = \frac{£285{,}000}{0.8} = £356{,}250$$

Variable Costs and the Break-Even Formula

What about the inclusion of the cost of sales? Where is that in the above equation?

We have to take into account *all costs* – both fixed costs and variable costs. We have already identified we need to broaden our definition of fixed costs to include depreciation and interest… *but where is the inclusion of the variable costs?*

It is of course already in the above equation in the form of the gross margin percentage. In the above example, our gross margin is 80% which means our cost of sales must be 20% (100% – 20%).

Service Businesses with 100% Gross Margin

It is possible that a service business could have a 100% gross margin. Under these circumstances the BEP Sales Level would be exactly the same as the fixed costs:

$$\textit{BE Sales Level} = \frac{£285{,}000}{100\%} = \frac{£285{,}000}{1.0} = £285{,}000$$

Corporation Tax and the Break-Even Formula

What about corporation tax? Should this be included in the broader fixed costs calculation?

Corporation tax is not a cost of the business. Similar to a dividend, it is a distribution of the profit made by the business. In the case of corporation tax, it is a distribution to the Government rather than the shareholders.

Finally, note that if a company is breaking-even it is, of course, not making a profit. Hence it is likely there would be no corporation tax to pay in any event!

> **The Break-Even Point Formula**
>
> - The formula for working out the BEP is:
>
> $$BE\ Sales\ Level = \frac{Fixed\ Costs}{Gross\ Margin\%}$$
>
> - When calculating the BEP, we must include depreciation and interest costs in our fixed costs calculation. Without them, we will not be including *all costs*.
> - Corporation tax is not relevant to the BEP calculation.

Break-Even Analysis Using Excel

Excel, or any other spreadsheet programme, arguably offers a far superior solution to calculate the BEP. Let us look at a simple example model for a café with a variety of costs – Carl's Café. We will be using Carl and his café to illustrate financial modelling later in the book, but for now we will look at his break-even point.

All the cells coloured in yellow are variables which can be changed – all the other cells are formulas. It is therefore possible to quickly and easily adjust the assumed gross margin percentage, any of the fixed costs, and the average spend per customer. As each of these variables are changed, the revised BEP of the business will be instantly calculated.

Carl's Café Break-Even Model

Play around with all the costs and the gross margin. You can then see how this affects the sales level you would have to achieve to break-even.

ONLY CHANGE YELLOW CELLS. THE REST ARE FORMULAS!

Gross Margin		**75%**
Fixed Costs (annually):		
Staff Wages	£	45,000
Rent	£	35,000
Heat & Light	£	6,000
Cleaning	£	9,000
Other Misc Costs	£	5,000
Interest	£	5,000
Depreciation	£	15,000
Total Fixed Costs	**£**	**120,000**
SALES BREAK-EVEN POINT	**£**	**160,000**

You can also look at the break-even point in terms of number of Customers required, depending on how much they spend:

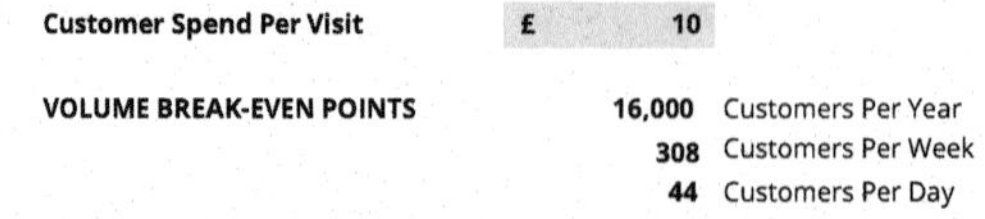

Customer Spend Per Visit	**£**	**10**
VOLUME BREAK-EVEN POINTS	**16,000**	Customers Per Year
	308	Customers Per Week
	44	Customers Per Day

Note that the break-even volumes are also shown in terms of number of customers required per year, week and day. Again, this is useful information in order to gauge the viability of a business prior to starting any trading.

If this was a start-up situation, all these figures could be verified by basic market research. Clearly some figures would be more accurate than others, but overall the BEP could probably be estimated with a reasonably high degree of accuracy.

This model template is available for you to download and adapt as you wish.

Margin of Safety Concept

The **margin of safety** (MOS) is the difference in sales between what the business is actually achieving at the moment and its Break-Even Point (BEP):

$$Margin\ of\ Safety = Current\ Sales\ Level - BEP\ Sales\ Level$$

Note the MOS can be expressed in either sales value or volume, or alternatively as the percentage either could fall before the BEP was reached.

The formula for calculating the percentage MOS would be:

$$Margin\ of\ Safety\% = \left(1 - \frac{BEP\ Sales\ Level}{Current\ Sales\ Level}\right) \times 100$$

Example

Let's look at a further example below of a business with sales of £250,000 per annum, and a BEP of £180,000:

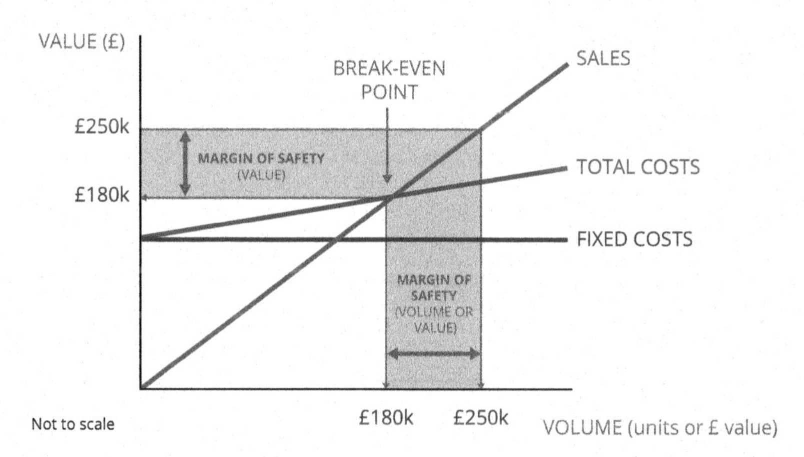

The MOS can be calculated as follows:

$$Margin\ of\ Safety = £250{,}000 - £180{,}000 = £70{,}000$$

Sales could drop by £70,000, or 28%, before the business would begin to lose money.

Businesses in Difficult Sales Environments

In a rapidly changing business environment, such as when sales fall unexpectedly, businesses may need to react quickly in order to survive.

Example

In the following different example, we can see that the company has a £0.9m margin of safety based on its current annual sales level of £6.7m:

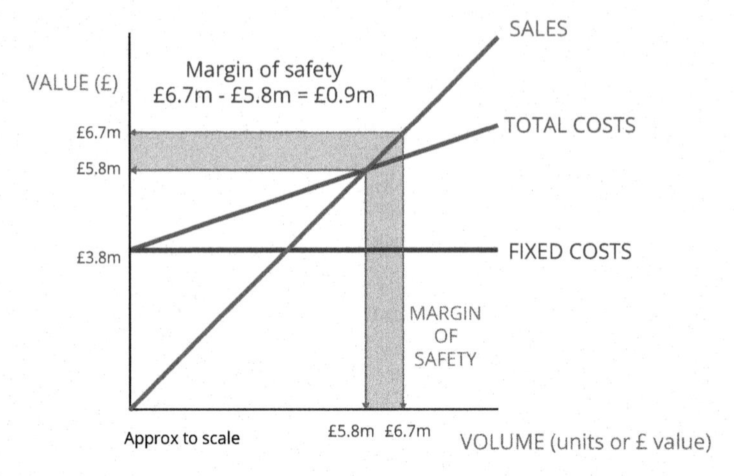

If faced with a severe decline in sales, what should it do? Should it wait until it starts losing money or perhaps begin to act sooner? This is a dilemma often faced by business managers – *do we cut overheads now, and risk losing good staff, or do we wait and see if sales will return to their previous levels?* Both strategies can be highly damaging to the business. What do you think? We will come back to this dilemma below when examining a case study.

If the above business took immediate action, and reduced its fixed costs by £0.5m per annum, then the revised chart would look like this:

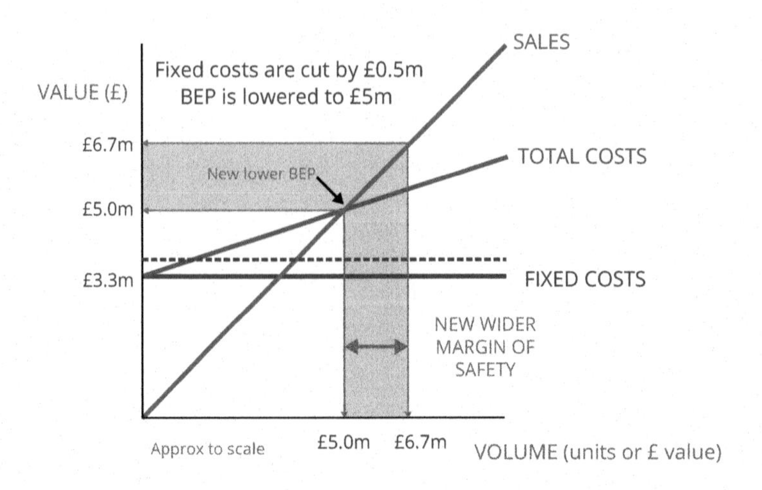

The new BEP has been reduced to £5m (from £5.8m). The MOS has also grown to £1.7m based on the previous sales level of £6.7m. The company has considerably more flexibility to remain profitable as the sales level declines.

Another way to help with the dilemma of deciding whether to take action on costs, is to have a range of forward looking KPIs, which could allow you to *know* your business is set to decline, or grow, well in advance. We return to this topic in the final chapter of the book.

Experience of Cook Trading

Cook Trading is a large and successful British company. It produces a wide range of frozen ready-meals, and sells them through a mixture of its own retail stores, its own franchised stores, and independent farm shops. In addition, it sells online direct to the consumer. Its products are not sold through the major retailers – Cook largely controls its own distribution channels. The business grew rapidly from its foundation in 1997 and by 2007 had just opened a new kitchen[2] in Sittingbourne, Kent, to meet the demand and provide extensive capacity for future growth. As a result, it was highly borrowed and was barely profitable due to its rapid expansion. But on their consistent growth trajectory, nothing looked like much of a problem. *That is until the 2008 financial crash.*

From the moment Lehman Brothers spectacularly collapsed, their sales dropped 15% 'overnight'. Their largely middle-class customer base immediately tightened their belts and some regarded Cook's delicious meals as an unnecessary luxury. Cook had experienced sales swings in the past – but nothing like this: there was no bounce back – the sales bumped along at their new lower level.

Edward Perry, the entrepreneur who had built the business (along with his brother James Perry and chef Dale Penfold), faced the reality of **receivership**.[3] They explored all options: receivership, cutting costs, and raising new capital. In terms of cutting their cost base they moved rapidly. They relocated their head office into the same building as the new kitchen. They approached all the landlords of their shops and asked for a suspension of rent payment, and in most cases received some assistance. Basically, they did all they humanly could to bring the cost base of the business into line with the new reality.

James later reflected: *'Our desperate straits became the mother of inventive ways of filling our cash flow. We threw everything we could overboard, got to know our balance sheet and all our creditors, begged shareholders for assets to use as security for subordinated debt (after using up all our own) and so on. Everyday felt like the trenches, doing just enough to stay alive until tomorrow.'*[4]

They also lined up new sources of capital, and in early 2009 were about to draw down some new funds on onerous terms when a miracle appeared to happen: sales started to edge up *at the same time* as their costs base was at a new lower level. Edward and James decided to decline the extra funds and Cook started making profits again!

The rest is history. The business has performed strongly ever since and for 2019, sales were £64m and profit before tax £2.5m – a truly extraordinary success story.

What Can We Learn from Cook Trading's Experience?

The Cook story is perhaps worthy of a book in its own right, but there are several quick lessons we can learn from this experience.

Move Quickly

The quick reaction by the directors almost certainly saved the company. The *certainty* was sales had fallen and the *uncertainty* was that they would recover anytime soon. In a severe crisis, it is best to act on *certain* information. The certainty was that their cost base was too high, and it was necessary to reduce costs across the business in whatever way they could.

This principle can be applied to any decisions on spending money during a crisis. Logic would suggest that a company in a sales downturn should spend more money on marketing to improve the revenue situation. But the *certainty* is the marketing expenditure is going to add to the costs base of the business, and the *uncertainty* is that the marketing activity will actually work. It may actually make the financial situation worse. Under these circumstances it usually pays to follow the *certainty path* – for example reducing the labour force is *certain* to reduce the overheads in the long-term (i.e. after initial redundancy costs).

Explore Other Opportunities

Cook Trading also explored additional equity and loan financing. Because the business had historically been very successful at an operating profit level, but was hampered by a large interest charge, it meant that additional **equity funding** was a realistic possibility. However, as they were in a crisis situation, the terms were not favourable[5]. But it was, at least, a far better option than receivership.

Finally, James made a very telling comment. Prior to this crisis, they had not sufficiently understood their balance sheet and the consequences of it being in a weak financial state. As mentioned at the very start of the book, in our experience this is very common amongst entrepreneurs – they gain a good understanding of the profit & loss but frequently overlook the importance of the balance sheet. Make sure you do not make this potentially fatal mistake too!

Margin of Safety Concept

- The margin of safety (MOS) is the difference in sales between what the business is actually achieving at the moment and its BEP:

  Margin of Safety = Current Sales Level – BEP Sales Level

- Businesses facing challenging trading situations are likely to cut their costs, thereby attempting to lower their BEP and widen their margin of safety.
- In a severe financial crisis, focusing on certainty (such as cutting costs) rather than uncertainty (such as marketing initiatives) is likely to be the better strategy for survival.

Limitations of Break-Even Theory

The neat break-even models shown at the start of this chapter are somewhat conceptual, and it is worth highlighting some of the limitations and weaknesses to this type of analysis. This does not take away its value – in fact by appreciating all the limitations we are able to use the concepts with greater confidence and a fuller understanding of their application and meaning.

Relevance of Volume as a Measure

Conventionally, the x-axis is shown as volume. In this chapter, we have shown it as *either* volume *or* sales value as either measure indicate the growth in the *scale of the business*. The problem with volume as a measure is defining what this actually means. In the case of a major manufacturer like Mercedes Benz, volume could simply mean vehicles produced (but even then, cars, vans, buses or trucks are all extremely different market segments and have widely differing cost and margin structures). But for a company like Amazon, other than 'parcels shipped', volume will be even more meaningless, as the business offers such a diverse and unrelated range of products at wildly different price points.

Finally, a **SaaS** company may have a variety of subscription packages. If 'volume' was defined in terms of number of subscribers, these may vary from single persons to large corporates, each with significantly different sales values attached.

Fixed Costs Usually Rise in Jumps

The second issue is that fixed costs may rise in a somewhat lumpy fashion. If a business is growing at a very steady pace, perhaps employing a few more staff each year, the fixed cost line would rise in a progressive fashion as the company grew along its sales line. But this scenario may be very unrepresentative of many companies' experience.

Cook Trading's move into their new kitchen in Sittingbourne was a major step-change in their overhead structure, and when combined with a severe sales downturn pushed them into a loss-making situation. This example nicely illustrates the fact that a business can theoretically have multiple BEPs as it progresses.

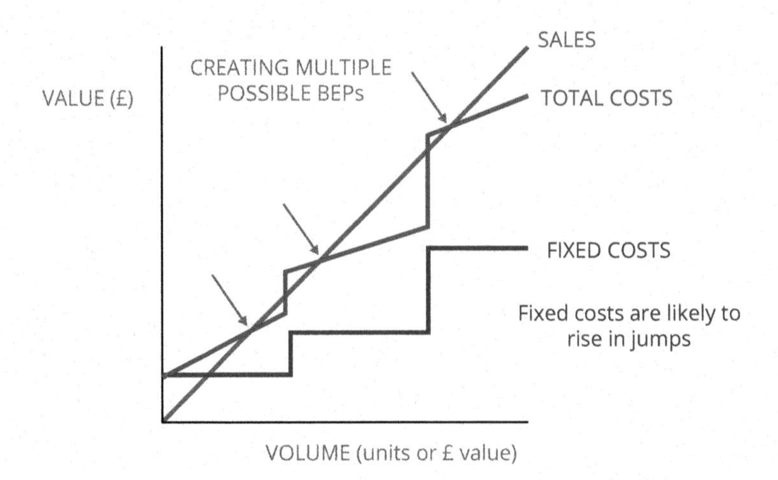

The Total Cost Line May Be Curved

Thirdly, the assumption that the variable costs rise in a linear fashion is likely to be erroneous. In most commercial situations, as a company progresses in size, it is able to lower its cost of sales. This comes about either through greater purchasing power or operational scale, or from both.

As a result, the variable costs could grow at a progressively slower rate than sales or volume grow over time and the total cost line would then be curved.

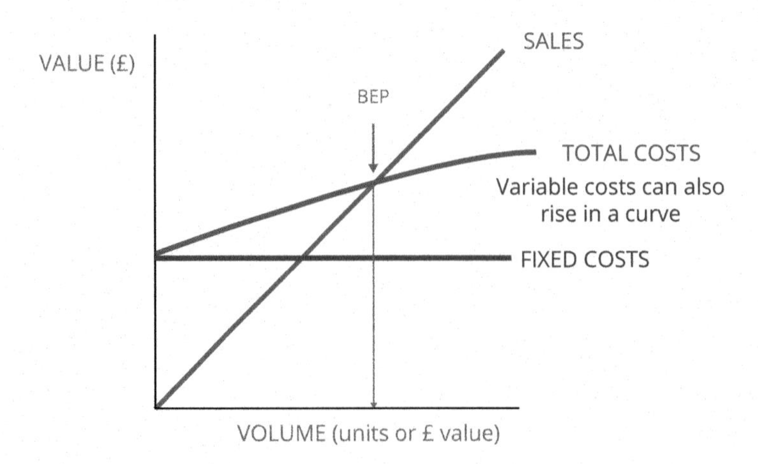

Limitations of Break-Even Theory

- The BEP concept has some weaknesses and limitations. For example, fixed costs tend to rise in jumps and the total cost line is unlikely to be linear.

Notes

1. There could, of course, be other variable costs other than the cost of sales alone. But we are trying to keep this example as simple as possible.
2. 'Kitchen' greatly understates the facility – it is an enormous factory. But the industry still refers to them as 'kitchens'.
3. Receivership is when the company runs out of capital and is placed into the hands of an official receiver. The receiver will then either sell off the business as a going concern (now without its past liabilities), or close it down and just dispose of the assets. In the case of Cook Trading the business would definitely have survived and have been relieved of its substantial debt burden and several shop leases that were a liability. However, the family would have lost their ownership of the company unless they had managed to buy it back from the receiver. Their reputation with creditors, suppliers and landlords would also have been severely damaged.
4. *Daily Telegraph,* 24 October 2018.
5. This highlights the fact that equity funding also carries a cost – generally *higher* than debt funding.

2.7 THE STOCK MARKET & PROFITABILITY

The Drivers of Share Prices

It is helpful to understand what drives share prices (also called stock prices) on the stock exchanges of the world.

The primary driver of the value of any share will be its long-term profitability (or earnings) potential, combined with the market value of any assets that it owns. So, even if a business is not profitable in the short term, but is perceived to have huge long-term potential, it can be extremely highly valued. Amazon is one such company – it has relatively limited profits when considering its size, but because of its domination of online retailing, it commands a massive valuation on the stock market. Similarly, companies such as Twitter, Snap and Ocado are all highly valued, yet their profits at the present time are either non-existent or low. But the *expectation* is they will be enormous in the future.

In the past, companies such as Google, Apple and Facebook may have been in similar situations, but now provide enormous profits and, as a result, continued growth in shareholder value. Over the past decade, many technology companies from the United States have managed to deliver just about everything the stock market could want – high earnings, strong sales growth, rising profitability and a promising outlook. No wonder these are the world's most valuable companies!

We can summarise by saying all the following factors will influence a share price:

- Current earnings
- Future potential earnings (or rather investors' expectations of future earnings)
- Stability and quality of earnings
- Generally perceived or real risk factors
- Market sector the company is operating in (i.e. is it attractive?)
- General market sentiment in wider economy (including the prevailing interest rates)

Earnings Per Share

This is a critical measure to help determine a company's share price, for both a privately-owned business, and in particular for a company quoted on a stock exchange. Its importance is derived from two key issues expressed on a 'per share' basis: 1) a company's ability to generate profit for reinvestment; and, 2) a company's ability to continue to pay out dividends to shareholders. Earnings per share (EPS) is calculated by taking the profit after tax and dividing it by the number of shares in issue:

$$EPS = \frac{Profit\ After Tax}{No.\ of\ Shares\ in\ Issue}$$

If a company made a £3.5m net profit after tax, and had 2.5m shares in issue, we could work out the EPS as follows:

$$\frac{£3,500,000}{2,500,000} = £1.40$$

For each share that is owned, £1.40 of wealth is being generated. *What would you be prepared to pay for one of these shares?* If the price was just £1.40 you would be getting your money back in a year, so clearly that price would be too low. Maybe 5 times, representing five years? Or even more/longer? So much depends on your view of the *outlook* for the business and the reliability of its earnings.

P/E Ratio

In fact, if we take the actual share price on the stock exchange, and divide it by the EPS, we can get the Price/Earnings (P/E) Ratio. Let's assume the share price is £11.20, then the calculation would be as follows:

$$P/E\ Ratio = \frac{£11.20}{£1.40} = 8\ times$$

In other words, the stock market is saying: *'We think 8 times the annual earnings is the correct valuation for this share.'*

As you can imagine, if the stock market analysts had good reason to believe the EPS would rise to £3 next year, and £6 the year after that, then they may believe 8 times next year's earnings of £3 is an absolute bargain. Hence, they may be prepared to pay £24 a share. This would make the current P/E ratio look like this:

$$\frac{£24.00}{£1.40} = 17\ times$$

This higher P/E ratio is *anticipating* the future earnings of the business. The higher the forecast EPS the greater justification there is to pay a higher price for each share. It also works in reverse. If profits are anticipated to decline, so will the share price.

If we search online or look in the financial press, we can see the P/E ratio shown for each share price. This gives us an idea of how valuable the business is as rated by the market. These figures can also be compared to a sector average.

In early January 2020, the P/E ratios for Apple and Amazon were 24 and 80 respectively. Both have high ratings, suggesting the market expects continued earnings growth, but the expectation is Amazon's will grow at a far faster rate (from a lower base) than Apple's.

Quality of Earnings

This is something that you understandably may not appreciate, but is of critical importance to the value of a business.

Consider the performance of the two companies below:

Profit After Tax

£million	2016	2017	2018	2019	2020	5-Yr Totals
Company A	1.1	1.2	3.2	(0.5)	2.3	7.3
Company B	0.5	0.7	1.7	2.1	2.3	7.3

They are both making the same profit after tax in their last financial year. Cumulatively they have also made the same amount of profit over the 5 years shown. Company A has demonstrated it can make even higher profits – it peaked at £3.2m – but, on the other hand, made a loss the following year.

Company B, however, has shown *consistent* growth and *stable* profitability. If this pattern continues, we can perhaps expect a profit of around £2.6m for the next financial year. On the data we have, this looks quite likely. However, we cannot say the same for Company A – it might be a record profit, but it could also be a loss. Company A's earnings history appears to be less reliable, i.e. of poorer quality.

If this is the only information you had, which company would you most want to own? *Which would you regard as more valuable?* Clearly, we would like to know a great deal more about the businesses and their markets, but the example does illustrate the value of stable and growing earnings. Stock markets always appreciate *stability* of earning as well as *growth* in earnings. The two combined tend to lead to a high stock market rating, or a high price/earnings (P/E) ratio being applied.

The Drivers of Share Prices

- When determining what each share of a company is worth, we consider many factors. But the key one is the perceived *long-term* prospects for the earnings per share.
- The price/earnings ratio allows us to look at the share price relative to its wealth generation for each share and hence determine whether it is good or poor value.
- When we look at the profitability of a business we should also look at the stability of those earnings and the likelihood of their future growth. If both these factors are strong, then the business will be worth significantly more than a comparable sized business without these features.

PART 3

THE BALANCE SHEET

3.1 THE BALANCE SHEET STATEMENT

The **balance sheet** is an extraordinarily powerful financial statement, yet most small business owners pay little attention to it. This is largely because of a lack of understanding – many entrepreneurs struggle just to grasp the profit & loss statement, so the balance sheet is often disregarded and treated as 'one statement too many'. In fact, of the three key financial statements, it is the master statement: the other two – profit & loss and cash flow – are, in effect, subsidiary to it.

The balance sheet contains vital information about a business. Described simply, it is a *statement of what a business owns, what it owes, and its ownership equity **(shareholders' equity**) at a particular point in time.* Put another way, it is a snapshot representation of assets held by a business and how those assets are financed.

This information is useful as it shows:

- What assets a business has, such as property, machinery, stock, cash, etc
- What liabilities it has, such as bank loans, creditors, or other debts
- Whether the assets are of greater value than the liabilities
- The book value of shareholders' equity in the business
- How liquid the business is – for example how able is it to pay off its short-term liabilities

The balance sheet also shows us some other interesting information:

- How the business has been funded, i.e. whether by the issue of share capital or by debt
- How it has deployed those funds
- An indication of whether the business has a history of making profits or losses
- An indication of whether the business is vulnerable to complete collapse in the short term
- And a series of balance sheets (two or more), showing the financial health of the business at different points in time, is a powerful way of understanding the evolution of the business' financial status

All this knowledge can be gleaned very rapidly if you understand what you are looking at, and hence is extremely useful and powerful.

The Balance Sheet Is on a Particular Day

The best way to try and understand the balance sheet is to think of it as a photograph of the company. It is a picture of the assets and liabilities of the business *on a particular day.* You will notice that the heading will always give the date, expressed, for example, 'As at 31 March 2020'. This means that this is how the company's assets and liabilities looked *on that day*. The date is always at the end of an accounting period, such as a month, quarter, or year.

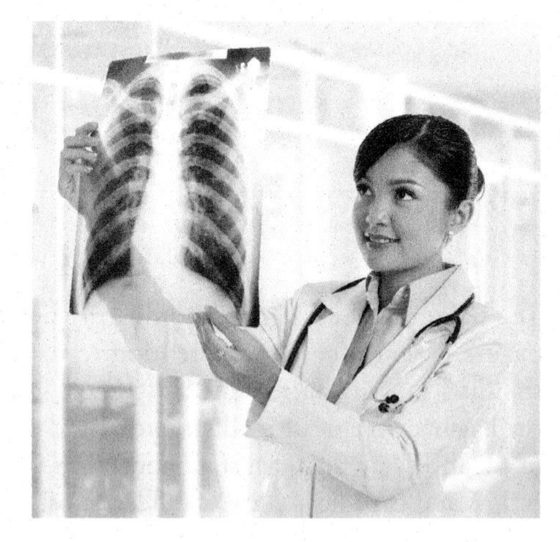

The balance sheet is like an X-ray of the 'bones' of the business on a particular day. It can also quickly show you the general health of the business.

The photograph analogy can be taken one step further by thinking of the balance sheet as an X-ray. The picture gives detailed insight as to what is happening within the business – you can see the assets or 'bones' of the business, and can determine how healthy it is all looking.

Note the profit & loss statement is always for a *period of time*. This period is likely to be for month, quarter, or full year. The profit & loss statement shows the *activity* throughout the period – hence it is more like a video. It is a recording of what has happened from a profitability viewpoint.

The Balance Sheet Formula

The balance sheet is viewed in a table format, or as a list. But behind this is an underlying formula:

For published accounts in the United Kingdom:

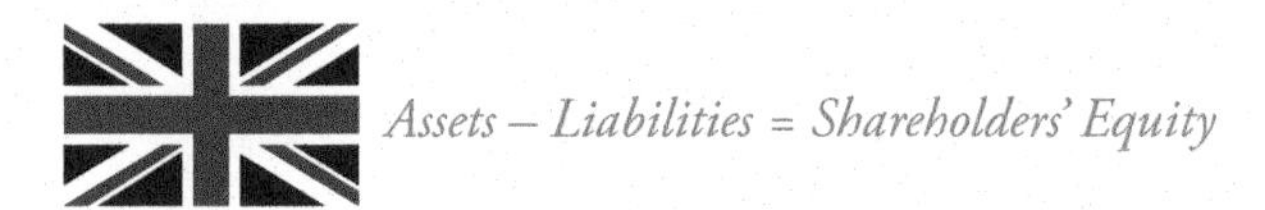

In the United States, it is customary to express it differently:

You do not need a degree in mathematics to realise this is exactly the same thing. It is just shown in a different way. But as you will see, most multinational companies simply show the balance sheet in a list format. We will, however, come back to the US version of the formula later as it raises some interesting issues in the way we consider the data.

Let's take a look at the conventional UK version of the formula and try to understand the implications of it. From here on, when we refer to the left- or right-hand side of the balance sheet, it is this format that we'll be referring to. Understanding this formula will help you appreciate the power and proper use of the balance sheet.

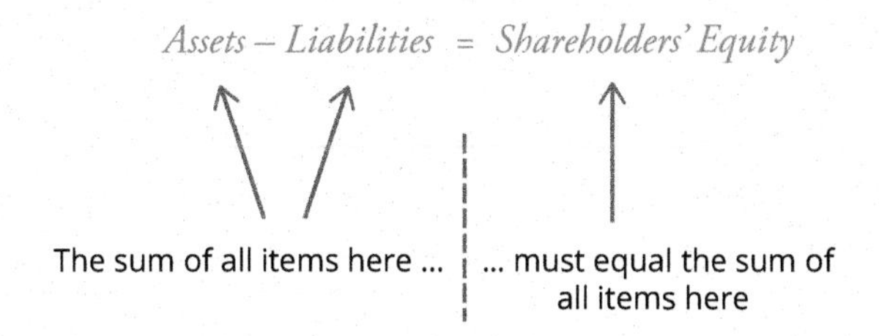

On this basis, it has to balance. Every movement will have a counter-movement that will maintain the balance. If you see or produce a balance sheet that is not balancing, then there is something wrong with the mathematics or the allocation of items within it.

The wonderful thing about the balance sheet (especially when combined with the profit & loss and cash flow statements) is that it leaves nothing out. *Nothing is forgotten, nothing is missed*, provided of course the accounts have been prepared properly. Like any snapshot, it becomes even more informative when compared to an earlier one of the same company, so that changes become apparent. *All* the differences between a business's

The balance sheet will always balance. If it does not there is an error.

balance sheet at two different points in time can be explained by the profit & loss or the cash flow statements or changes within the balance sheet itself, or a combination of the three. How exciting!

Debits and Credits

As we learned in Chapter 1.2, for all financial statements, one of the basic building blocks is the concept of **debits** and **credits**: *every* debit must have a corresponding credit. This goes to the very heart of double-entry bookkeeping. These debits and credits can be in the balance sheet, or in the profit & loss statement, or in both, but they must all balance out.

Debits and credits can be horribly confusing. Don't let this ruin your day!

Unfortunately, it is very easy to get confused about what should be a debit and what should be a credit. The best way to deal with this is to always keep in mind that debits are a *use of funds*, and credits are a *source of funds*. This is true whether you're looking at the balance sheet or profit & loss statement. In the latter, it is relatively straightforward: credits represent a plus to profit (i.e. a source of funds, such as sales), while debits represent a minus to profit (i.e. a use of funds, such as costs). *So that must mean credits are 'good', debits are 'bad', right?!*

Wrong! ... at least as far as the balance sheet is concerned, where debits represent an *increase* to assets and a *decrease* to liabilities and shareholders' funds – in both cases a *use* of funds. And, of course, credits are the reverse – that is, a source of funds. No wonder it's confusing – it all seems to be the wrong way around.

Debits, which are assets in the balance sheet, are now 'good'; credits, which are liabilities in the balance sheet, are now 'bad'. The flaw in this argument is to think of holding assets as solely 'good'. Assets, like employees, are a resource to be deployed in the efficient running of the business. A good business manager wants to have neither too much nor too little. Indeed, some assets, while sometimes unavoidable, are simply a drain on the cash resources of the business. A classic example of this would be **trade debtors**. By the same token, **trade creditors** – a liability – are a positive help to cash flow.

A further explanation as to why we struggle with this concept is because we think of debits and credits in terms of our own bank accounts. If the bank credits our account with money, we are pleased, as they have added money to it. If they debit our account it is 'bad', as they are taking money away from it. *But actually, the terminology is from the bank's viewpoint, not the customer's.* If your bank account is in credit, it is actually a *liability* to the bank. They owe you that balance, and should you require it, they will have to pay it to you. Crediting your account with money is *increasing* their liability.

The best way to get to grips with debits and credits in the context of the balance sheet is to look at some examples. Here are two simple examples of how different accounting activities will impact the balance sheet and keep it in balance. If whilst looking at these two examples, the debit and credit aspect starts to confuse you, just try remembering again that credits are the *source of funds* and debits the *application of funds*. Alternatively, think in terms of changes rather than just balances; i.e. if something gets 'bigger' or 'smaller' in the balance sheet there has to be another corresponding transaction to make it balance. Grasping this concept is the important part – the correct terminology can follow.

Example 1: The company buys a new £3,000 laptop for a staff member

In this example, let's assume the company pays for the computer in cash. Hence the cash balance in the assets column will fall by the amount paid (£3,000). This is the *credit* (where the money has been sourced). But at the same time the business now owns a new asset – the laptop – which will appear as a **fixed asset** worth £3,000. This is the *debit* (where the money has been applied). The point is the cash value has gone down and the fixed asset register has been increased by the same value. Therefore, the debits and credits balance out.

Interestingly, if the company had bought the computer with a loan, then the fixed assets would grow, as above. However, instead of the cash falling, the liabilities would rise by the corresponding amount. *The fixed assets would be debited and the liabilities would be credited.*

Another fundamental point to note about this example is that the balance sheet *does not grow or shrink in overall value* – the assets/liabilities have just been *re-arranged.* No wealth has been added to, or been taken away from, the business.

Has this purchase affected the profit & loss statement?

The answer is *'not yet'*. Both the debit and credit sides of the transaction occur only in the balance sheet – at this stage the profit & loss is unchanged. Once the asset starts to age, its value will depreciate, and it is at this point the profit & loss becomes involved. The depreciation will be charged to the profit & loss as a cost and the value of the computer will be reduced in the balance sheet by this exact amount of depreciation. *The profit & loss has been debited and the fixed assets have been credited.* If the £3,000 computer was depreciated over three years, then its value in the balance sheet would be reduced by £1,000 each year (or around £83 a month) and this amount charged to the profit & loss as a cost. At the end of the first month of the computer's life it would have a balance sheet value of £2,917. This simple asset purchase has now affected all three of the financial statements.

Example 2: The company issues some new shares to raise some capital

Note how in Example 1, all the activity took place on the 'left-hand' side of the balance sheet. We increased fixed assets and reduced cash (or increased liabilities if the money was borrowed). In this second example, the activity happens on *both* sides.

Again, it is a very simple change. Imagine the company has successfully completed a £180,000 fund-raising round by issuing new shares in exchange for cash. The company will receive £180,000 in cash from the new shareholders. This will go into the bank account and increase cash assets by that amount – *a debit* (the application of the new money).

So where does the credit side go? This will appear on the 'right-hand' side of the balance sheet under shareholders' equity. *The shareholders' equity has been credited by £180,000* (the source of the new money). In a nutshell, we have increased assets (debited) by £180,000 and increased shareholders' equity (credited) by the same amount. Everything remains balanced.

Finally note that this transaction has *increased* the value of the balance sheet (but *not* affected the profit & loss). This is because new wealth has been *added* to the business by the share issue. Investors have put in new cash (arriving on the left-hand side of the balance sheet) in exchange for new shares (the value of which is put on the right-hand side of the balance sheet).

Once you have grasped these examples, you are well on your way to understanding the balance sheet.

The Balance Sheet

- The balance sheet formula is *Assets – Liabilities = Shareholders' Equity*.
- The balance sheet is often shown as a list and the formula above can be expressed differently (but the meaning is always the same).
- The balance sheet will always balance. If it is out of balance, there is an error somewhere.
- Any changes to the profit & loss statement affect the balance sheet.
- Some changes just affect one side of the balance sheet, whilst others affect both sides.
- There is always a corresponding debit (application of funds) or credit (source of funds) for each change.
- In the profit & loss, sales are a credit, and hence are a positive to profitability, whilst costs are a debit and will reduce profitability.
- In the balance sheet, it all appears 'the other way around' and can be thoroughly confusing. For example, adding to cash is a debit and reduction to cash is a credit. Don't let this ruin your day! Once you've understood the logic it will all suddenly seem quite simple.

3.2 A TOUR OF THE BALANCE SHEET

If you want to get to know somewhere, it's quite helpful if someone gives you a quick tour of the place. We are going to do just that with the balance sheet, and we will dive into a little more detail in places, but overall we will try and explain it all as simply as possible.

We'll start by taking a detailed look at the items that make up a balance sheet. Some of these are conceptually very simple (e.g. cash, stock), whilst others are more complicated and somewhat confusing (e.g. share premium and revaluation reserves). Stay with us on the journey as you will be richly rewarded by – hopefully – a substantial advance in your understanding.

To make life a little more complicated, assets are divided into two types – **non-current assets** and **current assets.** And anything that we owe is divided into **current liabilities** and **long-term liabilities**. There is good logic and common sense behind these classifications, and fortunately, the concepts are relatively easy to understand.

Note that we talk in terms of the 'left hand' and 'right hand' sides of the balance sheet, reflecting the formula. This is to help you understand the concepts. But as previously explained, most large companies express their balance sheet in the form of a list of assets, liabilities and equity. It makes no difference – the formula is still clear to see.

Tulip Greeting Cards — **Balance Sheet as at 31 December 2019**

Assets - Liabilities			=	*Shareholders' Equity*	
		£'000			£'000
Non-current assets				**Capital and reserves**	
Fixed assets		1,920		Called up share capital	240
				Share premium	300
Current assets				Revaluation reserve	510
Stock	620			Retained earnings	750
Debtors	1,850				
Cash	250				
	2,720				
Current liabilities					
Falling due within 1 year	(1,740)				
Net current assets		980			
Long-term liabilities					
Falling due after 1 year		(1,100)			
Net assets		**1,800**		**Shareholders' Equity**	**1,800**

The above balance sheet is for **Tulip Greeting Cards**. As explained earlier, this is based upon our former greeting card business Card Connection Limited. The numbers have been changed slightly, but still give us a real-life example of a successful business.

The first thing to observe is the two sides of the balance sheet – the left-hand side being the **assets and liabilities**, and the right-hand side being the **shareholders' equity** (also known as shareholders' funds). The formula is written above in red as a reminder.

The second thing to observe is the relative simplicity of the statement. There isn't a lot of detail – what makes up the non-current assets of £1.9m? What are those current liabilities of £2.7m? *Isn't this all a bit vague?*

The answer to this is straightforward. For the purposes of looking at the big picture of the business, this statement is fine. It allows us to quickly see how the assets and liabilities are allocated and the net asset value of the business. If we require more detailed information, there are notes in the accounts to allow us to dig deeper. These notes are a key part of any set of accounts and they usually contain all sorts of breakdowns of the figures and explanations. Inevitably, the larger the company the more extensive these notes are likely to be. Take a look at a major listed company's accounts, and you will see pages and pages of them.

Let's look at each item in turn.

Non-current Assets

Non-current assets are best described as the assets the company owns which are not typically traded as part of the operation of the business, and, generally speaking, are not readily convertible to cash. Non-current assets are broken down into two types:

- **Fixed assets** (also called *tangible fixed assets*): these are usually the items that support the operations of the business, such as buildings, machinery, computers, cars, and office equipment.
- **Intangible assets**: these are assets that have no physical presence, such as trademarks, copyrights, patents and goodwill, but which are deemed to have a very real economic value all the same.

Non-current assets may even include assets that have nothing to do with the operation of the business, such as surplus land or buildings, or investments in other companies. So, non-current assets cover a broad range of potential items.

The term 'fixed' is quite helpful to focus on. These assets tend not to be traded: hence they are constant or *fixed* in their nature. Contrast this with stock, which is of course traded each day as part of the company's operations. They are both assets, but of a different nature.

Here is a breakdown of Tulip Greeting Card's fixed assets, which was provided in the notes of the accounts:

Fixed Assets	£'000
Freehold building	1,450
Plant & equipment	360
Vehicles	30
Fixtures & fittings	25
Freehold improvements	55
Total	**1,920**

We can see a variety of assets above, the largest of which is a freehold building. The other assets relate to plant & equipment (which in this case includes some wrapping machinery and computers), vehicles, fixtures & fittings (such as office furniture) and improvements to the property. The freehold improvements relate to the past installation of air-conditioning and other additions.

Freehold buildings are generally regarded as high-quality assets, since they are relatively easy to value and sell. This value in the balance sheet is therefore easier to verify and more likely to be a truer figure than some of the other assets listed.

But surely all these numbers are true? Well, yes and no! They will be true assuming correct accounting principles have been applied and the business is a going concern (i.e. has not ceased, nor is about to cease, trading). However, this does not mean the assets could immediately be sold at these precise values. In fact, this is most *unlikely* to be the case as we learned in Chapter 2.5. The valuations should be read more as an expression of the assets' cost rather their open market value. If we were buying the business, we should not take the values shown in the accounts are being true. We should carry out our own analysis to calculate their worth. This would be part of any **due diligence** process.

How Non-current Assets from the Balance Sheet Impact the Profit & Loss Statement

Give some thought as to how the balance sheet and the profit & loss statements are linked regarding non-current assets. *Does activity in one statement impact the other?*

The answer is most definitely *yes* – the two statements are inextricably connected with regard to non-current assets in particular. As we learned in Chapter 2.5, depreciation can be a significant cost line in the profit & loss statement, reflecting the *use* of assets. But, somewhat confusingly, the exact same item, depreciation, also appears in the balance sheet. *How can this be?*

The difference is that, whereas depreciation in the profit & loss statement represents the *use* of funds (a debit), in the balance sheet it represents the corresponding *source* of those funds (a credit). It is, therefore, the flip side of the depreciation double-entry. The source is the piece of an asset that has been used up or depreciated. Remember, if you are struggling with the concept of debits and credits do not worry – just think of it as two corresponding reductions. The asset value is reduced and this is balanced by a reduction in the profit.

Depreciation Example

Let's assume the company buys some new machinery on 1 January 2020 that cost £24,000. We are depreciating it on a **straight line** basis over five years, hence by 31 December 2025 the book value will be zero. This means the monthly depreciation will be:

$$\frac{£24{,}000}{60\ months} = £400\ per\ month$$

We can see from the table below how this depreciation is applied each month:

Fixed Asset Depreciation

£	Jan-20	Feb-20	Mar-20	Apr-20	May-20
Machinery value at start of month	24,000	23,600	23,200	22,800	22,400
Monthly depreciation	(400)	(400)	(400)	(400)	(400)
Machinery value at end of month	23,600	23,200	22,800	22,400	22,000

On 1 January, the asset is valued at £24,000 (what it cost new), but at the month end it is only valued at £23,600. This is then the value assumed at the start of the following month, and again a charge of £400 is applied, further reducing the value to £23,200. This process continues over the chosen five-year period.

The month-end values are the figures that will appear in the balance sheet each month, and the amount of depreciation – in this case £400 – is what is charged as a cost to the profit & loss statement. This principle is applied to all the assets where relevant.

As we learned in Chapter 2.5, different rates of depreciation may be applied to different types of assets. For example, a laptop computer may be depreciated over just three years using the straight line method. However, a car may be depreciated at a rate of 25% per annum using the **reducing balance** method. These applications are recognising the reality that the laptop may have no functional use or value at the end of this period, whilst a car will continue to have both for several years beyond its disposal by the company.

Treatment of Property in UK Accounts

Note that freehold land is not depreciated at all in the United Kingdom, since it is deemed to be one of the few types of an asset that do not have a finite life. This is not to say that its value will not rise or fall due to market conditions, but this is a different process requiring a different accounting treatment. Any building, or improvements to the property such as installing air-conditioning or redecoration, is deemed to have a finite life and *will* be depreciated.

In the case of a freehold building, the value of the land element and the building element need to be identified in order to depreciate the building element only. The rate of depreciation on this building element will be low (2.5% per annum is suggested). Given that buildings in the United Kingdom, providing they are properly maintained, tend to appreciate in value, it is arguable whether this is necessary. However, the correct process would be to depreciate them, then revalue them if appropriate every few years.

How Non-current Assets from the Balance Sheet Impact the Cash Flow Statement

If an asset is purchased outright (i.e. not from borrowed money), then the impact on the cash flow statement is immediate as the cash goes out of the business to pay for it. From then on there is no impact on the cash flow statement unless the asset is sold, in which case the cash obtained would then appear in the bank account.

But surely as depreciation is impacting the profit & loss statement, it must also impact the cash flow statement?

The answer is most definitely *no*. Depreciation is not a cash flow item – it is purely an accounting adjustment. This adjustment to the profit & loss ensures the cost of the assets of the business is taken into account in a progressive and consistent manner, regardless of how the asset has been paid for. In the earlier example of a £24,000 purchase of machinery, the cash may have gone out in January 2020 to pay for it, but it would be ludicrous to have a £24,000 cost charged to the profit & loss in January as a one-off item. This would not reflect the fact the machinery has at least a five-year economic life. Likewise, it would be equally foolish to ignore the fact that this machinery would decline in value and to make no allowance for its cost over the five-year period. If we did this, we would be overstating our profitability.

If an asset was purchased using bank debt, hire purchase, or leasing, then the cash flow statement *would* be affected. The bank account would go down by whatever monthly payment was required to repay the loan and pay the interest cost. However, this is a *finance* matter, not directly relevant to fixed asset costs and depreciation.

Intangible Assets

There are no **intangible assets** in the Tulip Greeting Cards balance sheet example, but as explained above these are items such as such as trademarks, copyrights, patents and goodwill.

Goodwill is a balancing figure that is created to account for the difference in value that might have been paid for an acquisition beyond the net book value of the business. For example, Company A buys Company B for £2.5m. The net asset value (i.e. balance sheet value) of Company B is £1.5m, hence Company A is paying £1m over this amount. This will go into the balance sheet as goodwill – a sum that reflects the value of the business beyond its simple assets. In terms of the balance sheet, the £1m will sit in the non-current assets (this is the debit), and the corresponding balancing item will be the reduction in cash (the credit).

Intangible assets are recorded in value over a time period in a similar way to depreciating the value of a tangible asset. The only real difference is that this process is called *amortisation* rather than *depreciation*. Some intangible assets may have a very specific lifespan (such as a patent or a copyright), whilst other intangible assets may not have such a specific lifespan but the value will be amortised over a timespan that is considered prudent (goodwill could be an example of this). Some intangible assets may even be deemed not to have a finite life (possibly a trade mark or goodwill). However, prudent management would require that the value is reviewed and adjusted for impairment at any stage.

Non-current Assets

- Non-current assets are best described as the assets a company owns that are not typically traded as part of the operation of the business, and/or are not readily convertible to cash. These assets can be either tangible fixed assets (e.g. a building) and intangible assets (e.g. a patent).
- Generally speaking, these assets are depreciated or amortised each month as they age. This depreciation is charged to the profit & loss statement, and the book value of the asset falls each month by this amount.
- The book value of an asset is just an accounting estimate based on its original cost – it does not mean this is what it would fetch on the open market.
- Depreciation and amortisation are accounting adjustments and only affect the profit & loss and balance sheet statements. They do not affect the cash flow statement.
- In valuing all non-current assets, it is assumed that the business is a going concern – that is, it has the ability to carry on trading.

Current Assets

As described above, current assets tend to relate to assets that are changing during the course of the trading of the business, and are, generally speaking, readily convertible to cash. In our example balance sheet, these include **stock** (inventory), **debtors** (receivables), and cash. We shall look at each in turn.

Stock (Inventory)

In the notes to the accounts, further detail is shown on what constitutes stock:

Stock	£'000
Raw materials	45
Work in progress	65
Finished goods	510
Total	**620**

We can see that the £620k related to raw materials and work in progress, as well as finished goods. This is because at the close of business on 31 December 2019, when the balance sheet is dated, not all the product had been fully manufactured. In fact, if you consider it logically, at any one moment a trading or manufacturing business is likely to be in a situation where production is incomplete, or goods are in transit. The balance sheet 'photograph' needs to capture this state of activity and to reflect the valuations of the goods as accurately as possible.

As explained earlier, the principles behind stock valuation are relatively simple. Stock is valued at the lower of cost or net realisable value.

What does this mean in practice? Well, *cost* is what it has cost the business to buy in or to manufacture, including materials and any direct labour. *Net realisable value* is what the goods would be expected to sell for (after deducting any costs associated with their sale – hence *net*). We take whichever is the *lower* as our valuation. If we believe the stock is no longer saleable at or above the price it cost us, we must reduce its value accordingly in our accounts. This may result in writing its value down to zero in order to be *prudent* – always a painful experience for management to face! You will often find that a company in difficulty has excessive levels of stock in the balance sheet. This is not just a reflection of past poor sales, it reflects the fact they have failed to dispose of worthless stock to avoid a further profit & loss hit. Beware of this situation – their balance sheet value *and* their past profits are likely to both have been overstated.

How Stock from the Balance Sheet Impacts the Profit & Loss Statement

When an item of stock is sold, the cost is charged, or debited, to cost of sales in the profit & loss statement. The corresponding credit is the reduction in the stock in the balance sheet. The stock item has left the business and been delivered to a customer. Assuming the sales price is greater than this cost of sale, then a gross profit is made and this is shown in the profit & loss statement. If the item is sold at *below* this cost price, then a loss will inevitably be made.

In the situation where stock is written down at a value below its cost price, but has not been sold, this loss is also taken in the profit & loss. Simply, the drop in value of the asset, in this case stock, has to be represented in the accounts. At a later date, if this stock is sold after all, the profit & loss is debited with the revised valuation. If this is zero, then the cost of sale is zero, of course – hence the profit & loss will treat the entire sale price as gross profit.

How Stock from the Balance Sheet Impacts the Cash Flow Statement

When stock or raw materials are purchased, they will only impact the cash flow statement when they are paid for. Depending on the trading terms involved, this may be 30 days later (or longer).

When stock is sold to a customer, the same principle applies the other way around. The cash flow statement will not be affected positively until the customer has paid the invoice, which could be 30 or more days later. If the business is a retailer, i.e. selling the goods to a consumer directly, then the sale and the arrival of the payment will, typically, happen simultaneously.

Debtors (Receivables)

Debtors are another form of current asset. They are made up of either: money owed to the business by customers (**trade debtors** and **accrued income**); money owed by other third parties (other debtors); or goods and services that the business has paid for but not yet consumed (**prepayments**).

Again, the notes to Tulip Greeting Cards' accounts provide us with more detail of how the debtor 'book' is made up.[1]

Debtors	£'000
Trade debtors	1,530
Accrued income	160
Prepayments	135
Other debtors	25
Total	**1,850**

In the example, we can see that **trade debtors** account for most of the debtor book. Trade debtors are what customers of the business owe for goods delivered and invoiced. The figure will clearly be linked to how much credit the company provides its customers; how efficient and effective the business is at collecting overdue balances; and how large the business is, or, specifically, the scale of its overall sales revenue.

Other debtors are not specified in more detail in these notes, but they are effectively a catch-all for other amounts owed to the company by third parties, such as loans made to staff, tax rebates due, etc.

Prepayments will relate to goods or services that have been paid for, but not yet received or consumed. For example, if a company pays its rent three months in advance, then after the first month, one month is charged to the profit & loss and two months are treated as prepayments. This is in accordance with the **matching principle**, which we learned about in Chapter 2.4. Although the money has left the company's bank account, the fact that the rent has not been 'consumed' yet means it is treated as an asset. Whilst there is little chance of this money being turned back into cash if the business ceased trading, we return to the **going concern principle**, i.e. the business is assumed to be carrying on trading. Hence this unused rent is of use to the business, and is a genuine asset to it. Therefore, it is treated as such in the accounts and listed as a prepayment. Again, this is another example of how everything has a logical place in a company's accounts, and nothing is ignored!

If the prepayment could no longer be used or had no value, the cost would be immediately taken in the profit & loss, and the asset would disappear from the balance sheet.

Other prepayment examples are payments in advance for raw materials that have not yet been received (and hence become stock).

Finally, Tulip Greeting Cards had £160k of goods or services that it had delivered to its customers, but for which it had not yet raised an invoice. Under the **revenue recognition principle**, this amount will have been registered as sales in the profit & loss statement (i.e. as a credit), but we cannot put the corresponding debit to debtors or cash as the customer has not even been asked for payment yet! How do we post the debit to make sure our accounts balance? The answer is that a *different type* of current asset category is created, called **accrued income**. Remember if the goods or services have been properly supplied to a customer, and there is no reason to believe the customer will not pay the invoice when received, then this is legitimately an asset of the business that should be accounted for.

Cash

Cash requires little or no explanation. It is the finest-quality current asset a business can have in terms of liquidity, and, to some extent, the more of it the better. It is also the most definite figure in the balance sheet – i.e. the least susceptible to manipulation. The main form in which this asset is held will, of course, be credit balances held in one or more bank accounts (possibly denominated in more than one currency); however, it can also be held in the form of cash in hand, such as petty cash (for minor purchases) or, in the case of a retail business, cash register floats.

The only possible argument against a business having too much cash, is that if it is not required for the normal operation of the business or to finance future expansion plans, it should be returned to the shareholders by way of a dividend.

When trading gets tough, a business with plenty of cash tends to still have plenty of options, whilst a business with no cash may have few.

Cash is widely regarded as the best form of current asset. Generally, the more of it there is in a balance sheet, the better!

Current Assets

- Current assets are usually assets that change during the course of the trading of the business.
- Stock (inventory) is often a key asset in a company's balance sheet.
- Debtors (receivables) are what the company is owed by others.
- Debtors include trade debtors, who are customers who have not yet paid for the goods and services they have already received.
- Debtors also include prepayments, which is the amount the company has paid for in advance for goods and services it has not yet received or used.
- Trade debtors are generally regarded as a high-quality asset by banks.
- Accrued income relates to sales that have been delivered to the customer, but have not yet been invoiced. This is also a current asset to the business.
- Cash is the most verifiable asset in the entire balance sheet. Generally, the more of it the better!

Current and Long-Term Liabilities

There are two categories of liability in a company's accounts: **current liabilities** and **long-term liabilities**. *So, what is the difference between the two?*

Like many aspects of accounting, the answer is extremely simple and logical. Current liabilities are due for repayment *within* the next 12 months, and long-term liabilities are due for repayment *beyond* 12 months. But there is a slight complexity to consider: what if the liability is a bank loan that is both repayable in the next 12 months *and* for a further three years beyond that? Do we treat this as a current or long-term liability? *How should this be treated in the balance sheet?*

Once again good old logic comes to our rescue. Why can't a particular debt be *both* a current and a long-term liability at the same time? The answer is it can. The proportion of any loan that is due to be repaid in the next 12 months is treated as current and the balance beyond this is treated as long-term.

Time Period Differentiation Between Current & Long-Term Liabilities

The decision to allocate a liability to either current or long-term may seem rather arbitrary at 12 months. Why not three months or three years? Why this particular cut off?

Clearly if a division has to be made, then a single year is a very tidy one. After all, we produce annual accounting statements so the year-end balance sheet is going to neatly show us the division of liabilities that need to be repaid during the next annual trading period, and those that are due beyond this period.

A year is also quite a long time in business and a great deal can happen during this period. Hence, if a business is likely to have difficulties repaying its debts, when they are due in over a year's time there is at least plenty of time to find a solution. Contrast this situation to a bank overdraft, which is repayable *on demand* (many entrepreneurs do not fully appreciate the implications of this fact). If the bank withdraws an overdraft facility, as frequently happens during turbulent economic times, a company may only have a matter of weeks to find alternative funding or face potential catastrophe.

The above example does illustrate that there is a clear distinction between short-term and long-term liabilities. So, when analysing a balance sheet this distinction is very useful. If a company has substantial short-term liabilities (i.e. current liabilities) and limited current assets then it could go bust very rapidly. Even if a business appeared to be trading well, a sudden event such as a major customer failing to pay its bill on time could result in an instantaneous financial crisis. We will look at the relationship between current assets and current liabilities later, but appreciate now the critical nature of this relationship – in essence your current assets should *ideally* exceed your current liabilities by a comfortable margin. By how much they need to exceed it is very much down to the individual type of business.

Current Liabilities (Payables)

Current liabilities (also known as *payables*) are the liabilities due to be paid by the business within the next 12 months, as at the date of the balance sheet.

In the Tulip Greeting Cards balance sheet summary, once again these are shown in a single figure. We need to go to the notes to see how these are made up:

Current Liabilities	£'000
Bank loans	250
HP finance	55
Trade creditors	670
Corporation tax	280
PAYE & VAT	165
Other creditors	85
Accruals & deferred income	235
Total	**1,740**

In all the cases above, these sums are due to be repaid within the next 12 months. With respect to the bank loans and hire purchase amount, these are the *proportions* of the entire loan that are due within this 12-month period.

The sharp-eyed reader will have spotted that these liabilities can be split into two broad types: 1) *trading* liabilities, and 2) *financing* liabilities. Trade creditors, accruals and deferred income are all examples of liabilities that arise directly from the company's *trading* activities, while bank loans and hire purchase finance are examples of liabilities that arise from the company's *financing* policies. This distinction is important, because only the latter are interest bearing, and, as we shall explore further in Chapter 3.3, only the former are netted off trading assets to calculate **capital employed** and, hence, **return on capital employed**.

Re-analysed in this context, the list of current liabilities would look more like this:

Trading Liabilities	£'000	Financing Liabilities	£'000
Trade creditors	670	Bank loans	250
Corporation tax	280	HP finance	55
PAYE & VAT	165		
Other creditors	85		
Accruals & deferred income	235		
Total	**1,435**	**Total**	**305**

Future Interest Payments Are Not Included

One interesting aspect to note with respect to debt in the balance sheet is that it does not include interest payments going forward. Although this is a commitment that cannot be avoided (unless the debt is paid off), as at the date of the balance sheet the interest is *not yet due*. This interest is a future event and a future liability that does not exist today. Of course, if the company had not paid interest that was due, say if it had defaulted on its loan terms, then this would appear as a liability in the balance sheet.

The *capital* elements of the loans, whether due to be repaid in the next year or thereafter, are very much a liability that exists at the date of the balance sheet. Hence, they *have* to be included, unlike the future interest payments.

If you find it hard to accept that future interest payment liabilities are not included in the balance sheet, remember that neither are future revenue and profits from contracts that the business may have secured. Once again, all of this follows the **matching principle**.

Accruals

Accruals relate to items that have been 'consumed' by the company but not yet invoiced for by the supplier. The company knows an invoice will come, so therefore makes a provision in advance for this. If these items were ignored, the accounts could not be described as a *true and fair view* of its financial situation.

A good example might be an external accountant's fee. The accountant may be doing work each month for the business, but only raises an invoice every three or six months. The accrual is an estimate of what is outstanding at the time of the balance sheet 'photograph' that has not yet been invoiced by the supplier.

Deferred Income

Deferred income relates to revenue received from a customer, but for which the goods or services have not yet been delivered. It is effectively the opposite of **accrued income.**

Example: The company receives full payment on the sale of an item that is currently out of stock

Let's imagine this has happened just before the year-end. The salesman responsible is excited because it would tip him over his quota for the year. Unfortunately, the accountant will have to pour cold water on his enthusiasm because the sale has not been completed until the item is finally dispatched (as indicated by the **revenue recognition principle** of accounting). It is not yet a sale as the goods have not been dispatched, despite the fact that the money is in the bank!

So how should this look in the profit & loss statement and balance sheet?

The company has received the money, so clearly cash is increased by that amount. However, if the accountant says we can't apply the credit to the profit & loss, where should we apply it? The answer is we credit it to an account called deferred income. So, cash has been debited and deferred income has been credited. Deferred income is a form of liability in the balance sheet. The company has taken money from a customer and has the obligation to fulfil the order, or failing that, return the money.

At this stage, both debit and credit apply only to the balance sheet and the profit & loss is unaffected. Once the goods finally come into stock, the transaction can be completed. The deferred income will be debited by the amount of the sale. In the profit & loss, sales revenue is credited and the cost of sale is debited, resulting in a gross profit. This profit generated will credit current year profit in the balance sheet under shareholders' equity.

Once again, this is an excellent example of how the balance sheet attempts to give a comprehensively representative picture of what is happening in the business on the date shown.

Long-Term Liabilities

Long-term liabilities relate to the proportions of any debt due for repayment *beyond* 12 months. This never includes trading liabilities, only financing liabilities.

In the case of Tulip Greeting Cards, it is primarily bank loans. In addition, there is a small residue of hire purchase debt.

Long-Term Liabilities	£'000
Bank loans	1,080
HP finance	20
Total	**1,100**

Long-term liabilities could also include items such as directors' loans, where the owners of the business have lent the company money in order to establish it or help it grow. These loans may not be interest bearing and may have no date by which they have to be repaid.

Current and Long-Term Liabilities

- Current liabilities (payables) are what the company owes *within* the next 12 months.
- Long-term liabilities are what the company owes *beyond* the next 12 months.
- Liabilities, such as a bank loan, may have elements in both these categories at the same time.
- Accruals relate to items that have been 'consumed' by the company but not yet invoiced for by the supplier.
- Deferred income usually relates to sales that have been made to a customer, but the goods or services have not yet been delivered.

Capital and Reserves

We now move to the right-hand portion of the balance sheet, or, put another way, the other half, which shows how the net assets (assets minus liabilities) of the company have been funded *by its shareholders*. Labelled 'capital and reserves', this represents **shareholders' equity** (also known as shareholders' funds) – the wealth that the shareholders have invested in the business, and which constitutes the equity part of the company's funding.

Called Up Share Capital

Every company has a document called its **articles of association**. This document is the company's constitution – it spells out the powers and responsibilities of the directors and the rights of shareholders. These articles specify the characteristics of each share class and their **nominal value**. For example, a company may have shares with a nominal value of £1 each, but could in theory be any value. Generally, companies tend to opt for smaller values to make them more divisible and tradeable amongst a number of different individual shareholders.[2]

When a company is formed, shares are issued to the founding shareholders at the nominal share price. This is the **called up share capital** and is generally paid up in full, in which case the full description would be 'allotted, called up and fully paid'.[3]

This share capital is equivalent to the initial funding of the business – it is where it begins.

In exchange for the shares, the shareholders pay money to the company, and this money is the founding capital of the business. This newly added 'wealth' will immediately appear on the other side of the balance sheet as cash, prior to being invested or spent. Hence from the very moment of the birth of the business, the balance sheet balances.

Share Premium

As time goes on, the company may issue further new shares in exchange for new capital. The balance sheet will grow in value immediately as new cash comes in and is represented as additional share capital. Although every share (in the same class) has the same nominal value, it does not necessarily mean that each owner has paid the same amount for their shares. In practice, it may have been able to issue shares at a higher price. The difference is counted as **share premium.**

In our Tulip Greeting Cards example, the amount of called up share capital is shown as £240,000. From the notes (not shown here), we can determine that these are £1 shares, and therefore there are 240,000 in issue.

Tulip Greeting Cards' initial share issue was as follows:

$$200{,}000 \times £1\ \textit{shares} = £200{,}000\ \textit{of Share Capital}$$

A subsequent share issue of 40,000 new shares took place at £8.50 each. A *premium* of £7.50 was paid by the purchasers of the new shares *over* the nominal value of £1:

$$40{,}000 \times £8.50 = £340{,}000\ \textit{of New Capital}$$

In terms of the effect on the balance sheet, on the left-hand side (under current assets) £340,000 will appear as cash. On the right-hand side (under shareholders' equity), called up share capital would have increased by £40,000 and share premium by £300,000. So, in short, cash is debited by £340,000, issued share capital is credited by £40,000 and share premium is credited by £300,000. Everything balances neatly.

Is the total value of all the share capital then what the business is worth? Most definitely not! It just represents what has been subscribed for in terms of the nominal value of shares issued. The actual value of the business may vastly exceed this, or even be zero if it has failed.

Share Capital Can Be Tiny

You may well come across a balance sheet with just £2 of share capital, with perhaps just 2 shares of £1 issued. This will typically be a small business where the owners have lent the company the capital to get going, which is usually referred to as a **directors' loan**. The advantage of funding a business in this way is that once it is trading profitably, the loan can be repaid tax-free. If the money had been invested as share capital, then any capital coming back to the founders would be either as a **dividend** or in salary, both of which are subject to income tax.

The disadvantage of this method of funding is that the balance sheet can look very weak. This is because unless it has made good profits, its liabilities could exceed its assets – hence the balance sheet could have a negative value. This will make raising money from banks difficult. It will also negatively affect a company's credit rating.

Revaluation Reserve

When an asset has been in the balance sheet for a while, its value may need to be revised. For example, if a company bought a building for £1m, but 10 years later it is now worth £2m, how is this dealt with in the balance sheet?

The obvious answer is to revise the fixed assets up by £1m, to reflect the new £2m valuation. But the balance sheet will not now balance, unless there is a corresponding change elsewhere. This is what the **revaluation reserve** is used for – a sort of balancing pot of accounting money sitting on the right-hand side of the balance sheet. In this example, the fixed asset would rise from £1m to £2m, and a revaluation reserve would be created for £1m. Fixed assets have been debited by £1m and the revaluation reserve has been credited by £1m.

Has the company therefore made a £1m profit?

Very simply *'no'* - not until it *disposes* of the asset. If the company did sell the building at the new value, it would generate a profit of £1m. This would probably be described in the profit & loss statement as an 'extraordinary profit' because it was not part of the everyday trading of the business.

The building's value would then come out of the fixed assets, and the revaluation reserve would fall from £1m to zero again (as the gain has now been realised). In addition, £2m of cash would appear (assuming it was owned outright) and £1m would be added to the retained earnings line in the balance sheet (explained further below). Or in accounting language, fixed assets are credited by £2m; cash is debited by £2m; the revaluation reserve is debited by £1m; and the profit & loss is credited by £1m.

So, to recap, a gain in the value of an asset that has not yet been realised is shown as a **revaluation reserve.** *But if the value of the property subsequently fell, what would happen to the revaluation reserve?*

If the building dropped in value from £2m to £1.5m, the revaluation reserve would just be reduced to £0.5m. Any continued fall in the value of the assets, which had previously been revalued, would follow this process until the revaluation reserve fell to zero. This process would have *no impact* on the profit & loss, as remember no profit has been taken. *The assets have not been sold, so no profit has been realised.*

Tulip Greetings Cards has just such a revaluation reserve, in this case £510k, which was directly attributable to the rise in value of its property asset.

If an asset like a building is revalued upwards in the balance sheet, a revaluation reserve is created under shareholders' equity. It is not taken as a profit until the building is actually sold.

Impairment Losses

What if the building were to fall in value below its original cost, i.e. £1m? What if it was only now worth £0.75m?

This is where the treatment varies. Following on from the logic above, you could argue that a negative revaluation reserve would reflect the situation adequately. It would show the depleted value of the balance sheet. However, as *prudence* is one of the six fundamental principles of accounting, this methodology is regarded as insufficiently cautious. Instead, the reduction in value would be taken straight to the profit & loss.

In terms of the balance sheet, the fixed assets would decline by the drop in value, and a corresponding reduction in the retained earnings line in the balance sheet. The fixed assets would be credited by £250,000 and the profit & loss would be debited by £250,000.

Retained Earnings

In order to fully understand **retained earnings**, consider what happens when a business makes a profit. Assuming the customer pays its invoice, this profit will turn up in the balance sheet as cash. But where else is it represented in the balance sheet? There has to be a corresponding balancing figure.

Clearly if a profit has been made, wealth has been created. The shareholders have just got richer – their wealth has literally grown. It is therefore appropriate that this is also represented under shareholders' equity.

Retained earnings can also be referred to as the 'profit & loss account' in the balance sheet. Do not confuse this with the profit & loss *statement*.

This is dealt with by having a special item within shareholders' equity in the balance sheet called the 'profit & loss account'. You might – quite reasonably – find that confusing because we know that the profit & loss statement is a separate thing, right? Well, no… it's not really! Remember we stated earlier that, of the three key statements, the balance sheet is the master: well here is an example of how that is true. The balance sheet is actually a list of running balances, at a given moment in time, of *all* the various categories of account on each side of the **accounting equation**, and the profit & loss account (as found in the balance sheet) is simply one of those accounts – albeit a particularly important one. The profit & loss account item in the balance sheet simply shows the net figure of all the debits and credits that have been posted through the profit & loss statement in the course of the current financial year. In other words, at any given moment during the current financial year it shows the bottom-line profit for the year-to-date.

At the end of the year, when the **profit after tax** for the year has been finalised and the dividends declared, the residual amount is transferred to another shareholders' funds account called **retained earnings**. Consequently, the profit & loss account itself is cleared to zero for the end of year balance sheet, which is why you will typically only see 'retained earnings', and not 'profit & loss account' listed in published balance sheets. You may see the two items listed separately in management accounts, depending on whether the directors wish to see a distinction in their monthly balance sheet between retained profit brought forward from previous years and profit made to date in the current year. Or they may consider that it is effectively the same thing and list it under 'retained earnings'. For simplicity, we shall use 'retained earnings' to denote the accumulation of both past and current year profits.

Retained earnings is an extremely appropriate description. *It is the wealth that the company has generated that has been retained in the business.*

Retained Earnings Are Cumulative

The retained earnings figure in the balance sheet is a *cumulative* one. It is the addition of all past profit & losses (after tax) ever made in the history of the business that has not been paid out as **dividend** (or capitalised as share capital). It is not just the profit or loss for that particular accounting period. So, a quick glance at this number can tell you a lot – if it is large, the business has a strong history of profitability. If it is negative, the trading has clearly been a little problematic! In this case, it would be referred to as **accumulated losses** or accumulated deficit.

Also, if you are looking at the balance sheet of two consecutive accounting years, a quick glance at the *change in the retained earnings figures* will give you an indication of the profitability between the two periods. Some small businesses are only required to file abbreviated annual accounts; these include the balance sheet but not the profit & loss statement. Hence this is a useful way of gleaning their profitability without actually viewing the profit & loss statement.

There are some important things to also understand about the retained earnings figure. It is only a cumulative history of profitability *net of corporation tax and dividend payments.* So, if a dividend was declared and paid to the shareholders, the cash balance would fall as the money was paid out, and this retained earnings balance would be reduced by the corresponding amount. The wealth that was generated has left the business in cash and, as when a profit is made, this change needs to be reflected in the shareholders' equity with the same reduction.

Conversion of Retained Earnings to Share Capital

If a company wishes, it can convert its retained earnings balance into share capital. This is done through a **scrip issue** – basically issuing new shares to the current shareholders for the value of the funds in retained earnings. This is often described as 'window dressing' as it is just a process of tidying up the balance sheet presentation. Note the balance sheet *value* will not change. The share capital will grow and the retained earnings will fall by the same amounts.

Retained Earnings and Dividends

It is an important principle in company law that share capital cannot be used to pay dividends.[4] Dividends must be paid only from profits, whether made in the year or accumulated from previous years.

Hence it is illegal to pay a dividend to shareholders if the retained earnings figure is negative (known as accumulated losses), or if the payment of the dividend would make it become negative. In essence, this is a fundamental feature of the limited liability company, to preserve its capital base. This stipulation reduces the opportunities for shareholders to remove wealth from a business ahead of the creditors.

Capital & Reserves

- Share capital (and any share premium) relates to the value of the shares the company has issued in exchange for cash. Note it is not what the shares are worth today as this is likely to be a totally different number, depending on how successful the business has been.
- Share premium arises where the company is able to issue new shares at a price higher than their nominal value.
- The revaluation reserve is a balancing figure to take into account any revaluation of fixed assets. It is not a profit, as the assets have not yet been sold.
- It is not possible to have a negative revaluation reserve. Instead an impairment loss is generated and will be taken in the profit & loss statement.
- Retained earnings are the cumulative history of profitability net of corporation tax, dividend payments, and any scrip issues.
- It is illegal to pay a dividend if retained earnings in the balance sheet is negative, or would be made negative by the dividend. This is a protection for creditors of the company.

Further Examples of How Transactions Affect the Balance Sheet

Here are some additional examples of how different types of transactions will impact the balance sheet. Note that the references to the left-hand side (LHS) and the right-hand side (RHS) of the balance sheet are purely used to help you understand the concepts. In practice, they are often shown as lists, as demonstrated with the **easyJet** example shown in Chapter 3.4.

Example	Effect on LHS of Balance Sheet	Effect on RHS of Balance Sheet	Comments
Company makes a trading profit.	Cash or debtors grow.	Retained earnings grow.	Real wealth has been created and the balance sheet grows in value.
Company makes a trading loss.	Cash falls or debts increase to fund the loss.	Retained earnings fall.	Real wealth has been destroyed and the balance sheet shrinks in value.
Company pays off a short-term liability, such as a supplier's invoice.	Cash falls to repay it, and simultaneously creditors (in current liabilities) also falls by the same amount.	No change.	No wealth has been created or destroyed. There is no change to the balance sheet value.
Company takes out a £100k loan over a 5-year period.	Cash grows by £100k. current liabilities grow by £20k and long term liabilities by £80k.	No change.	No wealth has been created or destroyed. There is no change to the balance sheet value.

(continued)

Example	Effect on LHS of Balance Sheet	Effect on RHS of Balance Sheet	Comments
Company pays a dividend.	Cash falls by the dividend amount paid.	Retained earnings reduced by the same amount.	Balance sheet shrinks as wealth has been ***removed*** from the business and passed to the shareholders.
New shares are issued to an investor in exchange for cash.	Cash grows.	Share capital grows.	Real wealth has been ***added*** to the business. Hence the value of the balance sheet grows.
The company buys an asset, such as a computer and pays with cash.	Cash falls. Fixed assets rise.	No change.	No wealth has been created or destroyed. There is no change to the balance sheet value.
The company buys an asset, such as a computer and pays with finance such as hire purchase.	Cash falls by the amount of any initial payment. Fixed assets rise. Current and long-term liabilities both rise, as per taking out a loan above.	No change.	No wealth has been created or destroyed. There is no change to the balance sheet value.

Notes

1. The term debtor 'book' originates from the fact it would once have been a hand-written ledger maintained by an accounts clerk!
2. Prior to 1 October 2009, following changes brought about by the Companies Act 2006, companies were required to have a maximum level of share capital that could be issued, which was known as the **authorised share capital**. You may still see this feature in some accounts. Note that the authorised share capital does not form part of the balance sheet because it does not represent the amount of share capital actually held by shareholders.
3. It is possible that share capital is not fully paid up, i.e. shareholders may have paid for part and have a liability to pay the balance when called to do so. Hence there is a technical difference between called up share capital and paid up share capital, but generally called up share capital in a balance sheet is already fully paid. The notes in the balance sheet will fully clarify the situation.
4. Companies Act, 2006.

3.3 ANALYSING THE BALANCE SHEET

Congratulations! If you have understood what you have read so far, you are close to mastering the balance sheet. Whilst balance sheets will vary in terms of format, content and terminology, you have seen and hopefully understood the fundamental principles. These do not change regardless of layout and terminology.

Let's go one step further and start thinking about the meaning of what you are looking at. Is this a 'good' balance sheet or a 'bad' one? Is this business giving a high return on the assets that are employed in it? Or is it about to fail?

We are only going to focus on a few key ratios here – our goal is to progressively introduce them to you. We will look at some additional balance sheet related ratios later in the book. A comprehensive list of all ratios, covering most aspects of financial performance measurement, can be found in Appendix 2.

Tulip Greeting Cards' Profit & Loss Statement

As you will learn below, several balance sheet ratios refer to numbers from the profit & loss statement. We have introduced you to Tulip Greeting Cards' balance sheet on page 91. Below is the corresponding profit & loss statement for the year to 31 December 2019:

Tulip Greeting Cards

Profit & Loss Statement 2019	**£'000**	**Margins**
Sales	6,980	
Cost of sales	(2,350)	
Gross profit	**4,630**	*66%*
Operating expenses	(3,560)	
EBITDA	**1,070**	*15%*
Depreciation	(170)	
Operating profit	**900**	*13%*
Interest	(60)	
Profit before tax	**840**	*12%*
Corporation tax	(270)	
Profit after tax	**570**	*8%*

You will notice we have added some margin percentages – notably, gross margin at 66%, and profit before tax margin at 12%. Get into the habit of doing this whenever you see a profit & loss statement – these are two of the most vital measures of your profitability. We can quickly observe that these figures are healthy (remember a very rough rule of thumb is a gross margin in excess of 50%, and a profit before tax margin in excess of 10% is generally where you want to be – although this will vary considerably between different types of business).

Profitability and the Balance Sheet

We have repeatedly banged the drum over the importance of profitability. But the profit figure itself in monetary value needs to be viewed in the context of the *scale of assets* used to generate that profit. A £1m profit after tax may be a brilliant result for a relatively small business, but a £1m profit after tax from a major company like Tesco would be considered disastrously poor performance. *But why is this? The result is surely the same?* Quite simply the result is only the same monetary value, but when taking into account the scale of Tesco's operations, with the billions of £'s in store assets, such a result would show the management is not making good use of the assets.

Return on Equity

The **return on equity** calculation looks at the profit after tax[1] relative to the size of the balance sheet:

$$Return\,on\,Equity = \frac{Profit\;After\,Tax}{Shareholders'\,Equity}$$

Remember that shareholders' equity and net assets are exactly the same thing – they are just the totals of each side of the balance sheet. So, the above formula is identical to return on net assets. It is showing us how much profit is being generated relative to the wealth the shareholders' have invested in the business, or put another way, relative to the net value of assets tied up in the business.[2]

Let's look at Tulip Greeting Cards' return on equity:

$$Return\,on\,Equity = \frac{£570{,}000}{£1{,}800{,}000} = 31.7\%$$

What it is telling us is that for every £1 of shareholders' equity, or net assets, we are getting back 32p profit after tax. *Is this figure good or bad?* By any measure this is a good result, especially when thinking about the low level of return a bank would offer for money on deposit. Here are some factors to consider when considering the return on equity figure:

- What is the average for the industry sector? Does the company out-perform or under-perform against comparative businesses?
- Highly capital-intensive businesses (such as a car manufacturer) are more likely to achieve lower rates of return, whilst a capital-light business (such as a software developer) may have higher returns.

But hang on a minute… return on equity only gives us part of the picture. What if a business was carrying a great deal of debt to achieve its results? Although the cost of the debt (i.e. the interest paid) would be taken into account in the profit after tax figure, the net assets figure would be net of any debt. Surely it is relevant to look at the *total capital* used to achieve the profitability, not just the net assets?

The answer is most definitely *yes*, and this is where **return on capital employed** comes in, arguably one of the most important ratios in the entire world of business.

Return on Capital Employed

Capital employed is defined as the *capital investment necessary for a business to function*. It can be calculated either in terms of the amount of *assets* required to run the business, or in terms of the amount of *funds* necessarily invested to run the business. Both methods produce the same result. The table below illustrates the two sides of the capital employed equation.

Asset Side (Use of Capital)				**Funding Side (Provision of Capital)**
Fixed Assets - Plant & machinery - Fixtures & fittings - Motor vehicles **Current Assets** - Stock - Debtors - Cash for working capital ***Less* Current Liabilities** - Trade creditors - Tax owed	=	**Capital Employed**	=	**Shareholders' Equity** - Issued share capital - Share premium - Retained earnings **Debt** - Director's loans - Bank loans - Overdrafts - Hire purchase ***Less* Investment Assets** (possibly including excess cash)

The exact definition can vary, so expect to see the formula written in different ways. The most common – and we would suggest most logical – definition is as follows:

$$\textit{Capital Employed} = \textit{Shareholders' Equity} + \textit{Bank Debt}$$

Note that the definition of bank debt above is fairly broad, and would include:

- Bank or other interest-bearing debt (such as overdrafts and hire purchase).
- Directors' loans, even if these are not interest bearing, as this is most evidently capital that has been put into the business.
- Hire purchase arrangements.

It would not include:

- Creditors.

Another way of looking at capital employed is in terms of the sum of assets, such as:[3]

$$Capital\ Employed = Fixed\ Assets + Stock + Debtors - Creditors$$

Cash and Capital Employed Calculation

It is debatable how cash should be treated. Every business requires a certain amount of cash for **working capital**. However, if the business is sitting on excessive quantities of cash that is not required for the operation of the business, it could be argued that this should be deducted from the capital employed figure.[4]

We would recommend sticking to the first formula we showed above, but being aware there are arguments for variations to this, depending on circumstances.

Confusion Between Capital Employed and Net Assets

It is easy to get confused between the balance sheet value (net assets or shareholders' equity), and capital employed. They are different things, but could of course be the same value depending on the structure of the company's debt. The easiest way to understand this is to look at two examples.

Example 1: A company is started with £20 of share capital injected as cash and this is the only asset

The balance sheet is made up of cash on the 'left-hand' side and share capital of £20 on the 'right-hand' side. The balance sheet balances and has a net asset value of £20. What is the capital employed? It is of course £20 – there is no other capital associated to this business.

$$Assets - Liabilities = Shareholders'\ Equity$$

$$£20 - £0 = £20$$

Example 2: The same company but with a £1,000 loan

The company now borrows £1,000 from Barclays Bank and let us assume it invests this into some form of asset. The capital employed is now:

$$£20 + £1{,}000 = £1{,}020$$

But, critically, note the balance sheet value remains £20, since on the left-hand side it has £1,000 of new assets but also a liability in the form of the £1,000 loan. Therefore, they cancel each other out in terms of calculating the net asset value.

$$Assets - Liabilities = Shareholders'\ Equity$$

$$£1{,}020 - £1{,}000 = £20$$

Significance of Return on Capital Employed

The balance sheet shows us what assets and capital are employed in the business. However, if we want to determine the *productivity* of these assets in terms of generating wealth, we need to again look at the balance sheet in conjunction with the profit & loss statement. This will produce a valuable indicator, which can then be compared to alternative investments or competitors to determine whether performance is 'good' or 'bad'. It can also be looked at over time, which will give us an indication of how the business is progressing.

When it comes to financial ratios, return on capital employed is a 'rock star'. It shows us both how efficiently assets are being employed and indicates how quickly a business could grow from its own capital resources.

At a very simple level, if the company above made £20 profit before it borrowed the money from the bank, we could reasonably say this was 'good' since it returned 100% of its capital back within a year. The return on capital employed was 100% (with obviously very small numbers though!).

In the second situation, having borrowed £1,000 from the bank, if the business had made the same £20 profit we might deem this result to be 'bad' since the return on capital employed would have been a mere 2%:

$$\frac{EBIT\,(Operating\ Profit)}{Shareholders'\ Equity + Bank\ Debt} = \frac{£20}{£20 + £1{,}000} = 1.96\%$$

This illustrates the importance of considering how much capital is actually tied up in the company. The rate of return, or return on capital employed, will profoundly influence both how fast the company can grow without new external capital and how rapidly the shareholders will get richer.

Imagine two different businesses, both with rapid sales and profit growth at 50% per annum. You might imagine they're both equally attractive businesses. However, one generates 50% return on capital employed, and the other, which is more capital-intensive, only 10% per year. Assuming the return on capital is maintained (and ignoring corporation tax for a minute), the former generates enough profit to fund the required growth in its capital. The latter, on the other hand, will need to raise additional capital (by either equity or debt) each year in order to maintain the same level of growth. This is an aspect of growth – and the significance of return on capital employed – that is often overlooked.

Tulip Greeting Cards Example

If we take the example of Tulip Greeting Cards, we can work out its return on capital employed:

$$\frac{Operating\ Profit}{Shareholders'\ Equity + Bank\ Debt} = \frac{£900k}{£1{,}800k + £1{,}405k} = 28.1\%$$

So, what does this 28.1% mean? What it is saying is that for each £1 of capital that is tied up in the business, it is yielding 28p a year in profit. This number can then be used for comparisons and for making judgements.

Note in the above examples we have used the year-end balance sheet figures. If there had been significant differences in balance sheet values from the beginning of the financial year to the end, using an average of the two may be more meaningful.

Why Operating Profit is Used in Return on Capital Employed Calculation

Simply put, the numerator and denominator in calculating return on capital employed (or, indeed, any ratio) need to be consistent with each other. In the case of return on capital employed, we are concerned with the operating profit in relation to the assets that are used to generate that profit, regardless of how those assets are funded. If you want to factor in financing costs, and the impact that has on shareholders' return, you need to look at return on equity.

Profitability and the Balance Sheet

- Return on equity shows us how much profit is being generated relative to the shareholders' equity (i.e. the return on the wealth the shareholders have left in the business). It is exactly the same as return on net assets.
- The return on capital employed is a different calculation from the return on shareholders' equity and takes into account how much other funding is used beyond the shareholders' equity. It is one of the most fundamental measures of a business's performance.
- Capital Employed = Shareholders' Equity + Bank Debt. The definition of what constitutes 'bank debt' can vary, but typically includes all interest-bearing debt as well as directors' loans to the company.
- In calculating return on capital employed, use operating profit (EBIT) as the numerator.

Liquidity Ratios

Regardless of the business sector, all companies are likely to face a major challenge during any 10-year period. Something nasty is likely to come and 'bite' them. It could be a major customer going bust, recessions, fraud, or a fire. The stronger the balance sheet is, the more able the business is to survive such challenges. A weak balance sheet could result in financial ruin.

Because these events can occur without much warning, a business needs to have sufficient resources to survive whilst it adjusts to the new environment. For example, a sudden drop in sales could rapidly push a business into a trading loss situation. The business will need time to reduce its cost base and cover these losses until it can become profitable again.

This is where liquidity ratios are useful as they provide an indication as to a company's likely ability to survive should things go wrong. More specifically, they are designed to measure the company's ability to pay down its short-term liabilities out of its current and/or liquid resources. But be warned: as we will see later in the two balance sheet case studies, easyJet and Vulpine, the ratios need to be looked at in conjunction with other information.

Beware of the crocodiles. A challenging situation is likely to come along and 'bite' a company in any 10-year period. The company needs the financial strength to survive.

The Current Ratio

The **current ratio** is widely used when evaluating a balance sheet. It provides a measure of how large current assets are when compared to current liabilities.

Let's return to our Tulip Greetings Cards example and see how their current ratio looks:

$$\frac{Current\ Assets}{Current\ Liabilities} = \frac{£2{,}720k}{£1{,}740k} = 1.6$$

In this situation, the current assets are 1.6 times greater than the current liabilities. Or, in other words, the company possesses £1.60 of current assets for every pound of short-term liabilities. This could be described as 'good', as the business could theoretically pay off all its current liabilities if it were able to liquidate all its current assets – and still have around £1m of working capital to carry on trading.

The Quick Ratio

The **quick ratio** (also known as the *acid-test ratio*) is a similar ratio, but focusses on the company's ability to pay down current liabilities from *liquid assets only* (i.e. assets that can be realised within a very short period of time without compromising value).

Instead of including *all* current assets in the numerator, it only includes assets that are *readily convertible to cash*. In other words, stock and other current assets that are *not* readily convertible to cash (e.g. **prepayments**[5]), are deducted from the asset side of the equation.

Give some thought to why stock and prepayments are removed?

Stock is not regarded as a particularly good-quality current asset in the event that a company ceases trading. Here are some of the reasons:

- If the business fails, the stock may only be worth a fraction of its normal selling price, particularly if large amounts of it are dumped on the market.

- The actual value in the accounts may not be true: frequently businesses fail to write-down the value of obsolete stock, especially if they have been trading poorly.
- If the business has failed there may simply be no market for their products any longer (for example if the product required extensive after-sales support).

Similarly, prepayments are expenses that have been paid in advance (such as rent), and which the company is committed to incurring. On that basis, they can never be converted to cash to pay down *existing* debts. By definition, they can only be used to redeem *future* expenses.

Contrast this to the **trade debtors** book. This is regarded as the next best-quality current asset after cash. If the goods/services have been delivered to a customer, and there is no reason to dispute the quality of what was provided, then the debt is nearly as good as cash as an asset. *But what if the customer refuses to pay?*

Unless there is a good reason, they cannot refuse and would face debt recovery proceedings if they did. The only risk then is whether the customer has the *ability to pay* (i.e. is not about to become broke itself). Banks, therefore, treat the trade debtor book in high regard.

Let's go back to the quick ratio. In the Tulip Greetings Cards example the calculation would be as follows:

$$\frac{Current\ Assets - Stock - Prepayments}{Current\ Liabilities} = \frac{£2,720k - £620k - £135k}{£1,740k} = 1.13$$

Again, this looks respectable since it is greater than one. This suggests all current liabilities could still theoretically be repaid out of current liquid assets, even removing stock and prepayments from the equation.

But how about if the mix of current assets was somewhat different, with stock valued at £1.8m (instead of £620k) and trade debtors at £535k? This is how it would then look:

$$\frac{Current\ Assets - Stock - Prepayments}{Current\ Liabilities} = \frac{£2,720k - £1,800k - £135k}{£1,740k} = 0.45$$

The picture looks very different indeed, even though total current assets (and therefore current ratio) are exactly the same. Two key issues emerge. Firstly, it is concerning that this ratio is now below 1 as, without taking into account stock as an asset, the business would not be able to repay its current liabilities. Secondly, stock seems to be a disproportionately large part of current assets. We would need to investigate whether this was just a feature of this business, or perhaps more likely, that the value of the stock was overstated. We will learn how we can analyse the stock situation in the next chapter – we can do this with another ratio without actually having to roll up our sleeves and go down to the warehouse and take a look at what's there on the shelves!

What is the correct level for these liquidity ratios?

There is *no specific number* that can be said to be correct and the ideal number would vary from business to business. For example, an airline needs to cope with some potentially very turbulent (excuse the pun) situations, such as recessions, fuel price spikes, terrorist incidents, extreme weather, etc. All of these could have a severe and immediate impact on its profitability. Contrast that to a major supermarket, where a bad year is one when sales slip by a mere 2%.

Clearly an airline needs to maintain a far higher level of liquidity than a supermarket chain. Hence the ideal current ratio or quick ratio will vary between them. Also, as we saw in the example above, it is not just a case of the ratio – it's also what makes up the assets and liabilities. Are the current assets made up of stock or cash? There's a world of difference between the two.

Balance Sheet Liquidity Ratios

- Ratios are a great way of determining the health of a balance sheet.
- The current ratio is current assets divided by current liabilities. Ideally this should always be comfortably greater than 1.
- The quick ratio is current assets *less* stock and prepayments, divided by current liabilities. This is a more rigorous measure as it removes illiquid assets. Again, this should ideally always be in excess of 1.
- The quality of the assets is of critical importance when looking at either ratio. For example, stock is not regarded as a quality asset by banks, since it may be hard to realise its full value in the event of the company's liquidation.
- Trade debtors is usually an excellent asset as it is just one step away from being converted to cash.
- Ideally if a business sold all its current assets it should be able to repay all its current liabilities and still have sufficient working capital to carry on trading.

Gearing Ratios

Consider a scenario where a special forces soldier is made to run up the side of a mountain with a load of building bricks in his backpack. He would probably find this an enjoyable challenge as it would push his strength and stamina to new levels. However, for most of us this would be a complete nightmare. Before the 1km mark, we would be worn out and start walking. We'd then probably have to give up the challenge part of the way up the mountain because of exhaustion!

When we examine a company's debt, we look to see if it is able to carry the burden.

Clearly the weight carried is the same in both situations; i.e. a backpack full of bricks. But the outcome is very different depending on who is carrying the load.

Debt is very similar. Debt problems rarely relate to the size of the debt in itself, but rather to the ability of the business, person, or country, to carry it. For example, a student with a £20k credit card debt may be in a far more precarious situation than a city banker with a £2m mortgage on her £3m house when supported by an annual salary and bonus of £1m! *We can begin to see that it is the debt relative to the assets, or income, that is of primary importance rather than the capital amount borrowed.*

When we look at a balance sheet, one of the things we are evaluating is the *ability* of the business to carry any debt it may have. This is of particular interest to banks, since they will be concerned as to whether the company will be able to repay any borrowings in the future. We are going to look at the three primary ratios banks use to evaluate **gearing** (also known as leverage). The first two, the **debt to equity** and **debt to capital** ratios look at the company's ability to carry the debt load, and the third, **interest cover**, looks at how easily the company can pay the interest charge each year.

Debt to Equity Ratio

For this we take the total interest-bearing debt and divide it by the shareholders' equity (which is the same as net assets of course). In the case of our example:

$$\frac{Debt}{Shareholders' Equity} = \frac{£1,405k}{£1,800k} = 0.78$$

Note this is not generally expressed as a percentage. Any number greater than one indicates there is more debt than equity. Whilst the lower this number is perhaps the better, other factors are also very relevant. If the industry sector is very volatile (i.e. profits fluctuate wildly) then a low ratio is probably essential. Conversely in a very stable business it can be higher. Banks will be familiar with what is 'normal' for each industry and therefore acceptable to them.

In our example of Tulip Greeting Cards, the debt is primarily long-term in nature and relates to a mortgage on its freehold offices. This makes the situation considerably more secure than if the debt was from a short-term **overdraft**. Once again, we are seeing a situation where our evaluation is not just about the number, but what lies *behind* the number.

Note the definition of debt can vary. It normally refers to bank or other interest-bearing debt only (not trade creditors, for example) and we would obtain the detail from the accounting notes. We would suggest it should include directors' loans even if these are not interest-bearing.

Debt to Capital Ratio

The debt to capital ratio is less commonly used, but is helpful in showing us what proportion of the total funding of the business (as opposed to the net assets) is made up of debt:

$$\frac{Debt}{Capital\ Employed} = \frac{£1,405k}{£1,800k + £1,405} = 0.44$$

We can see that in the case of Tulip Greeting Cards 44p in every £1 of capital used in the business is sourced from debt. Once again, this tells us that there is plenty of equity in the business. However, as mentioned above, we would also consider the nature of the debt (whether long- or short-term), the company's operational gearing (explained below) and the specific industry sector concerned before making a final judgement on whether the figure was 'good' or 'bad'.

Interest Cover Ratio

As well as wanting the capital value of the loan being repaid, banks want a company to be able to pay the annual interest charges from the profits it is generating. Measuring how many times it could do this shows how much risk they are facing. The **interest cover** ratio is not actually derived from the balance sheet and is solely generated from the profit & loss. But it is fundamentally linked to the debt to equity ratio in the context that a bank will be considering both these ratios simultaneously when evaluating their risk exposure to a business. Note in calculating the ratio, we use operating profit rather than profit before tax, since the profit figure needs to exclude the interest charge itself.

In our Tulip Greeting Cards example, the company could pay its interest costs 15 times over:

$$\frac{\textit{Operating Profit}}{\textit{Interest}} = \frac{£900k}{£60k} = 15$$

This again suggests the debt situation is in safe territory. However, a sharp rise in interest rates can cause problems for companies, as not only does the interest charge go up, but their sales and profits may simultaneously be coming down as consumers reduce their spending. The ratio may then fall to a point below what the bank requires (this is known as **bank covenant**). You may have read in the press about large troubled companies being 'in breach of their bank covenants'. If this happens, the bank can ask for the loan to be repaid, which can then lead to the collapse of the business.

A further variance on this ratio is the **debt service ratio**, which includes the interest costs in the denominator as above, but also adds any capital repayments due in the next 12 months. This then becomes an indicator as to whether the company has sufficient cash flow to meet these obligations. Note it is only an indicator because operating profit is not, of course, necessarily the same as the business's cash flow.

Operational Gearing

Businesses in more volatile market sectors are better off funding their businesses with equity (i.e. issuing new shares) rather than debt. When deciding what level of gearing is right for a particular business, a major factor to be taken into account is the level of **operational gearing** inherent in the business. This can arise from both the *volatility of the sector* and the *cost structure* of the business. As touched on in Chapter 2.6, the profits of a company that faces high fixed costs will be more sensitive to changes in sales volumes (i.e. more highly geared) than a company with low fixed costs. Therefore, the management might seek to offset this risk by making sure their *financial* gearing is kept low.

Gearing Ratios

- The actual debt amount is of far less significance than the ability of the business to carry the debt.
- To help us determine the ability of a business to carry debt, we look at the debt burden relative to its equity (or net assets).
- We also consider how many times its profit covers its interest cost burden – this is the interest cover ratio.
- Companies that operate in volatile markets and with high operational gearing should carry lower levels of debt as a proportion of their balance sheet value. Under these circumstances, equity funding is likely to be preferable for ensuring their long-term survival.

Notes

1. It would also be reasonable to use profit before tax as an alternative. If corporation tax is being distorted by past year's trading (e.g. from trading losses carried forward from large capital allowances), then the before-tax figure may be more suitable for consistent comparisons.
2. This simple ratio can also be applied to any individual asset. For example, if you purchased some machinery to reduce your manufacturing costs, you could divide the savings made by the cost outlaid to see a simple rate of return on the new investment.
3. Other definitions, such as fixed assets minus current liabilities, are arguably erroneous, as current liabilities could include bank debt due for repayment within the next 12 months.
4. Cash will already be included if using shareholders' equity figure in a calculation. This would therefore give a different figure than if using the stock + debtors – creditors method of calculation.
5. The prepayments figure may only be visible from the notes in the accounts. A simpler, although less meaningful, version of the acid-test may just remove stock and ignore prepayments.

3.4 BALANCE SHEET EXAMPLES

It's worth taking a look at any major company's accounts. You should find that you now understand them… to a point! Inevitably, you will find different terminology for the same items and you may also may find the order of the items reflects the US format, despite being a UK company.

easyJet's Balance Sheet

easyJet is a great British success story, having grown from an entrepreneurial start-up in 1995 to a multi-billion pound company with over 14,000 employees. It is also an interesting company to look at, due to the challenges an airline must face operating in a complex international market.

Its 2019 balance sheet (together with the preceding year) is reproduced on page 124. We have simplified a few items from the published accounts to make it easier to understand, but the figures in aggregate are the same. What can we see from taking a quick look at this?

The first thing to remember is that this is effectively only an extract as it does not include any of the notes to the accounts. These are an essential part of any published account, and are a rich source of additional information. We shall pick up on some of this additional information in the comments below.

The first observation you might make is that, contrary to our earlier suggestion that a financially healthy company's **current ratio** should exceed 1, easyJet's current ratio is in fact *under* 1, at 0.8 (down from a fraction below 1 in the previous year). Does this mean that they have a liquidity problem? The simple answer is no. You will also see that the company has over £1.5 billion of *cash-based assets* and is actually maintaining a very high level of liquidity.

Did you also notice that a key balance sheet item – that we explored in Chapter 3.2 – is missing? That's right, there is no stock! Well, of course there isn't – easyJet is a service company and has no requirement to hold stock. Although this means that their current assets are lower than they might otherwise be – with the consequent impact on current ratio – it is, in fact, highly *beneficial* to their cash flow as there is no need to tie up valuable capital in goods waiting to be sold.

Another important clue to the nature of the company's working capital requirements can be found under current liabilities, labelled 'Unearned revenue' with a massive £1,069 million. This is another name for **deferred income**, and would mostly represent revenue from ticket sales for flights that have not yet happened (remember the **revenue recognition principle**). So, in fact, much of the cash pile on their balance sheet is cash received from customers who are still looking forward to their holiday. This is also hugely beneficial to easyJet's cash flow as it is zero-cost capital, but does of course mean that they need to maintain a suitable level of liquidity to cover the liability.

On the other hand, we can observe that the business is highly capital intensive in terms of fixed assets, which can be found here labelled 'Property, plant and equipment' at £5.2 billion. There are no prizes for guessing what type of plant and equipment would represent the bulk of this in an airline business. Indeed, the notes to the balance sheet show that nearly all of this is, of course, 'Aircraft and spares' – as might be expected.

While 'Property, plant and equipment' represents the bulk of the company's non-current assets, another significant component is made up of *intangible* assets, and, in particular, goodwill at £365 million. A quick ferret around in the all-important notes reveals that this is, in fact, the value that the company places on its route network, and is calculated by using the **net present value** method that you will learn more about in Chapter 6.3.[1]

Finally, it is interesting to see a lot of hedging assets ('Derivative financial instruments') on both asset and liability sides of the balance sheet, presumably held as part of the process of minimising risks from exchange rate and commodity (fuel) price fluctuations.

Can we determine how much profit the business has made in the last year, just from the balance sheet?

The answer is yes – to a point. The movement in retained earnings between the two years shown – £2,215 million minus £2,166 million – tells us that it was sufficiently profitable to retain £49 million of its after-tax profits after paying out any dividends to shareholders. We would, however, need to look at the profit & loss statement to get a more comprehensive picture of the profitability of the business, and how much it has paid out in dividends.

Note the 2019 Annual Report extends to over 180 pages of highly detailed information – there's lots more we could look at!

easyJet plc Balance Sheet	**30th Sep 2019**	**30th Sep 2018**
	£ million	£ million
NON-CURRENT ASSETS		
Tangible		
Property, plant and equipment	5,163	4,140
Derivative financial instruments	126	175
Other non-current assets	194	133
	5,483	4,448
Intangible		
Goodwill	365	365
Other intangible assets	196	181
	561	546
TOTAL NON-CURRENT ASSETS	6,044	4,994
CURRENT ASSETS		
Trade and other receivables *(debtors)*	372	406
Derivative financial instruments	147	220
Current tax assets	24	-
Cash, cash equivalents, & money market deposits	1,576	1,373
	2,119	1,999
CURRENT LIABILITIES		
Trade and other payables *(creditors)*	(1,050)	(1,023)
Unearned revenue *(deferred income)*	(1,069)	(877)
Lease liabilities	(219)	-
Derivative financial instruments	(138)	(24)
Other current liabilities	(192)	(136)
	(2,668)	(2,060)
NET CURRENT ASSETS	(549)	(61)
NON-CURRENT LIABILITIES		
Borrowings	(1,324)	(968)
Lease liabilities	(359)	-
Derivative financial instruments	(72)	(7)
Provisions for liabilities and charges	(397)	(335)
Other non-current liabilities	(358)	(390)
	(2,510)	(1,700)
NET ASSETS	**2,985**	**3,233**
SHAREHOLDERS' EQUITY		
Share capital	108	108
Share premium	659	659
Miscellaneous reserves	3	300
Retained earnings	2,215	2,166
TOTAL SHAREHOLDERS' EQUITY	**2,985**	**3,233**

Vulpine Performance Limited

Let's now move from a major quoted company to a business started in mid-2011, Vulpine Performance Limited, with £150k of seed funding. The business produced a range of cycle clothing that was suitable for both ride and destination – in other words, they were tailored to look fashionable when you were off the bike as well as on it. It was a great idea at the time, as cycling was booming in the United Kingdom and the prototype products were excellent.

The founding entrepreneur was extremely persuasive when it came to raising money. He had a vision of a substantial cycle clothing brand and he enthusiastically shared this with all he met. We were some of the seed investors, but declined to take part in the later rounds.

Let's look at the balance sheet as at 30 April 2014, which also shows the preceeding year for comparison purposes. The 2014 accounts are therefore at a point nearly three years after trading began. The format shown below is very standard for privately owned UK companies. Have a look at the balance sheet in isolation to the profit & loss statement, and see if you can answer these three questions:

1. Is the business profitable or unprofitable? And can you tell what the profit or loss was over the last year?
2. How has the business been funded in the past year?
3. What is the liquidity of the business like? Is it good or bad?

Without looking at the profit & loss statement you can begin to answer the above questions. Have a go!

Vulpine Performance Ltd					**Balance Sheet as at 30 April 2014**
		2014		**2013**	
	Notes	£	£	£	£
Non-current assets					
Intangible assets	4	3,942		5,913	
Tangible assets	5	27,852		14,167	
			31,794		20,080
Current assets					
Stock		599,287		229,527	
Debtors	6	32,459		35,748	
Cash		200,821		82,584	
		832,567		347,859	
Current liabilities					
Falling due within 1 year	7	(273,189)		(103,559)	
Net current assets			559,378		244,300
NET ASSETS			**591,172**		**264,380**
Capital and reserves					
Called up share capital	8		457,445		298,545
Share premium	9		505,585		95,450
Accumulated losses	9		(371,858)		(129,615)
SHAREHOLDERS' EQUITY			**591,172**		**264,380**

Profitability

We can simply look at the accumulated losses, which show £372k of losses to date. Subtracting last year's figure of £130k we can see than the trading loss for the past 12 months was the difference, i.e. £242k. Given the scale of these losses, we can be confident that nothing has been paid out in dividends or corporation tax (both of which are deducted from an annual profit to derive the retained earnings figure for the year). Glancing at the profit & loss statement below we can see we were right in our calculation.

We can also sneak at look at the sales whilst we're there – and, my goodness, a £242k loss on just £416k of sales appears to be quite a bad result. But note sales have more than doubled from the previous year – maybe it is just all down to the rapid scaling? We can also observe the operating expenses have grown by a staggering 300% – a great deal of overhead seems to have been added.

Vulpine Performance Ltd

Profit & Loss Statement		**2014**	**2013**
Year to 30 April	Notes	£	£
Sales		415,575	198,586
Cost of sales		(265,069)	(122,344)
Gross profit		**150,506**	**76,242**
Gross margin		*36.2%*	*38.4%*
Operating expenses		(393,715)	(131,783)
		(243,209)	(55,541)
Other operating income		875	5,067
Operating loss	2	**(242,334)**	**(50,474)**
Interest receivable		91	49
Profit (loss) before tax		**(242,243)**	**(50,425)**
Corporation tax	3	-	-
Profit (loss) after tax		**(242,243)**	**(50,425)**

Funding

We've established that the business was evidently not being funded by its own profits and cash flow. So how have these large losses been funded? Firstly, we can observe that the total share capital has grown by £569k, so new shares have been issued to shareholders in return for much-needed cash. Note the growth in *both* the called up share capital *and* the share premium. The latter is a result of the shares being issued at a higher price than their nominal value (see Chapter 3.2 for further explanation).

We can also observe that creditors have grown from £104k to £273k, suggesting £169k of extra money has come from suppliers or other short-term loans to the business. If we were to look at Note 7 in the accounts (not shown here) we could see more detail.

Liquidity

The **current ratio** is an apparently very healthy 3.0, but when we come to the **quick ratio** it drops to 0.85. This is not such a pretty picture – the stock value seems to be a disproportionately large part of current assets.[2] To determine if the business is carrying too much stock we can calculate how many months' stock the business is holding. To do this, we apply the following formula:

$$Stock\ Days = \frac{Average\ Stock\ Held}{Cost\ of\ Sales\ per\ Day} = \frac{(£229{,}527 + 599{,}287)/2}{£265{,}087/365} = 571\ days$$

That comes to just over 1.5 years' stock, which for any business in fashion clothing (albeit cycle clothing!) is an alarmingly long period of time.

Whilst it could be argued that the stock was being held in anticipation of continued sales growth, by this stage the business was regularly running clearance sales on its website. The stock situation was *not* under control and was one of the reasons why the gross margin (at 36%) was below the expectation of closer to 50%.

The stock issue does not rest there. Given there is likely to be stock that cannot be sold at the full asking price, it raises the question: is the stock actually worth what it cost to buy in? Since stock should be valued at the *lower* of cost or net realisable value, it is not inconceivable that some of it should have been prudently written down in value to zero? If this were the case – and we cannot determine this from the figures above alone – then the loss for the year of £242k could be *understated*. This would also mean the balance sheet's overall value was *overstated*.

Burn Rate and Runways

But the good news is the business has plenty of cash with a balance of £201k. *Cash is king,* we are told – so all is fine. *But is it really?* Putting the cash balance into the context of the trading losses, if the business continues losing money at the same rate, it is burning through around £20k a month (this is known as the **burn rate**).[3] This cash would be gone in around 10 months should no other sources of funding be found. This time period of remaining cash is known as the **runway** – a very apt way of describing the distance that can be travelled before take-off into profitability, or crashing at the end of the runway. Raising new capital is the alternative to either take-off or crashing, in which case new runway is added. But believe us when we say you cannot keep adding new runway forever – at some point you have to get into the air, or it's a tragic ending for all parties.

Whilst we cannot answer all the questions we may have about what is going on in the business, studying these accounts does provide us with valuable insights and pointers for further discussions with management. We would also urgently want to view more up-to-date trading figures, which would be available since the annual accounts had been prepared and published.

We will come back to the Vulpine story again later in the book. There is much more still to happen!

Vulpine's Balance Sheet

- By just looking at the balance sheet, without sight of the profit & loss, we are able to make meaningful observations about its historic profitability, funding and liquidity of the company. We can also do this in a matter of minutes!
- By looking at the balance sheet in conjunction with the profit & loss we are able to confirm some of our suspicions: namely, that there appears to be too much stock relative to the sales, and that the 'large' cash balance is not quite the safety net we might imagine it to be.

- The amount of cash being consumed in losses or invested into assets is called the burn rate. How long this burn rate can be maintained is known as the runway.
- We cannot answer every question from these financial statements, but they are valuable pointers for further investigations.

Notes

1. Once you have read Chapter 6.3, you may be interested to learn that, as indicated in the notes to its accounts, easyJet used a **weighted average cost of capital** of 9.4%.
2. No prepayments are specified in their accounts; hence we are only deducting stock in the calculation of the acid-test.
3. In reality, you might want to focus on the *projected* rate of 'burn', i.e. looking forward, to calculate the amount of runway a business has (assuming these numbers are credible, of course).

3.5 RETURNING TO THE BALANCE SHEET FORMULA

We just want to go back to the balance sheet formula before we move on. Sorry about that, but it's well worth the small effort required!

There are two insights we would like you to observe regarding the difference between the UK and USA variants of the formula. These will reduce potential confusion and also help you understand what this amazing statement is trying to say to us.

The Differing Balance Sheet Values

The first insight is the apparent balance sheet value will be different depending on which version of the formula we use.

Let's recap a moment: as we saw earlier, the balance sheet can be viewed in a table format, or as a list. But behind this is an underlying formula:

Assets – Liabilities = Shareholders' Equity

In the United States, it is customary to express it differently:

Assets = Shareholders' Equity + Liabilities

Clearly these formulas are the same but just expressed differently.

Let us revisit the simple examples we looked at when considering the **return on capital employed** ratio in Chapter 3.3, and see how the UK and US balance sheets would be presented.

Example 1: A company is started with £20 of share capital and this is the only asset

The balance sheet is made up of cash on the 'left-hand' side and share capital of £20 on the 'right-hand' side.

UK balance sheet presentation: £20 – £0 = £20
US balance sheet presentation: £20 = £20 + £0

There are no liabilities and the values therefore look the same.

Example 2: The same company but with a £1,000 loan

The company now borrows £1,000 from the bank; this is of course a liability.

UK balance sheet presentation: £1,020 – £1,000 = £20
US balance sheet presentation: £1,020 = £20 + £1,000

The UK balance sheet value remains £20, since on the 'left-hand' side it has an asset of the newly introduced £1,000 cash to add to the original £20, but also a liability of the £1,000 loan, which is now deducted.

The US balance sheet would appear to have 'grown' and has a value of £1,020! But it hasn't grown, of course, as the equation is the same, only expressed another way.

The US formula is saying: *'Here are our assets (now £1,020) and this is how they are funded: we put in £20 of our own shareholders' money and borrowed £1,000 from the bank.'*

The UK formula is saying: *'The net worth of the company is £20. We have put in £20 of our own shareholders' money but have borrowed £1,000 from the bank, giving us £1,020 in assets. But we recognise we have to pay this loan back at some point and are taking this into account in determining our net value.'*

The Differing Perspectives

These examples highlight the second insight – that the US formula takes a different perspective. It is as if they are looking at the same building but from a different angle – same structure but a contrasting view. In fact, we can suggest that the US version of the balance sheet is looking at it from the viewpoint of the company's *management* as opposed to its *shareholders* in the UK format.

US formula shown from the management perspective: *'We are employing these assets to operate the company and have funded it with these proportions of shareholders' money [equity] and from taking on these liabilities [the debt].'*

UK formula shown from the shareholders' perspective: *'This is the value of the equity in our business. It is shown by the difference between our assets [what we own] and our liabilities [what we owe].'*

For this reason, it is quite likely that the management of a British company might adopt the American, management-centric, format when drawing up their *management* accounts.

This, hopefully, explains why there is a different approach and seemingly different potential balance sheet values. Neither is right nor wrong – they are just differing perspectives of the same thing.

UK and US Balance Sheet Differences

- The UK and US balance sheet formulas are the same but expressed differently. Consequently, the US version may appear to have a higher balance sheet value.
- The US balance sheet takes the perspective of the *management*, showing how the assets employed in the business have been funded.
- The UK formula takes the perspective of the *shareholders*, showing the net asset value of the business after considering both its assets and liabilities.

PART 4

CASH FLOW MANAGEMENT & FORECASTING

4.1 THE CASH FLOW STATEMENT

Cash flowing through a business can be compared to blood flowing through the veins of the human body. Cash is the lifeblood of a business – if it stops flowing, just as with a human, the end can come very quickly.

Cash is continuously needed to pay employees, suppliers, for capital assets and numerous other items of expenditure. There is a continuous flow of money *out* of the business to fulfil these requirements. Likewise, there should be a continuous flow of money coming *in* to the business. This will be in the form of sales revenue, borrowings from banks or other sources, or injections of new share capital. The difference between the money coming into the business and the money going out is the **net cash flow**.

Presenting Cash Flow

The **cash flow statement** is the means by which this vital piece of information is recorded and communicated. It is the third of the 'holy trinity' of financial statements that we introduced you to earlier – thus completing the triangle, alongside the profit & loss statement and the balance sheet.

Whereas the profit & loss statement shows how the company has accrued profit or loss (created or diminished wealth) over a defined *period* of time, and the balance sheet shows the value of assets, liabilities and equity held by the company *at a particular point in time*, the cash flow statement accounts for how cash has moved through the company over a defined *period* of time (as with the profit & loss statement).

There are two, quite different, methods of compiling a cash flow statement: the **direct method** (sometimes known as the 'receipts and disbursements' method); and the **indirect method** (alternatively known as the 'adjusted net income' method). Both methods are entirely valid ways of calculating and presenting cash flow, but are very different from each other and have their own advantages and disadvantages. They do, however, have two things in common: 1) they will both break down cash flows into the same three categories; and 2) they will produce the same answer at the bottom line!

The latter might seem like an obvious truism, but, sometimes, calculating something by two different methods is a good way of verifying your answer – if they are different, something is wrong.

The three categories of cash flow that both methods display are:

1. **Cash flow from *operating* activities:** describing cash flowing through the company from day-to-day trading (e.g. cash in from customers, and cash out to suppliers and employees).

2. **Cash flow from *investing* activities:** describing cash flowing in and out of the company as a result of the purchase and sale of long-term (i.e. non-current) assets, such as property, plant and machinery, shares in other companies, etc.
3. **Cash flow from *financing* activities:** describing cash flowing in and out of the company as a result of its financing initiatives (e.g. money in from the issue of shares or from drawing down new debt, and money out for the payment of dividends or paying off loans).

We will explore these different aspects of cash flow in more detail later in this section. In the meantime, let's look more closely at the two different methods.

The Direct Method

As its name suggests, the direct method goes straight to the heart of the matter and simply lists and totals money in and money out in a given period of time. This gives it the obvious advantage of being easy to relate to, especially for anyone with limited familiarity with accounting and finance.

As mentioned above, this list will be categorised into the three broad types of cash flow, so, returning to the Tulip Greeting Cards example, it looks like this:

Tulip Greeting Cards

Cash Flow Statement 2019 - Direct Method	£'000	
Cash flow from operating activities		
Cash receipts from customers	8,356	
Cash payments to suppliers and payroll	(7,004)	
Interest paid	(60)	
Taxes paid	(742)	
		550
Cash flow from investing activities		
Receipts from sale of assets	3	
Payments for asset purchases	(237)	
		(234)
Cash flow from financing activities		
Receipts from issue of shares	340	
Receipts from new borrowings	-	
Repayments of borrowings	(305)	
Dividends paid	(120)	
		(85)
Net cash flow		**231**
Opening balance		**19**
Closing balance		**250**

As you can see, each line simply represents amounts coming in to or going out of the company's bank account in the period in question – it is easy to understand. However, you might be thinking to yourself, *'How can I relate the cash flow shown in this statement to the profit made by the company in the same period?'* This is a great question, and highlights one of the main shortcomings of this method. The answer is that, with the direct method statement alone, you can't – a separate reconciliation statement is required. This brings us neatly to the indirect method, which, quite conveniently, also happens to be a reconciliation between profit and cash flow.

In terms of building a **financial model**, covered in Chapter 4.5, we will use the direct method as this is generally easier to understand. If you struggle to understand the indirect method, do not worry – just stick with the direct method.

The Indirect Method

As indicated above, the indirect method, rather than looking directly at what cash has moved in or out of the business, instead starts with profit after tax for the period but then makes adjustments for non-cash items and movements on the balance sheet to get to cash flow.

For instance, as we've already learned in Chapter 2.5, depreciation is purely an accounting adjustment. It is, therefore, a non-cash item and needs to be added back in order to work out cash flow if starting from the profit after tax figure.

Give some thought as to what other items might need to be added or subtracted from profit after tax to deduce cash flow? To do this, it will be helpful to remember three key points:

1. All the values in the profit & loss, which hence give rise to the profit after tax figure, are based on the application of **accrual accounting** principles, as introduced in Chapter 2.4. With accrual accounting we are trying to get a true and fair view of the *profitability* of the business, which does not necessarily correspond to actual cash flows – there are likely to be differences.

2. All the differences between profit and cash flow can be traced to changes, *or movements*, in the balance sheet between the start and the end of the period.

3. With the indirect method (where profit after tax is our starting point), we are only interested to see how any particular balance sheet movement makes our cash flow larger or smaller than might be expected given the amount of profit after tax made.

So, for instance, if the value of trade debtors increases during the period, what impact does this have on cash flow *relative to profit after tax*? Think about what this means: more money remains outstanding from customers at the period end – it's not cash in the bank account. Therefore, cash flow will be *lower* than the profit after tax figure suggests. We will therefore need to *deduct* this movement to calculate cash flow from the profit after tax figure.

What about stock? Let's say that management has been successful in reducing stock over the period – what does this mean in terms of cash flow relative to the profit after tax figure? The answer is that with stock levels going down, less cash is tied up in it, and, consequently, cash flow relative to the profit after tax figure will be higher – we will need to *add* this movement to calculate cash flow from the profit after tax figure.

Debits & Credits

Let us think about this in a different way for a moment – in terms of debits and credits. Both **trade debtors** and stock have something in common: they are both assets, and hence any increase in them represents a deployment, or *application*, of funds. Therefore, an increase in these items in the balance sheet from one period to the next represents a *debit movement*, while a decrease represents a *credit movement.*

Remembering that every debit needs a corresponding credit, an increase in stock or debtors corresponds to a credit (decrease) movement in cash. It would be the reverse if stock or debtors were reduced – there would be a credit to them, and a debit to cash. A very simple way of thinking about asset versus cash movements is as the opposite sides of a see-saw – as one goes up, the other goes down.

So, what about the other side of the balance sheet – namely, liabilities such as **trade creditors**? Remember, liabilities are a *source* of funds (we are using someone else's money). So, if they increase in any particular period of time, cash is effectively coming in – therefore the cash balance *also* increases. The increase in liabilities is the credit, and the increase in cash is the debit. And, of course, should liabilities decrease, then the reverse situation is applied.

We can summarise the different positions in the table below:

Change to Balance Sheet	Implications to Cash Flow	In Terms of Debits & Credits
Increase in assets	Negative impact on cash flow (they have absorbed funds)	Assets are debited (the application of funds) and cash is credited (the source of funds)
Decrease in assets	Positive impact on cash flow (we have turned them to cash)	Assets are credited (source) and cash is debited (application)
Increase in liabilities	Positive impact on cash flow (we are using someone else's money to fund our business)	Liabilities are credited (source) and cash is debited (application)
Decrease in liabilities	Negative impact on cash flow (we are having to repay liability from our cash)	Liabilities are debited (application) and cash is credited (source)

Going back to the Tulip Greeting Cards example, here's how the exact same underlying numbers as displayed using the direct method would look set out using the indirect method:

Tulip Greeting Cards

Cash Flow Statement 2019 - Indirect Method	£'000	
Cash flow from operating activities		
Net profit/(loss), from P&L	570	
Add back depreciation	170	
Adjustments for movements in:		
Current assets		
Stock	(220)	
Accounts receivable	(60)	
Accrued income	40	
Prepayments	-	
Other debtors	-	
Current liabilities		
Accounts payable	(80)	
Accruals	10	
Tax & national insurance	10	
Other creditors	(5)	
Corporation tax	115	
		550
Cash flow from investing activities		
Receipts from sale of assets	3	
Payments for asset purchases	(237)	
		(234)
Cash flow from financing activities		
Receipts from issue of shares	340	
Receipts from new borrowings	-	
Repayments of borrowings	(305)	
Dividends paid	(120)	
		(85)
Net cash flow		**231**
Opening balance		**19**
Closing balance		**250**

You will notice a couple of points. Firstly, the bottom line is exactly the same as the direct method – phew, this is good news as it verifies our calculations! And, secondly, like the direct method, the line items are separated into three different categories. You'll notice that only the first one, cash flow from operating activities, is really any different and now shows quite a bit more detail. You will also notice that this method helps us to understand how profit and cash flow relate to each other, which is its main advantage over the direct method.

The Cash Flow Statement

- A business has to fully understand the flow of money into and out of the business both today and, indeed, into the future. The cash flow statement is the means by which cash flows are recorded and communicated.
- The difference between the flow of money in and money out in any given time period is the net cash flow. In the long run, net cash flow has to be positive, otherwise a business will run out of cash and is likely to fail.
- There are two methods by which a cash flow statement can be compiled and presented – direct and indirect. Both are equally valid, but show cash flow in a totally different way. Both methods break down cash flows into the same three categories: operating, investing and financing.
- The advantage of the direct method is that it is easier to understand, especially for someone with limited familiarity with accounting and finance. The advantage of the indirect method is that it also provides a reconciliation between profit and net cash flow.

4.2 THE CASH CONVERSION CYCLE

The **cash conversion cycle** is the process of turning a company's trading activity into cash. For example, a business may go through a process of buying goods, paying for them, perhaps adapting them in some way, then storing them, selling them to customers, and finally collecting payment. How efficiently this process takes place will have a considerable impact on how a business is funded and how quickly it can scale. In this chapter, we will explore the conversion process, and in the next chapter we will look at alternative structures or processes a company can use in order to improve its efficiency in this regard.

We will also see how this can be measured, both in terms of value (i.e. £'s) and in terms of the overall number of days that a business takes to convert cash it has laid *out* on stock purchases into cash coming *in* as revenue. This widely used metric is also known simply as the cash conversion cycle (CCC) or net operating cycle. It is, largely, only relevant to businesses that buy, hold and sell physical stock. It is generally accepted that, when comparing similar businesses, the lower the number, the more efficient (and profitable) the business.

In doing this calculation, we will introduce you to two more fundamental business ratios: **debtor days** (how long it takes us to collect in money from our customers); and **creditor days** (how long we take to pay our suppliers). We will also look at **stock days** (how long we are holding stock for) in a bit more detail – we briefly looked at this with the Vulpine case study in Chapter 3.4. Armed with your new-found knowledge of the balance sheet, you will recognise these as relating to the three key components of a company's working capital, but expressed in terms of periods of time.

All the above ratios, along with numerous others, have been comprehensively summarised for you in Appendix 2.

The Stock Period

Managing stock levels is a key component of managing cash flow.

The first element of the CCC is the **stock** period (also known as inventory period, or **stock days**) and is a measure of the average amount of time that a business is holding its product in stock before being sold. This could be in a warehouse if the business is a manufacturer or distributor, or in a retail store if the business is a retailer. This is generally a costly process, as holding stock consumes resources:

- It ties up capital.
- It occupies space, which can be costly.
- It needs to be kept secure and insured.
- It absorbs management and workforce time.
- It can become obsolete or unusable.

The secret of good stock control is ensuring that the quantity held is kept to a minimum, *whilst at the same time* ensuring availability is high to the customer. It is easy to assume that a company with high stock levels will always have good availability. In fact, the exact opposite is more likely to be true. In our experience, businesses that fail to manage their stock levels frequently run out of their best-selling lines, whilst they are simultaneously sitting on large quantities of redundant product.

Measuring the Stock Period

Measuring stock levels is of critical importance to a business. This can be done in several ways, but a commonly used formula calculates the number of days' stock that is being held:

$$Stock\ Days = \frac{Average\ Total\ Stock\ Held}{Cost\ of\ Sales\ per\ Day}$$

Example

$$Stock\ Days = \frac{Average\ Total\ Stock\ Held}{Cost\ of\ Sales\ per\ Day} = \frac{£630,000}{£7,000} = 90\ days$$

Average total stock held should represent the *average* total investment in stock throughout the period being examined, taking into account movements in stock levels. For example, if the business is growing rapidly and stock levels have, as a result, grown consistently throughout the period, the calculation should be based on an average of the opening and closing balances. Or, if we are looking at a business that is highly seasonal over the course of a year, and stock levels have fluctuated up and down as a result, we might want to go to the extra effort of calculating the average stock held across all 12 interim months (assuming that information is available). On the other hand, if there has been no significant movement in stock over the period, we may decide that simply the period-end balance provides a meaningful number. This would be a matter of pragmatic judgment.

In the calculation of any ratio, the numerator (top) and denominator (bottom) must be inherently consistent with each other. Stock days is no exception, so we must be careful that the valuation method of the bottom number must be compatible with the way stock is valued. As you will recall, stock is usually valued at *cost* (or net realisable value if less than the cost). This is why we divide average stock by *cost of sales per day*, rather than *sales per day*.

It should probably go without saying that cost of sales per day is simply cost of sales divided by the number of days in the period being examined. This might typically be 365 if you are calculating for a whole year, but remember to adjust accordingly if you are calculating for shorter trading periods, say 90 days for a quarter, or 30 days for a month.

The Debtor Period

The second element of the CCC is the debtor period, also known as **debtor days**. **Trade debtors** are customers who owe the company money for goods or services already delivered. They are shown in a company's balance sheet as a current asset. In most situations, the debtor book is made up of customers who have received products or services from the company but not yet paid their invoice. Note that, for the purposes of this calculation, we would *include* **accrued income**, but *exclude* **prepayments** and other debtors.[1]

The amount of time a company gives its customers to pay is known as the **credit period** (not to be confused with the credit*or* period described below), and in most business-to-business (B2B)-type relationships the terms would be 30, 60, or 90 days. It is typically set out in the company's terms of business. The factors that influence the length of time given to a customer will be driven by both the standard terms adopted in the industry, and the market power of the customer (or possibly supplier).

Trade debtors are customers who have not yet paid for the goods or services they have received. Measuring the time this is taking is vital for good cash management.

A major supermarket group like Tesco is able to demand 90 days' credit from its suppliers, and if a company does not want to accept these terms, it may find it cannot get to do business with such a dominant retailer. *This is an example of customer power over suppliers.*

Alternatively, a company such as Apple may be able to stipulate strict payment terms to any of its retail distributors (i.e. non-Apple Store customers). If these retailers want the privilege of carrying the Apple range they have to conform to all of Apple's stipulations, such as methods of display and service support, and of course its credit terms. Customers that do not pay on time may risk losing the product range. *This is an example of supplier power over customers.*

While the credit period represents the amount of time formally *granted* to customers for settling invoices, the debtor period is the amount of time actually *taken* by customers, on average, so they might not be the same. There may be one or two customers who pay up sooner than the credit period, but there are likely to be many more taking longer to pay. Any variance from the granted credit period needs to be watched diligently in order to avoid running into cash flow problems, and minimise the risk of bad debts. Hence the need to measure and monitor the debtor period on a regular basis.

Measuring the Debtor Period

As described above, measuring the debtor period can be of critical importance to a business. Like the stock period, this can be done in several ways, but one of the most widely used formulas calculates the average number of days it takes to collect money due:

$$Debtor\ Days = \frac{Average\ Trade\ Debtors}{Sales\ per\ Day}$$

Example

$$Debtor\ Days = \frac{Average\ Trade\ Debtors}{Sales\ per\ Day} = \frac{£1,080,000}{£24,000} = 45\ days$$

As with the stock period calculation, the numerator should represent, or at least approximate, an average balance over the course of the period being examined. But, also as with the stock period calculation, a certain degree of pragmatism can be employed in determining how this is best calculated.

Again, as with the stock period, the golden rule of ratios applies: the numerator and denominator must be consistent with each other. This raises two points to note about the denominator here:

- Because the numerator (trade debtors) describes *sales* that have not yet been paid for, the denominator must be *sales per day*, not the *cost of sales per day* used in stock days.

- The trade debtors figure will be *inclusive of VAT*, but the sales figure is always *net of VAT*, one or other needs to be adjusted accordingly – i.e. either the VAT component should be stripped out of trade debtors or it should be added to the sales number.

Creditor Period

The third and final element of the CCC calculation is the creditor period, also known as **creditor days. Trade creditors** are businesses, organisations or individuals to whom the company owes money. They are shown in a company's balance sheet as a current liability. In most situations, they will be made up of suppliers who have supplied a product or service to the company, but have not yet been paid.

The amount of time a company takes to pay its suppliers is known as the creditor period, and, as mentioned above, in most B2B-type relationships the terms would be 30, 60, or 90 days. Again, the length of time the company is able to take to pay its suppliers will depend on both the standard terms adopted in the industry, and the relative market power of the parties involved.

Measuring the Creditor Period

Measuring the creditor period is usually done by calculating the number of days credit the company is managing to achieve from its suppliers:

$$Creditor\ Days = \frac{Average\ Trade\ Creditors}{Cost\ of\ Sales\ per\ Day}$$

Example

$$Creditor\ Days = \frac{Average\ Trade\ Creditors}{Cost\ of\ Sales\ per\ Day} = \frac{£420{,}000}{£7{,}000} = 60\ days$$

Again, like stock days and debtor days, the numerator should represent the *average* balance over the course of the defined period, though applying pragmatic judgement as to how this is calculated. Once again, the golden rule of ratios applies: the numerator and denominator must be mutually consistent to produce a meaningful result. In the case of creditor days, this raises the following points:

- Again, as with debtors, the numerator and denominator must be consistent in terms of VAT (remembering that the trade creditors number in the balance sheet will be gross, while the purchases number will be net).

- Be aware that the numerator (trade creditors) represents stock purchases that have not yet been paid for, therefore the denominator of cost of sales may not necessarily be consistent if there have been significant movements in stock during the period being measured. Items could, for example, have been purchased yet are still sitting in stock, and would not therefore feature in the cost of sales. The longer the trading period being measured, the less of a distortion this is likely to be, and in most circumstances can be ignored.

- It is possible that the trade creditors number may include an amount that relates to expenses or capital expenditure purchases (rather than stock purchases). If this is a material amount, and we want to focus on the efficiency of the trading throughput of the business (e.g. for the purposes of calculating the cash conversion cycle), then we might want to deduct these from the total.

Calculating the Cash Conversion Cycle

Above, we have looked at all the components that make up the calculation and given some numerical examples. These can be illustrated all together in the chart below:

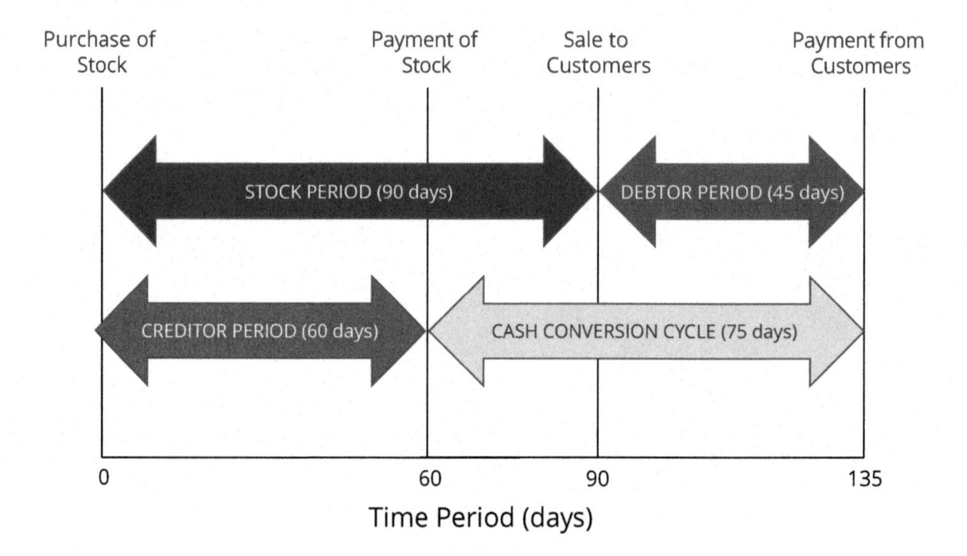

Along the bottom of the chart we have the timeframe, which in this example stretches for a total of 135 days. The company purchased its stock on Day 0, and sells it to its customer on Day 90, representing a 90-day stock holding period. The customer then pays for the goods 45 days after receiving delivery, which is on Day 135 in the cycle. Both these periods require capital in order to fund the outlay, and hence are a financial drain on the company's resources.

Part of this funding requirement, however, comes from the supplier, who gives the company 60 days credit. The company receives the goods into its warehouse on Day 0, but does not have to pay for them until Day 60.

The cash conversion cycle period, i.e. the period which requires funding net of credit from the supplier, is the difference and is illustrated by the yellow period above.

The Cash Conversion Cycle Formula

We can use this simple formula in order to work out the CCC period:

$$\textit{Cash Conversion Cycle} = \textit{Stock Period} + \textit{Debtor Period} - \textit{Creditor Period}$$

In our example, this is:

$$Cash\ Conversion\ Cycle = 90\ days + 45\ days - 60\ days = 75\ days$$

This tells us that the company takes a net total of 75 days to convert its investment in stock into cash. This is, of course, a continuously rolling average. The higher the number, the more working capital will be required and the greater likelihood of other operational inefficiencies. A rising number should be of considerable concern to the company's management. The lower the number, the more operationally efficient the company is, and, probably, the more profitable.

Multiplying this number by sales per day will give an indication of the cash flow impact of this cycle:

$$CCC\ Cash\ Flow\ Impact = No.\ of\ Days \times Sales\ per\ Day$$

In our example:

$$CCC\ Cash\ Flow\ Impact = 75\ days \times £24{,}000 = £1{,}800{,}000$$

The logic being that the company's cash flow could receive a one-off boost of £24,000 for every day the CCC can be reduced. Like most business ratios, it is most powerful as a metric when compared either to earlier periods in the same company, or to other similar companies in the same sector.

Businesses with a Positive Cash Conversion Cycle

It is possible for the CCC to actually *generate* working capital for a business. Consider the scenario illustrated below:

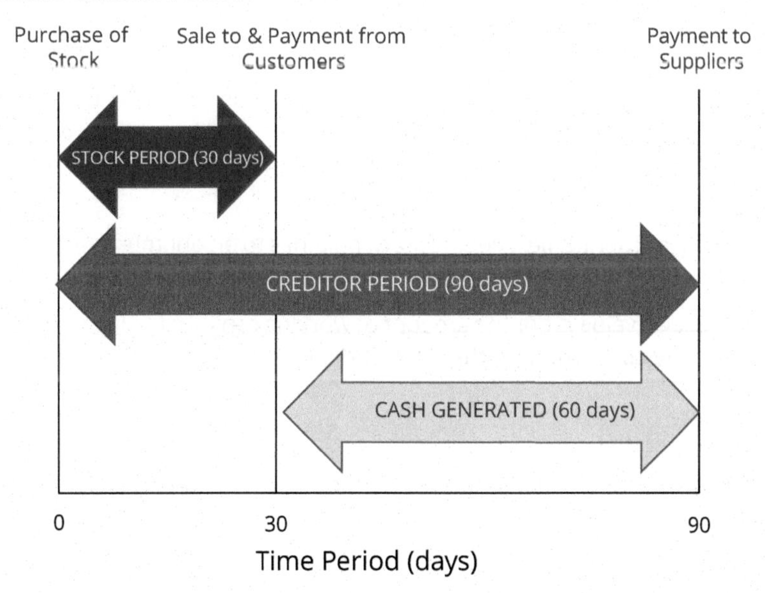

In this example, the company is equivalent to a major retailer, such as Tesco. The stock arrives into the business and is sold to customers 30 days later. The supplier, however, is not paid for 90 days from delivery, which consequently generates a positive cash flow.

$$\textit{Cash Conversion Cycle} = \textit{Stock Period} + \textit{Debtor Period} - \textit{Creditor Period}$$

$$\textit{Cash Conversion Cycle} = 30\ \textit{days} + 0\ \textit{days} - 90\ \textit{days} = -60\ \textit{days}$$

Note that the CCC is now negative, meaning that it is having a *positive* impact on cash flow. If we use the sales per day of £24,000 from our earlier example:

$$\textit{Cash Generated} = 60\ \textit{days} \times £24,000 = £1,440,000$$

The company's finances are boosted by £1.44m from this component of its trading operations. *Note that this is definitely not the net cash flow of the business.* As outlined above there will be many other operating expenses that require working capital (e.g. rent and payroll). But in this situation, the funds generated are a positive contribution to the total working capital requirement.

Also note that, in reality, major retailers such as supermarkets will not hold 30 days' stock. They are likely to operate on considerably lower numbers of days, particularly on food. In this respect, they would perform better than in our example.

The Cash Conversion Cycle

- To work out the cash conversion cycle (CCC) period we use this formula:

  Cash Conversion Cycle = Stock Period + Debtor Period - Creditor Period

- The CCC can be expressed either in terms of a number of days or as a value.
- The stock period and debtor period are 'negative' in the sense that the company has to find the funds to finance them. The creditor period can be seen as 'positive' insofar as it is working capital that is provided free by the supplier.
- Operating efficiently, i.e. keeping stock holdings to an optimum level, and collecting debtors on time, will greatly improve the cash flow of a business.
- Note the CCC value is not the amount of working capital a business may need. It is just one component of the total working capital requirement.

Free Cash Flow

The **free cash flow** (FCF) of a business is the surplus cash that the company generates after taking into account all its operational needs. This is after corporation tax, any increases in working capital requirements, and any capital expenditure.

As always, we can express it as a formula:[2]

$$FCF = EBITDA - Corporation\ Tax - Net\ Change\ in\ Working\ Capital - Capital\ Expenditure$$

Or expressed another way:

$$FCF = Net\ Cash\ Flow\ from\ Operations - Capital\ Expenditure$$

The reason why we use **EBITDA**, and not profit after tax, in this calculation is because:

- Depreciation and amortisation do not exist in the context of cash flow, since they are just accounting adjustments.
- Interest is excluded since we wish to see the cash generated from the operations of the business itself prior to the cost of any funding.

Why is FCF another important measure?

There are several reasons:

- FCF will take into account changes in the working capital requirements a business is facing. For example, a business with positive sales growth is likely to experience a drain on cash as its stock levels and debtor balances rise (though, possibly, also partially offset by increased creditor balances). Equally, if customers are taking longer to pay their invoices, debtors will increase; or, if suppliers are demanding faster payment, creditors will decrease; or if more goods for sale are being bought than sold for whatever reason, stock levels will increase. All these movements will adversely affect the cash flow of the business, but none will be visible from examining the profit & loss statement, which could, theoretically, be looking increasingly healthy, whilst disguising an emerging fundamental cash flow problem.
- The FCF will be important to investors, such as a venture capitalist. They will want to see whether the business can generate sufficient cash to fund any debt financing (both in terms of interest payments and capital repayments) and may also want to ensure they are able to receive a dividend flow.

Changes to the working capital requirements of the business can be both positive and negative. If, for example, the company was able to reduce stock levels (and still maintain the level of availability to customers) then it would be a positive change as less capital would be tied up in stock. Regardless of what the changes actually are, they need to be taken into account when looking at the overall cash generation.

The free cash flow is essential to monitor, as well as profitability. Rising profitability can disguise a deteriorating cash position.

Finally, we need to take into account capital expenditure. A business such as a luxury hotel will constantly have to upgrade its facilities – this will impact the amount of cash the business has left over and can return to its shareholders. Likewise, an airline will need to replace its aircraft as they age – the capital generated from its operations will not be the cash that can be given to its shareholders – *we have to consider the replacement of worn out assets.* This type of capital expenditure, which is maintaining the operational efficiency of the business, is different from *growth* capital expenditure (e.g. building a new factory for an entirely new product range). It should be noted this is a subtly different kind of capital expenditure.

Free Cash Flow and Capital Investment Appraisal

Projected FCF can also be used as the starting point when attempting to value a business as a potential acquisition, or evaluate a capital project as a potential investment. Alternatively, a similar analysis of projected FCF can be used to compare two or more competing projects to consider which one gives the greatest return from the investment.

In order to do this, we take the estimated future FCF figures of a business or project and discount them by a chosen rate (the **discount rate**) such that they are converted into an amount representing their hypothetical value to us as if we had the cash in our hands today. This amount is called the **present value**. The level of the discount rate used is set so that it reflects the lower value we (or our investors) place on uncertain cash flows in the future. We will come on to this topic in Chapter 6.1 – the point now is to recognise that FCF is the building block of this process.

Free Cash Flow

- The free cash flow (FCF) of a business is the surplus cash that the company generates after taking into account all its operational needs.
- We can calculate the value using this formula:

$$FCF = \text{Net Cash Flow from Operations} - \text{Capital Expenditure}$$

- The FCF figure is of importance when using capital investment appraisal techniques.

Notes

1. Accrued income is for goods or services that have been delivered but not yet invoiced, hence are highly relevant. Prepayments are advance payments on items like rent, but not yet used, and are not relevant to the sales revenue of the business. Other debtors could include all sorts of items, such as a tax refund due, that are also not directly relevant to the sales revenue. Hence these non-relevant items should be excluded for greatest accuracy of calculation.
2. Technically, the amount of corporation tax deducted here should be only that arising from operating profit (EBIT).

4.3 IMPROVING CASH FLOW

Start with the Business Concept!

In the last chapter, we looked at the **cash conversion cycle** and understood how this can impact the working capital requirement of a business. It pays to consider this cycle *when a business concept is first conceived and developed*, as this can greatly influence both the amount of start-up capital required and the speed at which the business could grow. Consider, for example, that you are planning to start selling a range of clothing imported from overseas. You have a choice of either selling through major High Street retailers or going direct to consumers by selling online. Whilst there would be numerous issues to consider about how to reach your target customers, one thing is very clear – you would be paid a lot quicker if you sold directly to the customer.

Our Top 10 Ways in Which You Can Improve Your Cash Flow

But what if you are way past the concept stage of your business – how do you improve cash flow?

You can be forgiven for being tempted by the obvious method of delaying paying anyone you owe money to. True – this will improve your cash flow, but it is a momentary fix and can only be pushed so far. There are also many negative consequences of this action. How about coming up with some strategies that are *permanently* good for cash flow and may actually improve harmony with your suppliers, customers, and perhaps surprisingly, your employees? Being clever with cash flow management means looking deeply into the *operations* of the business.

We have come up with our Top 10 ways to improve the cash flow of a business, with No. 1 being the best way in our opinion. Let's look at these in turn. Give them a read, then give some thought as to whether we have put them in the right order.

Rank	Action	Significance
1	Improve profitability	This has to be the first and foremost action to take. It will be made up of many factors, but here are the obvious ones: - Increase sales volume. - Improve gross margin % by raising prices and/or reducing unit cost of sales. - Reduce overheads. Profits flowing into a business will either arrive as cash (as per a retailer) or debtors. Whilst debtors are not cash, they are just one step away, and if this represents a problem to cash flow there are ways of resolving it, as set out below.
2	Get customers to pay with order	This is great if you are a retailer or an online business, but not possible for many companies. Maybe this should be ranked No. 1 on this list? But there isn't much point in collecting payment promptly on unprofitable sales transactions, hence we've put it at No. 2.
3	Collect payments using Direct Debit	If it is not possible to get your customer to pay with the order, how about obtaining their permission to help yourself from their bank account? This is what happens with the Direct Debit process and is operated by many service suppliers (such as telecoms and electricity). Small companies can also use this process, but will need a strong balance sheet to convince their own bank to operate this facility on their behalf. If they cannot achieve the required financial status, there are third-party companies that will operate Direct Debit on their behalf for a fee.
4	Optimise stock levels	Stock is capital tied up and has to be funded. Keeping stock levels to a minimum, whilst ensuring that availability to customers is kept as high as possible, requires careful management. Done properly, it can make a considerable contribution to the positive performance of a business.
5	Speed everything up	Think of a movie speeded up… everything happens at an unreal speed and the scene quickly ends. If you were to speed up *every step* in the process of doing business, inevitably your cash would arrive quicker. Some obvious examples would be: - Raise invoices the moment goods or services are delivered. Once raised, the clock is ticking on any credit terms given to customers. - Reduce the time products take to manufacture and/or are held in stock. - Reduce time to process orders and deliver the goods. - Improve the speed of every other aspect in the business (even seemingly unrelated functions such as recruiting staff) thus making you awesomely efficient. - Treat your suppliers as partners and try to make them more efficient. This benefit will be returned to you in the long term.

Rank	Action	Significance
6	Factor your debt	If you are sitting on a debtor book that you really need to turn into cash, you can use a debt factoring service or other form of debtor financing. This process involves the bank (or other financial institution) paying you most of the invoice just after you have raised it. They will then collect the money on your behalf. The drawbacks of this service are firstly it is costly (the bank takes some of your gross margin) and secondly it may tell your customers that you are not exactly flush with funds. Finally, an aggressive bank chasing one of your customers for payment may not be good for long-term customer relations!
7	Negotiate better supplier terms	This is an extremely obvious suggestion. Just ask your suppliers for longer payment terms when negotiating the supply contract. If you are strong financially and a reliable payer, suppliers will be reasonably receptive to this request. However, if you are a poor credit risk and do not honour the terms when agreed you risk being treated as a poor customer, and even being dropped as not worth doing business with.
8	Invest in credit control procedures	If you cannot collect your money with the order, nor by Direct Debit, you are left reliant on your customers to pay you on time. Unfortunately, many will need chasing, otherwise your receipts of payments may stretch well beyond your set terms. Employing effective credit control procedures is essential. These will include sending out monthly statements to customers, following up late payers, and doing credit checks on all new customers. Employing a dedicated credit controller to chase up slow payers may also be beneficial. In our experience, they need to be robust individuals who are extremely persistent. If you allocate the task as an additional add-on role to another unsuitable member of staff, they are likely to make this unpleasant task their lowest priority. So, recruit the right person, possibly part-time if it is not a full-time role. The management reports for the credit controller should be looking at: - Amount of credit outstanding within the allowed credit period (e.g. 30 days). This highlights your exposure to any individual customer. - The amounts outstanding in time bands (e.g. 30 to 60 days, 60 to 90 days, and 90 days+). This highlights the level of efficiency of your credit control function, particularly for the time bands that are beyond your set credit period. - Details of all individual customers who represent a potential payment problem (i.e. amount outstanding and time overdue). This highlights the customers that are now hindering cash flow.

Rank	Action	Significance
9	Asset financing	All of the above have focused on trading with your customers. Let's give some thought now to finance asset purchases. This could be done in a number of ways, for example paying from operational cash flow or from a bank loan. But if the asset is leased or bought on hire purchase, then the cost of the item can be paid on a monthly basis. The security for this lease or loan is the asset itself, i.e. if the monthly payments are not met the asset is repossessed by the lender. This is a great way of funding items such as vehicles and machinery.
10	Delay paying your suppliers	Oh dear! If you are resorting to this strategy, then you have not been effective in Nos. 1 to 9 above (or are under-capitalised). Your biggest problem is probably with No. 1 – you are not making a sufficient profit and your balance sheet has been slowly depleting. Not paying your suppliers within the agreed timeframe will create resentment with them and you will not get the best prices, nor performance, out of them. They may even drop you as a customer. You will also face constant chasing phone calls, emails/letters and even the occasional court summons to resolve. As well as developing a bad name within the industry, what does it say to your employees? They are likely to become dispirited and look for alternative employment. This is really something to do as a last resort and only to be done in extreme circumstances, and ideally with the specific prior agreement of friendly suppliers.

As you can see, item Nos. 1 to 9 can be regarded as positive solutions, whilst item 10 would clearly be a negative one. Is the order above correct in terms of importance? What do you think, and have we missed any others?

This list is also incredibly relevant to improving that rock-star ratio we keep going on about: **return on capital employed**. Almost every action above will either contribute to improving the operating profit of the business, or reducing the capital employed. Given that the former is divided by the latter, you can see how the ratio will consequently improve with each incremental improvement shown above. And in case you have had a momentary lapse of memory, the higher the return on capital employed is, the faster you will generate wealth, and the faster you will be able to grow without external funding!

Moody Sewage Example

Moody Sewage was a small business we helped several years ago, run by a friend called Darren Hall. The business was in trouble – it had been losing money and owed its main supplier over £130,000. The supplier had simply not chased up Darren for payment and this had given him a false sense of security with respect to his cash flow. The financial management focus had also been on short-term cash planning, not on long-term profitability. Consequently, the business was operating at a loss, and the cash position was bolstered by not paying this and other suppliers on time.

Moody Sewage kept a positive net cash flow by continually extending its credit with a key supplier. Needless to say, this strategy nearly led to financial disaster.

Darren took active steps to improve profitability, which we will look at later. But one significant change he made for improving *both* his cash flow *and* his operational efficiency, was to start using Direct Debit to collect the payments from his own customers. These had previously been costly to collect, and often involved chasing-up telephone calls and trying to obtain credit card payments over the phone. In addition, because the sums were relatively small, the chasing process was a disproportionately large cost of the whole transaction.

Moody Sewage's balance sheet was nowhere near strong enough for the bank to allow the company to perform the Direct Debit service itself. So, Darren engaged a third-party company to operate it on the company's behalf. They also printed and posted the invoices as part of the service.

From the customer's perspective, paying by Direct Debit took away some of the tedious headache of managing the septic tank in their garden. From Moody Sewage's viewpoint, it both improved cash flow and reduced overhead costs simultaneously.

Improving Cash Flow

- There are numerous ways a company can improve cash flow. Improving profitability and efficiency are far superior methods to delaying payments to creditors.

4.4 THE CASH FLOW FORECAST

The Importance of Cash Flow Planning

As we described in Chapter 4.1, cash is the lifeblood of every business – its continuous flow is essential to the business's survival. It follows, therefore, that monitoring and managing the company's cash position is a key management responsibility – not just in the present, but in the weeks, months and even years ahead.

As you can imagine, if more money keeps going out of the business than comes in, a serious problem is likely to arise. This is a common situation with an early stage business: they have yet to reach profitability and hence are not generating sufficient cash to meet their expenditure requirements. However, providing they are meeting the growth goals promised to their investors, it is usually possible to keep raising new capital to bridge the gap until they reach profitability and the ability to generate sufficient cash themselves.

As we have mentioned when looking at the Vulpine case study in Chapter 3.4, for a start-up waiting to achieve profitability, the amount of cash it is consuming each month or year can be described as the **burn rate** and the time period the company can survive before requiring further funding is known as the **runway**. For example, a company burning cash at a rate of £1m a year, and is sitting on £1.5m of cash, has a theoretical runway of 18 months.

A flashpoint of potential failure for a business is to find itself running out of cash, and, worse still, running out of the means to bring in more cash. This generally immediately precedes going bust, and the more imminent this moment is, the harder it becomes to raise new equity capital, or to persuade a bank to lend money. Hence, planning ahead for cash resources and capital-raising facilities is vital. Remember Benjamin Franklin's quote from the very first chapter of this book: *'If you fail to plan, you are planning to fail'!*

We have already referred to the overused expression *cash is king* – there is much truth to this statement, although as we will repeatedly remind you throughout the book, you should be focusing on both cash and profitability simultaneously. The sooner profitability is reached, the less vulnerable a company will be to running out of cash: firstly, it should be generating cash from the profits made; and secondly new investors are more likely to be attracted to a profitable company.

The Cash Flow Forecast

With so many items of expenditure going out in the future, and different sources of money coming in, we need a method of planning what is happening, otherwise we will be driving in the dark. Add to this a further complexity – some, in fact most, of the items of cash flow may be *uncertain in their nature*. The best and most obvious example of this is sales revenue: we can rarely be absolutely certain of our sales in the months, let alone years, ahead.

This is where the cash flow forecast comes in – it is effectively a list of projected money in and projected money out in the months and even years ahead. The difference is the net cash flow for each period. As always, let us start by looking at a very simple example. Below is a cash flow forecast for six months ahead:

Cash Flow Forecast

£	Jan	Feb	Mar	Apr	May	Jun
Opening cash balance	-	50	100	150	(150)	(100)
Money in	200	200	200	200	200	200
Money out	(150)	(150)	(150)	(500)	(150)	(150)
Net cash flow	**50**	**50**	**50**	**(300)**	**50**	**50**
Closing bank account	**50**	**100**	**150**	**(150)**	**(100)**	**(50)**

We can observe the business starts with a zero opening bank balance. It is projecting a consistent flow of 'Money in' of £200 a month, and a consistent flow of 'Money out' of £150 – with the exception of April, where £500 is projected to go out.

Note the 'Closing bank account' forecast is projected to be negative in April. Unless the business has an **overdraft facility** in place with its bank, it will run out of cash. Under these circumstances the bank could stop all payments out of the bank account, with all the corresponding chaos this could cause. But by planning ahead, the business can, not only identify the potential problem in April four months ahead of time, but also take steps to resolve the problem before it occurs. Solutions could be many, such as: ensuring fresh share capital is raised well in advance; or arranging extra funding from a bank; or talking to suppliers and asking to make payments over an extended period.

Timeframe for a Cash Flow Forecast

The cash flow forecast can be for a variety of time horizons into the future. The further out it goes, however, the more uncertain the projection will be, until eventually it becomes a pointless exercise. We would suggest a rolling 12-month period[1] is both useful from a planning viewpoint and meaningful in terms of reliability. By rolling we mean updated each month to always be looking at least a year out – we will cover more of this later in Chapter 7.2. Many very small businesses may be looking at their cash flow only *a few weeks ahead*, often simply juggling their finances to meet the immediate payment deadlines. This is a potentially disastrous operating strategy as it leaves insufficient time to sort out problems in advance and can often lead to business failure.

The Cash Flow Forecast Is the Product of a Financial Model

It is important to recognise at this stage that a high-quality cash flow forecast can only be done accurately for any period of time exceeding a few months by producing a **financial model**. This will usually be produced in a spreadsheet programme such as Excel.

Every financial model has to be based on a set of **assumptions**. If these are well researched and sensibly applied, the subsequent model should be of good use – and, of course, if they are poorly researched, then the output is likely to be of limited use. The old expression *'rubbish in, rubbish out'* is extremely valid in this context!

Once you have a set of assumptions, the next step is to produce the profit & loss forecast. This is vital in order to determine whether the business can generate a profit. If it cannot do this within a reasonable timeframe, then clearly there may be something wrong with the concept. Alternatively, you may have a concept that is going to require a great deal of funding until it finally reaches profitability. Either way, the early results may require a substantial rethink of your initial assumptions and further modelling.

The third step is to produce the cash flow forecast. This should be a separate forecast from the profit & loss. It should *not* be a hybrid of the two statements – if anyone ever tells you to do a single statement, they are effectively just asking you to produce just the cash flow forecast. *This is because a cash flow forecast alone will not give you sufficient clarity on the profitability of the business.* Focusing just on the cash flow is a serious error – you are looking at the output, not what is creating that output, which ultimately is the profits or losses generated by trading. This apparent trading performance can be disguised by cash coming into the business from other sources, such as capital injections, or loan drawdowns; or alternatively from delaying payment to suppliers and the tax office. These actions may make the cash flow appear to be okay, when this may be far from reality. *In our role as mentors of hundreds of businesses, we have seen this mistake repeatedly. The consequences have usually been disastrous!*

Focusing just on cash flow alone is a terrible error in financial modelling. Disaster usually follows.

In fact, we would go a step further and suggest that a really first-class financial model would include a forecast for the profit & loss, cash flow and balance sheet. It should also adhere to the basic rule of accounting, that the two sides of the accounting equation must always match. This, then, helps to ensure the internal integrity of the forecast.

The Cash Flow Forecast

- Cash flow forecasting is an essential feature for any business. A business has to fully understand the flow of money into and out of the business both today and well into the future.
- The difference between the flow of money in and money out in any given time period is the net cash flow.
- In the long run, net cash flow has to be positive, otherwise a business will run out of cash and is likely to fail.
- Businesses should ideally be looking at their cash flow at least 12 months ahead on a continuous rolling basis.
- A well-produced cash flow forecast should be the product of a more comprehensive financial model. This will include a set of assumptions, and forecasts for the profit & loss and a balance sheet.
- There is no such thing as a 'hybrid' profit & loss forecast and a cash flow forecast. Any such statement is simply a cash flow forecast in isolation – a potentially dangerous management tool!

Note

1. 12 months is a suitable time period for most businesses, but note this may need to be longer for others.

4.5 BUILDING A FINANCIAL MODEL

Financial modelling is extremely useful and powerful. Once you have an idea for a new business, before taking it any further you would be well advised to test it in a simple **financial model** by using a spreadsheet programme, such as Excel. After making some basic financial assumptions, this can give you an early indication as to potential profitability and capital requirements. You can then make a judgement whether to investigate the concept further, and in the process further refine the model.

But that's just in the context of a potential start-up. What about businesses already up and running? Modelling is just as vital for them, of course, as it allows management to glimpse into the future – a financial crystal ball. They can see what their performance could be like in the next year or more – this is vital for budgeting purposes and cash flow planning. They can perform 'what if…' scenarios, such as the impact on profitability of a new product, or in a crisis situation the effect of falling sales in the months ahead.

So, financial modelling is both powerful and practical, and the actual process of building a financial model is a great way to understand the inter-relationship between all the financial statements. In this chapter, we are going to show you how to create and use a good financial model.

Your Starting Point

Most modelling begins with a blank Excel spreadsheet. This is fine if you know what you are doing but does mean you have a long road ahead of you before you start to see some meaningful data.

As an alternative, we have created two financial models that can be used as starting templates. Inevitably they will be imperfect for your particular requirements, and in most cases, they can be quickly adapted into something suitable. Even if these models are not used, they are good illustrations of what is required, and we will use them as examples to explain the process.

The two models are:

Carl's Café

This model is for a simple café. A café was chosen because everyone can understand the concept and its likely cost structure. It also has many features shared by more complex businesses, such as stock, premises, capital equipment, wages, bank loans, etc.

Whilst it might have been more appealing to take an exciting tech start-up as an example, comprehension of the concept might not be clear, and the business may have few features such as a physical product, stock or capital equipment. Our role is to give you the ability to understand all aspects of the finances of a business, which must therefore cover these items.

Meet Carl who has done a simple café start-up!

Davis Design

This is basically the same as Carl's Café in structure. The key difference is the front end, specifically the sales forecasting. This model is more flexible and has two sales forecasting templates. The first format is for a multiproduct business, which allows for the creation of a variety of products, each with different gross margins. The second format caters for a scenario such as a design agency, where they are constantly pitching for new work but never quite certain what will actually convert to sales. Both templates can either be used individually or in combination as appropriate. More on this later.

Meet the Davis Design team who sell both physical products as well a design consultancy service.

The Davis Design model also has a few other technical additions to it, and we would recommend using this model as your starting point, rather than Carl's Café. But for the purposes of explaining how such a model works, we will focus on Carl's Café.

> **The Power of Financial Modelling**
>
> - Financial models allow you to glimpse into the future and see the potential outcomes from your financial assumptions.
> - As a tool, it is vital for both start-ups and established trading businesses.
> - Building a financial model is a great way of properly understanding the interrelationship between the financial statements.

The Financial Modelling Process

There are four steps to building a financial model, and these are in a *strict order* entirely driven by logic. Here they are:

Step 1: financial assumptions
Step 2: the profit & loss forecast
Step 3: the cash flow forecast
Step 4: the balance sheet forecast

As explained in Chapter 4.4 it is essential to follow this order. Consider these points:

1. How can you produce a profit & loss forecast without knowing what the financial assumptions behind it are?
2. How can you produce a cash flow forecast if you do not know if your trading is actually generating or consuming wealth, i.e. making a profit or loss?

The answer is, of course you *can* do both, but in the first instance your profit & loss forecast is unlikely to be accurate without valid assumptions. In the second scenario, again it is reliant on assumptions, but the cash flow forecast is unlikely to be much use without a clear understanding of what is usually the main driver of cash flow, i.e. the profit & loss forecast.

Just to repeat again, the cash flow forecast should be a *separate forecast* from the profit & loss. Remember also there is no such thing as a hybrid profit & loss and cash flow forecast. Such a model is simply a dressed-up cash flow forecast (dressed up with some figures from the profit & loss, but not formatted in such a way as to allow the reader to clearly determine the profitability status, only the cash flow status). Using such a hybrid model is generally a way of planting the seeds of your business's later failure.

The final step is to produce the balance sheet forecast. This may *seem* challenging at first glance but is actually quite straightforward once some basic accounting concepts are understood. The balance sheet forecast *has* to follow from the cash flow forecast. *Why?* Simply because the balance sheet forecast has to contain the amount of cash in the bank account ... and you will only know this when you have done your cash flow forecast. *It's that simple!*

Finally having profit & loss, cash flow and balance sheet projections that are all consistent with each other ensures the integrity of the overall model, helping to iron out any errors.

General Principles of Financial Models

Rule 1: K.I.S.S. – Keep It Simple, Stupid!

Rule 1 has to be to not over-complicate it, particularly at the start. Of course, if you have a substantial trading business, your model is likely to be both complex and sophisticated. But this model will not have been built overnight – it will have come from a long process of development based on trading experience, possibly over many years.

You can handwrite a basic forecast on the back of an envelope, and therefore roughly sketch out the future performance and scale of a business. If you can do this, it illustrates the point that complexity is not necessarily required to get a picture of how the future looks. Your initial objective is to determine the rough direction of the business: *Will it make money? If so, roughly how much? And roughly how much cash will it consume or generate?*

We often say you are only trying to establish the approximate wind direction. *Is it coming from the North, South, East or West, or roughly any points between?* To know the direction down to the nearest degree of the compass may be completely pointless – if not impossible. At the end of the day, your assumptions are only guesses or estimates – though, hopefully, well-informed ones. So, however hard you try, the output of your model can only be estimates too. We once consulted for a business that took the modelling so seriously that, during the course of a year, they still had not finished it. They were too obsessed with trying to get every detail correct at the outset; the net result being they still had no clear foresight of their trading position. Oh dear – they seemed to be more interested in building a model than building a business!

Rule 2: Your Forecast Is Wrong

Rule 2 says that, whatever forecast you produce, it *will* be *wrong*. If you forecast a bank balance of £253,681 in a year's time, the chances of it being exactly that figure are exceedingly slim – to say the least. Even if it is that figure, the way it was derived will *not be as you had forecast.*

When we started our second business, Card Connection Limited, we prepared a forecast financial model for ourselves and 3i, the venture capital group that helped fund the start-up in 1992. Before we had sold a single greeting card, we forecast a first-year loss of £55,000 (c.£120k in 2020 values). Astonishingly, we actually came in within a few hundred pounds of this number, which surprised us as much as 3i. However, in reality, sales were behind the forecast plan (they were too optimistic within the timeframe), but the unit gross margin on the hundreds of display spinners we supplied to our franchisees was considerably higher than we had anticipated. So, the shortfall on sales had been made up from an unexpected source. Despite this piece of luck, we could justifiably congratulate ourselves on a good piece of financial modelling. Every model will be up or down in numerous places, and hopefully they all balance out to give a reasonably sensible picture of the future. We certainly did just that!

So, even if your forecast turns out to be relatively accurate, the chances are the way it has been generated will *not* be as you expected. This, of course, primarily applies to early stage businesses – mature businesses can be forecasted with a higher degree of accuracy.

Knowing that your model is almost certainly wrong is important to bear in mind. Firstly, do not take the numbers too literally, and secondly remember to have plenty of contingency funding. Inevitably, the most common error is to overstate the sales forecast. In the case of Card Connection, we went on to beat all the sales and profit forecasts we had made, but it took longer to get there than we anticipated.

Rule 3: You're Damned Either Way

We often view financial forecasts at business angel pitching events with mild amusement. The chances of any Year 1 profits being greater than £1m are probably similar to those of winning the National Lottery twice running. Hence, when we see this, the forecast is dismissed as (probably) nonsense, and the management has little credibility in the eyes of the investor. In fact, any Year 1 profit at all is extremely unlikely in most situations.

Much the same applies to the 'hockey stick' forecasts – exponential growth on an astonishing scale. Not impossible, but most unlikely unless they have an extraordinary product and team.

Then there are the forecasts with a very slow build in profitability, or even losses for years ahead. These are instantly regarded as unattractive and investors lose interest. *It seems you cannot win!* You are damned if you are too optimistic, and damned if you are too pessimistic.

Clearly somewhere between the two extremes is what is wanted, backed up by credible assumptions. This is the magic sweet-spot that potential investors will look for – nesting precariously between being unexciting and being unrealistic. Every investor knows forecasts will be wrong (and usually over-optimistic), but they will want to see the upside potential. That potential, however, must look credible.

When pitching it is often hard to make your numbers seem credible!

Investors also want to see that the management has a financial plan – i.e. a financial model – even if the numbers are of somewhat dubious value at the outset. The existence of a good robust model indicates that the management at least understands the process, and as a business scales, the forecasting system is in place for when the numbers progressively become more meaningful.

Make Your Model Easy to Use

A good financial model should be easy to understand and use. Remember that it could be looked at by a large number of individuals, such as other members of your management team, investors, and bank managers.

One simple rule to follow, which we apply to all our spreadsheets, is to make sure all input cells are clearly indicated, for instance by colouring them in yellow. This means that the user can instantly see which cells can be changed and appreciate that all the other cells contain formulas.

Having clear segregation between the assumptions, profit & loss, cash flow and balance sheet forecasts is also vital. Finally, there should be some summary pages where the busy executive or investor can quickly grasp the big picture of what is happening. These can be supported by a series of graphs highlighting key aspects of the performance of the business. We illustrate these principles in our café example.

Treatment of Inflation

A common question asked is how to treat inflation. You have a choice of producing a model entirely in today's prices, known as 'in real terms', or putting in price and cost changes as you see them likely to occur, known as 'in nominal terms'.

If you were doing a capital investment appraisal, calculating the **net present value** or **internal rate of return** of an investment, you would do these calculations in real terms. However, a financial model is serving a different purpose. Here, you may primarily be producing a budget for next year, and in this case the inclusion of inflationary pressures is essential. For example, the cost of your premises may be rising next year, and you know you need to increase your staff salaries to retain your team. In fact, seeing these inevitable cost changes may be a key component in helping you decide whether to raise your own prices next year. The impact of this decision can then be clearly seen in your financial model.

In conclusion, you need to consider the purpose of your model before deciding whether to adjust it for inflation. Either way, you need to clearly state what you have chosen to do in your assumptions.

The Financial Modelling Process

- Strictly follow a four-step process of producing assumptions, profit & loss, cash flow and balance sheet forecasts in that order, ensuring they are separate elements of the model.
- Avoid making the model too complicated to begin with. Add complexity and sophistication over time.
- A useful tip is to use a colour for the input cells. This makes it easier for others to use.
- Where a financial model is to be used for internal financial planning purposes, figures should be in nominal terms (i.e. showing any inflationary changes that might occur).

This next section is best read in conjunction with viewing the **Carl's Café** and **Davis Design** financial model examples. Please note that the models are frequently amended, so the version that you download may differ from the screenshots below. However, all the principles remain the same.

Assumptions in the Financial Model

What assumptions might there be for a coffee shop? These are likely to fall under three simple headings:

Sales Assumptions
How many customers come into the café each day?
What is their average spend per visit?
How much of what they spend is on food and how much on beverages?

Gross Margin Assumptions
What level of gross margin is there on food and beverages?

Operating Expenses Assumptions
How many staff will be needed and what are the wage rates?
What is the rent for typical café premises?
What will the heating and lighting cost?
What other costs apply (such as marketing)?

Capital Equipment
What equipment will be required, and how much will it cost?
What rate of depreciation should be applied?

Funding
How much money is needed to start the business?
Will this money be sourced from the founder, investors, or bank loans, or perhaps a combination of them all?

Whilst this is far from a comprehensive list, it does illustrate the principles. The model itself will also help reshape some of your early assumptions, such as how much funding you will require.

How to obtain most of this information is not covered by this book – that's market research. But some obvious ways to research a café model would be: sitting in or outside various coffee shops and watching the customer flow and cash register readings; talking to café owners and staff; talking to estate agents about example properties; and talking to equipment suppliers, shop fitters, etc. This type of work is invaluable, as not only do you gain a better handle on the statistics, but you can also learn more about the actual operation of the business.

Fixed and Variable Assumptions

Our example models work on the basis that some assumptions are *fixed throughout the year*, and others *change from month to month*. For example, rent is generally constant throughout the year, hence this assumption is entered for the year, and the figure is then automatically copied down to the profit & loss and applied on a monthly basis.

Here are some examples of fixed assumptions. All the boxes in yellow can be changed, and the model will automatically recalculate after each change is made. There are also some spare lines – 'Other 1' and 'Other 2' – which allow for additional overheads to be created and they will automatically be added into the profit & loss forecast beneath (further lines can be expanded out in the actual model).

Carl's Café Financial Model

1. Assumptions *The assumptions as the vital first component. These drive the P&L below. Divide them between those that change annually and those that change month to month.*

Fixed Assumptions *These assumptions are fixed for each trading year.*

ONLY CHANGE YELLOW CELLS. THE REST ARE FORMULAS!

Overheads:	2021	2022	2023
Staff Salary Rate (incl NI)	£20,000	£21,000	£22,000
Annual Rent	£32,000	£40,000	£40,000
Annual Rates	£12,000	£12,000	£12,000
Annual Heat & Light	£4,000	£4,500	£5,000
Annual Cleaning	£9,000	£9,300	£11,000
Annual Other Misc Costs	£5,750	£6,500	£8,000
Other 1	£0	£0	£0
Other 2	£0	£0	£0

<--- Expand here to see more inputs

Finance Costs:	
Bank Loan	£70,000
Interest on Loan	6.0%
Loan Period (Months)	48

<--- Expand here to see loan payment breakdown

Plant & Equipment:		Property:	
Shop Fitting Costs	£80,000	Purchase Cost	£0
Machinery Purchased	£22,000	Revaluation	£0
Depreciation Period (Years)	5	Current Value	£0

Investment Capital:		VAT Rate	20%
Investment in Share Capital	£45,000		
Directors' Loan Loans	£15,000	Corporation Tax Rate	20%
Opening Bank Balance	£0		

An example of an assumption that varies from month to month is 'No. Customers per Day' – this may be higher (or lower) during the summer months when compared to the rest of the year. In the example below, you can see the variable assumptions run across the spreadsheet from left to right. Only the first 9 months are shown below, but in the Excel model they run for 36 months:

Variable Assumptions *These assumptions vary for each month.*

Month:	Jan-21	Feb-21	Mar-21	Apr-21	May-21	Jun-21	Jul-21	Aug-21	Sep-21
No. Customers per Day	1	40	70	90	100	110	110	110	110
Spend per Customer (incl VAT)	£8	£8	£8	£8	£8	£9	£9	£9	£10
Total Sales per Day (incl VAT)	£8	£320	£560	£720	£800	£990	£990	£990	£1,100
No. Trading Days (per Week)	6	6	6	6	6	6	6	6	6
Gross Margin	65%	65%	65%	65%	65%	65%	65%	65%	65%
No. Staff	1.0	1.0	2.0	2.0	2.0	2.0	2.5	2.5	2.5

Once again, changing the assumptions in these yellow boxes is easy, and the impact can be seen immediately on the key financial statements elsewhere.

More Complex Sales Assumptions for a Multi-product Business

As stated earlier, the Davis Design example can cater for a multiproduct business. The exact layout can of course be amended as appropriate – this is just an example:

		Month:	Jan-21	Feb-21	Mar-21	Apr-21	May-21	Jun-21	Jul-21	Aug-21	Sep-21
PRODUCTS (FORMAT A)		*This is a list of products the company sells, each at a different Gross Margin, and also allows for different order sizes and invoice values for each month.*									
Product 1		Sales Volume (units)	100	150	200	250	300	350	400	400	400
		Product Price	£12	£12	£12	£12	£12	£12	£12	£12	£12
		Sales	£1,200	£1,800	£2,400	£3,000	£3,600	£4,200	£4,800	£4,800	£4,800
Gross Margin on Product %:	50%	Gross Profit	£600	£900	£1,200	£1,500	£1,800	£2,100	£2,400	£2,400	£2,400
Product 2		Sales Volume (units)	50	50	50	50	50	50	50	55	55
		Product Price	£30	£30	£30	£30	£30	£30	£30	£30	£30
		Sales	£1,500	£1,500	£1,500	£1,500	£1,500	£1,500	£1,500	£1,650	£1,650
Gross Margin on Product %:	60%	Gross Profit	£900	£900	£900	£900	£900	£900	£900	£990	£990
Product 3		Sales Volume (units)	5	5	5	5	5	15	15	15	15
		Product Price	£40	£40	£40	£40	£40	£40	£40	£40	£40
		Sales	£200	£200	£200	£200	£200	£600	£600	£600	£600
Gross Margin on Product %:	68%	Gross Profit	£135	£135	£135	£135	£135	£405	£405	£405	£405

Note that the gross margin shown above is driven from another simple model for each of the individual products, which allows for changing the cost structure of each component part of a product:

VAT Rate:	20%		
	Product 1	**Product 2**	**Product 3**
Selling Price (incl VAT)	**£ 14.40**	**£ 36.00**	**£ 48.00**
VAT	£ 2.40	£ 6.00	£ 8.00
Selling Price (excl VAT)	**£ 12.00**	**£ 30.00**	**£ 40.00**
Component Part 1	£ 1.00	£ 5.00	£ 3.00
Component Part 2	£ 3.00	£ 6.00	£ 4.00
Component Part 3	£ 0.50	£ 1.00	£ 6.00
Component Part 4	£ 1.50	£ -	£ -
Total Costs	**£ 6.00**	**£ 12.00**	**£ 13.00**
Gross Profit	**£ 6.00**	**£ 18.00**	**£ 27.00**
Gross Margin %	50%	60%	68%

More Complex Sales Assumptions for a Consultancy-Type Business

The Davis Design model also has a template suitable for a business that has to pitch for projects. This is always a forecasting challenge, since clearly *only a proportion of the work that is pitched for is going to be won.* By attaching a probability of success to each project, the sales outcome can be weighted accordingly.

Whilst this is clearly wrong – as each individual project will either be won or lost in its entirety – if applied over a *large number* of projects with meaningful likelihoods of success attached, then the resulting overall forecast could be very accurate. Clearly the greater the number of projects involved, the better the forecast is likely to be.

		Month:	Jan-21	Feb-21	Mar-21	Apr-21	May-21	Jun-21	Jul-21	Aug-21	Sep-21
SERVICES (FORMAT B)		*Note that here a probability is attached to the likelihood of winning the business.*									
Client/Project A		Sales	£12,000	£12,000	£12,000	£12,000	£12,000	£12,000	£12,000	£12,000	£12,000
Gross Margin on Project %:	45%	Gross Profit	£5,400	£5,400	£5,400	£5,400	£5,400	£5,400	£5,400	£5,400	£5,400
Likelihood of Gaining Business:	20%	Expected Sales	£2,400	£2,400	£2,400	£2,400	£2,400	£2,400	£2,400	£2,400	£2,400
		Expected Gross Profit	£1,080	£1,080	£1,080	£1,080	£1,080	£1,080	£1,080	£1,080	£1,080
Client/Project B		Sales	£0	£0	£6,000	£18,000	£22,000	£0	£0	£0	£0
Gross Margin on Project %:	45%	Gross Profit	£0	£0	£2,700	£8,100	£9,900	£0	£0	£0	£0
Likelihood of Gaining Business:	50%	Expected Sales	£0	£0	£3,000	£9,000	£11,000	£0	£0	£0	£0
		Expected Gross Profit	£0	£0	£1,350	£4,050	£4,950	£0	£0	£0	£0
Client/Project C		Sales	£0	£0	£0	£0	£3,000	£7,000	£12,000	£4,000	£2,000
Gross Margin on Project %:	55%	Gross Profit	£0	£0	£0	£0	£1,650	£3,850	£6,600	£2,200	£1,100
Likelihood of Gaining Business:	75%	Expected Sales	£0	£0	£0	£0	£2,250	£5,250	£9,000	£3,000	£1,500
		Expected Gross Profit	£0	£0	£0	£0	£1,238	£2,888	£4,950	£1,650	£825

None of the above templates are intended to be definitive. They are only simple examples of what you can do. Consider what are the important criteria for your business and build your model around them.

> **Assumptions**
> - A financial model lives or dies by its assumptions. Regardless of how sophisticated the model is, if the assumptions are weakly derived, the final output will be of limited value.
> - Keep your assumptions in defined areas, allowing the user to be able to easily make changes.

The Profit & Loss Forecast

The profit & loss forecast is relatively straightforward. In the Carl's Café example, sales, gross profit and overhead structures are determined from the assumptions above it. You will notice that, with the exception of one line, none of the cells are yellow. This is because all of the cells (other than those coloured yellow) are formulas. Change any of the assumptions shown above, and the profit & loss recalculates for each month.

2. Profit & Loss *All the cells below are formulas working from the assumptions above.*

Month:	Jan-21	Feb-21	Mar-21	Apr-21	May-21	Jun-21	Jul-21	Aug-21	Sep-21
Sales (excl. VAT)	**£172**	**£6,880**	**£12,040**	**£15,480**	**£17,200**	**£21,285**	**£21,285**	**£21,285**	**£23,650**
Cost of Sales	(£60)	(£2,408)	(£4,214)	(£5,418)	(£6,020)	(£7,450)	(£7,450)	(£7,450)	(£8,278)
Gross Profit	**£112**	**£4,472**	**£7,826**	**£10,062**	**£11,180**	**£13,835**	**£13,835**	**£13,835**	**£15,373**
		65%	*65%*	*65%*	*65%*	*65%*	*65%*	*65%*	*65%*
Overheads									
Wages	(£1,667)	(£1,667)	(£3,333)	(£3,333)	(£3,333)	(£3,333)	(£4,167)	(£4,167)	(£4,167)
Rent	(£2,667)	(£2,667)	(£2,667)	(£2,667)	(£2,667)	(£2,667)	(£2,667)	(£2,667)	(£2,667)
Rates	(£1,000)	(£1,000)	(£1,000)	(£1,000)	(£1,000)	(£1,000)	(£1,000)	(£1,000)	(£1,000)
Heat & Light	(£333)	(£333)	(£333)	(£333)	(£333)	(£333)	(£333)	(£333)	(£333)
Cleaning Services	(£750)	(£750)	(£750)	(£750)	(£750)	(£750)	(£750)	(£750)	(£750)
Other Misc Costs	(£479)	(£479)	(£479)	(£479)	(£479)	(£479)	(£479)	(£479)	(£479)
Other 1	£0	£0	£0	£0	£0	£0	£0	£0	£0
Other 2	£0	£0	£0	£0	£0	£0	£0	£0	£0
Advertising	(£40)	(£40)	(£50)	(£50)	(£60)	(£60)	(£60)	(£70)	(£70)
Total Overheads	**(£6,936)**	**(£6,936)**	**(£8,613)**	**(£8,613)**	**(£8,623)**	**(£8,623)**	**(£9,456)**	**(£9,466)**	**(£9,466)**
EBITDA	**(£6,824)**	**(£2,464)**	**(£787)**	**£1,450**	**£2,558**	**£5,213**	**£4,379**	**£4,369**	**£5,907**
Depreciation	(£1,700)	(£1,700)	(£1,700)	(£1,700)	(£1,700)	(£1,700)	(£1,700)	(£1,700)	(£1,700)
Operating Profit (EBIT)	(£8,524)	(£4,164)	(£2,487)	(£251)	£858	£3,513	£2,679	£2,669	£4,207
Loan Interest	(£350)	(£344)	(£337)	(£330)	(£324)	(£317)	(£311)	(£304)	(£297)
Profit Before Tax	**(£8,874)**	**(£4,507)**	**(£2,824)**	**(£581)**	**£534**	**£3,195**	**£2,369**	**£2,365**	**£3,909**
Corporation Tax	£0	£0	£0	£0	£0	£0	£0	£0	£0
Profit After Tax	**(£8,874)**	**(£4,507)**	**(£2,824)**	**(£581)**	**£534**	**£3,195**	**£2,369**	**£2,365**	**£3,909**
Break-Even Point (Sales Excl VAT)	**£13,824**	**£13,814**	**£16,384**	**£16,374**	**£16,379**	**£16,369**	**£17,641**	**£17,646**	**£17,636**

The yellow line (titled Advertising) has been put in to illustrate that you can actually input straight into the profit & loss for each month, rather than having each cell as a formula. One limitation of the formula method when applied to overheads such as rent is that all of it is applied evenly throughout the year. This may not be the case – there might be a rent increase mid-year, for example. So, where a linear approach is inappropriate, just create more yellow coloured input lines directly into the profit & loss forecast.

Once again, the monthly columns continue for 36 months across the spreadsheet. Whilst this is good for providing month-by-month detail, it makes it quite difficult to view the big picture of the business's performance. However, this is dealt with by a tidy summary page, as explained below.

Finally, note that the projected *profitability* of the business is clearly shown for each month. You can see above that the business is not making a profit until the fifth month. It would be very hard to determine this from a hybrid profit & loss and cash flow forecast, as we will see below when viewing the cash flow forecast.

The Profit & Loss Forecast

- The profit & loss forecast must be a standalone section in the model, clearly showing the profits or losses into the future.
- This forecast can be largely made up entirely of formulas if you prefer, and hence it will immediately recalculate as your assumptions are changed.

The Cash Flow Forecast

In Chapter 4.1, we learnt that you can produce a cash flow statement in two ways, either the **direct method** or the **indirect method**. Both methods break down the cash flows into three categories and will also produce the same answer. The three categories of cash flow activity are operating (i.e. trading); investing (e.g. buying and selling fixed assets); and financing (e.g. flows from issuing new equity and taking on or repaying loans). A cash flow *forecast* can be done using precisely the same principles as a cash flow *statement.* The key difference is that the input numbers are forecasts rather than actual figures, and that the forecast is likely to be for individual monthly periods for a number of months or years ahead.

Because the indirect method is easier to understand, we will look at this in some detail and would recommend this method be used when first attempting cash flow forecasts.

Cash Flow from Operations

The first component of the model is the cash flow from the normal trading activities of the business. This is shown in the screenshot below of the first 9 months only. Note, as before, the model is actually for 36 months.

3a. Cash Flow (Direct Method)

Month:	Jan-21	Feb-21	Mar-21	Apr-21	May-21	Jun-21	Jul-21	Aug-21	Sep-21
Cash Flow From Operating Activities									
Money In:									
Receipts from Customers	£206	£8,256	£13,848	£17,976	£21,840	£25,542	£25,542	£23,142	£30,780
Money Out:									
Payments to Suppliers for Stock	£0	(£8,472)	(£2,890)	(£5,057)	(£6,502)	(£8,424)	(£9,540)	(£10,740)	(£8,940)
Payroll Payments	(£1,667)	(£1,667)	(£3,333)	(£3,333)	(£3,333)	(£3,333)	(£4,167)	(£4,167)	(£4,167)
Payments for Other Expenses	(£10,269)	(£2,269)	(£3,279)	(£10,279)	(£2,289)	(£3,289)	(£10,289)	(£2,299)	(£3,299)
VAT Payments to HMRC	£0	£0	(£1,082)	£0	£0	(£6,715)	£0	£0	(£8,409)
Interest Payments	(£350)	(£344)	(£337)	(£330)	(£324)	(£317)	(£311)	(£304)	(£297)
Corporation Tax Payments	£0	£0	£0	£0	£0	£0	£0	£0	£0
	(£12,286)	(£12,752)	(£10,921)	(£19,000)	(£12,448)	(£22,079)	(£24,306)	(£17,510)	(£25,111)
Net Cash Flow From Operating Activities	(£12,079)	(£4,496)	£2,927	(£1,024)	£9,392	£3,463	£1,236	£5,632	£5,669

The 'Money In' is made up of the 'Receipts from Customers', which shows when the sales revenue is forecast to be *received* into the bank account, rather than when the sales are forecast to take place. In the case of Carl's Café, it is assumed that most of this money is arriving at the same time as the sale takes place, so it is very simple. But if trade credit was given, then these receipts would be lagged according to the assumed time given to customers. Note that these inflows will *include the VAT* charged, whereas you will recall VAT is not included in the sales figures in the profit & loss forecast. More detailed workings showing how the figure is arrived at are shown further down the spreadsheet, beneath the actual cash flow forecast. These workings will feed the numbers shown above and allow the forecast to be kept visually clean and tidy, whilst also giving the user clarity on how the figures have been derived should they wish to see more detail.

The 'Money Out' consists of forecast payments to suppliers, and any VAT or other taxes due to be paid. Again, it is when is it actually paid, rather than when allocated to the profit & loss statement.

The 'Net Cash Flow from Operating Activities' figure on the final line shows us that more cash is going out from trading activities in the first two months and in the fourth month. From the fifth month on, the cash flow is positive.

Cash Flow from Investing Activities

The second section of the cash flow forecast is simpler to understand:

Month:	Jan-21	Feb-21	Mar-21	Apr-21	May-21	Jun-21	Jul-21	Aug-21	Sep-21
Cash Flow From Investing Activities									
Money In:									
Receipts From Sale of Assets	£0	£0	£0	£0	£0	£0	£0	£0	£0
VAT Refund on Purchase of Assets	£0	£0	£20,400	£0	£0	£0	£0	£0	£0
	£0	£0	£20,400	£0	£0	£0	£0	£0	£0
Money Out:									
Payments for Purchase of Assets	£0	(£74,400)	(£48,000)	£0	£0	£0	£0	£0	£0
Net Cash Flow From Investing Activities	£0	(£74,400)	(£27,600)	£0	£0	£0	£0	£0	£0

The 'Money In' relates to the sale of any assets (in this case none) and the refund on VAT from the earlier purchase of assets. The 'Money Out' is for the purchase of

Carl's shopfitting and equipment. Note these are forecast to be purchased in January 2021 but paid for in February and March. Once again, the cash flow shows us the figures for when the actual payments are made.

Overall, we can see that there are substantial cash outflows expected in February and March relating to the investing activities.

Cash Flow from Financing Activities

The third, and final, section of the cash flow forecast relates to the financing activities. This will cover funds coming in and out from bank loans, directors' loans, and any share issues. It will also show the outflow of any dividends paid.

Month:	Jan-21	Feb-21	Mar-21	Apr-21	May-21	Jun-21	Jul-21	Aug-21	Sep-21
Cash Flow From Financing Activities									
Money In:									
Issue of Shares	£45,000								
Receipt of Director's Loan	£15,000								
Receipt of Bank Loan	£70,000								
	£130,000	£0	£0	£0	£0	£0	£0	£0	£0
Money Out:									
Repayment of Bank Loan	(£1,294)	(£1,300)	(£1,307)	(£1,313)	(£1,320)	(£1,327)	(£1,333)	(£1,340)	(£1,347)
Repayment of Director's Loan	£0	£0	£0	£0	£0	£0	(£5,000)	£0	£0
Payment of Dividends	£0	£0	£0	£0	£0	£0	£0	£0	£0
	(£1,294)	(£1,300)	(£1,307)	(£1,313)	(£1,320)	(£1,327)	(£6,333)	(£1,340)	(£1,347)
Net Cash Flow From Financing Activities	£128,706	(£1,300)	(£1,307)	(£1,313)	(£1,320)	(£1,327)	(£6,333)	(£1,340)	(£1,347)
Net Cash Flow	**£116,627**	**(£80,196)**	**(£25,980)**	**(£2,337)**	**£8,072**	**£2,136**	**(£5,097)**	**£4,293**	**£4,322**
Opening Bank Balance	£0	£116,627	£36,431	£10,451	£8,113	£16,185	£18,321	£13,224	£17,516
Closing Bank Balance	**£116,627**	**£36,431**	**£10,451**	**£8,113**	**£16,185**	**£18,321**	**£13,224**	**£17,516**	**£21,838**

You will notice that after the initial draw-down of the capital in January 2021, the cash flow in this section is negative each month as the loan is progressively repaid.

Generating the Forecast Bank Balance

The 'Net Cash Flow' line is the aggregation of the three sections show above. This figure is added to the 'Opening Bank Balance' for the month, which will then give us the 'Closing Bank Balance'. This final line is of critical importance: *is there sufficient cash in the business to meet its future liabilities?* If any of the figures in the forecast cash balances were negative, it would suggest additional funding was needed, either from bank or directors' loans, or share issues. The loan from the bank could be in the form of an **overdraft facility**, which would allow the bank balance to go into negative territory up to the limit agreed.

Note how the 'Closing Bank Balance' line is not very helpful in determining the profitability of the business – focusing on this alone could be disastrous and is a common business mistake, as explained earlier. You need to focus on *both* profitability *and* cash simultaneously.

A further interesting point to observe is that Carl's lowest bank account forecast is to be £8,113. Given that all forecasts are subject to significant swings either way, this suggests his level of funding is worryingly tight. He would be well advised to raise perhaps another £25k, so this minimum was more like £30k – a number that feels to us more appropriate for this business's scale. The level of this minimum forecast liquidity will be influenced by how volatile the trading is likely to be, and whether there are other risk factors. For example, could Carl face unexpected delays in the start-up or unexpected shopfitting costs? Whilst there is no hard and fast rule, a general guide is to maintain a *minimum* liquidity of between 10% and 20% of forecast annual revenue. The more volatile the trading situation, the higher up this range you would need to be.

The Indirect Method as an Alternative

The indirect method starts with profit after tax for the period, but then makes adjustments in each of the three sections above, for non-cash items and movements on the balance sheet to get to cash flow. The Carl's Café model also shows the cash flow forecast on this basis, and it can be used either as alternative to the direct method or simply as a reconciliation between projected profits and cash flows. Further details of the methodology can be found in the earlier Chapter 4.1.

The Cash Flow Forecast

- The direct method of cash flow forecasting is easier to produce and understand.
- As with a cash flow statement, the forecast is divided into three sections, covering operating activities, investing activities, and financing activities. When aggregated we can see the net cash flow of the business each month.
- The net cash flow for the month is added to the forecast opening bank balance, to then produce a closing bank balance figure. This figure needs to be positive, otherwise the business will require additional funding.
- Note that the closing bank account line is not a reliable indicator of profitability. To determine future profitability, you need to refer to a separate profit & loss forecast.

The Balance Sheet Forecast

Whilst the profit & loss and cash flow forecasts are absolutely essential from the outset, the fourth and final component of a financial model, the balance sheet, is arguably less so – at least to start with. As time goes on, however, the opening balances shown in the balance sheet at any point in time play an important role in indicating likely cash flows in subsequent months. For instance, the running balance of outstanding debtors will tell you a lot about how much cash is likely to come in from customers over the next month or two.

Also, as we will see below, the balance sheet can be a good way to check there are no errors anywhere in the model.

Exactly how important a balance sheet projection is, though, will very much depend on the scale of your start-up, its trading situation, and whether you are obtaining external funding.

All of the information required to compile a balance sheet projection is already present in the profit & loss and cash flow projections. The example balance sheet in the Carl's Café financial model is made up entirely of formulas, i.e. there are no yellow input cells. Everything is driven from the initial assumptions, profit & loss and cash flow forecasts. As these are amended by the user, the balance sheet forecast will recalculate.

4. Forecast Balance Sheet

Month:	Jan-21	Feb-21	Mar-21	Apr-21	May-21	Jun-21	Jul-21	Aug-21	Sep-21
FIXED ASSETS									
Property	£0	£0	£0	£0	£0	£0	£0	£0	£0
Shopfitting Costs	£78,667	£77,333	£76,000	£74,667	£73,333	£72,000	£70,667	£69,333	£68,000
Machinery	£21,633	£21,267	£20,900	£20,533	£20,167	£19,800	£19,433	£19,067	£18,700
	£100,300	**£98,600**	**£96,900**	**£95,200**	**£93,500**	**£91,800**	**£90,100**	**£88,400**	**£86,700**
CURRENT ASSETS									
Stocks (Inventory)	£7,000	£7,000	£7,000	£7,000	£8,000	£8,500	£10,000	£10,000	£9,500
Debtors (Receivables)	£0	£0	£600	£1,200	£0	£0	£0	£2,400	£0
Prepayments	£5,333	£2,667	£0	£5,333	£2,667	£0	£5,333	£2,667	£0
Cash	£116,627	£36,431	£10,451	£8,113	£16,185	£18,321	£13,224	£17,516	£21,838
	£128,960	**£46,097**	**£18,051**	**£21,647**	**£26,852**	**£26,821**	**£28,557**	**£32,583**	**£31,338**
CURRENT LIABILITIES (< 1 YR)									
Creditors (Payables)	(£130,872)	(£50,890)	(£5,057)	(£6,502)	(£8,424)	(£9,540)	(£10,740)	(£8,940)	(£9,333)
Accruals	(£333)	(£667)	£0	(£333)	(£667)	£0	(£333)	(£667)	£0
Bank Loans (< 1 YR)	(£16,041)	(£16,122)	(£16,202)	(£16,283)	(£16,365)	(£16,447)	(£16,529)	(£16,611)	(£16,694)
Tax & NI	£21,778	£20,883	£0	(£2,012)	(£4,048)	£0	(£2,467)	(£5,234)	£0
Corporation Tax	£0	£0	£0	£0	£0	£0	£0	£0	£0
	(£125,469)	**(£46,795)**	**(£21,259)**	**(£25,131)**	**(£29,504)**	**(£25,986)**	**(£30,069)**	**(£31,452)**	**(£26,027)**
NET CURRENT ASSETS	**£3,491**	**(£697)**	**(£3,208)**	**(£3,484)**	**(£2,652)**	**£835**	**(£1,512)**	**£1,131**	**£5,311**
LONG TERM LIABILITIES (> 1 YR)									
Bank Loans (> 1 YR)	(£52,665)	(£51,284)	(£49,896)	(£48,502)	(£47,101)	(£45,692)	(£44,277)	(£42,854)	(£41,424)
Directors' Loans	(£15,000)	(£15,000)	(£15,000)	(£15,000)	(£15,000)	(£15,000)	(£10,000)	(£10,000)	(£10,000)
	(£67,665)	**(£66,284)**	**(£64,896)**	**(£63,502)**	**(£62,101)**	**(£60,692)**	**(£54,277)**	**(£52,854)**	**(£51,424)**
NET ASSETS	**£36,126**	**£31,619**	**£28,795**	**£28,214**	**£28,748**	**£31,943**	**£34,312**	**£36,677**	**£40,587**
CAPITAL & RESERVES									
Called up Share Capital	£45,000	£45,000	£45,000	£45,000	£45,000	£45,000	£45,000	£45,000	£45,000
Revaluation Reserve	£0	£0	£0	£0	£0	£0	£0	£0	£0
Retained Earnings	(£8,874)	(£13,381)	(£16,205)	(£16,786)	(£16,252)	(£13,057)	(£10,688)	(£8,323)	(£4,413)
SHAREHOLDERS' EQUITY	**£36,126**	**£31,619**	**£28,795**	**£28,214**	**£28,748**	**£31,943**	**£34,312**	**£36,677**	**£40,587**
DIFFERENCE CHECK LINE	£0	£0	£0	£0	£0	£0	£0	£0	£0

As with the cash flow forecast, there are the extensive workings (not shown above) beneath the balance sheet summary on the spreadsheet. These show the way in which the balance sheet values are derived, and again allow the balance sheet itself to remain uncluttered.

The Difference Check Line

You will observe there is a line beneath the balance sheet called 'Difference Check Line'. This is simply the difference between the 'Net Assets' and 'Shareholders' Equity' totals. Given that these should be the same, this check line should always be zero. If it is not zero, the balance sheet is not balancing and there is an error somewhere.

You will quickly discover that it can go out of balance very easily the moment you start playing around with the profit & loss or cash flow parts of the model. Remember that a balance sheet *always has matching debits and credits*, so inevitably if any of your changes just deal with one side of this equation, the balance sheet will be thoroughly unhappy about what you have just done!

A good working technique is to continually keep an eye on this check line whilst making changes elsewhere in the model. You can then, hopefully, see immediately what change has caused any imbalance that arises. There are always two clues to help you determine where the imbalance has occurred. The first relates to the *month* where the imbalance first occurs, and the second relates to the *amount of the imbalance*. These clues are only likely to be of much use if you can catch the fault early – otherwise you are likely to find that the imbalance amount is made up of a multiple of different items. You are then trying to sort out tangled spaghetti!

Assuming you have spotted the imbalance early, start by going through the profit & loss and cash flow workings and formulas line by line to try and spot the problem in the month the imbalance first occurs. Look out for the value amount of the imbalance – if it happens to be a nice round £5,000, for example, initially hunt for that same number in the forecast statements. But remember the £5,000 is the *net imbalance* so it could be the result of two or more imbalances aggregating to £5,000. Also remember that, if the fault is a minus where there should be a plus or vice versa (an easy mistake to make), you will need to look for an amount that is *half* the imbalance.

If you find the number, think in terms of where there should be a corresponding debit or credit. An example would be if you have added a new asset to your model, you will have debited fixed assets. But have you accounted for the *payment* of the asset, which is the credit? You would need to take the payment out of your cash flow forecast (which then credits the cash line in the balance sheet forecast).

The Balance Sheet Forecast

- The balance sheet forecast may seem relatively complex to produce, so, as it is not as essential as the profit & loss and cash flow, it can be left until later. However, it can be useful in spotting errors in the rest of model, and, as time goes on the running balances are an important input to cash flow forecasts.
- All of the information that goes into the balance sheet can be derived from the profit & loss and cash flow forecasts, consequently this part of the model should be entirely made up of formulas. As with the other parts of the model, all complex workings should be set out separately beneath.
- Keeping a constant eye on the 'Difference Check Line' helps resolve imbalance issues early. Finding the imbalances can be time consuming and frustrating!

Summary and Graphs

The summary is one of the key points of the whole modelling exercise. *It is the output* – the big picture of how the business is expected to perform. In Carl's Café there are various summaries under the *Summary* tab – again these are just examples. In the case of the profit & loss summary, it neatly shows the key performance over the next three years.

2. Profit & Loss	2021	2022	2023
Sales (excl. VAT)	£210,227	£361,200	£469,560
Gross Profit	£136,648	£234,780	£305,214
	65%	*65%*	*65%*
Total Overheads	(£105,127)	(£147,030)	(£187,590)
EBITDA	£31,521	£87,750	£117,624
Operating Profit (EBIT)	£11,121	£67,350	£97,224
Profit Before Tax	£7,355	£64,569	£95,488
Profit After Tax	£7,355	£62,424	£72,310

Our model has some flexibility and can be shown in more detail by using the plus(+) and minus(–) symbols in the far-left hand margin of the spreadsheet. These expand out the lines, providing more details on the overheads, etc. The above shorter extract would be ideal to cut and paste into a PowerPoint presentation where too much detail may be unnecessary.

Note our model only shows a three-year forecast. An investor may expect to see a five-year forecast. In this case, two more years could be extrapolated on the end, produced only on a yearly (rather than monthly) basis. It is somewhat pointless producing a forecast on a monthly basis beyond three years – forecasting at that level of detail is unnecessary for most businesses.

Ratios

The financial model has a summary of key ratios for each of the forecast three years. These can be produced on a month-by-month basis, but generally speaking this is probably too much data. The simple annual summary, as in our model, is adequate in most cases.

Profitability Ratios				
	Year:	2021	2022	2023
Gross Margin		65%	65%	65%
EBITDA		15%	24%	25%
Operating Profit (EBIT)		5%	19%	21%
Profit Before Tax		3%	18%	20%
Debt to Equity		1.2	0.4	0.2
Interest Cover		3.0	24.2	56.0
Current Ratio		1.7	3.0	2.9

Whilst there is a set of standard ratios in our model, identify what additional statistics really matter to your business and create some key performance indicators of your own.

Graphs

Adding graphs can greatly improve the visual impact of a financial model. The three examples in our model are somewhat limited, but nevertheless demonstrate how powerful they can be. Below we can see the cash flow forecast for the next three years.

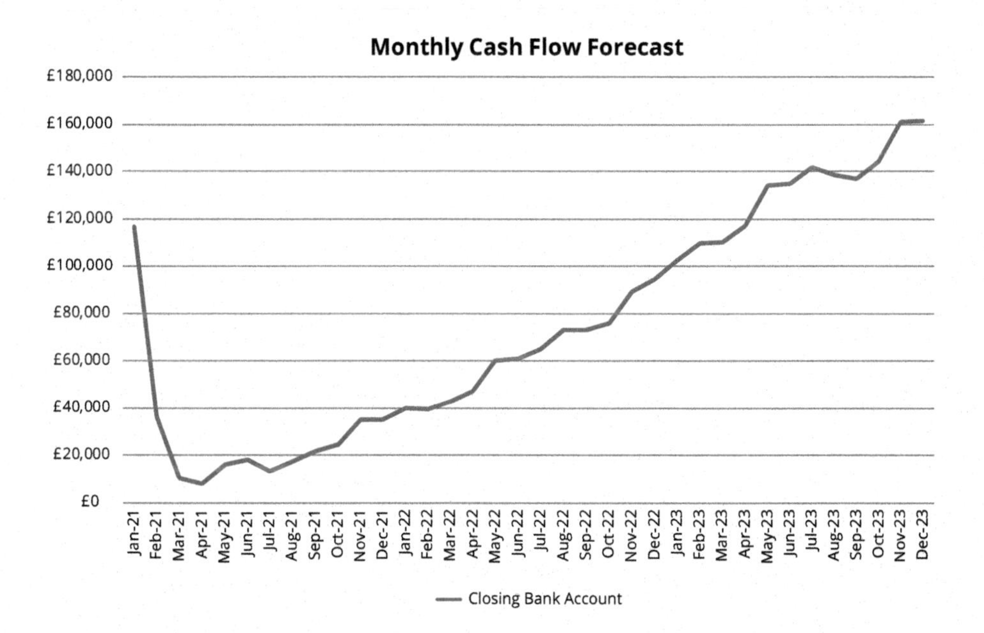

A quick glance at this graph tells us that the business has a consistent cash flow after the start-up period, but, as discussed above, the cash contingency appears to be dangerously small.

It is very satisfying to create a unified model, where just one change to the profit & loss assumptions is instantly reflected in your graphs. They are a great way of being creative and for showcasing your business in an exciting fashion.

Some Final Thoughts About Financial Modelling

Remember your financial model will always be a work in progress. Whilst at the start of a financial year, the next 12 months may be frozen to give you a firm budget to measure your performance against, the model can be continuously updated each month to provide a rolling forecast of the final outcome for the year. You will also find, as events change, that your assumptions need revising. Again, this is all part of the process. Finally, as time progresses, you can make the model increasingly more sophisticated.

Summary Sections

- The summary of the model is the final output and should allow the reader to quickly digest the forecast performance of the business.
- The summaries can include the profit & loss, cash flow, balance sheet, a table of key ratios and a selection of graphs.

PART 5

FINANCIAL CAPITAL

5.1 SOURCES OF CAPITAL

Equity Versus Debt

Every single pound (or any other unit of money) that makes up a company's capital originated from somewhere, whether the business was newly formed yesterday, or has been in existence for over 100 years.

These sources fall into one of two fundamental – and fundamentally different – categories: equity and debt. Each of these has its own particular set of characteristics that can bring differing advantages and disadvantages to the company and its shareholders. The choice of how much of the company's capital requirements should be funded by equity and how much by debt is one of the key strategic financial decisions faced by a company's directors.

All funding for a business comes from just two fundamental sources.

Equity can be defined as capital provided by the company's shareholders – whether injected as new funds or reinvested from earlier profits – which gives them a claim on all assets owned by the company *after* all liabilities have been paid, and on all future net profits that the company might make. *All* companies have some level of equity funding, whether great or small.

Debt can be defined as capital provided by third parties (e.g. banks, hire purchase companies, private individuals, etc.) as a loan or other form of debt instrument. The lender, therefore, has a claim on the company's assets (or a specific asset) limited to *only* the amount that has been loaned and is still outstanding, plus any interest (and any other costs) that has accrued. Note that this claim *takes priority* over any claims by equity holders. Providers of debt may themselves be in a priority queue with each other. Not all companies choose to use debt as a source of capital.

We will explore both of these sources of capital and their advantages and disadvantages in more detail later in this section, but the table below provides a preliminary outline of the key characteristics of each:

Characteristic	Issuing New Equity	Taking on Debt
Claim on assets and profits	Full claim on all assets, *net of liabilities*, and on all future profits after tax.	Priority claim (*ahead of equity*) on assets, or a specific asset, *to extent of amounts owed only*.
Cost	Carries a higher cost of capital than debt, because shareholders expect higher return to compensate for higher risk.	Generally, a lower-cost source of capital than equity.
Risk	Lower risk to the company, as all risk is transferred to equity holders. The company is not legally obliged to ever repay capital or distribute profits.	Higher risk for the company, which must repay capital in accordance with the terms of each loan, and pay interest when due. Debt providers can force the company into liquidation if amounts outstanding are not paid.
Impact on cash flow	Positive impact of new funds. The company is free to invest as it sees fit and is not legally obliged to repay the capital.	Positive impact of new funds. Negative impact when capital and interest payments come due.
Impact on shareholdings	New equity issued can cause potentially significant dilution to existing shareholdings, and hence reduction in claim to future profits.	No impact, other than risk (see above).

Grants and Tax Credits

Grants and **tax credits** are additional sources of potential funding available to businesses, especially in their start-up and developmental phases.

There are a huge variety of grants available – from both government and non-government organisations – which can be an excellent source of funding, and they are well worth investigating. One approach is to engage the services of a grant writer to advise on what grants might be available and put together a successful application. It is important to note that grants will appear as 'Other revenue' (i.e. not sales) in the profit & loss statement.

Similarly, businesses can also benefit from tax credits on research and development expenditure. For businesses already making a profit, these can be used to reduce their corporation tax liability. However, for businesses yet to make a profit, these can result in an actual cash payment from the Government, in exchange for a reduction in taxable losses carried forward and offset against future profits. We recommend looking at HMRC's website and consulting an accountant.

Are You Ready for Funding?

Any investor or lender is going to want to understand what is unique about your business and your team. They will also want to see your financial model, which will give an indication of your sales revenue, gross margins, and cost structure for three to five years ahead. This model will give an estimate of the capital you need to raise, as well as the potential returns the funding should generate. It is essential that you, as a team, can provide detailed answers to questions about how the sales forecast is derived; i.e. what are the assumptions behind it, and how do these assumptions translate into forecast revenues? How has your product or service been priced? Why is your cost structured in the way shown?

Investors or lenders will also want to know:

- How much, if anything, have you raised so far? What have you done with the funds to date?
- How much capital do you estimate you will need to achieve the next planned level of growth?
- What milestones are you hoping to achieve with the capital raised?
- How much ownership and control are you willing to give away?
- What do you expect in terms of support/commitment from each of the investors you are seeing?
- What is your cash burn rate?
- What runway would this fundraising round give you? It's common for start-ups to think of raising for an 18-month runway.

Advantage of Self-Funding

As indicated above, equity funding can come from either the issue of new shares or from the retention and reinvestment of past profits.

If you wanted to pick out the number one funding choice that is optimum for both the company and existing shareholders alike, it would have to be the latter – retained profit. It involves no costs, no dilution to existing shareholders and is largely at the discretion of the management. However, in the case of start-up or early stage businesses, this is unlikely to be an option. For this reason, in the subsequent chapters of this section, our examination of equity as a source of capital shall focus exclusively on raising equity capital from the issue of new shares.

5.2 DEBT FUNDING

Debt funding is a powerful way of making an investment happen that would otherwise be impossible. If the investment is a good one – i.e. it returns positive results (however those are defined) – then it has worked for the benefit of the person or company that took on the debt.

Perhaps the easiest way of seeing how useful debt can be is to consider a mortgage for an individual homeowner. Imagine someone wants to buy her own apartment for £500k, but understandably does not have the entire capital. She does, however, have £50k in savings. A mortgage provider, having considered her annual salary, is prepared to loan her the £450k difference, secured by the apartment itself. This mortgage process allows her to become a homeowner immediately, whilst if she had to wait until she had saved the full £500k, it may have taken her several decades to reach the required capital sum. In addition, during this period of saving, she would have had to pay rent to someone else for a place to live. The mortgage has made homeownership a reality for her, and, under these circumstances, debt finance has been extremely beneficial.

Banks are an excellent source of finance and can be a good alternative to issuing equity. But understanding the contractual implications of any loan is vitally important.

This example can also be used to highlight another feature of debt as far as the borrower is concerned: namely, that it leverages the investor's return. What do we mean by this? Let's imagine that our proud new homeowner sees her property go up in value by 10% in the year after she purchased it. As a result, her property is now worth £550k, which means that the value of her equity stake has *doubled* to £100k, even though the underlying asset has risen only 10% – her return has been leveraged (or amplified) by debt funding. Alas, as we all know, there is no such thing as a free lunch, and the price to be paid for this apparent financial wizardry is that her risk has also increased enormously. Imagine that, instead of rising, her property *falls* in value by 10%, and is now worth only £450k. In this scenario, the hard-earned savings that she put in as equity have been wiped out completely. This highlights both the upside and downside of using debt as a source of capital – it allows equity holders to keep a larger share of upside gains, but, at the same time, exposes them to greater downside risks.

Do these same principles apply in a commercial context, i.e. for a trading company? Yes, they do, but in the corporate world the types of investment – the application of the funds – are considerably more varied and consequently carry greater risks than simply buying a home.

Advantages of Debt Funding	Comments
Investments may become possible that could not otherwise be easily made (e.g. buying a property asset with a mortgage).	The key issue here is whether the investment turns out to be worthwhile. The more the return on the capital employed exceeds the cost of the debt finance, then the more worthwhile it is likely to be. But there may be many factors involved to determine what success means.
Debt finance, as opposed to equity finance, avoids shareholder dilution, and loss of control.	This can be a key issue for an early-stage entrepreneur. Repeated equity rounds can mean the founders end up as minority shareholders at an early stage, with the consequential potential loss of control. Using debt finance as an alternative avoids this problem.
Can be fast to arrange	Equity funding can take months to organise, but a bank loan can be arranged within days or weeks. The fastest type of bank finance is likely to be an overdraft facility.
Can be repaid or restructured relatively easily	Loans can always be repaid (although early repayment can attract penalties under some circumstances). They can also be extended by the lender, or refinanced by another lender, all subject to their agreement and circumstances.
Likely to require less reporting/oversight, and 'interference' in management decision-making	The reporting requirements of a debt (as opposed to equity) provider are likely to be less onerous, and lenders are less likely to want to get involved in decision-making processes. However, there is a flipside to this advantage in that a good investor, whose interest in the success of the business is aligned with the entrepreneurs/management, may well cause better decisions to be made – perhaps simply by asking challenging questions.
Interest payments reduce the corporation tax liability	Unlike dividend payments, interest charges are deductible against corporation tax.

So, debt funding has some great advantages. But what about the disadvantages? There are several to be aware of:

- Risk of default on loan should trading deteriorate, with the consequential risk of receivership.
- The repayment schedule, as well as interest costs, are a drain on ongoing cash flow.
- The interest charges reduce profits, and consequently surplus capital available for distribution to shareholders or reinvestment in the business.

Let's now look at the two main types of debt finance from banks. The following is not intended to cover all types of debt funding, but rather to give you an introduction to the key ones, and, most importantly, to understand the implications of taking on debt. Regardless of the actual type of debt, many of these issues remain the same.

Term Loans

A **term loan** has similarities to a mortgage insofar as it is for a specified period of time, with a clear structure of interest charges and a repayment schedule. Unlike a mortgage, however, it is generally likely to be for a shorter time period.

Typical Features of a Term Loan

- **Term of loan:** a typical commercial bank loan will be for three to five years, but the period can vary between anything from one to ten years, or more. Providing the borrower is meeting all the terms and conditions of the loan, the lender cannot demand its money back. This aspect of a term loan can be very important for a company's long-term financial planning and security.
- **Interest charges:** usually these will be variable and linked to the **LIBOR** or **SONIA**[1] rate (or other benchmark), plus a premium, which is the profit for the lender. The amount of this premium will depend on the level of perceived risk faced by the lender in making the loan. The terms may, for example, be SONIA + 2%. This means that as SONIA moves up or down, the interest rate charged will move accordingly, plus the fixed 2% margin on top. The interest rate may, however, be fixed for part or all of the term.
- **Arrangement fees:** this is likely to be a fixed fee, and usually a small percentage of the capital value, e.g. 3%. As well as arrangement fees, there can also be early repayment penalties. There can also be monitoring fees, often paid annually or quarterly.
- **Security:** typically, the bank will have a **fixed and floating charge** over the assets of a business. This is known as a **debenture.** In the event of default, this debenture can be enacted in order to recover the outstanding loan, plus any interest due, and potentially further financial penalties for default. Debentures generally ensure that the bank ranks ahead of other creditors in the event of the **liquidation** of the company. Alternatively, or in addition, the bank may seek personal guarantees from the directors of the company.
- **Covenants:** the terms and conditions within the loan agreement will include specific banking covenants to protect the lender. These would relate to **interest cover**, or **debt service cover** (see Chapter 3.3 for more explanation on these ratios), requiring profits to exceed the interest charged, or debt servicing cash flows, by a specified multiple. If this criterion is not met, the bank could ask for the loan to be repaid.
- **Balance sheet implications:** the amount of the capital that needs to be repaid in the next 12 months is a current liability. The amount due beyond 12 months is a long-term liability. Therefore, from a balance sheet perspective, a term loan is likely

to make the liquidity ratios appear healthier when compared to shorter term finance (such as an overdraft).[2]

In their enthusiasm to grow their business, few entrepreneurs will fully appreciate the power and reach of the bank (or other lender) when things go wrong. This is why it is so important to read and understand the terms and conditions of a loan, and to ensure the business is in a suitable state to carry the debt itself.

Example of how events can quickly turn sour

Let us imagine that a company borrows £2m from a bank at an interest rate of SONIA + 2% over a term of five years. There is a banking covenant that specifies interest cover must be 5 times the annual operating profit. With SONIA at 2%, the annual interest paid is therefore 4%, i.e. £80k a year. As operating profit is a very healthy £720k, the Interest Cover is 9 times. Everything is looking fine!

Some changes in the economy then occur. After a period of rapid economic growth, inflation rises sharply. The Bank of England responds with a series of interest rate rises, with SONIA now ending up at 5%. The annual interest charge is now 7%, i.e. £140k a year. But this is not the only worry: because of rising interest rates, consumers have reduced their spending. The company trades in a sector sensitive to consumer sentiment (e.g. home furnishings) and its sales fall by 25%, and operating profit slumps to £200k. The business is now in breach of its banking covenants and the entrepreneur just hopes the bank will remain supportive and not call in the loan. If the bank did, it would mean potential receivership.

This scenario is far from unusual in a recession. In our example, the business at least remains profitable, but in the worst-case scenarios the business could be losing money and require *further* funding. Note how the squeeze has appeared from *two directions* – falling sales *and* rising interest rates. The Great Recession of 2008–09 was unusual insofar as interest rates fell to record low levels, with a Bank of England base rate of 0.5%, but in all past recessions since the 1970s interest rates have often spiked following a painful dose of inflation. For example, in 1990–91 recession, inflation peaked at 9.5% and interest rates at 14.8%.[3] Ouch!

Unfortunately, most young entrepreneurs have no memory of past recessions, nor an appreciation of how quickly events can deteriorate. One particularly vulnerable group of entrepreneurs are property developers. Because of their high gearing in acquiring property, when markets are buoyant and property prices are rising, they tend to make exceptionally good profits. But in a recession, should property prices fall, they can quickly end up with assets worth less than their debt. Business collapse quickly follows, and the shiny Porsche 911 (no doubt also acquired on debt) is returned to the leasing company!

Personal Guarantees

Banks may also require personal guarantees from one or more of the directors of the company in addition to a debenture over the assets. In this situation, the liability will continue beyond liquidation of the company. These guarantees are also usually 'joint and several'. This means that, in the event of two directors sharing the risk of the guarantee and one defaults on their half, the other would be liable for the entire amount. Whilst it is easy to think of refusing to give these guarantees, frequently the debt funding may not be possible without them.

Overdrafts

An **overdraft** is a short-term flexible debt facility from a bank. This is likely to be reviewed annually, hence its term would typically be for a maximum of one year. A limit is agreed with the bank, and then a company can borrow anything from nothing to the full amount and will only pay interest on the money borrowed.

Typical Features of an Overdraft Facility

- **Term of loan:** as all overdrafts are subject to regular review by the bank, the maximum period is likely to be for one year. There is no defined term, though – the bank can demand repayment at any time.
- **Interest charges:** as per a term loan, but likely to be at a greater premium, e.g. SONIA + 5%. However, interest is only paid when the facility is used. Interest rates applied could change at very short notice if there is a change in the benchmark used, unlike with a term loan where the rates may be fixed for all or part of the term regardless of the movement in the benchmark rate.
- **Arrangement fees:** as per a term loan, but there will be no exit fees as the facility can be repaid at any time. Note the arrangement fee will be applied annually, unlike with a term loan, which will be applied only once for the whole term. This makes the effective annual interest rate higher than it appears at face value.
- **Security and covenants:** likely to be the same or similar to term loans; however, the bank can ask for full repayment 'on demand' (in practice likely to be within a month).
- **Balance sheet implications:** as the overdraft is repayable on demand, all the facility's value will appear as a current liability. This will adversely affect the liquidity ratios.

Press this button with caution! Overdraft balances are repayable to a bank 'on demand'.

The fact that these facilities can be withdrawn on demand should be raising concerns in your mind. In a period of recession, banks frequently reduce their own exposure to this type of debt in order to maintain the liquidity of their own balance sheets, and this withdrawal or reduction in facilities may come at the worst possible time for a business if it is also suffering from trading difficulties. Borrowers should also be aware that breaching the facility limit can lead to additional penal rates of interest beyond the original terms, as well as the possible freezing of the bank account.

Example of good use of an overdraft facility

Our former business, Card Connection Limited, had all its Christmas cards manufactured in China. Unlike the regular everyday cards, such as birthdays, the low margins did not make it viable to print them in the United Kingdom. This created substantial logistical and financial challenges, as the cards were printed around April, then arrived in the United Kingdom in June for distribution from 1 September (Christmas cards go on sale in shops from around Halloween). So how did the money flow? Well we had to pay for all the stock around July, but did not collect payment in full until January the following year, just after Christmas.

Normally we funded this from our own working capital, but one year we realised several months in advance that we needed some additional funding – but only for a period of a few months. The most logical and low-cost solution was to arrange a temporary overdraft facility. As our balance sheet was strong, the bank readily made this available, and we used part of the facility. As with all good financial planning, we had a greater facility than we actually needed. Whilst this would have cost us a little more in arrangement fees, the security of being adequately funded was worth the extra – never plan to run out of cash!

This is an excellent example of how an overdraft facility should be used. Here are some golden rules on overdraft facilities:

- The amount borrowed should be low in proportion to the total assets of the company.
- The size of facility should also be in proportion to the sales of a business. As a rule of thumb based on our own experience, we would recommend not exceeding 5–10% of annual sales revenue. Whilst this will be very much down to individual circumstances, anything beyond this is likely to create excessive short-term financial exposure.
- The facility should not be the main source of the funding of businesses and should be kept for short-term funding requirements such as in the example above.
- If the economy looks at risk of going into recession, overdrafts should be fully repaid, or greatly reduced, as early as possible.
- Should the bank seek repayment on demand, the company needs to have contingency plans. These may include taking loans from the directors or seeking extended payment terms from friendly suppliers.

Directors' Loans

These require relatively little explanation. Founders or owners of companies may loan their business capital in order to start in the first place, or to grow further. These are generally 'soft' loans without complex terms and conditions and usually at a zero rate of interest.

The main advantage of these loans to the directors is that they can take the capital back without any tax on the return of the money. If, for example, the same funds had been invested as new equity, then the capital can only be recovered when the shares are subsequently sold. Whilst dividends can be paid on the newly issued shares, income tax will be charged on these withdrawals.

If founders are funding the start-up using their own capital, this must be the best way of doing it? Well, not quite. One major disadvantage is that the business could have a negative balance sheet and be technically insolvent. Remember, the money put in as a director's loan is a liability, so the capital adds no overall value to the net assets of the company. Should a start-up trade at a loss initially, it would quickly develop a negative balance sheet. This could make obtaining credit (e.g. from suppliers) challenging.

Debt Funding

- Debt funding has some considerable advantages insofar as it avoids shareholder dilution and is relatively easy to arrange and manage. However, it is important not to be overexposed to debt as inevitable problems of repayment can occur.
- Term loans are, by definition, fixed over a specific time period, and with a consistent application of an interest rate (which can vary according to the prevailing benchmark rates).
- Overdrafts are for short-term funding requirements and are extremely flexible for the borrower. They are, however, repayable on demand and can be expensive when all the charges are considered. Interest rates charged can also change on short notice.
- Directors' loans have the advantage that they can subsequently be repaid without incurring a tax liability. However, the capital injected will not increase net assets and as a result the balance sheet could appear to be weak, particularly in a start-up situation.

Notes

1. Sterling Over Night Index Average, an important interest rate benchmark administered by the Bank of England. The UK financial industry is planning to move to this benchmark in place of LIBOR (London Interbank Offered Rate) from 2021.
2. If the entire outstanding balance was due within the next 12 months, i.e. the loan was in its final year, then all of it would be a current liability.
3. Source https://en.wikipedia.org/wiki/List_of_recessions_in_the_United_Kingdom

5.3 UNDERSTANDING SHARE CAPITAL

Equity funding involves the issue of shares by a company to shareholders in return for new money. Every company begins its life with some form of equity funding. At the miniscule end of the scale, that could simply be a small number of shares issued at £1 (or even less – nominal values can be a fraction of 1p!). *Regardless of how small it is, the formation equity is the first piece of capital that is injected into a business.* At the other extreme there is no theoretical limit to how much equity can be raised: the limiting factor will only be the market for the shares. As long as investors are willing to buy them, then a company can keep issuing them.

Advantages of Equity Funding	Comments
Theoretically an unlimited source of funding for a business	The only limit on the amount of share capital that can be created is the willingness of investors to buy such shares. This, in turn, will be influenced by how successful the company is at generating wealth for the shareholders, and how successful it is expected to be in the future.
No obligation to repay capital	Unlike debt finance, once shares are issued and paid-up, the company is not obliged to repay the capital to the shareholder, nor to pay a dividend (unless this is specifically stipulated in a shareholders' agreement).
Different classes of shares can be issued	Different classes (i.e. types) of shares can be issued to investors. These may give selected investors preferential treatment regarding dividends and liquidation, for example. Such flexibility may be important in attracting new capital to the business.

Different Types of Share Capital

Ordinary Shares

Ordinary shares are just that – the common stock issued to most of the shareholders. They will share the same rights (regarding voting, dividends, etc.) as each other, as set out in the company's **articles of association**. Assuming there are no other types of shares in issue, which is normally the case with most small businesses, then the number of these shares owned by each shareholder, relative to the total in issue, will determine their percentage share of the business. At the simplest level, two shareholders who own one share each, out of the two issued, will each have a 50% share of the company's equity.

Preference Shares

There may be different classes (or types) of shares issued. For example, there may be preference shares, 'A' shares, or 'B' shares, which have different rights compared to the other ordinary shares. These rights could be:

- Rights to distribution of capital ahead of other shares in the event of a liquidation event (i.e. a sale or the company's winding up).
- Dividend rights ahead of other shares.
- An interest payment as well as a dividend.
- Voting rights ahead of other shares.
- Pre-emption rights on the issue of new shares (i.e. the right to subscribe to new share issues in proportion to the existing holding).

Form an orderly queue: ordinary shareholders at the very back please!

The implications of shares with different rights can be profound, and venture capitalists widely use preferred stock as a means of protecting their downside and can also be used to ensure a healthier upside ahead of the ordinary shareholders. We will see specific examples of this later.

The Different Equity Rounds

Depending on how a company develops, it can have a series of different funding rounds. It is, of course, possible that there may only be one equity round at the start of the company's life, and that those shareholders remain the same until its eventual sale or liquidation. Much will depend on whether the business requires funding by issuing new shares to investors and is able to persuade them to invest.

The key metrics for each round are as follows:

A. **Number of shares currently in issue** (a matter of fact)

B. **Pre-money valuation** (a matter of negotiation)

C. **Number of shares to be issued** (a matter of decision)

D. **Issue price per share** (B divided by A)

E. **Total amount raised** (C multiplied by D)

F. **Post-money valuation** (B plus E)

Example

A company has 250,000 shares in issue, and is raising new money for which it has negotiated a pre-money valuation of £1,000,000 with existing and prospective new investors.

The share price will be:

$$\frac{Pre\text{-}money\ Valuation}{No.\ of\ Shares\ in\ Issue} = \frac{£1{,}000{,}000}{250{,}000} = £4$$

How much new capital has been raised? Well, that depends on how many new shares they decide to issue. Let's say it is 50,000, which means the amount raised is:

$$No.\ of\ New\ Shares \times Share\ Price = 50{,}000 \times £4 = £200{,}000$$

The post-money valuation will be:

$$Pre\text{-}money\ Valuation + Funds\ Raised = £1{,}000{,}000 + £200{,}000 = £1{,}200{,}000$$

The amount of equity, in terms of percentage, the new shareholders shall own shall be:

$$\frac{Funds\ Raised}{Post\text{-}money\ Valuation} = \frac{£200{,}000}{£1{,}200{,}000} = 16.7\%$$

A growing company can participate in a series of fund raising rounds from launch to public flotation. These are summarised below:

Different Equity Rounds	Explanation	Round Size in UK 2019 (Note this is a rough guide only and figures are continually changing in the industry)
Pre-Seed	Formation round, which could include friends, family, and other small investors. Can also include venture capital funds who have adapted their model to focus on investing at the earliest stages of company development. Generally, businesses at concept stage only, with investment decisions being predominantly influenced by the potential of the founding team.	Anything from £5k to £500k, but typically £250k–£350k if venture capital is involved.
Seed	First post-formation funding round, usually at commercial validation stage. Investors could be any of those in the pre-seed stage and also more likely to include accelerator programmes, angel syndicates and crowdfunding.	Anything up to £3m, but typically £1.5m to £2m where venture capital is involved.

Different Equity Rounds	Explanation	Round Size in UK 2019 (Note this is a rough guide only and figures are continually changing in the industry)
Early/ mid/late stage	These rounds could be with any type of investor and several could take place. Many businesses may not get beyond this point. At each subsequent round the business should have scaled and be demonstrably commercially successful, although unlikely to be profitable yet.	Depending on the size of the seed round, these rounds should be progressively greater in scale and pre-money valuation.
Series A	First major funding round, usually led by venture capital funds. Business is likely to be scaling rapidly and will command a substantial pre-money valuation. May still not be profitable at this stage due to the high costs associated with rapid scaling.	Anything from £3m to £10m, but typically £5m to £7m where venture capital is involved.
Series B, etc.	Further additional major rounds. A new letter is added for each different round. Further venture capital funds may be added.	Depending on the size of the Series A round, these rounds should be progressively greater in scale and pre-money valuation.
IPO (Initial Public Offering)	Flotation on a stock exchange. Very few companies ever reach this stage!	This will be dependent on the market chosen and funds raised. Valuations can run to £bn's.

The funding landscape is constantly changing and evolving. Where start-ups were rarely funded by venture capital at the pre-seed or even seed stage, it is now possible to obtain equity funding from them at concept stage. Some, such as Forward Partners in London, will even provide office space to entrepreneurs and actively assist in the customer validation process. Consequently, any neat lines and other boundaries to define where each category of investor begins and ends is likely to be misleading. There are also significant variations across markets and industries. Consequently, the above table should be treated as guidance only to the general equity funding landscape at the time of publication.

Progress through the different funding rounds will be almost entirely dependent on the commercial success of the business. Unless the company can demonstrate it can scale, with a profit ultimately down the road, then new sources of equity funding will dry up. Each additional round should be a step forward in terms of valuation and generally will be greater in terms of amount raised.

Issues of Share Dilution and Control

As more shares are issued, unless the founders add more capital themselves, they will face equity dilution. This is simply mathematics: as more shares are issued, the proportion of the total they own starts to fall. If founders are not careful, then they could quickly end up with below 50% of the equity and lose voting control of the business they founded. They could even get thrown off the board of the company they have created! Giving away too much equity early on might also negatively impact the company's ability to raise further equity investment. Investors want to see that founders are sufficiently incentivised, with percentage ownership in the company being considered a proxy for that.

This is another reason why moving to profitability quickly is advantageous. If you are making money two things can simultaneously happen: firstly, you may have less need of outside capital as you are generating some yourself; and secondly, if you do need funds you should be able to command a higher price per share. Alternatively, if the business is *scaling rapidly*, but far from profitable yet, then although funding will be required to cover the trading losses, investors will be keen to have a piece of the action. Under these circumstances there should be a ready market for the shares and high pre-money valuations can also be obtained. In summary, *profitability* and *scaling* are the desirable features for driving a good equity deal from a founder's viewpoint.

Another word of caution: consider who you are dealing with before taking their money. If for some reason you do not like a potential shareholder, we would advise following your instinct and steering clear of them. Early investors could end up with a disproportionately large amount of equity. Imagine the scenario where a founder gives up 45% of the equity at the pre-seed stage to a friendly investor introduced by the family's solicitor. This person may help make it all happen, but you become stuck with them as a partner and possibly a board director. We have heard variants of this story over the years – part with equity cautiously and ideally spread amongst many, rather than few, individuals.

Up Rounds and Down Rounds

An 'up round' is a new share issue with a *pre*-money valuation *above* the previous *post*-money valuation – in other words, the price per share has gone *up*. All existing investors love to hear that the next round is an up one, as it indicates their original investment has grown in value – at least on paper. The down round, as you've already guessed, is one at a lower share price than the previous round. Completing a down round is

Down rounds rarely have a happy ending!

uncomfortable for all existing shareholders, and they face the dilemma of participating and risking further potential wealth loss, or not participating and suffering a dilution of their shareholding percentage. The more severe the down round is, the worse the latter scenario will be for existing shareholders. If pre-money valuations start to fall, investors will become increasingly nervous and can quickly disappear: the saying, '*Success has many friends; failure is an orphan*' certainly applies in the funding world!

In our somewhat painful experience of investing in around 80 equity rounds over the years, we have seen many down rounds and participated in some. It is hard to recall any that have ended well. Our current position is that we tend to walk away, and avoid throwing good money after bad. But that's a personal view!

Convertible Notes

As an alternative to going through the complex process of issuing shares, it is possible to issue a **convertible note**. This is a short-term loan to the company which can be converted into equity at the next round. It has the advantage of being relatively quick to organise and does not require as much documentation as an equity round. Although the equity round will, in theory, take place in the future, it does mean the money can be raised beforehand.

Some of the key features of a convertible note are:

- It is unsecured debt, with a *maximum price* at which the investor (i.e. lender) can convert into equity at the next round. This is known as the cap. For example, the cap could be £2m, which means that even if the equity round took place at a pre-money valuation of £3m, the convertible note holder would only pay a pre-money valuation of £2m.
- The convertible note will also usually feature a discount as a form of reward for the early stage investor. Typically, such a discount is 20%, and would mean that if the round took place at £2m, the convertible note holder would buy shares at a pre-money valuation at £1.6m, having received a 20% reduction. Note that if the round took place at £3m with a £2m cap on the convertible note, then the cap would come into force as it is lower than £2.4m (£3m less 20%).
- Convertible notes can also carry interest, which could either be paid out to the holder or roll up to be converted into shares when the round takes place.
- The convertible note will have a time limit within which it must be converted to equity, or be repaid (the latter being at the investor's discretion).

So, it seems these convertible notes are the perfect solution to early fund raising. Not so fast: there is a rather large potential snag. Think back to the balance sheet chapters – taking on debt does not increase or decrease the size of the net assets of the business. Consequently, if the business trades at a loss it is possible the balance sheet will become negative and conceivably insolvent.[1] Additionally, the convertible note could potentially be off-putting to new investors at the equity round stage. Much would depend on the scale of the convertible note's value relative to the equity round, and any onerous terms attached to the conversion of the note that could affect the ongoing control of the company.

Different Equity Rounds

- The investment community has attached different terminology to the equity rounds dependent on the stage of the company's development and the amount of funds being raised. These are known as pre-seed, seed, Series A, B, etc. The boundaries between all these are somewhat blurred and continuously changing.
- Convertible notes can be used as an alternative to an immediate equity round. At a later stage these notes are converted to equity. They have the advantage of being an administratively simpler process to manage, but will not enhance the balance sheet value of a company.

Enterprise Investment Scheme (EIS)

The **Enterprise Investment Scheme (EIS)** was launched by the UK Government in 1993 to help early-stage businesses based or started *in the United Kingdom* to obtain growth capital from private investors. The scheme is open to most types of businesses that can issue new shares to investors under the scheme. The investors can then receive generous tax relief on this investment. Since the scheme's inception, over £20bn of funds have been raised and invested into around 30,000 businesses.[2] Following the success of this scheme, the **Seed Enterprise Investment Scheme (SEIS)** was added in 2012, offering even more tax incentives to investors who invest in seed stage businesses.

These schemes are of considerable significance to any business raising early-stage funding. Many angel investors will only invest in EIS/SEIS-eligible businesses – for understandable reasons: their capital risk is greatly reduced and any upside return is considerably enhanced. The key features of the schemes are set out below, but note these may have changed since publication and it is best to check on the **HMRC** website.

	EIS	SEIS
Investment size limits	£5m in any year, up to a lifetime max. of £12m	£150k in total
Company size limits	< £15m of gross assets < 250 employees	< £200k of gross assets < 25 employees
Time period	Capital must be spent within 7 years of first commercial sale	Capital must be spent within 3 years of first commercial sale
Excluded businesses	Excluded businesses include legal and financial services, property development, hotels, nursing homes, farming, electricity generation (and various others).	

Note additional criteria apply: see HMRC website. https://www.gov.uk/government/organisations/hm-revenue-customs

The benefits for investors are tax relief both on the investment itself, and also the gain (if any!) should the business be sold after three years. Again, this is a summary of the key features for investors at the time of publication.

	EIS	SEIS
Relief on Income Tax	30% of investment	50% on investment
Investment size limits	Up to £2m (with conditions)	£100k
Capital Gains Tax on sale	Gains are tax free providing investment held for at least 3 years	

Note additional criteria apply: see HMRC website. https://www.gov.uk/government/organisations/hm-revenue-customs

Example for Investor

An investor buys £10,000 of shares in a company that qualifies for EIS or SEIS relief. Investors can offset 30% or 50% (depending on scheme chosen) against their Income Tax, resulting in a net investment of £7,000 or £5,000. Let us assume this shareholding is then sold for £20,000 over three years later. The returns would look as follows, depending on which scheme was applied:

	Without EIS/SEIS	With EIS	With SEIS
Cost of investment	£10,000	£7,000 (after 30% relief)	£5,000 (after 50% relief)
Sales proceeds 3 years later	£20,000	£20,000	£20,000
Capital gain	£10,000	£13,000	£15,000
Capital Gains Tax (assumed rate at 28%[3])	£2,800	Nil	Nil
Overall net gain £	£7,200	£13,000	£15,000
Overall net gain %	72%	186%	300%

Note in this example it is assumed the investor can claim the full tax relief and would pay Capital Gains Tax at the highest rate. Additional factors may also apply: see HMRC website.

The EIS/SEIS schemes, therefore, make an investment potentially far more lucrative, and consequently can encourage greater risk taking. There is also a key additional factor – should the investment fail, the investor would be able to offset their loss against Capital Gains Tax in all the above circumstances, but in the case of EIS/SEIS the loss can also be offset against Income Tax as an alternative. For a top rate taxpayer, this can provide additional levels of tax relief – consequently, the downside of an investment loss is slightly less painful under EIS/SEIS.

Convertible Notes and EIS/SEIS

As explained above, angel investors are likely to require that their investment is eligible for EIS/SEIS. A straightforward convertible note is not eligible for the tax relief under these schemes. However, there may be ways around this, such as making it an Advanced Subscription Agreement (ASA) and/or including an agreement specifying that, in the event of the company's impending **liquidation**, the convertible note is converted into equity just beforehand. The key difference between an ASA and a convertible note is that the ASA is an equity instrument rather than a debt one, and cannot be repaid in cash, whilst a convertible note could theoretically be repaid on demand (depending on the terms agreed with the investor).

Enterprise Investment Scheme

- The Enterprise Investment Scheme (EIS) offers private individuals substantial tax incentives to invest in early stage businesses based in the United Kingdom. The Seed Enterprise Investment Scheme (SEIS) offers even more generous incentives to encourage investment in start-ups.
- Because of the scale of the tax incentives, businesses that do not qualify will be significantly less attractive to angel investors in the United Kingdom than ones that do qualify.

Notes

1. An insolvent business is one that cannot meet its financial liabilities. A company director has a legal responsibility to creditors to ensure that it can meet potential liabilities before taking them on (Insolvency Act 1986).
2. Enterprise Investment Scheme and Seed Enterprise Investment Scheme and Social Investment Tax Relief, May 2019 Statistics on Companies Raising Funds, HMRC.
3. 28% is the highest rate at time of publication. Lower rates may apply, depending on individual investor's personal tax circumstances.

5.4 SOURCES OF NEW EQUITY FUNDING

In this chapter we are going to look at some of the most common sources of equity funding for entrepreneurs. Inevitably these tend to merge into one another, as boundaries are not strictly defined. For example, anyone who subscribes to a crowdfunding round is technically an angel investor. But small-scale crowdfunding investors are certainly not the same type of investor as an experienced business angel, as you will see.

The main categories of equity funding are summarised below:

Type of Equity Funding	Explanation
'Friends, family and fools'	This category of investor is often the one that kick-starts a business. Great if the business works out and problematic if it does not!
Angel investors	Angel investors come in all shapes and sizes, from friends and family through to professional business angels who have made multiple investments. They are private individuals who invest in early-stage businesses and hope to make a great return.
Equity crowdfunding	An online platform where entrepreneurs can pitch their businesses with a video and prospectus. Now a popular route primarily for early-stage businesses, but tends to attract inexperienced, small-scale investors.
Venture capital and private equity	A wide range of venture capital (VC) funds which offer funding from early stage through to many £m's. In addition, there are corporate VCs, accelerator programmes, family offices and sovereign wealth funds.
Stock markets	The world's stock markets offer a potentially enormous supply of capital. But floating a business, known as an IPO (Initial Public Offering) is extremely complex and expensive. Only for the larger scale businesses.

'Friends, Family and Fools'

One of the 'three Fs' is often the starting place of funding for many entrepreneurs. Advantages are relatively obvious: there are less likely to be legal or economic consequences of failure. A bank, for example, could require a personal guarantee that would require full repayment of a loan should the business fail. Not only could an entrepreneur suffer the pain of business failure, but they could also end up having an ongoing debt hanging over their head or even face bankruptcy. The bank of Mum and Dad tends to be a little more lenient. Should the business take off ... well, Mum and Dad, or Aunt Molly, could end up exceedingly wealthy as a result of your endeavours!

The downsides are also obvious. Family wealth can be eroded and this can cause arguments and a blame-game within families. There could also be considerable embarrassment if friends are involved, with the inevitable possibility of friendships being ruined.

Perhaps one of the most famous such investors was Ian McGlinn, who, as the boyfriend of one of Anita Roddick's first employees, gave her £4,000 to open the second branch of The Body Shop in Brighton in 1977.[1] This followed her initial failure to obtain funding from the bank. In return, McGlinn acquired a 50% shareholding of the company. In 2006, The Body Shop was acquired by L'Oréal, and McGlinn's shares, though now diluted to 22%, were sold for £146m. Ian McGlinn could certainly never be called a fool!

Anita Roddick was ahead of her time, and campaigned throughout her life for human rights, the protection of the environment, and promoted ethical business practices. She was also hugely generous with her time: as young entrepreneurs in the late 1980s, we wrote to her and asked if she would come out to lunch with us! She obliged and we were privileged to be able to pick her brain about the retail business sector, having just given her a tour of one our own shops. Sadly, she died in 2007.

Ian Cook/The LIFE Images Collection/Getty Images

Pioneering entrepreneur Anita Roddick, founder of The Body Shop.

Business Angels

Heaven sent: business angels can bring both funding and expertise.

Business angels are individuals who invest equity into businesses with a view to growing their capital. The stage of funding will usually be at the pre-seed or seed stages but angels could conceivably take part in any later rounds. However, the general focus will be on early-stage businesses, and the EIS/SEIS tax incentives provided by the UK government further drive angels to this sector of the funding market.

Business angels usually invest as part of an angel group or syndicate and there are now numerous such clubs around the United Kingdom, but predominantly concentrated in the South East of England. These syndicates are not usually formal funds – every member invests as an individual, and not all will participate in each investment. In fact, in our experience of The Surrey Investors' Club, no more than 5 to 10 angels from the club are likely to invest at any one time out of over 100 members. But, when combined with other angel syndicates, numerous angels can participate in a single round. Companies may also simultaneously be obtaining capital from other sources. For example, it is not unusual for a company to be seeking top-up funds from angel groups to supplement funding from a venture capitalist.

The UK Business Angel Association published a comprehensive report on the British angel market in 2018.[2] They surveyed a total of 658 angels and held in-depth interviews with 159 of these. They identified the following profile of a typical UK business angel:

- The typical business angel in the UK is male, white and most likely to live in London and the South East.
- The average age from their survey was 52, with the largest group of their sample aged 55–64.
- Business angels are highly experienced, with typically eight years of investment experience.
- The median initial investment is £25,000, and the median follow-on investment is £7,500.
- On average, a typical angel spends 1.6 days a week in the business they invest in and holds their investment for 6 years.

Business angels represent an excellent source of expertise for young companies. Because the angels tend to have plenty of 'grey hairs' (i.e. experience!), come from a wide variety of industry sectors, and usually have time on their hands, they are often keen to get involved. If they are invested in the business, they are likely to give their time for free – at least initially.

Most Important Investment Criteria to Angels

The survey identified the five most important criteria for making an investment. Here they are in order of importance:

1. **Team:** the entrepreneurs involved must have the relevant skills and experience.
2. **Scalability:** the business and revenue model needs to show potential to achieve growth and scale.
3. **Expected returns:** there has to be the chance to make a substantial upside in return for taking the risk (angels often talk about a 10x return on initial investment).
4. **Realistic valuation:** the pre-money valuation has to be sensible.
5. **Idea:** the product/service/business model shows strong potential for being disruptive in the sector or market. In other words, a great idea!

Are you surprised that the idea comes out fifth on the list and not first? Having made many poor investment decisions ourselves over the years, we are not at all surprised – a great idea is worthless in the wrong hands. In fact, it is worth noting that few companies will stick precisely to their initial idea (i.e. as presented to their early-stage investors), and many go through a testing and iteration process that shapes the idea further. It is not uncommon for a start-up to do a full pivot if they struggle to scale.

This list is highly relevant to any entrepreneurs seeking investment from angels (or, indeed, any professional investor). First and foremost, you need a great team with a balance of skills (covering sales, product, and finance), and ideally with experience from the sector itself. Sector experience can often be brought in with board advisers or non-executive directors. A sole entrepreneur, with no significant sector knowledge, will be at a distinct disadvantage. The lead entrepreneurs also need a bit of the 'X-factor': some sort of combination of charisma, determination and intelligence.

There must also be a *substantial upside* for the angel investor. This is a function of the team, sector, idea, and the pre-money valuation – all have to be favourable to the investor. For example, if the team and idea were superb and in a growth market, but the pre-money valuation was unreasonably high, there would be little incentive for the angel investor, despite all the other factors being very positive.

Business angels tend to be relatively sector agnostic. They will, however, tend to avoid sectors they do not understand and will favour businesses that can scale rapidly.

Cost of Angel Funding

If the funding comes from a professional angel syndicate, they are likely to charge a fee of around 5% on funds raised. If the pitch session at one angel syndicate leads to a referral at another, then both are likely to seek a fee. Under these circumstances, it is generally customary for the two syndicates to share the fee, so the pitching company only pays the 5% and no more. Angel groups may also charge a relatively nominal fee to pitch at their events, regardless of whether funds are subsequently raised.

Double Dutch Case Study

Raised in the Netherlands (the birthplace of gin), twin sisters Joyce and Raissa de Hass always had a natural affinity with premium drinks. They were, however, frustrated with the limited selection of high-end mixers available to accompany the wider array of premium spirits. In response to this, during their years at university in Antwerp, where they studied finance, they started experimenting with making their own syrups and sodas, which became a true passion. In 2014, they decided to move to London to study MSc Technology Entrepreneurship at the UCL School of Management. Whilst on the programme they focused on the mixer market. At graduation, they won the UCL Bright Ideas prize for most promising start-up and received some initial funding, which they used to produce the first batch of product in order to obtain customer feedback.

This feedback was extremely positive, but they simply had no funds to start the business. They needed around £260,000 in pre-seed investment.

'As we had started Double Dutch right after university in a foreign country, we didn't have any professional network in the UK, let alone in the food & beverage sector. We didn't know where to start finding potential investors', Joyce said. *'We decided to start connecting with potential investors on LinkedIn, looking at profiles of people that either owned hotels/ bars/restaurants, had a food & beverage marketing background, or had extensive work experience and knowledge in the spirits industry. In the end, we found all the investors of our first round via LinkedIn, both from the direct contacts we made, and from the subsequent introductions they made to their respective networks.'*

One individual invested over 75% of the total capital raised and four other angels together invested the other 25%. Raissa continued:

'While it was great to have a lead investor, upon reflection if we could do it all over, we would have gone with a more equal split of capital input per investor. The challenge was that because he became the biggest minority shareholder, he received extra rights over the other investors which, in hindsight, wasn't good for the culture within the business. In terms of investors, it's also very important to not only look at their CV and background but at what their vision is as an investor and how they see their involvement currently and in the future. Do they want to get involved? Or not all? And if they do, to what extent, i.e. which parts of the business?'

Great success followed, and in 2017 and 2018 they followed up with two more rounds totalling £2m. At the time of publication, they are selling around 1m bottles a month.

Key lessons from Double Dutch:

- Even if you have no capital, it is perfectly possible to find it.
- In this situation, they used LinkedIn to target individuals from the relevant industry sector who could bring both capital and expertise.
- With hindsight, they felt it would have been better to have had a greater spread of smaller investors, rather than one major lead investor.
- If the investors are to be involved in working with the business, be clear about their role at the outset.

Business Angel Funding

- Business angel investors are usually members of a syndicate or club where they find the opportunities, but will invest their personal funds as an individual.
- Entrepreneurs can pitch at angel events in order to seek funding. The syndicate will typically charge a 5% fee on funds raised.
- Business angels represent a good source of knowledge and can often help with the development of an early-stage business.
- Angel investors can be found through the numerous angel syndicates, or by simply searching for relevant individuals through a network such as LinkedIn.

Crowdfunding

Although **crowdfunding** may be perceived as a more recently invented method of funding, it actually dates back centuries. Authors and publishers have funded book projects this way by advertising the projects to the public since at least the eighteenth century. All have involved using a large group of individuals to collectively fund a project.

In terms of equity funding, the internet has enabled platforms such as Crowdcube, Seedrs, and numerous others to grow in the United Kingdom over the last decade. These platforms are extremely flexible in terms of the funding available, with round sizes typically from £100k up to many £m's. BrewDog is one of the United Kingdom's fastest-growing food and drink brands and has raised a total of £39m through the Crowdcube platform, and now has an astonishing 80,000 investors.[3] These funds were raised in a series of four rounds over the period 2015–18, demonstrating that these platforms can be used as an alternative to venture capital. There are also few limits on pre-money valuations. In 2017, Revolut, the financial services business, raised £3.9m at a pre-money valuation of £276m on the Seedrs platform.

There are a number of determinants for success on a crowdfunding platform. These will generally include having a consumer-centric product that small investors can relate to (such as beer) and a snappy video featuring the founders. The pre-money valuations can also be unrealistically high from an angel investor viewpoint. Whilst at first sight this may appear to be a good thing, it can in fact be a problem when further funding is required, and makes the risk of a down round more likely.

But it is not just a simple process of uploading a snappy video of your consumer product idea. The platforms require a proportion of funds to have already been raised, meaning that the fund should be partially complete at the launch stage. This is important from a marketing viewpoint – nobody wants to feel as if they are the first investor. So those first investors will tend to come from 'friends, family and fools', or experienced angel investors. The latter group are unlikely to agree to excessively high pre-money valuations. The crowdfunding platforms will also seek to do a level of due diligence on the investment proposition, i.e. they will do their best to ensure it is a properly constituted investment offer with meaningful supporting information.

As with angel syndicates, fees will be charged on funds raised (typically 7%) and further charges may be applicable.

Crowdfunding

- Equity crowdfunding has become increasingly popular and offers entrepreneurs access to substantial levels of capital, at sometimes unrealistically high pre-money valuations from an angel investor's perspective.
- Crowdfunding is likely to be more successful in sectors which appeal to consumers.
- It is expected that the round is partially completed at the time of launch.

Private Equity and Venture Capital

The British Private Equity & Venture Capital Association (BVCA) has over 340 private equity and venture capital houses as members, and in 2018 a total of £34bn was invested by them.[4] Just as there are a wide variety of business angels, the terms private equity and venture capital cover a wide variety of different funding sources.

Venture Capital Funds

Venture capital (VC) funds are usually made up of the **general partners** (GPs), which is the venture capital company itself, and the **limited partners** (LPs), who are the sources of the capital. The LPs will include pensions funds, other financial institutions, and even private high-net worth individuals. The GPs will find the deals and invest the capital, and will charge an annual fee to the LPs for the management (typically 2% of the funds invested). Additionally, the GPs will take around 20% of any profit made when the fund is liquidated.

Different funds may specialise in different sectors, so if seeking a VC then it is important to do some research before approaching them. Their reputation is also of critical importance, and it is worth seeking out entrepreneurs who have received funding from them in order to determine their level of satisfaction, both with the terms they received and any ongoing support. As well as specific favoured sectors, the funds may concentrate on early-stage, mid-stage, or late-stage investments.

An important feature to understand about VC funds is they are likely to be *finite*, both in capital raised and in the length of time they intend to hold their investments. For example, a £250m fund could be created from LPs. Once raised, no more capital will be added to this particular fund. Over time, typically a few years at most, this fund itself will be *fully invested.* It is then a case of the GPs monitoring the investments and, when appropriate, liquidating them in a sale or IPO. This has certain implications:

- Firstly, despite the fund having made an investment in a company that has been highly successful, the fund may not have the capital to participate in further rounds. Although it will have held some capital back for such purpose, and to draw their fees from, this may not be sufficient.
- At some stage the VC will want an exit. This may be 10 years down the road, but the pressure to return capital to the LPs will exist. This could be in conflict with the goals of the investee company.

Successful VCs will, of course, be creating subsequent funds and these could participate in the later rounds. But the timing may not necessarily coincide with the company's requirements, or the VC may not be able to raise additional funds from LPs. Nothing can be assumed. VCs who choose not to participate in future rounds can also send out the wrong signalling to other VCs who could be considering an investment themselves.

Corporate Venture Capital

Instead of funds being sourced from LPs, they could come from a large corporation. Google Ventures, Intel Capital and Samsung Ventures are some of the best-known ones, but most large corporations are now seeking a piece of the entrepreneurial landscape themselves.

There are several reasons behind this interest. Firstly, they recognise that they are not the nimblest of beasts, and, when compared to a team of young enthusiastic entrepreneurs, are positive dinosaurs. Secondly is fear – the notion that a large corporation will be leading its sector in the decades ahead is now far from certain. All sorts of challenger businesses are emerging and reinventing the commercial landscape in their own backyard. Their logic, therefore, is to try and participate in these ventures at an early stage.

Inevitably, a corporate VC is likely to be highly focused on their own trading sectors. They have the advantage of potentially bringing sector knowledge and expertise to entrepreneurs. But one possible disadvantage is they may seek to fully acquire the business at some stage, and the timing may not be in alignment with the entrepreneurs who founded the business.

Accelerator Programmes

Whilst VC funds can be focused on any stage of a company's development, **accelerator programmes** are firmly rooted in the start-up funding space. Not only do most of them offer some seed funding, but they can provide mentorship and training to entrepreneurs, as well as physical office space from which to work. The largest such accelerator programme in the world at present is Techstars, which in 2019 operates in over 150 countries. A typical process for any accelerator programme will look something like this:

- Entrepreneur presents their idea and joins the competitive selection process to get in the programme.
- Some initial pre-seed capital (e.g. c.£25k) is provided in exchange for a small equity share (typically 5–10%).
- An intense period of development takes place over a 3-to 6-month period, which includes mentoring and seminars.
- A loan may also be made to the fledgling business (e.g. c.£100k) in the form of a convertible note.
- At the end of the programme there is a pitch day event, where outside investors, such as business angels, can attend.

There are many variants on this model. There are corporate accelerator programmes, which will operate with similar objectives to a corporate venture capital fund. Other accelerator programmes, such as Entrepreneurs First, work in a similar way, but the entrepreneurs do not join with a particular idea. Instead the focus is on selecting a highly talented group of individuals who are thrown together to form teams and come up with ground-breaking new ideas.

Envio Case Study

Launched in 2017, Envio is a technology start-up that lets brands offer home demos and rentals of expensive products. James Wilkinson, the founder, had won a handful of start-up competitions in his final year at Leeds University. This had helped with the very early stages of developing the concept, but he realised he was going to need capital beyond his own limited resources.

After firstly gaining some small grant funding, he had early interest from venture capital funds, but held back:

'I was very cautious around raising substantial capital for equity before I had a formula that fully worked. Venture capital has been described as a power tool, when used correctly it can be very effective, but when misused it can have devastating effects often leaving the founders with nothing.'

As a stepping-stone, he joined Techstars' three-month accelerator programme in New York.

'Whilst they took 6% of my equity for me it was highly valuable. Not only did I receive some more funding, but I had some amazing opportunities to learn from previous founders on everything from fundraising to running development teams. I think accelerator programs are best for technology / high growth companies – their culture encourages you to go big, or go home!'

The programme helped James to refine his idea and subsequently move forward with angel funding, primarily introduced from the programme.

Other Venture Funding

Family Offices

Highly affluent families can either have their own, or use the services of, a family office. These will oversee the investment of their capital, as well as advise on accounting, tax and legal advice. They can be a source of capital for entrepreneurs and, as with VCs, they may be more likely to invest in sectors that are familiar to them.

Sovereign Wealth Funds

Sovereign wealth funds manage the surplus wealth of countries that have generated large fiscal surpluses over the years. These funds are likely to focus on major investments in large-scale equity investment, property and other infrastructure.

Venture Capital and Private Equity

- The terms venture capital and private equity cover a wide variety of funding sources.
- Venture capital funds have a finite source of capital within each fund. Once fully invested it is then managed and eventually liquidated. The general partners are the creators of the fund itself and the limited partners are the providers of the capital.
- Other venture funding sources include corporate VCs, accelerator programmes, family offices and sovereign wealth funds.

Stock Markets

Many entrepreneurs dream of an **IPO** (Initial Public Offering), which is perhaps one of the ultimate symbols of their success. This is the listing of the shares of a company on a stock market, and, at this stage, companies can be valued at many £bn's. In 2018, Swedish music streaming service Spotify listed its shares on the New York stock exchange and achieved an immediate valuation of close to $30bn.

There are many advantages and disadvantage of a stock market flotation:

Key Advantages	Key Disadvantages
Access to seemingly unlimited new growth capital.	Enormous costs to obtain a listing.
An opportunity for founders and employees to convert their equity to cash.	Demanding legal compliance issues, both to list shares and on an ongoing basis.
Ability to acquire other companies by issuing new shares.	Continuous public scrutiny of the company's financial performance and operational behaviour.

Key Advantages	Key Disadvantages
Opportunity for the general public, and other institutions, to participate in the ownership of the business. Easy mechanism to reward all employees by granting tradeable share options. Raised public profile enhances PR and marketing opportunities.	Risk of a hostile takeover by another company. This will be particularly true should the share price became depressed.

The London Stock Exchange has two key markets. Firstly, and predominantly, the main market where companies have a full listing. The FTSE 100 index is derived from the top 100 of these companies in terms of their market capitalisation. There is also a secondary sub-market, AIM (Alternative Investment Market), which is for smaller capitalisation companies, and has a lower threshold of regulatory requirements, both to list initially and on an ongoing basis. Listing on the main market will cost many £m's and on the AIM market £0.5m upwards. In both cases, the fees will be extremely variable and dependent on the scale and complexity of the listing. But what is evident is that the cost is substantial and the ongoing scrutiny of performance is relentless!

Notes

1. https://www.managementtoday.co.uk/uk-ian-mcglinn-body-shops-missing-body/article/408754.
2. The UK Business Angel Market published by The UK Business Angel Association and produced by British Business Bank, June 2018.
3. Crowdcube.com, 2019.
4. BVCA Report on Investment Activity, 2018.

5.5 THE EQUITY FUNDING PROCESS EXPLAINED

In this chapter, we shall explore the actual mechanics and process of a funding round in more detail.

The Process in Outline

The typical series of events and actions for a funding round is as follows:

1. **Prepare the ground**
   a. Preliminary homework.
   b. Prepare financials and decide funding details (notably how much needs to be raised).
   c. Research target investors.
   d. Prepare pitch deck and financials.
   e. Research EIS/SEIS status.
   f. Approach potential investors.
   g. Attend initial meetings.
2. **Agree the deal**
   a. Attend follow-up meetings.
   b. Receive opening offers.
   c. Negotiate outline terms.
   d. Agree on the term sheet.
3. **Seal the deal**
   a. Due diligence.
   b. Execute key legal documents.
   c. Receive funds.

The actual timescale of this process can be anything from one to nine months, though three months would be fairly typical. The actual length of time involved would depend on: the scale and complexity of the deal; the attractiveness of the proposition; the efficiency of the potential investors and their advisors; and the level of preparedness of your business plan.

Fundraising is a time-consuming process that often takes longer than founders anticipate. With running out of cash being the second most common reason why start-ups fail, founders are encouraged to start thinking and planning the fund-raising process early.[1]

The Term Sheet

The **term sheet** is a non-legally binding document that sets out the terms and conditions agreed between investors, company and, if applicable, founders/directors prior to the actual legal documents being drafted by the lawyers. It serves a very important purpose in avoiding misunderstandings and wasted time – there is no point in instructing lawyers to create legal documentation that has not already been agreed in principle. The legal documents that will eventually be drafted or amended will include:

- Investment agreement, or sale and purchase agreement (SPA)
- Representations and warranties
- Disclosure letter
- Board minutes
- Articles of association
- Shareholders' agreement
- Contracts of employment for key personnel
- Other documents (e.g. assignment of intellectual property)

Negotiating the term sheet is of critical importance. Whilst it is technically possible to deviate from it in the final legal documentation, this could be problematic and cause ill-feeling. In addition, walking away from the term sheet could involve certain penalties, depending on what has been agreed. Hence from the outset it is essential to understand its contents and to be clear on all the terms.

The term sheet is a critically important document. It sets out the basis of the terms and conditions of the deal, and it needs to be fully understood by all parties.

The complexity and scope of the term sheet will vary according to the scale of the investment and the type of investors. In the case of early-stage angel investment, it is likely to be relatively straightforward and the company may issue the draft themselves. In the case of venture capitalists, they are likely to provide their own term sheet draft. Control of this document will depend greatly on the respective power of the two sides in the negotiation. If a company is desperate to raise the money, but there is relatively low level of interest by investors, then inevitably it will be in a weaker position and may end up accepting any terms on offer.

The key elements of any term sheet will relate to the *economics of the deal* and the *control of the business*. Let us look at each in turn. In doing so, and for simplicity, we will make a broad assumption that the company's shareholders are the *founders* (but in reality, they could be any number of existing shareholders prior to an investment round), and that the investor is a *venture capital fund* (but again, this could be any type of investor).

Economics of the Term Sheet

Price

A great deal of emphasis will be placed on the value of the business. This is defined in terms of **pre-money** and **post-money valuations**. For example, if a business is valued at £6m pre-money, and raises exactly £2m in new equity, the post-money valuation will be £8m. Note the new shareholders will hold 25% of the equity (i.e. £2m/£8m).

The determination of the pre-money valuation is significant for both parties. In the above example, if the pre-money valuation was £8m instead of £6m, with the same fund-raising of £2m, the new shareholders would only have 20% of the equity. The higher pre-money figure would benefit the existing shareholders and cause less dilution of their shareholdings. It would also reduce the potential returns for the investor, who would have a smaller share of the cake when the company is ultimately sold. Evidently, when in discussions with investors, it is vital to know whether discussions are about *pre-* or *post-*money valuations.

The price negotiated in any deal does, however, need to be looked at in the context of the other terms. As we will see from the Vungle case study below, it is easy to be side-tracked by the headline pre-money valuation figure at the expense of the other terms.

Warrants

Warrants are similar to stock options and could be included in a term sheet by the venture capitalist (or other investors). The warrant holder is granted the right to purchase more shares at a later date at a pre-agreed price. If the business was subsequently very successful, then these could be extremely beneficial to the holders, and their overall gain is enhanced. *So, if they are the winners, who are the losers?* Arguably, if the warrants have been exercised then there are no *absolute* losers, as every shareholder's wealth has grown due to the rising value of each share. But the warrant holder will receive more shares overall, and consequently the shareholdings of the non-warrant holders will be diluted, so they will be the *relative* losers.

Liquidation Preference

If, for some reason, you have been dozing off a bit when reading about term sheets, now is a good time to wake up. Trust us – these can have a devastating effect on the entrepreneurs' final exit value and it is vital to fully appreciate the significance of all types of **preference shares**.

The first thing to appreciate is that the term '**liquidation**' does not just apply to a company being wound up. In the context of equity funding rounds, the word 'liquidation' also refers to the realisation of the *VCs' investment*, not of the company itself. A liquidation event is, therefore, also likely to include the sale of the shares, or the merging of the business with another. The preference shareholders can be the first to receive any funds (this is the preference). These preference shares can also be *participating*, meaning that after investors have had their investment back, they then share in the proceeds left over pro-rata to their shareholding as if the shares were **ordinary shares** (this is the participation). Preference shares can, therefore, be 'participating' or 'non-participating'.

The final thing to note, before we look at some examples, is that preference shares can always be converted to ordinary shares should it suit the holder.

Example 1

In this example, a venture capitalist invested £2m for 20% of the company, and the founders have retained 80%. The founders started the business with relatively little capital, demonstrated some early scaling, and successfully persuaded the venture capital fund to invest. For simplicity, there are no other shareholders.

Three years down the road, the performance of the business has been a big disappointment compared to what had been expected at the time of investment, and the company has been sold to a buyer for £5m, well below the original expectations of the venture capitalist.

Below are three different scenarios for the sale at £5m, depending on what type of shares the venture capitalist held. The first is where the venture capitalist has ordinary shares – the same as those of the founders, and they carry no preferential rights. In the second and third scenarios, the venture capitalist has preference shares – and the third case is shown *with participation.*

Company Sold for £5m	**Scenario 1** **No Preference Shares**	**Scenario 2** **Pref. Shares with No Participation**	**Scenario 3** **Pref. Shares with Participation**
Venture capitalist's shareholding	20% (Ordinary shares)	20% (Preference shares)	20% (Preference shares)
Founders' shareholding	80% (Ordinary shares)	80% (Ordinary shares)	80% (Ordinary shares)
Proceeds to venture capitalist	£1m	£2m	£2m + (20% × £3m) = £2.6m
Proceeds to founders	£4m	£3m	£2.4
% of proceeds to founders	80%	60%	48%

In Scenario 1 the founders receive what you might reasonably expect – 80% of the proceeds, i.e. £4m. But in the second scenario, because the preference shares are paid out first, the venture capital fund gets its capital back but nothing more. At this stage, pause and consider that Scenario 1 may be rather unfair to the venture capitalist fund, which has taken significant risk injecting the growth capital into the business. Although the outcome may have been disappointing compared to what the founders had hoped for, they are still walking off into the sunset with £4m (most of which is capital gain to them), whilst the venture capitalist will be suffering a bruising £1m loss. Now the preference shares make a bit more sense to protect the venture capitalist's downside.

In Scenario 3, the preference shares also have participation. Now the venture capitalist not only gets its capital back, but also makes a modest return. The founders receive only 48% of the funds. And, here is the really important point, if the sale price dips below £2m, under both scenarios 2 and 3, the founders would get nothing – *yes nothing!*

Give some thought as to which of the three scenarios was, on balance, the fairest deal for both parties considering the original investment by each, and the final sale outcome.

Example 2

Let's look at the same scenarios but where the sale price of the business was £20m. All parties receive a far better outcome that was in line with expectations at time of investment by the venture capitalist.

Company Sold for £20m	Scenario 4 No Preference Shares	Scenario 5 Pref. Shares with No Participation	Scenario 6 Pref. Shares with Participation
Venture capitalist's shareholding	20% (Ordinary shares)	20% (Preference shares)	20% (Preference shares)
Founders' shareholding	80% (Ordinary shares)	80% (Ordinary shares)	80% (Ordinary shares)
Proceeds to venture capitalist	£4m	£4m	£2m + (20% × £18m) = £5.6m
Proceeds to founders	£16m	£16m	£14.4
% of proceeds to founders	80%	80%	72%

In Scenario 5, the preference shares are simply converted to ordinary shares in the context of the sale. This is because the £2m of preference is lower than the £4m they would receive if they were converted to ordinary shares.

In Scenario 6, despite the more onerous terms of the preference with participation, the founders still end up with 72% of the proceeds. The effect of the preference plus participation makes relatively little difference to the founders if the sale proceeds are at the higher end, as in this scenario.

Liquidation Preference with Multiples and Caps

Hopefully you now understand the significance of preference shares, and appreciate the significance of the added participation. We will now look at the additional complication of multiples and caps.

The multiples relate to the initial investment. For example, a venture capitalist could specify that they require a return of 3x the original investment, in which case there would be absolutely nothing left for the founders in Scenarios 2 and 3 of our examples.

In Scenario 5, at a £20m exit valuation, the venture capitalist would take their 3x £2m, i.e. £6m. In Scenario 6 they would take:

$$(3 \times £2m) + (20\% \times £14m) = £8.8m$$

Evidently these multiples work well in favour of the preference shareholders! Perhaps too well? This is where the concept of a cap comes in where a multiple is involved, with or without and participation.

Example 3

Using the investment as set out in Example 1, with the preference shares having a 1x multiple, with participation, but with a 3x original investment cap. If the business was sold for £5m or £20m, the cap would not be reached and hence would not be relevant. But if the sale proceeds were £40m, the cap would come into play:

	Company Sold for £5m	Company Sold for £20m	Company Sold for £40m
Pref. shares with participation, no cap	£2m + (20% × £3m) = £2.6m (Scenario 3 above)	£2m + (20% × £18m) = £5.6m (Scenario 6 above)	£2m + (20% × £38m) = £9.6m
Pref. shares with participation, but 3x investment cap	As above because cap of £6m not reached	As above because cap of £6m not reached	Cap of £6m reached for preference shares, so they are converted to ordinary shares: 20% × £40m = £8m

With the maximum that the preference shareholders could receive being £6m, which is 3x their original investment, it makes sense to convert the shares to ordinary ones. Hence the conversion takes place, and as ordinary shareholders they would receive £8m.

Many other combinations of a deal are possible. For example, there could just be 5x the preference shares with no participation, with a cap set at this level. Once this cap was reached, the preference shareholder would convert to ordinary shares.

Whilst a decade ago, venture capitalists were able to drive more onerous terms regarding multiples of their original investment, these multiples have been eroded down, both in the United Kingdom and United States, as an increasing number of venture capital funds have emerged chasing the deals available and have tended to settle at 1x for now. These terms are more reasonable to all parties, as they ensure some protection to the venture capital fund in the event of a poor outcome, whilst allowing the founders to be treated more fairly in the event of a higher outcome. The key point of the above explanation is to recognise this is a complex area, and some business founders could easily end up agreeing to an *apparently* satisfactory term sheet, but with terms that they do not fully understand. It is of paramount importance to obtain good legal advice, and to be prepared to walk away from onerous term sheets.

Pay-to-Play

Pay-to-play provisions are generally beneficial to the entrepreneurs raising further funds in the future. In essence, they require the preference shareholders of a previous round to fully participate in any subsequent rounds, pro-rata to their shareholding. The penalty for not taking part would mean their preference shares are then converted to ordinary shares. The inclusion of this clause is therefore useful, but would need some protective provisions to stop the price being driven deliberately downwards by the preference shareholders. They may, for example, be unenthusiastic about taking part in the next round and would rather leave it to new investors, but be even less enthusiastic about losing their preferred stock status. Hence, if they feel obliged to invest, they may wish to drive the price of the round downwards, which could seriously negatively impact the interests of the founders.

Pay-to-play: if you want to remain a key player in the game you had better get some chips onto the table.

Vesting

Share options may be issued to key employees within the business with the intention of both incentivising and retaining them. Typically, these will be for a period of 3–4 years, over which time they will accumulate the new shareholding. This period is known as the **vesting period**. The term sheet will contain provisions covering the granting of these: firstly, specifying to whom (whether directors, or all employees), and in what quantity. In addition, details of how these options are dealt with under certain events, such as if an employee leaves before the end of the vesting period, or if the company is sold or merged with another during the period.

If a minimum period is specified – perhaps 12 months – before any shares are granted, this is known as the 'cliff'. Once the cliff is passed, share options may then accumulate on a pro-rata basis to the time served, which could be on a monthly or annual basis.

Example

An employee has options over a four-year period, with a one-year cliff. The employee leaves after two years. As this is past the cliff, the employee will receive 50% of their options.

Additional criteria could apply, covering whether the employee is a 'good leaver' (i.e. not leaving for any form of misconduct or serious underperformance) or a 'bad leaver' (for example having been dismissed for misconduct or underperformance). The meaning of these would be carefully defined in the legal agreements, which are a product of the term sheet.

Any shares that have not been allocated, such as the balance of the shares that a leaving employee had not taken up, would remain unallocated. The existing shareholders would benefit, through reduced dilution of their holdings. This is known as reverse dilution.

Option Pool

A proportion of the equity may be notionally set aside to allocate to current employees, or future employees who have yet to be hired. Being able to grant them shares in the business may be key to motivating them and attracting them to the business. There needs to be agreement on the size of this pool at the time of any investment by a venture capitalist (or other outside investors). Otherwise, down the road, they may refuse to allow these new shares to be granted. In negotiating the pre-money valuation of the business, the option pool will need to be considered, as it effectively adds to the price for the investor (as their shareholding will ultimately face dilution). Founders need to be wary of investors insisting that the option pool comes out of their equity alone, in which case the investment terms may be less attractive than they first appear.

Anti-dilution

In the event that there is a 'down round', i.e. new equity is being issued at a price lower than the previous round, then a venture capitalist may slip in some rather unpleasant clauses reducing the impact on their own shareholding. This could mean that either all, or the greater part of the dilution, would fall upon the ordinary shareholders, rather than the preference shareholders. Prepare to be blinded by the mathematics involved in these clauses!

Vungle Case Study

Back in 2010 Zain Jaffer was playing around with a business concept whilst studying on the MSc Technology Entrepreneurship at UCL's School of Management. *'We were a video production company making 2-minute advertising videos for app developers. It wasn't a very unique or scalable business idea at the time'*, said Zain.

One thing he discovered was that his clients were not very good at generating views for the videos that Zain's company, Vungle, produced. Vungle initially operated as a video production studio and marketing agency trying to promote video ads across different channels in an attempt to drive video views. But then Zain took the concept one step further: *'We soon realised what developers wanted were downloads of their app, instead of video views.'* As a result, they changed their business model and offered to charge their customers *per download* rather than *per view*. The concept of Pay Per Install for Video had been born and the business took off.

Zain quickly realised he could divert spending away from the existing platforms (like Facebook or YouTube) if he built his own platform from the ground up. After a small $25K pre-seed round with friends and family, Vungle was all set to embark on an epic journey. In early 2011, Zain went off to Silicon Valley to join an accelerator programme for a few months where he obtained $120k in a second pre-seed round, whereby $20k came as equity (for a 6% share of the business) and $100k as a convertible note on reasonable terms.

The business achieved explosive growth and a seed round was launched.*'We planned to raise just $200k but we received a ton of interest from all the top investors that the round quickly became oversubscribed. We said yes to most of the offers as the pre-money valuation seemed great at $4m, and we also knew that was far higher than what we could have achieved in London at the time. We ended up taking in 10x the amount we expected and raised $2m.'* The seed round was one of the biggest that year in Silicon Valley.

By his own admission, though, Zain did not fully appreciate the implications of the term sheet. *'We knew the terms weren't great but did not fully appreciate the consequences at the time, particularly as the round had become so large for us'*. The new convertible note was for preference shares which could convert at 3x the initial investment of $2m, plus participation. Consequently, the first $6m would go to the investors plus any participation. But that was not all. In addition, they accrued interest at a rate of 7% per annum that could be taken in equity at the next round. *'This meant we were being diluted every day we delayed a new round'*, Zain lamented.

Fortunately, Vungle carried on scaling rapidly and a $6m Series A round was put together within a year. *'Now things were very different. We had enormous interest in the round and were surrounded by great advisors. We wrote our own term sheet this time and told interested investors that the terms were non-negotiable. After the conversion of the $2m convertible note into equity we were able to wipe out all the previous onerous terms.'* The pre-money valuation was also a substantial multiple of the previous seed round.

Vungle, by then profitable, went on to have a final $17m Series B round. *'I made sure that during the Series A round I spoke to as many VCs as possible, even though we had no need of their money as the round was full. But I made many contacts and kept them all up to date with our progress. Consequently, when the Series B came along, we had 7 offers and stopped taking new meetings as the median pre-money valuation was yet again many times the size of our previous round. The terms were truly great for us and the tables had turned. I even felt guilty as we got such an amazing valuation with very clean terms.'*

In July 2019, the private equity firm Blackstone acquired the entire share capital of Vungle in a $750m all-cash offer. Vungle remains one the most successful tech start-ups to originate from the United Kingdom.

Key lessons from the Vungle case:

- Understand the term sheet you are offered, and do not get blinded by the bright lights of the pre-money valuation. Whilst the onerous terms Vungle were given at the outset are now (fortunately) unusual, the case does create awareness of what can happen.
- Get good professional advisors to help you navigate through a round.
- Appreciate the importance of *scaling* and *profitability* as key drivers for obtaining strong interest in your round.
- Raising money when you're successful gives you leverage to obtain favourable terms.
- Build a network of investors and keep in touch with them: they can be useful at a later stage.

Control Terms in the Term Sheet

In the section above, we have looked at the economics of the term sheet, the issues that make up the *value proposition* for each of the parties. Changes to any of the criteria either will, or could, significantly alter the financial outcome for the investors or founders. We will now turn to the issues of *controlling the business* once the investment has been made. These will all be specified in the term sheet and will include the make-up of the board of directors, management reporting, dividends, and consent on key decisions (also known as protective provisions). Let's look at some of these in more detail.

The Board of Directors

Perhaps the most fundamental issue of control will relate to the make-up of the board of directors. The number of directors, how they are appointed, how frequently they meet, and the way their remuneration is reviewed will all be specified.

Large investors will insist on some form of board representation, either with the appointment of directors or in the form of board observers.[2] Additional investment rounds may bring more

The makeup of the board of directors can have a profound effect on a business. A good balance between the executive directors, investors, and industry experts is advisable.

directors to the board, which could adversely affect the speed and quality of decision making.

In David G. Thomson's 2006 book *Blueprint to a Billion*, which analysed the success factors in businesses that had rapidly scaled to a billion US$ in revenue, he found that the make-up of the board was a key determinant in their success. Companies that had boards dominated by investors did not perform as well as companies that had more diverse boards, which included alliance partners, customers, and CEOs who had scaled a business before. In other words, a board made up of experienced industry experts is preferable to one dominated by investors unfamiliar with the sector.

Whilst founders should welcome experienced venture capitalists onto their board, they should ensure that the numbers are balanced in a suitable way with industry experts and other key partners.

Shares

The criteria for issuing new shares, and process for the sale of any shares, will be specified. In private companies it is usual, for example, for the shares to be offered to other existing shareholders first. Pre-emption rights will also feature: these ensure that existing shareholders, should they wish, can participate in any future funding round pro-rata to their shareholding size.

Management Reporting

Details of frequency and type of management information provided to shareholders, and the frequency it is provided.

Dividends

Details of the policy concerning the distribution of profits (e.g. stating a certain percentage of profit after tax must be paid out each year). Note that preference shares can have rights ahead of ordinary shares concerning dividends.

Confidentiality and Non-compete

Requirement of shareholders to keep information confidential and potentially not to be involved with competing businesses. Further provisions would also be included in the contract of employment of any directors.

Consent on Key Decisions/Events

The board of directors may require consent from shareholders to make certain key decisions or to trigger key events. These protective provisions usually include taking on debt beyond a certain level, the sale of major assets, and, of course, the sale of the business itself. A percentage of shareholders that need to approve these events would be specified. For example, for the business to be sold, a requirement might be that 75% of the shareholders must approve the decision. Setting a percentage can also be effective in bringing some balance to decisions in the event of a major shareholder. For example, if a single founder controls 70% of the equity, and several investors hold the remaining 30%, by insisting on a threshold of over 70% the founder has to convince at least some of the other investors this is the right decision to make.

Drag and Tag

The 'drag along' clause relates to the ability to complete the sale of a company even in the face of some shareholder resistance. Following on from the above example, where 75% of the shareholders have to consent to the sale of the business, providing this percentage threshold is reached, any remaining minority who disagree can be 'dragged' along to complete the deal. Without this ability, a sale could either flounder (the purchaser insisting that they buy 100% of the equity or none at all), or face the prospect of the hold-out shareholder demanding better terms than on offer. In this latter situation, the only way the majority shareholders can get the deal across the line may be in accepting slightly less for their own shares so the hold-out shareholder can get more. That's an ugly situation to end up in.

Don't forget me! Tag along provisions ensure nobody gets left behind.

The 'tag along' is the opposite – it ensures that the minority shareholders cannot be left out of a sale in the event of a buyer being happy to simply purchase a controlling interest (i.e. not all the equity). Without this, a long-standing faithful small shareholder could be left holding onto their 'worthless' shares, whilst the majority holder sells their stake for a fortune and jets off to their new villa in Mallorca!

In both of these drag and tag situations, all shareholders would be treated the same in terms of price paid/received.

Deal Exclusivity

When a term sheet is agreed between the parties, there is likely to be a period of exclusivity where the founders must commit to doing the deal with the venture capitalist whose term sheet they have accepted in principle. This period, usually 30 to 60 days, is also known as a 'no-shop agreement'.

Clearly once legal work is being undertaken, alongside other due diligence work, costs will then have been run up by the venture capital firm. The VC firm does not want to suddenly be told by the founders that they have just been made a better offer, weeks after their term sheet had been agreed. The consequences of such behaviour would inevitably be some reputational damage, and in some cases, if specified, could involve cost penalties, such as legal fees.

The Term Sheet

- The terms agreed between investors and a company will be set out in a term sheet. This is a highly significant document and will specify both the economics of any agreed deal as well as the issues surrounding the ongoing control of the business.
- The ability to drive the terms set out in the term sheet will largely be determined by the respective power of those negotiating. A company growing rapidly in an exciting market may be able to write its own term sheet, whilst an early stage unproven business may have to accept any terms on offer in order to obtain funding.
- Entrepreneurs need to be aware of all the issues in the term sheet, and in particular those relating to preference shares. It is essential for entrepreneurs to seek legal advice from experienced lawyers and, possibly, corporate finance advisors.

Other Key Documents

The Cap Table

The capitalisation table, or **cap table** for short, is a ledger setting out all the shareholders, their shareholdings, types of shares, and the percentage of the total equity they each own. When a new round of investment is made this picture will change, potentially significantly. Some of the existing shareholders may buy new shares, whilst others may not. New investors will be added, and there may also be an option pool, as described above. The cap table should show the position pre- and post-round, giving clarity to all parties.

During any funding round discussion, a request to see the cap table is likely to be made. It is usually maintained in the form of an Excel spreadsheet or by using an online platform.

Articles of Association

The **articles of association** (also known as articles of incorporation) are a necessary legal part of the formation of every company. The articles are the company's constitution and set out the object and scope of its trading activities (normally fairly broad), and will include the control term elements specified above by a term sheet. In the United Kingdom, the Companies Act 2006 brought in a revised standard form that is adopted by most businesses. This makes the drafting easy – i.e. the standard terms can be used at the outset, but can also be revised as needed. If a company agrees a term sheet with an investor, the articles of association are likely to face some revision to put the terms agreed into practice.

The articles of association must comply with statutory law, and, in the United Kingdom, a copy will be filed at Companies House. Consequently, it is a *publicly available* document and can be viewed by anyone.

The Shareholders' Agreement

Unlike the articles of association, the **shareholders' agreement** is an optional document. It is a *private agreement* between the shareholders and is not publicly available. Whilst all shareholders have to comply with the articles of association, they are not automatically bound by the shareholders' agreement. New shareholders have to sign an agreement to accept the terms. Any breaches of a shareholders' agreement will be a contractual dispute between the parties.

The shareholders' agreement can contain the items covered by the articles of association and will normally take precedence if specified in the document. It is important that the two do not conflict with each other.

The shareholders' agreement is likely to go through a series of amendments at each funding round, depending on the investors' requirements and ability to demand changes. A comprehensive shareholders' agreement is an essential feature of any company, even with just two founding shareholders. For example, where there are just two equal shareholders, the shareholders' agreement could specify how disputes are resolved in the event of a deadlock situation.

The Contractual Process

Once terms of an investment are agreed in a term sheet, there will be both a period of **due diligence** and drafting of legal documentation. Note that this process is broadly the same whether it is an investment by a venture capital source or the purchase of the entire company by a buyer. It is important to appreciate for both scenarios, as most entrepreneurs raising capital will also ultimately seek an exit. In the case of an investment, the lead document will be an **investor agreement**, whilst with the sale of the entire business it will be a **sale and purchase agreement**. Below we will refer to both scenarios.

Due Diligence

This is the verification process of the business proposition. The investors or buyers will want to look at:

- **The business concept:** verifying its likely success, which could include talking to its customers or potential customers.
- **The team:** checking out their backgrounds. Are they the capable individuals they appear to be? Are there any skeletons hidden in a cupboard somewhere?!
- **The finances:** do all the numbers stack up? Are all the assets actually in place and are they valued correctly?
- **Intellectual property (IP):** are the patents and trademarks owned as claimed and properly registered in the relevant countries?
- **Liabilities:** are there any liabilities or potential liabilities that the investor/buyer should be aware of that may not have been declared? These could include ongoing disputes with customers, suppliers, former employees or tax authorities.

If there is some problematic bit of news about your business or background that you do not want to share, it is likely to be discovered during this phase. It is always best to be upfront and open about any problems, such as a lingering dispute with another party. This is part of business life and can usually be dealt with satisfactorily in the contractual process, as we will explain.

Part of the legal process for dealing with these issues will involve the directors and/or key shareholders signing a **disclosure letter**. This will draw attention to issues where the company, directors, or shareholders have not met, or are unlikely to meet, an aspect of a clause in the investor agreement. This disclosure – being open and honest about the situation – means that the investor is fully aware of the facts and cannot pursue the vendors about this issue once the contracts have been signed. *They knew about it at the time of investment/purchase.* However, it is also likely that the investor may seek an indemnity against the liability disclosed.

Investor Agreement, or Sale and Purchase Agreement

This is the document that will cover the purchase of shares by the investor/buyer and the sale of shares by the company or shareholders. The parties to the agreement will be the buyer, the company itself, and the company's shareholders. The terms will be driven by what has been agreed in the term sheet.

Amendments to Articles of Association and Shareholders' Agreement

Documentation will be produced to deal with any required amendments to the articles of association, and, if there is one, to the shareholders' agreement. Again, these changes will be driven by the term sheet. The mechanism for these changes will include board minutes outlining the changes, and a deed of adherence for the new shareholders' agreement (i.e. an agreement by the new shareholders to abide by it).

Any sale of shares to a buyer is likely to have some form of warranties attached. These will be time limited in their scope.

Warranties and Indemnities

The **warranties** can be extensive, particularly if the company has a long trading history. For a start-up investment, these are likely to be simpler. Warranties are effectively guaranteeing that the information provided to the investor/buyer is true in all *material* respects. These will cover the items listed under the due diligence process, i.e. stating that all the information provided is correct, and additionally that no material information has been withheld that could have adversely affected their decision to purchase the shares. If, for example, the directors of the company knew in advance that they were about to lose a major customer, but deliberately withheld this information until after the contracts had been signed, this could be a major breach of a particular warranty. This information would certainly have influenced the investor/buyer's behaviour, who may have sought a lower purchase price or even pulled out completely. This potentially serious breach could then lead to major litigation post sale.

In the example above, if the directors suspected they were about to lose a particular major customer, but were not certain, this fact would feature in the disclosure letter. Consequently, if the customer was then lost, there would be no comeback on them or the shareholders (unless an indemnity had been put in place).

Just as when you buy any consumer product, the warranties are likely to be strictly time limited. If a problem has not been identified within this period, then any liability will lapse. These will typically be for up to three years on most specified items, but could be up to seven years for any undeclared tax liabilities.

The **indemnities** are put in place to deal with specific issues or problems (i.e. those 'skeletons in the cupboard') that have *not* been resolved at the time of sale. These may not necessarily be time limited. These are a guarantee by the vendors (whether this be the directors, the company itself, its shareholders, or all of them) that should the cost of the dispute/problem arise, or be beyond a certain level, then the vendors would pay it. These indemnities are actually very helpful – should a problem exist it may be extremely difficult to quantify the liability, which could range from nothing to millions of pounds. By having a guarantee in place, it can mean the deal can proceed without this liability impinging on the other terms.

Now you are probably wondering what is the mechanism for protecting the investor/buyer in the event of a breach of the warranties or the need to call up an indemnity? This is a good question and can be dealt with by the retention of funds. For example, a proportion of the proceeds may be held back and kept by the lawyers in an escrow account for a period of a year or more. Or the funds may be paid by the investor/buyer in stages rather than on the date of contract. Clearly, any use of these funds to cover a warranty or an indemnity ultimately has to be accepted by both parties, otherwise there is a risk of costly litigation to resolve the dispute.

Notes

1. https://www.cbinsights.com/research/startup-failure-reasons-top/
2. A board observer is someone who can attend board meetings, but does not have a vote nor the same legal responsibilities. Although they would not be able to vote as a director, key issues may require shareholder consent, in which case they may be able to exert substantial influence even with 'observer' status.

PART 6

CAPITAL INVESTMENT APPRAISAL

6.1 INTRODUCING CAPITAL INVESTMENT APPRAISAL

At first glance this may not seem the easiest of topics to understand, but it is well worth the effort to grasp the basic concepts and to be able to apply the principles.

If a business or an individual investor is faced with a number of investment opportunities, it may be difficult to decide which opportunity is the best one to adopt. Whilst there may be numerous issues to consider in making that decision, some of which are not financial, it can be helpful to at least look at the *financial aspects* in a consistent and robust manner.

We will look at the three key methods you can use: **payback period**, **net present value** (NPV) and **internal rate of return** (IRR). The mathematics behind the latter two may appear rather complicated. But you do not need to worry – it is easily done with functions in Excel. What you need to appreciate are the *concepts behind the mathematics*, rather than just the mathematics.

Here are some of the areas where capital investment appraisal is a useful tool:

- Placing a value on a business to either sell or acquire it (including valuing your own business during a funding round).
- Evaluating whether an investment in a new fixed asset (e.g. machinery) is worth doing.
- Helping choose between two different projects, i.e. judging which one offers the best return.

These chapters will build your confidence at understanding all the principles of capital investment appraisal. You should then be able to discuss them intelligently with banks, venture capital funds or professional advisors.

The Interrelationship Between Risk, Return and Time

The first concept to understand is how risk, return and timescale are interrelated.

Risk and Return

If an investor is offered a 5% return on £10,000 of savings by a major UK bank, backed by the Bank of England, they may be delighted with this rate of return. Currently, banks are tending to only pay around 0.5% or less, so 5% would be a high rate of return in today's market.

In this example, the investor is taking almost no risk with the capital invested, because the chances of the Bank of England failing are remote, as the bank is underpinned by the British state. Therefore the 5% return is effectively 'risk-free'. This makes the investment, offering a 5% return, look extremely attractive.

Now let's consider if the loan is being made to a known criminal, who is prepared to offer a 50% rate of interest on the money lent to him. This is ten times the rate of return the bank is offering! *Surely this is a far better investment?* But hopefully, common sense says that no rate of return would be adequate to compensate for this risk. The criminal may be unlikely to repay the capital in the future – not to mention what nefarious activities he might be using the money for!

The greater the risk an investor takes, the larger the return they will expect. The two issues are fundamentally linked.

In this second scenario, however attractive the return appears, it would be wise not to get involved with such an investment. *The simple fact is the risk is too great.*

How about something in between? A reliable friend of yours is doing a property development and trying to raise money. She is offering you a 20% return on your money… is this of interest to you?

The return is 15% greater than the bank is offering risk-free. But there are clearly risks involved in lending her money, as the property development could go wrong and your capital could be lost. Consequently, the extra 15% *premium* you are being offered over the *risk-free rate* may not be adequate for your comfort.

However, if she offered you a legal charge over the assets of the property (i.e. just like a bank receives when granting a mortgage), then the security has been greatly improved. In the event of the development going wrong, you would at least have a right over any remaining value. This will significantly reduce your risk, perhaps now making the 20% return sufficiently attractive to you.

We can see that in all three of these situations the risk exposure is driving the decision on whether or not to invest. *The risk factors involved are fundamentally interrelated to the return being offered.*

We will also introduce the concept of **risk premium** – the amount of expected return we are being offered *in excess* of the *risk-free* return. If this is not sufficiently attractive then we will not be prepared to make the investment.

Finally, consider how business angels view investments. They appreciate they are taking a risk on their investment, but they are prepared to do this in return for correspondingly high returns. If the investment cannot potentially deliver these high returns, they would not be interested.

Return and Time

Anyone investing money would ideally like his or her returns as quickly as possible. This is so they can either spend it or re-invest it in something else.

Banks tend to offer more attractive terms on savings if customers commit their money for longer periods. This, in turn, helps them plan their finances: if they have long-term depositors of money it is easier for them to commit to long-term loans to other customers. In this example, a long-term investment is offering higher rates of return in compensation for the time commitment.

We can see that the length of time investors have to wait for their return, or the time they have to commit their capital, will influence both their decision to invest in the first place and the amount of return they expect back.

This introduces the fundamentally important concept of the **time value of money**: a pound in the hand now (**present value**, or PV) is worth more to a rational investor than a pound to be received in future years (**future value**, or FV).

The longer investors have to wait for a return on their capital, the greater their expectation of overall return will be. The two issues are fundamentally interrelated.

Risk, Return and Time All Together

If we look at a business angel investment, the sophisticated investor will know that the time it takes to build and sell a business is likely to be 5–8 years (very few are likely to do this within 3 years, which is often misleadingly quoted as the exit timetable). Hence it is a long-term investment strategy, but hopefully matched by excellent financial rewards.

However, as we have already established in the case of business angel investment, the timescale is only one part of the decision to invest. The bigger aspect relates to the risk involved. *Can the management team deliver their business plan? What if their product or service is not accepted in the marketplace? What if everything takes much longer than planned and they run out of cash?*

This is a great example of where risk, return and timescales are all interrelated. Business angel investors have to balance these factors in their minds, and inevitably, the riskier and the longer-term nature the investment is, the higher their expectation of return will need to be.

Overview of Appraisal Methods

When a company is faced with an investment decision, many factors will need to be taken into account. For example, if it is considering two acquisition opportunities, one of these may be in their own market sector, whilst the other may be in a new market. Hence there are strategic issues to take into account, which go beyond just financial considerations. A new market is a new opportunity for a business and may deliver exciting future growth opportunities. However, it may be considerably riskier than acquiring a business in a familiar market sector.

Capital investment appraisal does not offer an evaluation on these strategic considerations. It attempts to create a level playing field of *financial information* so that you are comparing like for like taking into account risk and the time value of money. In the case of looking at two different acquisition opportunities, it can attach a value of worth to each one. This allows a clear means of evaluation *from a financial perspective.*

There are three main methods of making this evaluation. They are:

Payback Method

This method looks at how long it takes to get the amount invested back. This is a very simplistic, but also logical, approach. It makes no allowance for the time value of money, nor for risk.

Net Present Value (NPV) Method

This process converts the stream of future cash flows that are associated with the proposed investment (whether positive or negative) into a present value. The future values are discounted at the required rate of return of the investor (this is known as the **discount rate**, and should be based on the company's **cost of capital**). Then if we deduct the initial outlay of the project, this gives us the net present value.

Internal Rate of Return (IRR) Method

This shows the rate of return that a stream of future cash flows yields. Depending on whether this rate is high enough for the investor to cover his or her cost of capital, a decision is then made whether to invest or not. By definition, the NPV will be zero when IRR is used to discount cash flows – a fact that is initially a little confusing. This is explained in further detail below.

Choice of Metric to Use in Appraisal

When using any of the main appraisal methods to evaluate a possible investment or capital project, we must first establish what performance measure we should use.

Should it be operating profit? ... or EBITDA? ... or profit before tax? ... or profit after tax? ... or cash flow from operations? The short answer is none of the above ... at least directly!

In fact, we need to use the projected *marginal,* or incremental, impact of the investment on *cash flow.* What this means in practice depends on the nature of the investment:

- If we are considering buying shares in a company, cash flow is made up of the initial purchase cost of the shares, the subsequent expected dividend flow and the eventual expected sale value.
- If we are considering buying a piece of machinery that we expect will increase output while making cost savings, the cash flow might consist of the initial cost of purchasing the machine, the net impact on operating cash flow (including the expected cost savings), any net impact on working capital, any net impact on tax

payments and any salvage or disposal value (or, indeed, cost) at the end of the machine's viable economic life.

- If we are considering buying an entire business, the relevant impact on cash flow would consist of the initial purchase price (including any deferred payments), projected future **free cash flow** (adjusting for any capital expenditures that may be required, or any cost savings that can be made by combining with existing operations), and the expected future exit value of the business (if appropriate). An explanation of free cash flow can be found in Chapter 4.2.

The free cash flows of a business, or project, are used as the building blocks for capital investment appraisal.

Whatever the scenario, there are two key points to remember:

1. We are only interested in *cash*. Non-cash accounting adjustments such as depreciation can be ignored.
2. We are only interested in the *incremental* cash flow resulting directly from the investment.

Other points to bear in mind are:

- Interest charges that arise from debt incurred to fund the investment should not be used. As you will see in the later section on discount rates, this would mean that this cost is being double-counted.
- We will want to decide the frequency of the time periods used to make the evaluation – monthly, quarterly or annually. A more frequent time period (e.g. monthly) might provide a more nuanced evaluation, but is likely to be very cumbersome in calculation. Annual projections are generally thought to be adequate.
- Expected inflation rate going forward – the figures we use need to be in real terms. More on this later.

Opportunity Cost Concept

Opportunity cost is the term used to describe the situation where there are two or more possible investment opportunities open to a business, but it can only invest in one. Therefore, if it has a choice of doing investments A, B, or C, and decides to do C, it gives up the opportunity of doing investments A or B as alternatives. *They are no longer possible because of this decision.* We can say: '*The opportunity cost of investment C is A and B.*' That is, we cannot do A or B as a consequence of choosing C.

If we can only do one project from a selection of projects available, the opportunity cost of selecting it is the loss of the other potential projects.

Capital investment appraisal is a useful tool in helping to decide between projects. If one has a higher NPV or IRR than another, then we can see that the return from that one is better. If this is our sole measure, then we can be more confident in making the right decision.

Capital Investment Appraisal

- The amount of return an investment will potentially yield, the risks associated with it, and the time it takes to come to fruition are all fundamentally interrelated and of critical importance when appraising investments.
- The three common appraisal methods are payback period, net present value (NPV) and internal rate of return (IRR). They can be used for a variety of appraisals, such as looking at the value of a business based on its future cash flow or for comparing two competing investment projects.
- When evaluating a business investment, we use the free cash flows of the opportunity in our calculations.
- Opportunity cost is the term used to describe the situation where there are two or more possible opportunities that a business can invest in, but it can only invest in one.

6.2 THE PAYBACK METHOD

The **payback method** is a very straightforward method. It answers the question: *How long will it take for me to get my cash back?* This is simple to calculate and extremely logical to consider, but has some serious shortcomings as a capital appraisal method.

Example: Investment in Machinery

A company can invest £500k in a new machine that will save it £100k a year in costs. *What is the payback period on this investment?*

Clearly it is five years. The savings will have paid for the machine in this time period.

This method is easy to use and is a quick 'sanity check'. By this we mean that it is a way of quickly ensuring whether the investment is viable or not – if the payback was 100 years it could be labelled 'insane' instead!

But the method has some very fundamental weaknesses. Firstly, it does not allow for risk or the time value of money. In the example below, we can see three different scenarios of a £500k investment, all with a payback of five years. Do you consider all scenarios to be equal, or is one preferable to all the others?

Cash Flow Projections

			Years			
£'000	0	1	2	3	4	5
Scenario 1						
Initial capital cost	500					
Free cash flows (FCF)	-	100	100	100	100	100
Cumulative FCF	-	**100**	**200**	**300**	**400**	**500**
Scenario 2						
Initial capital cost	500					
Free cash flows (FCF)	-	450	-	-	-	50
Cumulative FCF	-	**450**	**450**	**450**	**450**	**500**
Scenario 3						
Initial capital cost	500					
Free cash flows (FCF)	-	-	-	-	-	500
Cumulative FCF	-	**-**	**-**	**-**	**-**	**500**

Without much effort, we can see that Scenario 2 is superior in the sense that most of the capital is returned by the end of Year 1. Scenario 3 is the least attractive, as we have to wait until the fifth year to get our money back. In fact, all three scenarios are very different from an investment yield viewpoint when taking into account *time*. Yet the payback method tells us they are all equally good! Also, no allowance is made for the possibility that these scenarios may carry different levels of risk and uncertainty, thereby making them more or less attractive.

The payback method also does not take into account the *scale of the investment,* but only looks at how fast the cash is returned. For example, an investment may have a fast payback, which is far superior to other opportunities available to an investor, but the *scale* is very small and hence not of much use.

The payback method simply looks at how long it takes to get the cash back from an investment.

Finally, an alternative investment may have a *higher percentage return on capital,* but a slower payback. For example, it may take ten years to get the capital back, but the subsequent returns are both substantial and long-lasting. An investment in an oil pipeline is a good example of this type of investment: there would be substantial upfront costs – from perhaps over a decade of planning and construction – prior to a single drop of oil being pumped. But, once built and the oil is flowing, the costs of operating are low and the lifespan long. On a time payback basis, it appears unattractive, but the return on capital on a long-term basis may be outstanding.

The Payback Method

- The payback method is simple and logical.
- It does, however, have serious weaknesses: it does not take into account the time value of money, nor risk, nor the scale of investment, nor subsequent returns on capital.

6.3 NET PRESENT VALUE

The Net Present Value Concept

Both net present value and internal rate of return are based on the concept of **discounted cash flow** (DCF).

Let's imagine we are trying to evaluate a proposed new capital project – perhaps a new factory, or a new restaurant, or a new shop, or simply a new machine. We've done all our projections, and produced a nice neat schedule of expected cash flows at different times, starting from now and going forward into the future. Some cash flows are negative, notably the initial outlay, and some are positive. One way to evaluate the economic benefit of these cash flows is to boil them down to a single number that is relevant and meaningful to us right now. *But we can't simply add up all the cash flow figures, can we?* That would produce a meaningless number: some would be in the very near future (or even immediate) and reasonably certain, but others could be way off into the future and highly uncertain. *These are not equivalent to us in terms of value now.*

The net present value calculation attempts to put a single value on a future stream of positive or negative cash flows.

What we need to do, before adding all the cash flows together, is transform them into an equivalent 'now' figure. This 'now' figure would be a *discounted* version of the expected future cash flow number, *such that we would be equally pleased to have either.* In other words, we need to discount our projected cash flows in such a way that we place the same value on receiving the larger, uncertain amount in the future as we would on receiving the smaller discounted amount today – the 'now' figure.

The amount we discount it by will depend on our view of the situation – the less we favour money in the future, the higher the rate we will discount it by. We call this the **discount rate**. This discount rate is usually expressed as an annual percentage, and for businesses, is generally derived from how much it costs them to raise capital – otherwise known as the **cost of capital**. We shall explore how to determine an appropriate rate later in Chapter 6.5.

The 'now' amount that we have calculated is called the **present value**, and because we *net off* all the cash outflows (notably any initial outlay) from all the cash inflows, the resulting single number is called the **net present value** (NPV).

In short, to calculate the net present value of a project, we transform all the associated cash flows – whether positive or negative, *including* the initial investment – into a single figure. If the resulting value, the NPV, is greater than zero, then the investment is yielding a positive return above the chosen discount rate, and will enhance the value of the business. If the NPV comes out as zero, then the return on the project will simply match the company's cost of capital, but no more (in fact, zero NPV has a special role, which will be explored later). On the the other hand, if it is negative, the investment can be expected to deplete shareholder wealth – clearly to be avoided!

The Net Present Value Calculation

The underlying calculation for net present value is as follows:

$$NPV = -C_0 + \frac{C_1}{1+r} + \frac{C_2}{(1+r)^2} + \ldots + \frac{C_n}{(1+r)^n}$$

where:
C_0 = *Initial investment*
C = *Free cash flow**
r = *Discount rate*
n = *Number of time periods*

* for each period (note this can be negative, especially in the early years)

which can be written as:

$$NPV = \sum_{i=1}^{n} \frac{C_i}{(1+r)^i} - C_0$$

where:
i = *the number of each individual time period*

Or expressed very simply:

$$NPV = Present\ Value\ of\ Future\ Cash\ Flows - Initial\ Investment$$

The discount rate ***r*** can also be referred to as the **hurdle rate**, and is usually derived from the company's cost of capital over the timeframe of the investment. The term 'hurdle rate' is more often used when evaluating the internal rate of return (explained in the next chapter).

Back to the above formula: ***n*** refers to the number of time periods that the investment is spread over (often expressed in years, but using months or quarters can provide a more finely tuned answer). A time period must be specified for this methodology to work.

The net free cash flow is the surplus *incremental* cash flow resulting from the investment after taking into account all necessary outflows (for example, capital expenditure, changes in operating expenses, and changes in working capital).

Example: A company is trying to establish the financial benefit of purchasing a new machine, with the following estimated values:

Investment:	£500k
Cost saving:	£100k per annum
Life of machine:	8 years
Final value at end:	£25k

This looks like a good investment, but what is it worth in *today's* terms? This can then be compared to the capital outlay of £500k. We can then see how worthwhile the investment is, both relative to its outlay cost and to alternative investment opportunities. When calculating this, we also need to consider the company's cost of capital. The simple payback method cannot give us this answer except in very crude terms.

The first step in the process is to establish the discount rate. 'Discount' is a very appropriate word because, remember, what we are saying is the money we expect to get in the future is of less value than the money we have today or in the very near future. *We use the discount rate to progressively reduce the value of the future flows.*

The discount rate must reflect what the capital costs us in order to make this investment – either in actual terms (e.g. the interest rate we pay a bank on a loan), or in terms of what opportunities we are giving up as a result – and, also, any associated risks. We will return to the subject of how to calculate or choose a discount rate. But for the moment, let's apply an assumed discount rate to some examples and get to understand the methodology of calculating the NPV of an investment.

At this point, it is worth expanding on what we mean by *incremental* cash flows. When performing a NPV analysis, it is vital to include *only* those cash flows that arise *directly* from the investment. Let's use an example to help clarify this. Imagine we are considering the purchase of a new packing machine to replace an old one. The latter still works well enough but can only deliver a certain level of throughput and is struggling to keep up with the demand. The new machine is slightly bigger than the old one, and will require three trained staff to operate it. It is easily capable of handling the higher levels of demand that the company is experiencing.

What cash flows should we include in our analysis? Is the fact that the machine is slightly bigger going to make a difference? Should we include the cost of employing the three operatives? Will they need retraining? These are all highly pertinent questions that need to be addressed in calculating the NPV. If the factory already has space to absorb the slightly bigger machine, then this has zero impact and can be ignored. If, however, extra space is needed, then the cost of providing this should be included. If the old machine also required three operatives, then the cost of employing them can also be ignored in our NPV analysis because it is not *incremental* (unless they get a pay rise as a result of using the new machine, in which case this should be factored in). However, if the operatives require retraining, then this cost should also be considered. These examples should give you a feel for what is, and what is not, incremental.

Calculating the Net Present Value (NPV)

The best way of calculating the NPV is to use an Excel, or similar, spreadsheet. For simplicity, we will just refer to Excel. Excel allows quick recalculations using different assumptions. You can either write the formulas for each year, which has the advantage of showing the individual discounted figures, or just use the NPV function. This will do everything for you. In the examples below, we have done both.

In the above example of a £500k investment returning £100k per annum for 8 years, we have assumed that the final value of the asset is £25k in the last year of the project. We need the opportunity to put in a final value figure to take into account the fact that there could be value at the end of the project. Clearly this could be zero, but in most cases, there may be a disposal value for the business or asset. Even if we may not actually dispose of the asset at this point, we need to consider what it would be worth. This is usually referred to as the terminal, or final value. This is another estimate we have to make.

Keeping it very simple, let's also assume an overall discount rate of 10% has been chosen. *What does the investment give us back?*

Below is an excerpt from an Excel model which is available for you to download. As with our other Excel models, all the variables are shown in yellow. The user can change these as they wish in order to try out different scenarios. The other numbers are generated from formulas (i.e. if the numbers in the yellow boxes are changed, the figures below them will recalculate).

NPV Method		**2021**	**2022**	**2023**	**2024**	**2025**	**2026**	**2027**	**2028**
Year	0	1	2	3	4	5	6	7	8
Capital Investment:	£500,000								
Discount Rate:	10.0%								
Free Cash Flows		£100,000	£100,000	£100,000	£100,000	£100,000	£100,000	£100,000	£100,000
Final Value									£25,000
Net Cash Flows	(£500,000)	£100,000	£100,000	£100,000	£100,000	£100,000	£100,000	£100,000	£125,000
Discounted Cash Flows	(£500,000)	£90,909	£82,645	£75,131	£68,301	£62,092	£56,447	£51,316	£58,313
NPV:	**£45,155**	<--- This is calculated using Excel's function.							

Note the timeframes. Although calendar years have been put above, the project years run from 0 to 8 in the model. Year 0 is effectively 'now' when we make the investment, and Year 1 is the end of the first year.

The 'Net Cash Flow' line takes into account the initial capital investment, the free cash flow from the project, and the final value at the end of the period. It is this stream of net cash flow that we discount.

The 'Discounted Cash Flows' line shows this stream of net cash flows discounted each year. We can clearly see that the numbers get smaller as the years go on. One year out from the investment, we are saying that £100k is only worth £90.9k, and five years out £100k is only worth £62.1k. These are the 'now' figures referred to above. *We are valuing future money less that money today. We are discounting the cash flow into the future.*

If we add up this stream of discounted cash flows, it comes to £45,155. In fact, in the actual Excel model the 'Discounted Cash Flows' line is superfluous as the NPV function works it out for you from the net cash flows. The figure from this function is shown as the last line – the NPV is £45,155. *But what does this £45,155 mean?*

It is in fact saying: *If you make this investment on the assumptions you have chosen, it should enhance the current value of your business by £45,155 allowing for the 10% cost of capital.* Or put another way: *If the cost of your capital is 10%, then this investment is worth £45,155 in today's values.* Therefore, based purely on this information, it looks like a good investment.

But what if the discount rate was higher, say 15%? This is shown below.

NPV Method		2021	2022	2023	2024	2025	2026	2027	2028
Year	0	1	2	3	4	5	6	7	8
Capital Investment:	£500,000								
Discount Rate:	15.0%								
Free Cash Flows		£100,000	£100,000	£100,000	£100,000	£100,000	£100,000	£100,000	£100,000
Final Value									£25,000
Net Cash Flows	(£500,000)	£100,000	£100,000	£100,000	£100,000	£100,000	£100,000	£100,000	£125,000
Discounted Cash Flows	(£500,000)	£86,957	£75,614	£65,752	£57,175	£49,718	£43,233	£37,594	£40,863
NPV:	**(£43,095)**	<--- This is calculated using Excel's function.							

Firstly, look at the 'Discounted Cash Flows' line. We can see that these numbers are shrinking at a faster rate. *Yes, we are discounting them more, as we are regarding future money as less valuable than we did before.* We are discounting them at 15% each year instead of 10%, so they are going to be smaller.

We can see that the value has come out as –£43,095, i.e. a negative figure. *What does this mean?*

What it is saying is: *If you make this investment on the assumptions you have chosen, it will give you £43,095 below a 15% return.* If you wanted a 15% return on your investment, you would not get it. You would be short by £43,095 in today's values. Therefore, based purely on this information, it looks like a poor investment. But it is only 'poor' in the context that it will not deliver you a 15% return… it will give you a return, but it is short of a 15% return by £43,095 in today's values.

But put another way: If the cost of your capital is 15%, then you will lose £43,095 from this investment in today's values. Clearly in that context it would be a poor investment.

Why might you want a 15% return, rather than the 10% from the earlier example? The answer could be that either you perceive more risk than the earlier example, or you are more averse to risk, or the cost of your capital is higher as a result of higher interest rates, or a combination of the these. Either way you are placing a lower value on the future cash flows and consequently the investment in today's values.

An Important Note About the Way Excel 'Thinks'

It should be noted here that the Excel NPV function assumes that all the cash flows occur at the *end* of each period. In the real world, this is unlikely and effectively understates net present value (potentially by a significant amount). If a higher frequency period than a year is used (e.g. monthly), then this is not really an issue. There are, however, easy workarounds for yearly periods that can address this – you can simply average out the free cash flows between two years creating an effective 'mid-year' point. An example of how to do this is shown in the spreadsheet.

Further details on how to create this model in Excel are shown in Appendix 3. It is also easy to adapt the downloadable spreadsheet model.

What If the NPV Is Zero?

In the above examples, a 10% discount rate return yields a positive NPV value (i.e. additional wealth in excess of a 10% return), whilst a 15% discount rate leaves us with a negative NPV. So surely at some point between 10% and 15% there would be a rate that would produce a zero NPV? At a *zero* NPV the investment would be giving exactly that percentage return... and we know it must be between 10% and 15% in the above example.

Why don't we just work out what this figure is in the first place? Well, we can and it's called the **internal rate of return** (IRR). We will look at this in the next chapter.

Confusion Between Present Value and Net Present Value

Before we move on to the IRR, it is worth highlighting the common confusion between **present value** (PV) and **net present value** (NPV). Sometimes a present value is mistakenly referred to as a net present value.

Present value is the value of a future cash flow, or stream of cash flows. Net present value is the present value of projected inflows *net of* the present value of projected outflows (most notably the initial investment) for a particular investment project.

Example: A company is offered for sale at £20m. Analysis of the free cash flows using a suitable discount rate shows these are worth £22m

The present value is therefore £22m. If you were to buy the company, i.e. outlay £20m, then the net present value would be the difference, £2m. You may hear of someone saying *'The NPV is £22m'*. Well it's not – that's the PV!

Remember the formula from above:

$$NPV = \sum_{i=1}^{n} \frac{C_i}{(1+r)^i} - C_0$$

In the example above this is:

$$NPV = £22m - £20m = £2m.$$

An Enhanced Version of NPV

An enhanced version of the NPV approach, called the **First Chicago Method**, still uses the discounted cash flow model described at the beginning of this chapter to determine a net present value. However, instead of just one set of projections, a number – usually three – are produced: a *base case* scenario; a *downside*; and an *upside*. An estimated probability is then assigned to each of these, which are then multiplied through and added up to create a probability-weighted NPV.

This approach has the benefit of being less dependent on the need for a high discount rate to deal with the uncertainties of the investment and is particularly useful for start-up and early-stage businesses where a stable pattern of positive cash flow has not yet been established. For this reason, it is widely used in venture capital and private equity circles.

To demonstrate, let's take as our base case the example used above with a discount rate of 10%. For the downside case, we shall assume the future cash inflows will be 20% *lower*, and, for the upside case, 20% *higher*. This will produce three different NPVs, to which we can then assign estimated probabilities as per the table below:

	NPV	**Probabilities**	**Probability Weighted Outcomes**
	£		£
Downside case	(61,543)	25%	(15,386)
Base case	45,155	60%	27,093
Upside case	142,524	15%	21,379
Totals		**100%**	**33,086**

As you can see, the investment is still indicating a positive return. But, what if we had been feeling the need to use the higher rate of 15% to allow for these uncertainties? Well, we wouldn't need to because we have already provided for them in this method. As a result, this more nuanced approach shows a green light to go ahead with the investment, as opposed to the red light suggested by just the base case discounted at the higher rate.

Net Present Value

- The net present value (NPV) calculation attempts to give the net value of an investment in today's figures after taking into account the cost of capital.
- To do this calculation, we discount the free cash flows, placing an increasingly lower value on the cash flows furthest in the future. The amount we discount the future cash flows by is known as the discount rate.
- The NPV of an investment project is the present value of the future cash inflows less present value of projected outflows, notably the initial outlay of the investment.
- The calculation of NPV is relatively straightforward (though somewhat cumbersome if done manually), but can also be done using an Excel function.
- The First Chicago Method is an enhanced version of NPV to deal with outcome uncertainties by using probability-weighted scenarios.

6.4 INTERNAL RATE OF RETURN

We use the **internal rate of return** (IRR) method to calculate an investment project's overall rate of return. More technically, it is the effective annualised compounded rate of return from an investment, expressed as a percentage. With this information, we can then decide whether or not it is good enough for us to proceed with the investment. For example, if the IRR of a project was 7%, but our expectation of a decent return was 20%, then this project is not for us and would be rejected.

The reason it is termed 'internal' rate of return, as opposed to just 'rate of return', is that it is a 'self-contained' calculation based solely on the financial projections. Other factors, such as cost of capital, interest rates, risk factors, inflation, etc., are not considered.

Calculating the IRR

The first thing to digest is the potentially confusing fact that, by definition, the NPV of an investment project will be equal to zero if its projected cash flows are discounted at the internal rate of return. This is both the very definition of IRR and is how it is calculated.

Whilst at first sight, this may seem hard to grasp, it is worth mastering the underlying logic. When we looked at the examples in the previous chapter, of using both a 10% and 15% discount rate, we got two different NPV figures:

Discount Rate	NPV
10%	£ 45,155
15%	£ (43,095)

At some point between the 10% and 15% we will get an NPV of zero. It is in fact at 12.4%. Plug that into the Excel spreadsheet, and the NPV will be zero.

What this is saying is: *Using the assumptions you have chosen, this investment will give you a 12.4% return on your capital.*

Or put another way: *At a 12.4% discount rate the investment is neutral in terms of value. It neither creates nor destroys any additional wealth beyond 12.4%.*

Or try this: *If the cost of capital is 12.4%, then this investment yields no value. It does not create or destroy any wealth.*

All these statements are valid; they just look at it in slightly different ways.

Again, let's return to the NPV formula:

$$NPV = \sum_{i=1}^{n} \frac{C_i}{(1+r)^i} - C_0$$

where:
C_0 = *Initial investment*
C = *Free cash flow*
r = *Discount rate*
n = *Number of time periods*
i = *The number of each individual time period*

To calculate IRR using this formula, we would set NPV equal to zero. We know the value of ***n***, so, in theory, we can calculate ***r***. However, ***r*** cannot be calculated analytically – it has to be done by trial and error, otherwise known to mathematicians as a reiterative calculation. In other words, start with a guess, run it through the formula, see if it gives the zero NPV that you're looking for; if not, revise the guess and start again – clearly a job for the computer! Unlike calculating NPV, which is relatively easy to do manually, this calculation is best left to our good friend Excel to sort out.

Using the IRR function in Excel, we can do the following calculation:

IRR Method		**2021**	**2022**	**2023**	**2024**	**2025**	**2026**	**2027**	**2028**
Year	0	1	2	3	4	5	6	7	8
Capital Investment:	£500,000								
Free Cash Flows		£100,000	£100,000	£100,000	£100,000	£100,000	£100,000	£100,000	£100,000
Final Value									£25,000
Net Cash Flows	(£500,000)	£100,000	£100,000	£100,000	£100,000	£100,000	£100,000	£100,000	£125,000
Discounted Cash Flows	(£500,000)	£88,981	£79,176	£70,452	£62,688	£55,781	£49,634	£44,165	£49,123
IRR:	**12.4%**	<--- If this IRR figure is used as the Discount Rate, the NPV will always be zero!							

We can see that the IRR comes out at 12.4%, and if you add up the 'Discounted Cash Flows' line, they will come to zero. Note the 'Discounted Cash Flows' line is shown purely for interest and understanding, and is not required by Excel's IRR function.

Incidentally, you may notice that the IRR function in Excel has two inputs. The first is the array of numbers representing the cash flows – obviously essential. The second is the initial guess, which we referred to above. For Excel, this is optional because, if omitted, Excel simply assumes 10%, which, in most cases, will do the job.

The Hurdle Rate

As stated above, the IRR calculation is effectively saying: *If you make this investment on the assumptions you have chosen, it will give 12.4% return on your investment.* We then may ask: *Well, is this a good investment or not?*

And the answer is actually quite simple: *It depends on what level of return you require. If you require a 15% return, it is not a good investment for you. But if you require a 10% return it is a good investment for you.*

This is where the term **'hurdle rate'** – also known as the **required rate of return** – comes in. Just like in a hurdle race, a 'good' or 'bad' outcome depends on whether the runner can jump the hurdle. If the runner cannot get over the bar that has been set, she has failed in the context of that particular race. The outcome can be deemed to be a 'bad' one. On the other hand, if she jumps the hurdles and goes on to win the race, then the outcome would be described as a 'good' one.

A business can set a hurdle height – or hurdle rate – over which the investment has to 'jump' (i.e. exceed) to be worth pursuing. Inevitably, the higher the investment jumps over this hurdle, the better. The riskier the project is, the more likely the hurdle will be set higher. Just as determining the discount rate for an investment is a challenge, the same difficulties apply to the choice of the hurdle rate.

(Getty Images/Image Source/ Pete Saloutos)

The hurdle rate is the minimum required return expected from an investment. It has to jump over this level.

For most intents and purposes, the hurdle rate is likely to equal the discount rate, as used to calculate NPV. We can say: '*Unless we receive an IRR of at least 20% (our hurdle rate), we will not make the investment as the return is insufficient*', which is effectively the same as saying: '*If a Discount Rate of 20% produces a NPV of less than zero, the project is not producing sufficient value to be of interest to us.*' We can start to see that the NPV and IRR methods are effectively applying the same underlying logic, but approached from different angles.

Modified Internal Rate of Return

The IRR capital appraisal methodology has a number of weaknesses. One of these is that it assumes any surplus cash flows generated in each of the periods are reinvested at the IRR rate of return of the project. In our IRR example above, it would mean that the £100k of free cash flow generated in Year 1 would be reinvested for the remaining 8 years at a return of 12.4%. In reality, this may be misleading, as the investment project does not need these funds – they are a surplus. So they would need to be reinvested elsewhere, perhaps at a completely different rate of return. This can result in a distorted assessment of the project's profitability.

The **modified internal rate of return** (MIRR) is an alternative approach to IRR and is likely to produce a more meaningful figure, or at least one with fewer biases. Once again, Excel offers an MIRR function, so it is not necessary to revert to the actual mathematical formula.

MIRR Method		**2021**	**2022**	**2023**	**2024**	**2025**	**2026**	**2027**	**2028**
Year	0	1	2	3	4	5	6	7	8
Cost of Capital:	6%								
Reinvestment Rate:	6%								
Capital Investment:	£500,000								
Free Cash Flows		£100,000	£100,000	£100,000	£100,000	£100,000	£100,000	£100,000	£100,000
Final Value									£25,000
Net Cash Flows	(£500,000)	£100,000	£100,000	£100,000	£100,000	£100,000	£100,000	£100,000	£125,000
MIRR:	**9.3%**	<--- This is calculated using Excel's function.							

The above screenshot shows the same FCFs using the MIRR methodology. Note we also have two new inputs to consider:

- **Cost of capital:** this is how much the funding is costing for the project.[1]
- **Reinvestment rate:** this is the assumed annualised rate of return we will receive on the surplus FCFs when invested elsewhere.

Note we have chosen to put the same rates for the cost of capital as the reinvestment rate – a reasonable, conservative assumption. The latter could, of course, be higher or lower than the cost of capital, and the Excel model caters for either scenario. For clarity, in our example, we are saying: *All the positive free cash flows generated by the project over the 8-year period will only be reinvested at a rate of 6% per annum.* This contrasts to the IRR model, which assumes we will receive a 12.4% return on this money. The MIRR comes out at 9.3%, as opposed to 12.4%, and is arguably a more realistic figure.

There is a further benefit of the MIRR methodology. The IRR calculation struggles to cope with negative FCFs after the initial outlay. If these alternate, for example, between positive and negative figures, the resulting IRR figure may be ambiguous or even meaningless. The MIRR calculation can cope with these fluctuations, and hence is a more robust methodology.[2]

Internal Rate of Return

- The internal rate of return (IRR) is the effective annualised compounded rate of return from an investment, expressed as a percentage. The term 'internal' comes from the fact that the calculation is based solely on the financial projections – other factors, such as cost of capital, interest rates, etc., are not factored in.
- By definition, the net present value (NPV) of an investment will be zero if discounted at its IRR.
- The hurdle rate is the minimum level of IRR that an investment must achieve in order for it to be deemed worthwhile.
- Unlike NPV, the calculation of IRR is extremely complex, and best left to an Excel function.
- Modified internal rate of return (MIRR) offers a less complex, arguably more robust, alternative approach.

Notes

1. Also known as the finance rate, which is the term used by Excel.
2. It should, however, be noted that both the IRR and MIRR calculations require at least one negative cash flow number – most likely the initial outlay – to work properly.

6.5 ESTABLISHING THE DISCOUNT RATE

In the previous chapters, we have looked at the methodologies for calculating net present value (NPV) and internal rate of return (IRR or MIRR). We have seen how using different discount rates will affect the NPV calculation for the same set of projected cash flows. *But how do we decide what discount rate should be used in the first place?*

We also illustrated how we can set a hurdle rate in the case of the IRR (or MIRR) calculation, which is the level of percentage return that a prospective investment must exceed (or 'jump') in order to be deemed worthwhile. *But how do we determine at what level this hurdle should be set?*

The answers to both these questions are effectively the same.

Factors Which Will Influence the Discount (or Hurdle) Rate

Numerous factors can influence the discount rate or hurdle rate chosen. These are summarised below:

- **Opportunity cost:** if investors have plenty or other opportunities available to them, all with a similar risk profile, they may be more demanding in their expectations (i.e. set a higher 'hurdle' to jump).
- **Risk:** the greater the risk involved in the investment itself, the higher the expected return is required to be.
- **Time:** the longer the investor has to wait for a return, the more demanding they are likely to be in their expectations of return.
- **Prevailing interest rates:** the higher the prevailing interest rates are, the greater the cost of both borrowing and equity will be.
- **General economic sentiment:** if the economic outlook is looking uncertain, investors may be more demanding in their expectations. Effectively this is just another aspect of risk, but at a macro level.

It is worth noting that the discount rate may be very different for a company as opposed to an investor, such as a venture capital fund. The company may also use a company-wide rate, reflecting the cost of its borrowing and shareholder expectations, or use a specific rate for an individual investment project. The latter may apply, for example, if it was a potentially high-risk investment.

To establish a suitable discount rate, we also need to take into account the capital structure of the company – that is, how much of its capital is funded by debt and how much by equity. From the relative weighting of these two sources of capital, we can calculate what is known as the **weighted average cost of capital** (WACC).

Having established the cost of the debt funding, and the cost of the equity funding, we simply apply the rates in proportion to the amount of debt and equity. So, let's now explore how we can determine the cost of these two distinct components, which, when combined, give us the total cost of capital and the figure we use for the discount rate.

The Cost of Debt Funding

The cost of debt is simply the average interest rate paid to banks or other lenders. A minor complication is that interest is deductible against corporation tax. This is known as the **tax shield** and needs to be factored in. Expressed as an equation, therefore, a company's cost of debt can be calculated as:

$$Cost\ of\ Debt(\%) = Average\ Interest\ Rate \times (1 - Tax\ Rate)$$

For example, if the company had borrowed from the bank at an interest rate of 6.25%, and the corporation tax rate was 20%, then the cost of the debt funding would be 5%.

It is important to note that this is only ever a *component* of the overall cost of capital, and, hence, the discount rate. Even if heavily funded by debt, a business enterprise will always have at least some equity component. A bank is most unlikely to lend without a **debenture** in place giving it security in case of a default on the terms of the loan. Under these circumstances, only a small part of the risk is being borne by the bank – all of the *residual* risk would be borne by the shareholders. Failure to repay the loan would have consequences for them.

The Cost of Equity Funding

Determining the cost of equity is more complicated since we need to consider the *expectation of return* for the shareholders, or investors.

Shareholders are taking a risk with their money, and anyone who takes a risk is expecting a return on their capital large enough to compensate them for that risk. *The riskier the investment, the greater the return they will expect.* In the case of debt, we have a clear cost – the interest rate charged by the bank. However, in the case of equity it is far more subjective because of this expectation of a return. If your mind is asking what this figure should be – well, that's a very good question!

Calculating a suitable discount rate when the funding is from equity is not easy. The reward shareholders expect for taking a risk is often just a matter of opinion.

The required level of return for any *individual* investor is a matter of subjective judgement. It should incorporate their own personal assessment of:

- **Their ability to tolerate risk:** the less tolerance to risk an investor has, the higher a premium they will require.

- **The riskiness of the investment**: if it is perceived to be risky, the investor will expect a higher level of return in compensation for having taken the higher risk.
- **Opportunity cost**: the availability of other opportunities, which would include being able to deposit their money in a bank for an entirely risk-free rate of interest.

At first glance you might think the first two above are the same point – they most definitely are not. For example, an investor may be very tolerant to risk, but still demand a high premium for a particularly risky venture. Alternatively, a very risk-averse investor may demand a high premium for undertaking a relatively low-risk investment. At the end of the day it will very much boil down to an opinion, for example: *'For the risk I am taking I expect to receive a 25% return on my investment.'*

If you are interested in exploring more technical ways of determining the discount rate, considering the expectations of return and risk, you could look at the Capital Asset Pricing Model. This is widely used by companies, but is beyond the scope of this book.

Establishing the Discount Rate for Combination of Debt and Equity Funding

Formulating the cost of capital, and hence the discount rate, for a company funded by a combination of debt and equity is not that difficult once you have already established both the cost of debt and cost of equity, as shown above. As previously explained, we apply the rates in proportion to the amount of debt and equity to give us the weighted average cost of capital:

$$\frac{Cost\ of\ Debt \times Debt\ Funding}{Total\ Capital} + \frac{Cost\ of\ Equity \times Equity\ Funding}{Total\ Capital} = WACC$$

The first element of the formula works out the cost of the proportion of the total capital that is funded by bank debt (or other forms of interest-bearing debt). The second element of the above formula works out the cost of the proportion of the total capital that is funded by equity (i.e. shareholders' funds). The two added together give the WACC, which we could use as the discount rate taking this mix of funding into account.

Example: A company's total capital of £500k consists of £200k of bank debt and £300k of equity

The cost of debt (taking into account the tax shield) is 5% and the cost of equity as indicated by investors' expectations (or the Capital Asset Pricing Model if used) is 20%.

We can therefore calculate the overall discount rate (i.e. the weighted average cost of capital) as follows:

$$\frac{5\% \times £200k}{£500k} + \frac{20\% \times £300k}{£500k} = 0.02 + 0.12 = 14\%$$

The left-hand part of the equation says: '*Our borrowings are costing us 5% on the £200k we owe, after taking into account the tax shield.*'

The next portion of the formula effectively says: '*For the £300k of shareholders' money being risked, a total return of at least 20% is required.*'

Combined together, we can see that the overall cost of capital is 14%. This is the discount rate that we will use in our NPV calculation. We are saying: '*This is what the capital costs us overall, taking into account the mixture of debt and equity funding.*'[1]

Impact of Gearing on the Weighted Average Cost of Capital

Assuming that the cost of debt is always lower than the cost of equity, it would seem that the greater the proportion of debt within the WACC equation, the lower the WACC would *theoretically* become. However, as we established above, no matter how high the debt component gets, there is *always* an equity component and all or most of the burden of risk ultimately falls on the shareholders. As a result, the higher the gearing in a business (i.e. the debt to equity ratio), the greater the risk will be to the equity element. Consequently, the expectation of return demanded by shareholders can rise exponentially, making the cost of the equity element increasingly higher.

For example, an investor may be happy with a 20% return on their capital for a business with no debt. However, should the business decide to borrow £1m from the bank, for which their equity capital is ultimately liable, their expectations of return may jump to 50%. *The equity is effectively now more expensive.*

There are mathematical models that can be used to calculate this effect, including the Capital Asset Pricing Model mentioned above. However, at the end of the day there has to be a level of judgement weighing up all the factors outlined above in order to determine the suitable discount rate.

When a Higher Discount Rate Leads to a Higher NPV

Can you think of a situation where a higher discount rate could counter-intuitively produce a *higher* NPV? This is not supposed to happen because, as we've now learned, the higher discount rate should set a higher bar to compensate for risk, not lower it!

There is such a situation though (fortunately a reasonably unusual one), and this is something to be aware of when applying the NPV method. If the project carries a substantial exit cost, then the higher the discount rate, the less significant that cost becomes in the NPV calculation, thus inflating present value. Examples of projects where this might occur could include a nuclear power station or oil drilling operation where there will be substantial decommissioning costs at the end of the facility's economic life. By applying a higher discount rate, we are, of course, reducing the size of this final financial obligation in present value terms. The sensible approach to resolve this situation would be to apply a lower discount rate to this final element of the cash flow, i.e. the negative residual value.

Establishing the Discount Rate

- A company's, or an investor's, choice of discount rate will be influenced by many factors. These include the availability of alternative investments (opportunity cost); the risks involved; the timescale of the investment; whether it is funded by debt or equity, or a combination of both; and the prevailing rate of interest.
- To determine a suitable discount rate, we need to calculate the weighted average cost of capital (WACC). This is derived from the proportion of funding from debt, and the proportion from equity.
- The cost of debt is simply the rate of interest charged by the lenders, net of the tax shield. The cost of equity is harder to determine, but is primarily based on investor expectations.

Note

1. As a real-life example of the practical use of the weighted average cost of capital, observant readers may recall from Chapter 3.4 that easyJet use a rate of 9.4% to calculate the value of goodwill in their balance sheet.

6.6 APPLICATIONS OF CAPITAL INVESTMENT APPRAISAL

Perhaps the first question to ask before applying capital investment appraisal techniques is: which method is the best one to use? All the methods have their merits and in some cases considerable limitations. Understanding these will help us answer this question.

Payback Method Limitations

As we learnt in Chapter 6.2, just because an investment pays back faster in terms of time does not make it necessarily the best investment. The payback method does not consider the scale of the investment, nor the potential long-term return on capital. A small investment giving a small return very quickly may be considerably inferior to a longer-term investment that returns more money in pounds. Clearly using the payback method as the sole measuring criteria is flawed.

IRR Method Limitations

The IRR method can be misleading when comparing two or more investment opportunities with either: very different *scales* in terms of value; or very different *time horizons* over which the project is expected to run.

Scale of Investment

Imagine you have £1m that you need to invest. Project A will need all of that money and it looks like it will deliver a very satisfactory IRR of 30%. Project B requires just a quarter of that money and is expected to generate an even better 35% IRR.

On the face of it, using IRR comparison, Project B is the obviously better option. However, you might be left scratching your head about what to do with the rest of the money – you might only be able to invest this in a bank at a 2% return! *In this case Project A might well be the better option after all.* You would want to consider which project is best in the context of both your total capital budget – how much money you have to invest – and what other investment opportunities may be coming up in the near future.

Just as with the payback method, the IRR Method does not take into account monetary value in terms of pounds. *It is a percentage return, not a value return.*

Duration of Investments

To compare two projects using IRR methodology, they must be of the *same, or similar, time duration* for an effective comparison to be made.

For example, if Project C had an IRR of 20% and was completed within 2 years, it would not be comparable to Project D which had a 15% IRR over a 5-year period. Project C may appear to be 'better', but the return of 20% is only for 2 years. To compare it to Project D we would have to know what would be done with the capital at the end of the 2 years. *How would it then be invested, and what IRR would it yield during years 3 to 5?* Clearly re-investing your capital at the end of the project may not get the same level of return.

In both of these examples, the problem is called the **reinvestment risk**, and is not addressed by the IRR method.

Bias Towards Earlier Returns

Even within the project's own timeframe, IRR does not address the issue of how the cash flows are reinvested as they arise. In fact, the implicit assumption is that they are reinvested at the same rate as the project's IRR. In the case of an investment that is expected to generate a high rate of return with early positive cash flows, this could be highly misleading and creates an unrealistic bias towards early returns.

The modified internal rate of return (MIRR) method addresses this issue, as explained in Chapter 6.4.

Other Issues

Because of its rather clumsy reiterative method of calculation, IRR also raises some other issues in practical use. It only produces a meaningful result if cash flows conform to the standard pattern of *out*flows at or near the start of the project followed by a series of *in*flows. However, if there are no outflows (an investor's dream – unlikely but not impossible!), it simply will not work at all. Also, in a long-term project with cash flows that fluctuate between positive and negative, IRR can produce ambiguous or meaningless results. NPV is not affected by either of these issues, and MIRR can cope with any mix of cash flows so long as there is at least one outflow.

MIRR, on the other hand, requires – and is sensitive to – additional assumptions about financing and reinvestment rates of return.

NPV Method Is Most Reliable

Although not without its own issues, the NPV method is widely regarded as the most robust, especially when applied in conjunction with IRR or MIRR.

It is a powerful technique for assessing the likely enhancement (or dilution) of shareholder value, in monetary terms, as a result of investment in any capital project. If one project is very small, and the other very large, the values in terms of pounds will show clearly.

NPV and IRR are like two sides of the same coin. You are just looking at the same object from different perspectives.

If in doubt, use this method, but in effect NPV and IRR are just different sides of the same discounted cash flow modelling coin, i.e. you are just looking at the same thing from different angles. There is no reason why both methods cannot be used in any capital project appraisal.

That said, if the project you are considering involves heavy exit costs (e.g. decommissioning) please remember the point at the end of Chapter 6.5 about how this can distort the NPV calculation.

The main issue when using NPV methodology is that the calculation is dependent on, and highly sensitive to, the application of an appropriate discount rate. This is especially challenging in the uncertain environment of a start-up or early-stage business. The enhanced approach to NPV used in the First Chicago Method deals more robustly with the issue of uncertain projection assumptions.

A Word About Inflation

When using capital investment appraisal tools, it is usual practice to assume future free cash flows are in today's prices. In other words, you do not adjust the future figures for the effects of inflation. This means that any NPV figures are consistent with today's values, and the discount rate would then be a real (as opposed to nominal) target rate of return.

If you are presented with nominal figures (i.e. including the effect of inflation) and you intend to do a discounted cash flow, you must firstly adjust them to bring them into real values. You would then discount these adjusted figures, which are all in today's prices. If you did not do this, the data would be inconsistent and the calculated NPV or IRR would be of dubious value.

Powerful Uses of Discounted Cash Flow Modelling

In the previous examples, we have looked at straightforward project investments. Let's look at some other examples of applications where DCF methodology is very powerful.

Company and Share Price Valuations

DCF is undoubtedly a very powerful tool when determining whether a share price is a 'good' or 'poor' value at its present price on the stock market – in other words, is it mispriced? In theory, the share price of a public company should represent the sum of discounted future dividends – *but in theory only!*

By forecasting the free cash flows and terminal value of a company's operating business into the future, and using a chosen discount rate, it is possible to establish the present value of the business.[1] Dividing the resulting value by the number of shares in issue will give us the present value per share. If this is materially different from the quoted share price, then there is an indication as to whether the shares are worth buying or should be sold.

Whilst assumptions again have to be made, the ability to forecast the future earnings of major corporations is a great deal easier than for smaller, more speculative, investments/projects. This is because a great deal of financial data is published by the companies for just this type of purpose, and their scale generally makes their trading less volatile than a small business, and hence more predictable. A suitable discount rate also has to be chosen, but despite these constraints, this methodology, if applied well, is a powerful tool in evaluating potential acquisitions, or other equity investments.

Evaluating an Angel Investment – Vulpine Performance Ltd

In October 2015, Vulpine Performance Limited launched a crowdfunding round on the platform Crowdcube. The business had originally started in 2012 and we were early-stage investors in the business.

The Crowdcube round set a pre-money valuation of the business at exactly £5m. Having witnessed the company miss many of its previous sales and profit forecasts, we thought it would be interesting to do an NPV calculation to see whether this figure was justified or not. However, based on our experience to that point, we had no intention of investing further funds ourselves. We were merely watching with interest.

We built a model in Excel which used *their numbers* from *their prospectus* for the next few years, and then made relatively modest projections for the remaining years to take us out 10 years in total. To make the model flexible we created variable inputs for the sales growth and gross margin – this would allow us to see what happened if we put in more modest expectations. These variables are shown in the yellow cells in the excerpt of the model below:[2]

Vulpine Performance Ltd Investment Appraisal											
	2014/15 Last Actual	**2015/16** Year 1	**2016/17** Year 2	**2017/18** Year 3	**2018/19** Year 4	**2019/20** Year 5	**2020/21** Year 6	**2021/22** Year 7	**2022/23** Year 8	**2023/24** Year 9	**2024/25** Year 10
Assumptions											
Sales Growth		*32%*	*93%*	*60%*	*40%*	*30%*	*20%*	*10%*	*10%*	*10%*	*10%*
Gross Margin	*31%*	*50%*	*52%*	*53%*	*53%*	*53%*	*53%*	*53%*	*53%*	*53%*	*53%*
Profit & Loss											
Total Sales	£ 995,590	£ 1,311,271	£ 2,528,500	£ 4,045,600	£ 5,663,840	£ 7,362,992	£ 8,835,590	£ 9,719,149	£ 10,691,064	£ 11,760,171	£ 12,936,188
Net Profit After Tax	£ (301,938)	£ (222,394)	£ 233,879	£ 479,650	£ 572,042	£ 672,676	£ 810,312	£ 892,408	£ 938,722	£ 1,084,904	£ 1,196,741
Free Cash Flow from Operations		**£ (191,872)**	**£ 96,100**	**£ 168,406**	**£ 301,157**	**£ 423,209**	**£ 546,277**	**£ 232,675**	**£ 810,742**	**£ 896,616**	**£ 991,078**
NPV Analysis											
Discount Rate	25%										
Terminal Value P/E Ratio	12										
Terminal Value	£ 14,360,891										
Year	0	1	2	3	4	5	6	7	8	9	10
Cash Flow from Operations		£ (191,872)	£ 96,100	£ 168,406	£ 301,157	£ 423,209	£ 546,277	£ 732,675	£ 810,742	£ 896,616	£ 991,078
Cash Flow Adjusted for Timing	£ (95,936)	£ (47,886)	£ 132,253	£ 234,781	£ 362,183	£ 484,743	£ 639,476	£ 771,708	£ 853,679	£ 943,847	£ 495,539
Discounted Cash Flows	**£ (95,936)**	**£ (38,309)**	**£ 84,642**	**£ 120,208**	**£ 148,350**	**£ 158,841**	**£ 167,635**	**£ 161,839**	**£ 143,224**	**£ 126,681**	**£ 53,208**
	Pre-Funding Round										
Present Value	**£ 2,510,000**										
Post-Money Valuation	**£ 5,500,000**										
Net Present Value	**£ (2,990,000)**										

We assumed a discount rate of 25%, which we felt would be reasonable for an angel investor taking a risk. We also assumed the business would have a **P/E ratio** of 12 at the end of the period (see Chapter 2.7 for explanation of this ratio).

The resulting figures were somewhat disappointing – the investment would fall well short of the desired return:

$$NPV = \sum_{i=1}^{n} \frac{C_i}{(1+r)^i} - Initial\ Investment$$

$$= £2,510,000 - £5,000,000 - £500,000$$

$$= -£2,990,000$$

In other words, if you bought the company for the £5m pre-money valuation, invested the £500k requested, based on the above assumptions in the model, you would be nearly £3m short of a 25% return. In reality, each new Crowdcube shareholder would purchase a piece of this wealth-destruction in proportion to the number of shares they purchased. Note that this is wealth-destruction entirely in the context of expecting a 25% return.

The internal rate of return is actually 14.5%, hence if your 'hurdle' had been 25% it would not have met your wealth-building expectations. *Assuming Vulpine's figures to be accurate*, this *would* give the Crowdcube shareholders a return on their investment, but not a very exciting one when considering the risks that they were taking.

Vulpine's History of Poor Performance

As described above, the management had a poor history of meeting its financial forecasts, and consequently we felt that the figures presented to the prospective shareholders could be over-optimistic. For the year 2016–17 they were forecasting a 93% growth in sales, as well as a 52% gross margin. As you can see from the 2014–15 actual figures, their historical gross margin had been 31% and sales growth was only forecast to be 32% for 2015–16.

We decided to put in some lower forecasts that we thought were achievable. We reduced the immediate years ahead to a growth rate of 30% and reduced the gross margin to 45%. This is how the model then looked:

Vulpine Performance Ltd Investment Appraisal											
	2014/15 Last Actual	**2015/16** Year 1	**2016/17** Year 2	**2017/18** Year 3	**2018/19** Year 4	**2019/20** Year 5	**2020/21** Year 6	**2021/22** Year 7	**2022/23** Year 8	**2023/24** Year 9	**2024/25** Year 10
Assumptions											
Sales Growth		*32%*	*30%*	*30%*	*30%*	*30%*	*20%*	*10%*	*10%*	*10%*	*10%*
Gross Margin	*31%*	*45%*	*45%*	*45%*	*45%*	*45%*	*45%*	*45%*	*45%*	*45%*	*45%*
Profit & Loss											
Total Sales	£ 995,590	£ 1,311,271	£ 1,704,652	£ 2,216,048	£ 2,880,862	£ 3,745,121	£ 4,494,145	£ 4,943,560	£ 5,437,916	£ 5,981,707	£ 6,579,878
Net Profit After Tax	£ (301,938)	£ (292,901)	£ 37,745	£ 74,697	£ 74,178	£ 103,634	£ 129,861	£ 145,112	£ 162,896	£ 183,196	£ 206,062
Free Cash Flow from Operations		**£ (262,379)**	**£ 88,517**	**£ (65,972)**	**£ (75,699)**	**£ (79,973)**	**£ (27,375)**	**£ 49,458**	**£ 60,404**	**£ 72,444**	**£ 85,689**
NPV Analysis											
Discount Rate	25%										
Terminal Value P/E Ratio	12										
Terminal Value	£ 2,472,744										
Year	0	1	2	3	4	5	6	7	8	9	10
Cash Flow from Operations		£ (262,379)	£ 88,517	£ (65,972)	£ (75,699)	£ (79,973)	£ (27,375)	£ 49,458	£ 60,404	£ 72,444	£ 85,689
Cash Flow Adjusted for Timing	£ (131,190)	£ (86,931)	£ 11,273	£ (70,835)	£ (77,836)	£ (53,674)	£ 11,042	£ 54,931	£ 66,424	£ 79,066	£ 42,844
Discounted Cash Flows	**£ (131,190)**	**£ (69,545)**	**£ 7,215**	**£ (36,268)**	**£ (31,882)**	**£ (17,588)**	**£ 2,894**	**£ 11,520**	**£ 11,144**	**£ 10,612**	**£ 4,600**
	Pre-Funding Round										
Present Value	**£ (30,000)**										
Post-Money Valuation	**£ 5,500,000**										
Net Present Value	**£ (5,530,000)**										

We can see that using a 25% discount rate, the negative NPV rises to -£5.5m. In fact, the present value also becomes negative. *What does this mean?*

The negative present value is saying: *in the context of a 25% discount rate, the company is already worthless!*

New shareholders, it follows, are highly unlikely to see their money back should this be the performance of the business. Their IRR would be close to -8% per annum, assuming the business is able to carry on trading. One could reasonably argue that at these slower rates of growth, less capital expenditure would be required. But even if the £500k of extra funding sought was reduced, it would not change the picture from one of a potentially dire investment. Even lowering the discount rate to 5% would still result in a negative NPV of -£4.25m. *The pre-money valuation of £5m is simply unsupportable.*

What Actually Happened to Vulpine

The Crowdcube round was an astonishing success – but only insofar as they raised £1m. The promotional video was outstanding, featuring the support of a famous former Olympic cyclist. The video was emotive and passionate, making a strong case for building a lasting cycle clothing brand like Rapha, which had already been a great commercial success.

But remember we said that the management had a poor record of meeting their targets? Unfortunately, matters did not improve within the business, and poor choices were made concerning investing the new capital. All the ambitious sales forecasts were missed, and by early 2017 the business had run out of cash. It actually attempted a second Crowdcube round. This rescue funding, presented as a need for more growth capital, was soon exposed and Crowdcube cancelled the round part way through the process.

In April, the business had run out of options, and unfortunately went into receivership. All shareholders – both early stage (including us!) and from the first Crowdcube round – lost every penny of their investment. On 14 May 2017 the *Sunday Times* published an article on the front page of its business section, citing Vulpine as one of the worst cases of crowdfunding gone wrong. The brand does, however, live on – the name and assets were bought by an established business from the receiver.

What Can We Learn from Vulpine?

There are several lessons we can learn from the Vulpine case study, both in relation to the topic of this chapter and in broader commercial terms:

- The first and most obvious lesson is to pay attention to valuation at the outset. A straightforward capital investment appraisal would have told you that this was not a good investment at a £5m valuation.
- Secondly, to question the assumptions: their forecasts did not look credible, especially when considering their past performance. As well as their published prospectus, past accounts were also available to see. It was evident that sales growth had been modest and trading losses disproportionately high. Whilst we all know that past performance does not necessarily predict future performance, in our experience it is an excellent indicator.
- Finally, to consider the management of the business. Whilst the published financial information gave a sufficient clue that all had not been well managed in the past, further investigation (such as talking to other shareholders, customers or even staff) would have revealed this was a business to avoid.

Uses in Negotiation

We will relate just one of several personal experiences using NPV as a powerful negotiating tool.

When selling our first business, Frame Express, in 1989 to a fairly large public company, we produced a comprehensive financial model that gave a present value to the business. Frame Express was a chain of 16 shops in and around London offering a fast picture framing service. Inevitably, during the initial negotiations (over an expensive lunch, for which they very generously picked up the tab!), the managing director

of the company finally asked us what we wanted for the business. Our somewhat ambitious reply was *'£2m'* (around £5m in today's prices).

His response was brutally swift: *'In that case'*, he said, *'let's just all enjoy the lunch and go our separate ways'.* But we remained unfazed and stuck to our position, which we stated was supported by our financial model giving a present value of £2m. This became our opening position and was supported by 'hard' financial facts. Note the inverted commas! Our figures were certainly credible, but naturally on the optimistic side. Furthermore, we, rather cheekily, incorporated cost savings that *they* could make post-acquisition by merging their existing business with ours.

What followed was interesting – in the subsequent days the discussions were about bringing the price down from £2m to a more acceptable level to them. *Our model had created a credible benchmark from which the negotiations started.*

Undoubtedly what they should have done was to robustly challenge the *assumptions* – the forecast cash flows and the discount rate. They could have rightly argued that the forecasts were over-optimistic and that the chosen discount rate was too low for the risks they were taking. And, most importantly, they should never have allowed *us* to factor in to the price the savings and economies of scale that *they* might make. By doing so, they effectively passed this economic benefit to us before they'd even begun.

The final sale took place at £1.75m. The price they paid was undoubtedly at the very top end of any reasonably supportable range of values, but as young entrepreneurs we were naturally delighted!

Key Lessons from Frame Express

There are several lessons worth highlighting:

- Justifying your valuation with a NPV model is extremely powerful in negotiation. Unless the opposing negotiating team is familiar with capital investment appraisal, they may struggle to argue with your numbers.
- If you are presented with a NPV model, challenge all the assumptions used as well as the chosen discount rate. Changing these in your favour could considerably alter your negotiating position.
- Never allow an opposing negotiating team to do the financial appraisal for you. Do this yourself.

Applications of Capital Investment Appraisal

- NPV is the most consistently reliable method of capital investment appraisal. IRR and payback methods have biases. MIRR addresses some of IRR's weaknesses.
- Forecast free cash flows should be adjusted for inflation and presented in real terms (i.e. today's prices).
- There are some excellent applications of these methodologies, such as valuing a potential acquisition, or an angel investment, or being used in negotiations as a tool to justify a particular valuation.

Notes

1. To establish the present value of the company itself, it is essential to add any non-operating assets (that are not factored in the cash flow projections – notably cash) and deduct all non-operating liabilities (notably interest-bearing borrowings).
2. Note that these are just excerpts from the model. There are considerably more workings not shown, including the calculations for IRR. Further assumptions have been made in producing the NPV calculations, but all are regarded as fair and reasonable for the purpose of the exercise.

PART 7

RUNNING A FINANCIALLY INTELLIGENT BUSINESS

7.1 A FINANCIALLY INTELLIGENT BUSINESS

The management team of a financially intelligent business knows *everything significant* about the performance of their business. They understand exactly how their sales are made up: by individual product line or category, and from which customers. They understand how much money is generated *from each of the individual products* – what they cost to create and the gross margin they make on each one. They understand how *the entire operating cost structure* of the business is put together, and consequently how *their final profit figures have been derived.*

Not only do they understand how their profits are made, they are continually measuring their performance against a plan – known as a **budget** – to check they are on track. The moment something drifts out of line, they are aware of it and immediately act to correct the situation. It could be that a product's sales have declined against expectations; or, a large customer has suddenly reduced their purchasing; or, a cost has risen out of line with the budget. *The point is the financially intelligent company knows about the situation immediately*. It can then take action in a timely fashion.

A financially intelligent business is one that goes beyond just producing a set of accounts. They start to apply the information to bring about change.

It is one thing understanding the profit & loss, balance sheet, and cash flow statements, but quite another putting them to effective use. In our experience, so many **SMEs** (Small or Medium-sized Enterprises) produce what they feel are adequate accounting statements and then do very little with them. The profit produced 'is what it is' rather than what they have *deliberately and consciously* created. They fail to appreciate how the generation of better financial data can open their eyes to what is happening in their business, and doing so will in turn profoundly affect their decision-making.

In this final section of the book we are going to see how you can take accounting information and effectively use the data to understand what is happening within the business. This understanding is the first step in increasing *control* and ultimately the *profitability* of a business. We will learn how to become a financially intelligent business!

Good or Bad Performance?

Consider the following statement and subsequent question:

> *'My business made a £10,000 profit last month.'* Is this a good or bad result?

Surely this must be good? Isn't it a decent profit?

> *'Actually, it's **bad**! We'd planned to make £50,000 and are way behind on our plans. We're extremely concerned by this result – it suggests we're heading towards break-even and even a potential loss-making situation in the coming months.'*

Evidently, we misunderstood the situation. It is not good at all.
How about this one:

> *'My business lost £120,000 last month.'* Do you think this is good or bad?

This seems very clear-cut – it is bad. No company can sustain these types of losses…

> *'Actually, it's **very good**. We've been growing rapidly and investing heavily in new infrastructure. Sales are well ahead of plan and we had forecast a loss of £250,000 last month. The £120,000 loss is a terrific result. We're on track to make our first profit in the following quarter.'*

Well, we got that one wrong too! Clearly this is an extremely good result.

What is happening here? It seems our judgement based on the initial statements was entirely wrong. We had not understood *the background* – we had not taken into account the *expectations* of performance. Once we saw the performance in the context of what was *expected* we changed our minds about the situation.

Tesco's Result in 2012

Tesco reported its performance for the six months to 31 August 2012. It came in with a profit of £1.7 billion. Surely by any measure, this is an astonishing profit and shareholders would clearly be popping some of Tesco's own-brand Finest Vintage Champagne? Actually, no, some of them decided to dump their shares. This result was 11.6% down on the previous year and marked the start of Tesco's much-publicised decline from grace. Those who sold the shares then made a good decision – the stock continued to fall over the next three years.

Setting the Benchmark

It is impossible to answer the question of whether a result is 'good' or 'bad' without a clarity of what the *expectation* was in the first place. We need a 'post in the ground' to measure how far we have travelled from that point. We can then state how far we have travelled to meet our goals. In business, this expectation is called a **budget**.

The budget for a business is a key document. It sets out what we expect to achieve during the accounting period in terms of our sales and cost structure, and consequently our profitability and cash flow. We can then very easily measure our progress each month against this *expectation*, and instantly see if some element has gone adrift. The management is then alerted and can either accept the situation as it is or take some corrective action. *The key point is the business has a clear awareness of what is happening.*

Benchmarking Beyond the Profit & Loss Statement

The concept of benchmarking performance against a budget or target can go far beyond the profit & loss statement, which will include sales and costs. We can set benchmarks for sales volumes, percentage gross margins, stock levels, stock turn, debtor days, creditor days, sales per employee, employee turnover… the list of potential measures is almost endless. As well as looking backwards to see how we have done historically, we can also set benchmarks looking into the future. For example, we could monitor the forward order book, which will give us an early warning of potential future increases or decreases in sales (and hence profit) performance.

But just as under-measurement can be a problem, so can over-measurement! Managers can be overwhelmed by too much data and consequently could end up missing or ignoring the figures that are really important. The key is to determine a set of meaningful measures for each component part of a business, and to ensure one individual person is ultimately responsible for the delivery of that measure against the plan. Making this all work – choosing the right measures, ensuring they are monitored by the right team members, and acted upon when necessary – is what outstanding financial intelligence is all about. Whilst we cannot cover all the issues surrounding this topic, this final section of the book will give you a clear idea of where to start.

A Financially Intelligent Business

- A financially intelligent business understands everything significant about the performance of the business, whether this is related to sales, profits, or any other meaningful measure.
- We cannot say whether performance is good or bad without first creating an expectation. In business this is called a budget, and we measure performance against these figures.
- Benchmarking performance can go well beyond the profit & loss statement. However, it is important to be selective to avoid overwhelming management with data.

7.2 THE ANNUAL BUDGETING PROCESS

The budgeting process, if done properly, is a comprehensive appraisal of the expected sales revenues, margins, cost structures and financial resources of the business in the financial year ahead. The clarity of this information is fundamentally important at many levels, including providing an indication of the likely funding requirements the business may have in the period ahead. It will define a key level of expected performance for directors and managers throughout the business. It will ultimately define whether trading has been going well or badly. Welcome to the world of budgets and forecasts.

The Difference between Budgets and Targets

Before we start looking at the process in more detail, it is worth clarifying the difference between a **budget** and a target. The two are frequently muddled up and treated as the same thing. They can, of course, actually be the same thing if you want, but this is potentially a mistake and may cause management disappointment and confusion. Here's our view of the situation.

A budget is a set of figures that you *expect* to achieve for the year. The management team, given a normal set of trading conditions, are expected to deliver this result as a *minimum* performance. All cash flow planning and capital investment are based around these numbers. Clearly things can go wrong, in which case the budget may not be delivered. But there has to be a good reason, otherwise management has failed in some capacity. A target is quite different:

- It is something *aspirational* – a goal to reach for, a number to stretch the management team.
- It will be higher than the budget and is okay to miss.
- If the management team is properly incentivised, it will receive additional remuneration in the form of bonuses if they meet, or get close to meeting, the target results. They should be driving the business *beyond* budget performance levels in order to gain their bonuses.

If the budget is set at the target level, i.e. the aspirational level, then you are setting up a situation for failure and disappointment. If a fairly basic bonus is paid out for meeting the budget, and the budget is actually not very achievable, then part of the way through the year the management team is likely to abandon all hope of getting the desired result and consequently their bonuses.

Love Taste Company Example

The Love Taste Company makes fruit smoothies for the catering and retail trade under the Love Smoothies brand. During good weather, sales spike dramatically, so a generally good summer period results in very substantial sales and profitability.

The UK summer of 2014 proved to be a great year for hot weather, resulting in a superb sales and profit performance. Partly as a result, the 2015 budget was set very high – after all, it did not appear to be such a stretch given the amazing 2014 performance. However, as it turned out, the summer weather in 2015 was a disappointment, and hence actual sales levels fell far short of what – with hindsight – was an overly ambitious budget. Ironically, the business still had shown great progress, but nothing like the budget.

For 2016, the business set a less ambitious budget – one based on the assumption of the poor to average weather of a typical UK summer. They could be certain of meeting this under normal circumstances. A target was also set stretching and incentivising the management to reach beyond this performance.

Fixing the Budget for the Year Ahead

The budget, as described above, is the financial forecast that the company expects to achieve in the accounting period. Budgets are normally set for a single 12-month period, but for large companies with significant capital expenditure, budgets may be for longer periods.

We have already learned how to produce a three-year financial forecast in Chapter 4.5, giving us a month-by-month profit & loss forecast. When we are happy with this model, we 'freeze' the forthcoming 12-month period as our budget. These numbers become the definitive markers against which we measure performance.

Unless there are overriding reasons to do so, this budget will *not change* throughout the 12-month period. It is a fixed point of reference, and the numbers within it will be used for comparison purposes each month in our management accounts, which are explained later.

Profit & Loss

Month:	Jan-21	Feb-21	Mar-21	Apr-21	May-21	Jun-21	Jul-21	Aug-21	Sep-21	Oct-21	Nov-21	Dec-21	Totals
Sales (excl VAT)	**£172**	**£6,880**	**£12,040**	**£15,480**	**£17,200**	**£21,285**	**£21,285**	**£21,285**	**£23,650**	**£23,650**	**£23,650**	**£23,650**	**£210,227**
Cost of Sales	(£60)	(£2,408)	(£4,214)	(£5,418)	(£6,020)	(£7,450)	(£7,450)	(£7,450)	(£8,278)	(£8,278)	(£8,278)	(£8,278)	**(£73,579)**
Gross Profit	**£112**	**£4,472**	**£7,826**	**£10,062**	**£11,180**	**£13,835**	**£13,835**	**£13,835**	**£15,373**	**£15,373**	**£15,373**	**£15,373**	**£136,648**
		65%	*65%*	*65%*	*65%*	*65%*	*65%*	*65%*	*65%*	*65%*	*65%*	*65%*	*65%*
Overheads													
Wages	(£1,667)	(£1,667)	(£3,333)	(£3,333)	(£3,333)	(£3,333)	(£4,167)	(£4,167)	(£4,167)	(£4,167)	(£4,167)	(£4,167)	**(£41,667)**
Rent	(£2,667)	(£2,667)	(£2,667)	(£2,667)	(£2,667)	(£2,667)	(£2,667)	(£2,667)	(£2,667)	(£2,667)	(£2,667)	(£2,667)	**(£32,000)**
Rates	(£1,000)	(£1,000)	(£1,000)	(£1,000)	(£1,000)	(£1,000)	(£1,000)	(£1,000)	(£1,000)	(£1,000)	(£1,000)	(£1,000)	**(£12,000)**
Heat & Light	(£333)	(£333)	(£333)	(£333)	(£333)	(£333)	(£333)	(£333)	(£333)	(£333)	(£333)	(£333)	**(£4,000)**
Cleaning Services	(£750)	(£750)	(£750)	(£750)	(£750)	(£750)	(£750)	(£750)	(£750)	(£750)	(£750)	(£750)	**(£9,000)**
Other Misc Costs	(£479)	(£479)	(£479)	(£479)	(£479)	(£479)	(£479)	(£479)	(£479)	(£479)	(£479)	(£479)	**(£5,750)**
Total Overheads	**(£6,936)**	**(£6,936)**	**(£8,613)**	**(£8,613)**	**(£8,623)**	**(£8,623)**	**(£9,456)**	**(£9,466)**	**(£9,466)**	**(£9,466)**	**(£9,466)**	**(£9,466)**	**(£105,127)**
EBITDA	**(£6,824)**	**(£2,464)**	**(£787)**	**£1,450**	**£2,558**	**£5,213**	**£4,379**	**£4,369**	**£5,907**	**£5,907**	**£5,907**	**£5,907**	**£31,521**
Depreciation	(£1,700)	(£1,700)	(£1,700)	(£1,700)	(£1,700)	(£1,700)	(£1,700)	(£1,700)	(£1,700)	(£1,700)	(£1,700)	(£1,700)	**(£20,400)**
Operating Profit (EBIT)	(£8,524)	(£4,164)	(£2,487)	(£251)	£858	£3,513	£2,679	£2,669	£4,207	£4,207	£4,207	£4,207	**£11,121**
Loan Interest	(£500)	(£491)	(£481)	(£472)	(£463)	(£453)	(£444)	(£434)	(£425)	(£415)	(£405)	(£396)	**(£5,380)**
Profit Before Tax	**(£9,024)**	**(£4,655)**	**(£2,968)**	**(£723)**	**£395**	**£3,059**	**£2,236**	**£2,235**	**£3,782**	**£3,792**	**£3,801**	**£3,811**	**£5,741**
Corporation Tax	£0	£0	£0	£0	£0	£0	£0	£0	£0	£0	£0	£0	**£0**
Profit After Tax	**(£9,024)**	**(£4,655)**	**(£2,968)**	**(£723)**	**£395**	**£3,059**	**£2,236**	**£2,235**	**£3,782**	**£3,792**	**£3,801**	**£3,811**	**£5,741**

Above, we can see a typical 12-month forecast budget summary. These numbers are what the management of the business believe is achievable over the next year. We use these figures as a benchmark against which our actual performance can be measured.

The Rolling Forecast

Once the trading year is under way, we need to have sight of how the year will eventually turn out. At any point during the year, senior management should be able to state the likely annual sales and profit figures based on the performance so far during the year. We are often astounded that many business owners are unable to answer the simple question *'What annual sales and profit are you expecting for this financial year?'* An estimate of these figures should roll off their tongue with ease!

If performance had been running exactly at the budgeted figures, then we can easily see what the outcome will be. But most businesses inevitably perform differently from their original budget. Perhaps, with the benefit of hindsight, the market was considerably more challenging than expected and the budget was too optimistic. Alternatively, management may have been overly cautious, and the budget figures should have been more demanding. Regardless of the reasons, as the year progresses we need clarity on what the *outcome* is going to be.

The way to do this is to make a second copy of the Excel document that was used to make the budget. This document is then called a **rolling forecast**. As the months go by, we input the *actual performance* into the spreadsheet, overtyping the original budget figures. After each number is input, the year-end forecast will begin to change.

Profit & Loss	Actual Performance —->						Forecast —->						
Month:	Jan-21 Actual	Feb-21 Actual	Mar-21 Actual	Apr-21 Actual	May-21 Actual	Jun-21 Actual	Jul-21 Budget	Aug-21 Budget	Sep-21 Budget	Oct-21 Budget	Nov-21 Budget	Dec-21 Budget	Totals Forecast
Sales (excl VAT)	**£320**	**£7,540**	**£13,890**	**£17,600**	**£19,300**	**£23,100**	**£21,285**	**£21,285**	**£23,650**	**£23,650**	**£23,650**	**£23,650**	**£218,920**
Cost of Sales	(£112)	(£2,800)	(£4,830)	(£6,050)	(£6,300)	(£7,900)	(£7,450)	(£7,450)	(£8,278)	(£8,278)	(£8,278)	(£8,278)	**(£76,002)**
Gross Profit	**£208**	**£4,740**	**£9,060**	**£11,550**	**£13,000**	**£15,200**	**£13,835**	**£13,835**	**£15,373**	**£15,373**	**£15,373**	**£15,373**	**£142,919**
		63%	*65%*	*66%*	*67%*	*66%*	*65%*	*65%*	*65%*	*65%*	*65%*	*65%*	***65%***
Overheads													
Wages	(£1,750)	(£2,250)	(£3,200)	(£3,200)	(£3,200)	(£3,500)	(£4,167)	(£4,167)	(£4,167)	(£4,167)	(£4,167)	(£4,167)	**(£42,100)**
Rent	(£2,667)	(£2,667)	(£2,667)	(£2,667)	(£2,667)	(£2,667)	(£2,667)	(£2,667)	(£2,667)	(£2,667)	(£2,667)	(£2,667)	**(£32,000)**
Rates	(£1,000)	(£1,000)	(£1,000)	(£1,000)	(£1,000)	(£1,000)	(£1,000)	(£1,000)	(£1,000)	(£1,000)	(£1,000)	(£1,000)	**(£12,000)**
Heat & Light	(£333)	(£333)	(£333)	(£333)	(£333)	(£333)	(£333)	(£333)	(£333)	(£333)	(£333)	(£333)	**(£4,000)**
Cleaning Services	(£750)	(£750)	(£750)	(£750)	(£750)	(£750)	(£750)	(£750)	(£750)	(£750)	(£750)	(£750)	**(£9,000)**
Other Misc Costs	(£650)	(£300)	(£550)	(£460)	(£550)	(£479)	(£479)	(£479)	(£479)	(£479)	(£479)	(£479)	**(£5,864)**
Total Overheads	**(£7,190)**	**(£7,340)**	**(£8,550)**	**(£8,460)**	**(£8,560)**	**(£8,789)**	**(£9,456)**	**(£9,466)**	**(£9,466)**	**(£9,466)**	**(£9,466)**	**(£9,466)**	**(£105,674)**
EBITDA	**(£6,982)**	**(£2,600)**	**£510**	**£3,090**	**£4,440**	**£6,411**	**£4,379**	**£4,369**	**£5,907**	**£5,907**	**£5,907**	**£5,907**	**£37,244**
Depreciation	(£1,700)	(£1,700)	(£1,700)	(£1,700)	(£1,700)	(£1,700)	(£1,700)	(£1,700)	(£1,700)	(£1,700)	(£1,700)	(£1,700)	**(£20,400)**
Operating Profit (EBIT)	(£8,682)	(£4,300)	(£1,190)	£1,390	£2,740	£4,711	£2,679	£2,669	£4,207	£4,207	£4,207	£4,207	**£16,844**
Loan Interest	(£500)	(£491)	(£481)	(£472)	(£463)	(£453)	(£444)	(£434)	(£425)	(£415)	(£405)	(£396)	(£5,380)
Net Profit Before Tax	**(£9,182)**	**(£4,791)**	**(£1,671)**	**£918**	**£2,277**	**£4,258**	**£2,236**	**£2,235**	**£3,782**	**£3,792**	**£3,801**	**£3,811**	**£11,465**
Corporation Tax	£0	£0	£0	£0	£0	£0	£0	£0	£0	£0	£0	£0	**£0**
Net Profit After Tax	**(£9,182)**	**(£4,791)**	**(£1,671)**	**£918**	**£2,277**	**£4,258**	**£2,236**	**£2,235**	**£3,782**	**£3,792**	**£3,801**	**£3,811**	**£11,465**

The above is an example of a rolling forecast in action. The first six months are actual performance, whilst the remaining months are the original budget numbers. This then produces an up-to-date forecast of the final year-end result, shown in the far right-hand column.

We can see that with actual figures entered up until June, the year-end result is showing a higher profit before tax of £11,465. This is the result *assuming* the remainder of the year runs to the budget figures. As always, this is just a guide as to the final outcome because few businesses will run exactly to their budget.

What If the Budget for the Rest of the Year Looks Unrealistic?

It may well be that performance is so far ahead, or so far behind, the original budget that using the budget figures for the period July to December (in this example) is now a nonsense. Under these circumstances, the management of the business should produce a revised forecast for these remaining months, reflecting the new reality. The headings of the revised columns will now change from 'budget' to 'forecast'. These changes will provide the necessary validity for the forecast year-end result.

Note this scenario does not mean the budget has changed. The budget remains constant throughout this process – remember it was frozen at the start of the financial year. Here, we are merely making the forecast outcome more accurate.

The Cash Flow Forecast

When updating the rolling forecast model, the cash flow and balance sheet forecasts will also update automatically; this is essential for good management. For example, if the business was trading substantially behind its original budget, it may be that there will be cash flow difficulties in the months ahead. By having clear visibility of this potential problem, management can arrange additional funding or make other adjustments to the cost structure as appropriate. *The point is, future problems should be identified and addressed early.*

Looking Beyond the Year-End

Remember that the rolling forecast is a 3-year model (often with further, less detailed, forecasts stretching out to five years). Whilst the focus has been on the financial year – a 12-month period – as we get to the end of this period our visibility needs to look beyond the year-end. Otherwise, if we only looked ahead as far as the financial year-end, by October we would only be forecasting up to December (assuming a January to December accounting period). This is only looking two months ahead – not a very long period. And by November the situation will be even tighter, and by then we should at least be working on finalising the next year's budget.

If you are using the 3-year financial model, it is relatively easy to look ahead 12 months on a continual basis. As you type in actual figures each month, and review the remaining period of the financial year, you can also keep an eye on the figures in the subsequent financial year. Ask yourself, *do these look logical and achievable?* If not, start to adjust them. Even if they are only fairly crude estimates, they will still give you an indication of profitability and cash flow 12 months ahead.

It is vital to be looking at cash flow projections beyond the end of the current Financial Year – ideally always 12 months ahead.

We learnt this lesson the hard way. We were once approaching our financial year-end, and did not maintain a rolling forecast. As with most businesses, we started the budget too late, often only finalising in January (after the new financial year had started). We discovered that by February we would have a significant cash flow problem. All this was entirely predictable had we been operating the correct procedures described above. As it was, we ran in panic to the bank and hastily arranged some extra short-term funding. Fortunately, we were fundamentally in a sound financial state, and we received funding. But had we been in a precarious financial state, with a weak balance sheet, it would not have been so easy. Trying to arrange funding from a position of weakness is a bad place to be, and can on occasions be fatal for the business. Needless to say, we never repeated this mistake again.

Circumstances When the Budget Can Be Changed

As described above, the budget is frozen at the start of the financial year and is not normally changed throughout the period so we can consistently measure performance against a fixed benchmark. We once met a business owner who said *'We are always on budget'.* When asked *'How is that possible?'* the person replied *'Because we constantly change it each month'.* Clearly, they were somewhat muddled as to the purpose of a budget, and would consequently be unable to accurately determine whether they were doing well or poorly against expectations.

There are, of course, *exceptional* scenarios where a budget may need to be re-drawn mid-year. This would be justified if there were fundamental changes to the cost structure of the business. For example, if the business acquired a competitor and started to integrate the two businesses, then both the sales plans and costs structures in the original budget may be relatively meaningless.

Likewise, if near the start of the financial year there was such a significant shift in the outlook for the business – either upwards or downwards – it may be appropriate to sit down and revisit the budget. *The key determinant is whether it is still meaningful or not.*

The Annual Budgeting Process Steps

As the financial year comes to a close, the rolling forecast is used to develop next year's budget. If the 3-year forecast has been kept up-to-date, then the process should be relatively easy. The more times this annual cycle has been done, the easier it gets.

The process can be summarised as follows:

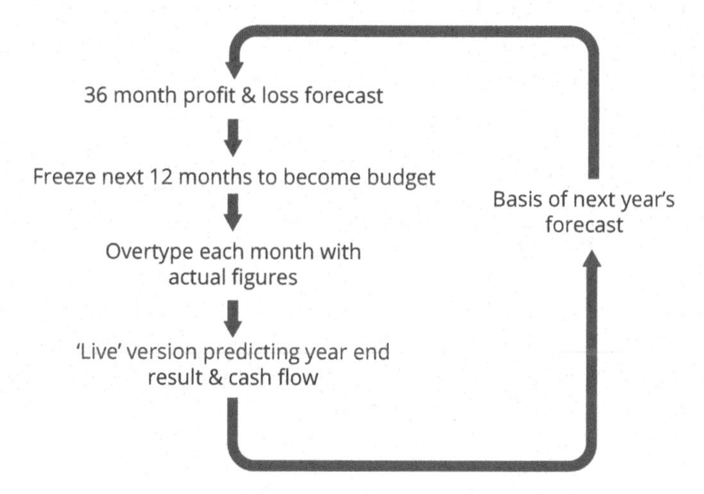

In our experience, the first time a company produces a budget it is never very satisfactory. Part of the problem is down to the fact there is limited historical data in the desired format. As explained in the next chapter, we recommend that the management accounts are reformatted into departmental cost centres. In addition, the formatting of the sales reports may change to give a better understanding of where revenue is coming from.

The budget should mirror these new formats precisely, but the data for the previous year might not be readily available with the same level of detail. It is generally counterproductive to spend too much time trying to reformat the previous year's trading data to reflect any new formats – the energy is better spent looking forward.

Consequently, the first budget should be regarded as somewhat of an estimate. In fact, all budgets are by their nature estimates – it is just this first one is more of an estimate than future ones will be. After the first year's trading, the correctly formatted historic data will make the creation of the second year's budget considerably easier. The management team will also be starting to get used to the approaches outlined below. Each year the accuracy of the budget should improve and become an easier task and the processes should become embedded into the culture of the business.

Internal Management Process

There are no set ways on how a budget should be produced, but the process below is one method that we would recommend. There are two distinct parts to the budget: the sales revenue plan and the cost structure plan. The approach to each of these will be slightly different.

Sales Revenue Plan

The complexity of this will vary from business to business. With our greeting card publishing business, Card Connection, we were able to forecast future volumes very accurately. We had around 15,000 shops selling our cards and knew that each store sold around 90 cards a month on average. We knew which major accounts (who had multiple outlets) were growing and were likely to give us more retail space in the coming year. We also knew of other major customers where the business was declining. Finally, we knew our pricing strategy, and where we were increasing or reducing our prices. All this information could be fed into the Excel model to produce a detailed and cautious sales forecast, which was usually extremely accurate, often to within a few percentage points.

This principle, of working from the bottom up customer by customer, is a way of ensuring a highly accurate sales forecast. For most companies, especially those with a high gross margin percentage, the sales figure will have the greatest impact on the bottom-line profit. Investing time and energy here is a worthwhile exercise.

Forecasting for some other types of business can be more challenging. For example, if selling a consumer product or service online, it may be hard to predict sales if the market is extremely competitive. Customer loyalty may be low and, should competitors' prices suddenly become more attractive, customers could switch completely, causing orders to stop altogether rather than just slow down. Under these circumstances, any sales forecast needs to be on the conservative side.

The important thing is to understand what are the underlying *drivers* of sales volumes and revenues, and build these into your budgeting/forecasting process. In the case of our former greeting card business, the high-level drivers were: number of retail stockists; and sales volume per month per stockist. You will remember in the Carl's Café model, the key drivers were: number of trading days (per month); number of customers per trading day; and average spend per customer.

Cost Structure Responsibilities

The cost structure of the business should be broken down into *logical departments*. For example, there may be sales, product, marketing, customer services, accounts, logistics, and IT departments, all with their own individual budgets. Each department should have a director or manager who is *specifically responsible* for this individual budget, both in terms of its creation *and* delivery.

All cost items in their budget should be their responsibility – there should not be any costs outside their control. Throughout the business every cost should be allocated to the most appropriate department. Because one person is ultimately responsible for each department, then someone is accountable for every single cost. There should be no exceptions.

Creating a good and sensible budget requires strong teamwork between all directors and managers.

Often early-stage businesses have little clarity on how their cost base is made up, and who is individually responsible for managing each element. *Everyone taking responsibility for the cost structure means – in reality – nobody is.* Until this is clearly resolved, a business's costs are likely to run consistently over budget. This was certainly our own painful experience of early-stage growth – each year we would make great progress on sales development, but the final profit would be disappointing because of cost over-runs.

Having identified the appropriate departments and their managers, each should submit to the CFO their plan for the year. Any form of empire building – i.e. putting in large costs to allow for pet projects should be frowned upon in the extreme. In fact, the culture of the business should be the exact opposite. One of our very best directors always managed her budgets extremely responsibly and made every effort to save the company money, so when she asked for some extra funding we knew it was justified, and spent little time evaluating her request. She was always right in her assessment! This is the type of culture you want to encourage – prudence and responsibility. *It is vitally important that the CEO takes an interest in the budgeting process, and places strong emphasis on the team approach.*

Once the CFO has all the sales and departmental cost structures, they are able to build the budget. The first draft is usually a thoroughly disappointing experience, as, when all the costs are taken into account, the profitability appears to be less than expected.

The CEO Now Throws a 'Wobbly'

So far, we have produced the budget from the bottom up. It's now time for a bit of top-down work. Typically, the CEO now gets a little agitated and says *'We've simply got to do better than this!'* This marks the start of the second phase of the budgeting process – further fine-tuning, consultation, and horse-trading begins.

It may be that the sales forecast needs to be a little more ambitious after all. Although this is a budget, and not a target, is it too cautious or pessimistic? Also, the pricing policy could be reviewed – could we maybe put some prices up?

On the cost structure, inevitably there will be costs and projects that have been added, but which are not critical. Can these be removed or delayed? What value do they really add to the business? Is there a better way to achieve the same result without spending so much money?

A useful tool to help establish whether a department's budget is appropriate in size is to measure it as a percentage of sales. For example, if last year the business spent 8% of sales on marketing, and this level of spend worked well for the business, then logic suggests that 8% may be appropriate for the next financial year. Assuming the sales forecast is greater, the new marketing budget would be 8% of this larger sales figure.

Even if it was decided to increase, or decrease, from this 8% level, at least the change would be done in context; in essence saying, '*We have deliberately chosen to increase marketing spend next year. Normally we spend around 8% of sales, but given the increased competition we are consciously increasing it to 10% of sales.*'

A good team of managers and directors will cooperate to come up with a budget that is both realistic and meets the aspirations of the business.

Avoid Creating an Excel Beast

When it comes to building the financial model in Excel it is important to avoid the temptation to have an all-encompassing model that contains every detail from across the company. Should this end up the case, it is likely that too many people will be inputting into the same document, or alternatively that just one individual controls and understands the monumental document. A beast has been created that has consumed the budgeting process and an over-reliance will be placed upon the sole individual who understands it.

A far more sensible approach is for the CFO to get each department to produce its own detailed budget in individual Excel spreadsheets. The broad format for these will be specified by the CFO. For example, the sales team may have a substantial sales spreadsheet with a month-by-month forecast for each individual customer. Likewise, the marketing department may have a spreadsheet with detailed spending on all the various marketing activities throughout the year. The company's financial model does not require all this data in such detail. The CFO can take the *summary data* from all the departmental forecasts and input this into the master financial model.

The Annual Budgeting Process

- The budget is the financial plan produced for the forthcoming or current financial period. We can measure the business's actual performance against this template as the financial year progresses.
- The rolling forecast is a separate financial model, which starts life with the budget figures for the first 12 months. As the months go by, it is updated with actual performance data and, if appropriate, revised projections to give a more accurate forecast of the year-end result.
- The budget is only ever likely to be re-written under extreme circumstances. For example, as a result of the acquisition of another business, or extreme changes in the market.
- Producing a good, meaningful budget requires extensive cooperation between the directors and managers within the business. It is vitally important that the CEO takes an interest in the budgeting process and places strong emphasis on the team approach.

- All costs should be allocated to a specific department, which in turn should have a single person with overall responsibility for its performance against budget.
- Avoid putting all the data into a single Excel document. Instead, allow individual departments to produce their own budgets using a specified template. The CFO can then take the summary data from these when creating the company's master financial forecast.

7.3 MANAGEMENT ACCOUNTS

Properly compiled and presented **management accounts** are a vital component of a financially intelligent business. As the name suggests, their primary purpose is to inform management as to what is happening in the business. They may be produced internally by a suitably qualified employee, or by an external accountant as a service. They may also be produced automatically from bookkeeping software (such as Sage, Xero or QuickBooks), though it is still advisable to get an accountant to set up the initial structure. The key difference from annual statutory accounts is that management accounts can be in whatever format the management finds useful – though it would be unwise to deviate from generally accepted accounting practices and principles. Most well-managed companies produce management accounts every month.

Accounts Unfit for Purpose

The quality of management accounts produced by many small businesses – and even a few larger ones – can be wholly inadequate. Take a look at the profit & loss statement opposite from a real business, which was run off from standard accounting software:

	Jun-13
Income	
Carriage Contribution	60
Interest Income	5
Sales	14,288
Wholesale Sales	33,432
Total Income	**47,786**
Less Cost of Sales	
Standard Cost of Sales	27,414
Stock Movement	(8,283)
Total Cost of Sales	**19,132**
Gross Profit	**28,654**
Less Operating Expenses	
Advertising	475
Bank Charges	34
Bookkeeping	80
Creative consultancy	2,435
Directors' Remuneration	4,000
Ecommerce Fees	318
Employers National Insurance	470
Entertainment-100% business	120
Garment Repairs & Alterations	135
Hotels - UK	1,103
IT Software and Consumables	255
Light, Power, Heating	13
Marketing - Frees & Contras	1,711
Office Costs	28
Packaging Products	46
PayPal fees	41
PR and Marketing Services	1,047
Rent	498
Salaries	2,742
Service charge on premises	158
Storage - Office & Event	247
Telephone & Internet	37
Travel & Subsistence - UK	874
Total Operating Expenses	**16,869**
Net Profit	**11,785**

Firstly, note the terminology varies slightly, with 'Income' being the US term for sales. Net profit is the same as profit before tax. Take a look at the figures and see what you can observe about the company's performance.

On the positive side:

- We can see the business is making a net profit.
- We have visibility of overall sales.
- We can see the costs of achieving this profit.

But that's about it! On the negative side:

- The sales and gross profit analysis is extremely limited and arguably confusing. We need considerably more detail, i.e. sales and margins by individual product group.
- The costs are shown in a long list in alphabetical order. Tiny items are given the same level of importance as more major expenditure. No attempt has been made to group them in logical departments.

- There is no budget to compare the figures against. Should we be pleased or disappointed with a net profit of £11,785? *We have no idea.*
- As well as not having a budget, we have no idea as to how these figures compare to the same period a year ago. *Is performance higher or lower?*
- Finally, this report does not tell us how we are trading year-to-date. Was the profit for this month a one-off, or part of sustained profitability throughout the year? Whilst the above accounting software would be able to produce such a report on a separate sheet, it would be better to see it on the same page if possible.

The Ideal Template for Management Accounts

Whilst inevitably there are numerous ways you could display management accounts, the format below is about as good as you can get and is widely adopted by larger companies.

YOUR COMPANY LIMITED **Month: March 2020**

Month						Year to Date				
2020 Actual	2020 Budget	*Var %*	2019 Actual	*Var %*		**2020 Actual**	2020 Budget	*Var %*	2019 Actual	*Var %*
					SALES					
£ 122,300	£ 115,000	*6%*	£ 98,050	*25%*	Sales	**£ 366,900**	£ 345,000	*6%*	£ 294,700	*24%*
£ 30,300	£ 23,800	*27%*	£ 25,700	*18%*	Cost of Sales	**£ 90,900**	£ 71,400	*27%*	£ 77,100	*18%*
£ 92,000	£ 91,200	*1%*	£ 72,350	*27%*	**GROSS PROFIT**	**£ 276,000**	£ 273,600	*1%*	£ 217,600	*27%*
75%	*79%*		*74%*			***75%***	*79%*		*74%*	
					DEPARTMENTAL COSTS					
£ 16,580	£ 15,500	*7%*	£ 12,600	*32%*	Sales & Marketing	**£ 51,600**	£ 53,000	*-3%*	£ 42,900	*20%*
£ 15,700	£ 12,800	*23%*	£ 12,800	*23%*	Product Development	**£ 39,800**	£ 42,300	*-6%*	£ 41,400	*-4%*
£ 14,750	£ 14,700	*0%*	£ 7,800		Operations	**£ 42,900**	£ 44,100	*-3%*	£ 36,400	*18%*
£ 2,920	£ 3,100	*-6%*	£ 3,580	*-18%*	Accounts & Legal	**£ 9,400**	£ 10,400	*-10%*	£ 10,740	*-12%*
£ 9,200	£ 8,900	*3%*	£ 7,230	*27%*	Admin & HR	**£ 27,300**	£ 23,800	*15%*	£ 21,690	*26%*
£ 7,600	£ 8,100	*-6%*	£ 6,500	*17%*	Directors	**£ 22,800**	£ 21,000	*9%*	£ 19,500	*17%*
£ 66,750	£ 63,100	*6%*	£ 50,510	*32%*	**TOTALS**	**£ 193,800**	£ 194,600	*0%*	£ 172,630	*12%*
55%	*55%*		*52%*			***53%***	*56%*		*59%*	
£ 25,250	**£ 28,100**	*-10%*	**£ 21,840**	*16%*	**EBITDA**	**£ 82,200**	**£ 79,000**	*4%*	**£ 44,970**	*83%*
£ 2,100	£ 2,100	*0%*	£ 2,300	*-9%*	Depreciation	**£ 6,300**	£ 6,300	*0%*	£ 6,900	*-9%*
£ 612	£ 600	*2%*	£ 750	*-18%*	Interest	**£ 1,260**	£ 1,260	*0%*	£ 1,480	*-15%*
£ 22,538	£ 25,400	*-11%*	**£ 18,790**	*20%*	**PROFIT BEFORE TAX**	**£ 74,640**	£ 71,440	*4%*	**£ 36,590**	*104%*
18%	*22%*		*19%*			***20%***	*21%*		*12%*	

This page would be the front page of a management accounts report. It is immediately evident that we can see the big picture of what is happening in the business. Here are some of the things it shows us:

- The left-hand column shows us the performance for the month. We can make comparison for each item against the budget, and also against last year.
- We can see the same analysis year-to-date. This allows us to put the month into context. For example, we can see that the profit before tax is 11% behind the budget for the month, but year-to-date it 4% ahead.

There would be supporting pages for sales – such as a breakdown by various product categories and appropriate gross margins. We can see that sales were £122,300 (against a budget of £115,000) for the month, and that the gross margin was 75% (against a budgeted 79%). The supporting page would show how these figures were made up and which products were responsible for the overall change in gross margin.

Likewise, each department would have a supporting page giving the detail behind the cost structure. Below is the Sales & Marketing Department extract:

SALES & MARKETING DEPT **Month: March2020**

Month						Year to Date				
2020 Actual	2020 Budget	Var %	2019 Actual	Var %		2020 Actual	2020 Budget	Var %	2019 Actual	Var %
£ **2,670**	£ 2,670	*0%*	£ 1,420	*88%*	Salaries & NI	£ **8,100**	£ 8,100	*0%*	£ 4,900	*65%*
£ **360**	£ 360	*0%*	£ 310	*16%*	Pensions	£ **1,080**	£ 1,080	*0%*	£ 930	*16%*
£ **2,440**	£ 900	*171%*	£ 1,445	*69%*	Temporary Staff	£ **3,230**	£ 3,000	*8%*	£ 1,290	*150%*
£ **300**	£ 300	*0%*	£ 430	*-30%*	Staff Training	£ **900**	£ 1,000	*-10%*	£ 860	*5%*
£ **3,470**	£ 3,500	*-1%*	£ 2,400	*45%*	Web Marketing	£ **10,960**	£ 11,000	*0%*	£ 9,840	*11%*
£ **1,300**	£ 1,900	*-32%*	£ 1,980	*-34%*	Other Marketing Media	£ **7,890**	£ 8,000	*-1%*	£ 8,500	*-7%*
£ **2,100**	£ 2,500	*-16%*	£ 1,230	*71%*	Printing	£ **6,300**	£ 7,600	*-17%*	£ 7,840	*-20%*
£ **400**	£ 500	*-20%*	£ 400	*0%*	Samples	£ **1,200**	£ 1,500	*-20%*	£ 1,200	*0%*
£ **1,160**	£ 500	*132%*	£ 460	*152%*	Design Fees	£ **4,800**	£ 4,500	*7%*	£ 1,240	*287%*
£ **50**	£ 50	*0%*	£ 45	*11%*	Magazine Subscriptions	£ **150**	£ 150	*0%*	£ 135	*11%*
£ **120**	£ 120	*0%*	£ 110	*9%*	Telecoms	£ **360**	£ 360	*0%*	£ 330	*9%*
£ **450**	£ 600	*-25%*	£ 580	*-22%*	Entertainment	£ **1,350**	£ 1,800	*-25%*	£ 1,740	*-22%*
£ **1,210**	£ 1,100	*10%*	£ 1,320	*-8%*	Travel & Subsistance	£ **3,630**	£ 3,410	*6%*	£ 2,685	*35%*
£ **550**	£ 500	*10%*	£ 470	*17%*	Misc	£ **1,650**	£ 1,500	*10%*	£ 1,410	*17%*
£ **16,580**	£ 15,500	*7%*	£ 12,600	*32%*	**TOTALS**	£ **51,600**	£ 53,000	*-3%*	£ 42,900	*20%*
14%	*13%*		*13%*			***14%***	*15%*		*15%*	

We knew from the summary page that the Sales & Marketing Department was 7% ahead of budget for the month, but we have no further insight. By looking at the supporting page we can instantly see that there has been substantial spending on Temporary Staff and Design Fees – the CEO is now in a position to question *'Why?'* should she so wish. But in actual fact, when these individual costs are looked at in the context of the year-to-date figures, neither of these are significantly out of alignment with the budget, and overall the Sales & Marketing budget is 3% below the plan. The CEO may therefore decide there are no issues of concern here.

The key issue here is that the CEO is *empowered with information*. She may ignore the overspend on temporary staff; ask for some clarity; or just make a mental note that the business is spending a lot on temporary staff. This might be relevant when talking to her team, or something to watch closely in the subsequent months' accounts.

Moody Sewage Example

We first introduced Moody Sewage in Chapter 4.3 when we described how Darren Hall, the owner, greatly improved his cash flow by collecting payments from customers by Direct Debit. But there is more to this story, which pre-dated this improvement to cash flow management. You may recall the business had been in financial trouble – it had been losing money and owed its main supplier over £130,000. This amount was significant at the time, and Darren was considering entering into **receivership** as a way out of the problem.

The business had three distinct service offerings: emptying septic tanks of sewage sludge; installing new septic tanks; and servicing existing septic tanks by inspecting them every few months. All costs were bundled together in a set of accounts of extremely limited value.

The financial management focus had also been on *short-term* cash planning, not on long-term profitability. Consequently, the business was operating at a loss, and the cash position was bolstered by not paying suppliers. Inevitably, this situation was not sustainable, and a crisis ensued.

The solution was relatively simple, and because Darren was extremely responsive to suggestions, rapid progress was made to correct the situation. We suggested he create three distinct profit & loss statements for each sub-business, or division. Hence all sales and appropriate costs related to the emptying of septic tanks were matched together, and likewise for the installations and servicing parts of the business. A Head Office department was also created for shared services, such as accounting.

The resulting information showed what each business division was contributing to the overall performance. The emptying business was breaking even, the installations business (the largest part) was losing significant amounts of money, and the servicing business was making a small profit.

Once Darren saw this he moved fast. He dramatically improved efficiency and reviewed his pricing across the business. For example, the installations side of the business now operated using strict cost guidelines for each quotation given. Within months the business moved from a loss to making over a £25,000 profit each month, and has made steady progress ever since. The debt mountain of £130,000 no longer seemed to be such a problem and was gradually repaid.

This was a fine example of two things: firstly, how good-quality profit & loss management information can transform a business; and secondly the folly of just focusing on cash flow. It also demonstrates the importance of prompt and appropriate action once equipped with the necessary information.

Gartenart Swimming Ponds Example

Gartenart Swimming Ponds is a successful business run by entrepreneur Tim Evans. The business builds custom-made swimming pools with a difference – the water is naturally purified without the use of chlorine. Not only are they better to swim in, but they also look great and blend into the natural landscape of a garden.

Tim's typical sales value is in excess of £120,000. Each project is a substantial sale and requires considerable oversight to ensure it runs profitably. Unfortunately, Tim was finding that, in a typical year, half of his projects ran over budget on time and cost, which consequently wiped out most of the profit he made on the jobs that went well.

As with the Moody Sewage example, Tim set about ensuring every cost was properly allocated to an individual project, for which a budget had been set. *This allowed detailed analysis of where costs were running adrift.*

Tim also went further. His biggest single cost was labour and if this overran on a project, the consequences were serious. He would either make no money on the job, or worse still actually *lose* money. Our advice to Tim was simple: *align your labour costs more closely to the performance outcome.* Tim introduced a flatter pay structure but with a bonus system whereby his workforce was rewarded for completing work on time or ahead of schedule, but lost all bonus if they overran. Initially, this proved to be unpopular, but the reality for Tim was that the business would never make a proper return unless he took this step.

Within a relatively short period of time, productivity on site started to improve. After their initial reticence, the workforce realised there was an opportunity to earn more money. It was a win–win situation and almost all projects started to complete on, or ahead, of budget. *The key issue was that Tim had aligned his greatest cost – the labour force – with the key performance outcome for the business, i.e. completing the task on time.*

Management Accounts

- Management accounts are produced for the management of the business, and can be in whatever format is most suitable for the business concerned – though still complying with generally accepted accounting practices and principles.
- Ideally, the front summary page of the management accounts should be able to give the CEO an accurate view of the performance of the entire business.
- The ideal template shows the performance for the month, and year-to-date, against both budget and last year. The template should also break costs down by department.
- The supporting pages allow the CEO to delve into more detail. If he or she is not satisfied with what they find, they can then seek further explanation from the director or manager responsible for the individual department.
- The Moody Sewage example shows us how allocating sales and costs appropriately can highlight where we are making or losing money within the business, and how this influences our decision-making. The example also highlights the folly of focusing primarily on cash flow. We need to focus on profitability *and* cash flow simultaneously.
- The Gartenart Swimming Ponds example shows us the power of not only proper budgeting for a project, but aligning the key costs element (in this case labour) with the key desired outcome (completing the project on time, and profitably).

7.4 TRAILING 12 MONTH GRAPHS

If your business is following all the processes described in the previous three chapters, then you are well on the road to outstanding financial intelligence. By this we mean your business has an extremely well-thought-out set of performance reports, and the management team have a keen understanding of their implications.

But let's 'pump up the volume' a bit further and look at what is an extremely easy-to-produce and easy-to-understand tool – trailing 12 Month Graphs (or T12Ms for short). This tool allows you to take your management accounting data to *a new level of usage and understanding*. Used effectively, you can really tune into the pulse of the business and instantly see when something is slipping off-track. You can use them to create knowledge tentacles into all the far-flung places of your business. And, perhaps most importantly, you can share this knowledge with all of your team in a way that they can easily understand. Welcome to the fabulous world of T12M Graphs!

What Is a T12M Graph?

The best way to explain a T12M graph is with an example showing sales, although as you will learn below, their usefulness extends a lot further. Consider the first graph below:

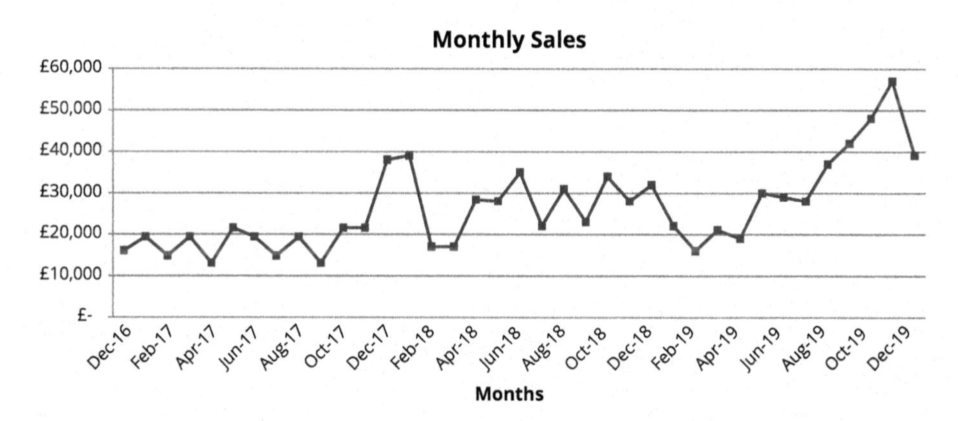

We can see that it shows sales on a monthly basis over a three-year period, and that they jump around a great deal from month to month. It is hard to determine a trend, except in the later months, where there does appear to be an upward trajectory.

We could say, for example, *'February 2018 was a bad month'.* But it may be that February is *always* a 'bad' month because of the seasonality of the business. The seasonality may be unhelpful in determining the trend from a graph viewpoint.

The second graph (below) shows the same data on a T12M basis. Here, we have plotted the previous 12 months' sales *as a total for each point on the graph*. What you are viewing is the *annual sales* of the business at *any point in time*.

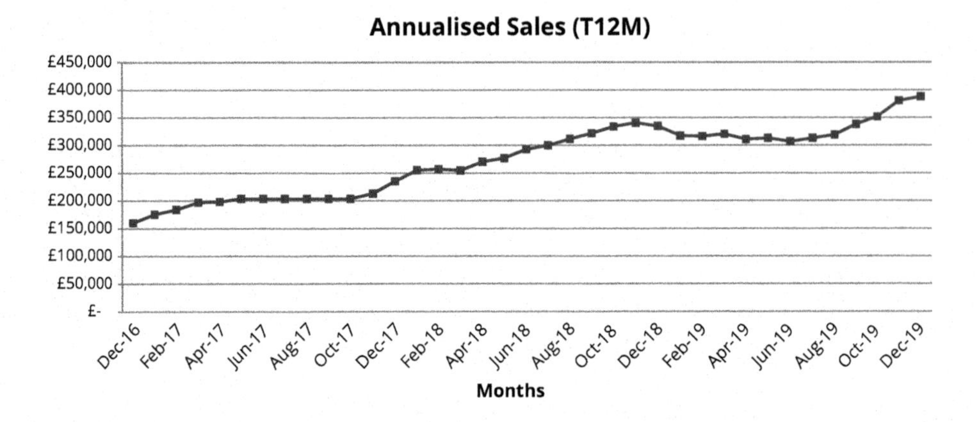

We are, of course, very accustomed to looking at annual sales at the end of each accounting period, but not on a month-by-month basis. Well, this graph is just that – the *annual sales on a monthly basis*. For example, in January 2018 the annualised sales were around £250,000, and in October 2019 they were £350,000.

In case you are still struggling to understand, each plot is exactly 12 months' figures. The plot for December 2017 is January to December 2017 *in aggregate*. The plot for January 2018 will include January 2018 figures, but now exclude January 2017. As each new number comes in, one goes out from the corresponding month in the previous year.

Your Business has Just Shrunk!

What is interesting to see in the above graph, is that in December 2018 the graph dips. Instead of a steady rise over the previous two years, it has started to fall. In fact, during this short period, the company has shrunk in size, and *it is immediately visible*. In many situations such a fall may go unnoticed, possibly for months, and valuable time is lost by the management – if they had known sooner, then some action could have been taken.

T12Ms for Major Customers

An extremely powerful application for T12M sales graphs is to create them for your top customers. Each business is individual, but if, for example, your Top 5 biggest customers accounted for 80% of your sales, tracking their movement is of critical importance. Using T12M graphs is one such way of doing this effectively.

Let's consider the graph below of the fictitious 'Major Customer 4'. Again, each point on the graph shows the annualised sales of this customer, i.e. the annual size of the account at any moment along the graph.

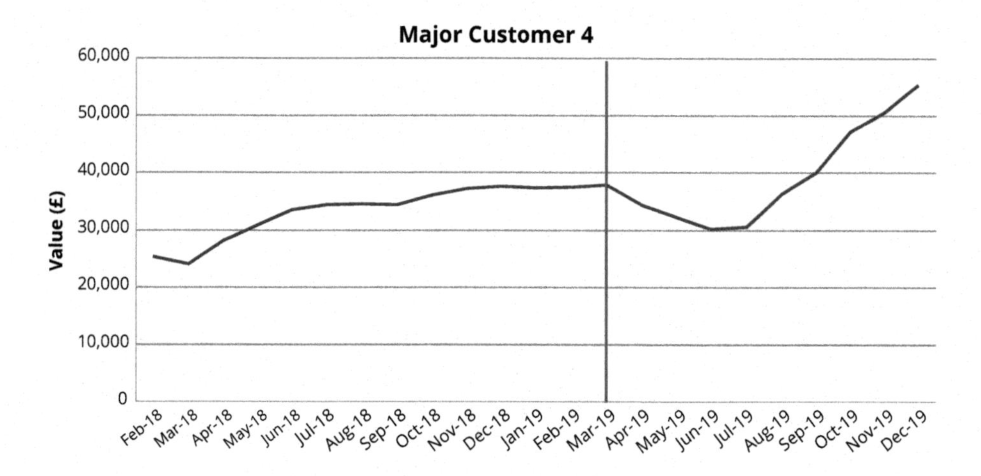

In April 2019 something happens – *the account starts to decline.* In most cases, this may take several months to notice, especially if the figures happened to be larger than the preceding *month*. But what is missed is that they are down on the preceding *year*. However, the above T12M graph shows us that April, May, and June 2019 were *definitely* lower than April, May, and June 2018. The new figures coming into the annualised plotted figure are smaller than the figures coming out, hence the graph is falling.

You could argue that the sales team would immediately notice that April 2019 was below April 2018 without needing the graph to point this out. Yes, maybe they would see this, but if they are busy and have many other customers to worry about, they may have registered one monthly fall and dismissed it as a one-off. Issues of seasonality, or timings of deliveries, can all contribute to disguising what is really happening to the underlying sales with a customer. And, by June, they might have missed such a clear downward trend. Often it is months later before trends are truly realised by management teams. They then take action – but rather belatedly.

Such a simple tool allows for *immediate notification of a downward trend.* There is no long trawl through numbers to work it out – it is plain to see that by May 2019 this customer is going backwards. More to the point, it is also clearly visible to the CEO. He or she is able to see this at a glance and begin to ask the team what is happening about this particular customer. Otherwise they are certainly unlikely to notice, as the data may be buried in a sales report, for which there is insufficient time to study in depth each month.

Once the trend is noticed, clearly action can be taken. Someone can call or visit the customer. *Are they experiencing downward sales pressure, or are they now buying from one of your competitors?* You need to know – both these eventualities are different and each is highly significant. And quick action may make all the difference.

T12Ms for Individual Product Lines

All of the above analysis for a single customer can also be applied to a single product line. This may be helpful to a product manager, for example, who has to keep track of the performance of multiple products or product categories. This simple tool would quickly highlight when progress had stalled.

T12Ms and Departmental Costs

In the above examples we have focused on sales performance T12M graphs. But can we use them to see what is happening to our cost base? The answer is of course yes, and it can be done in two ways.

Looking at the Actual T12M Cost in Pounds

Let's imagine that the graph below is the T12M of the Customer Services Department of a company. It is very helpful in showing us visually that the cost of running this department has been going up in recent months, but it is difficult to say whether this is 'good' or 'bad'. We need to relate it to another criteria, such as sales, in order to get a clearer picture of what is happening.

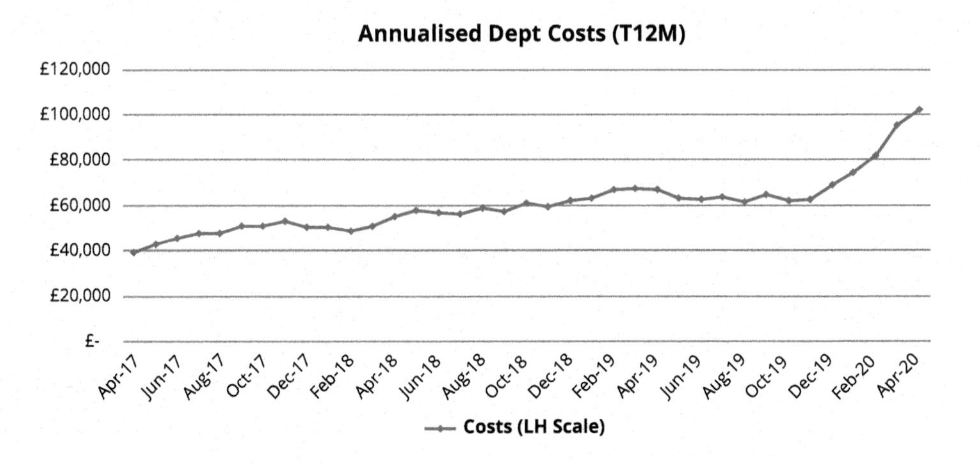

Looking at T12M Cost as a Percentage of Sales

If we now look at the T12M costs as a percentage of the T12M sales, shown in the graph below, we see a very different picture:

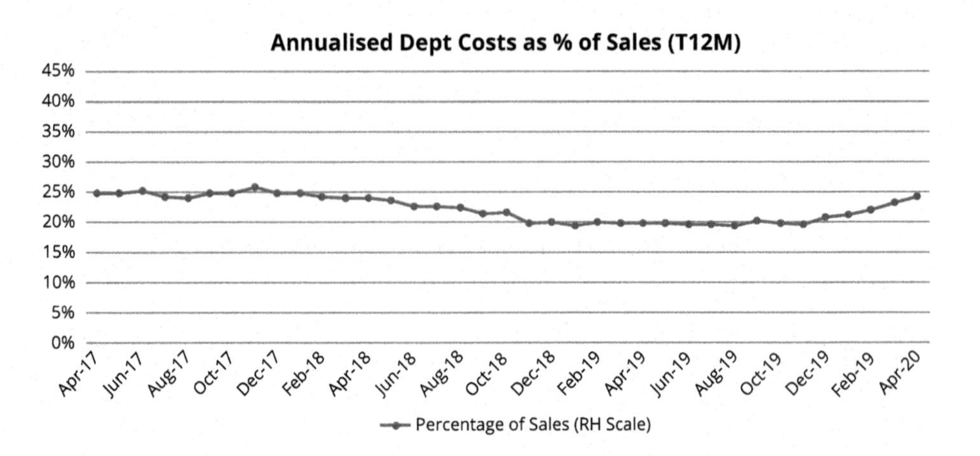

We can see that this department's costs amounted to 25% of sales in December 2017 and steadily fell to being 20% of sales by December 2018. Productivity had improved considerably – *we were spending less on Customer Services than previously.* Assuming the quality of service had not suffered, this could be described as 'good' performance.

From around December 2019 costs begin to rise steadily relative to sales. Whilst sales may have been increasing, the amounts spent on this department have increased at a faster rate. Clearly, the graph alone cannot tell us whether this is 'good' or 'bad' – we need more information. But if there has been no logical reason for this additional cost (i.e. no deliberate enhancements to service) then costs may be rising too fast. It could be that, with the growth in sales, the Customer Services manager has got one step ahead of himself and has enthusiastically over-recruited staff! Maybe this is acceptable; maybe it is not. But the point is the CEO needs to be acutely aware of this trend in the business.

Plotting Both Simultaneously

We recommend plotting both the actual pounds spend and the spend as a percentage of sales on the same graph:

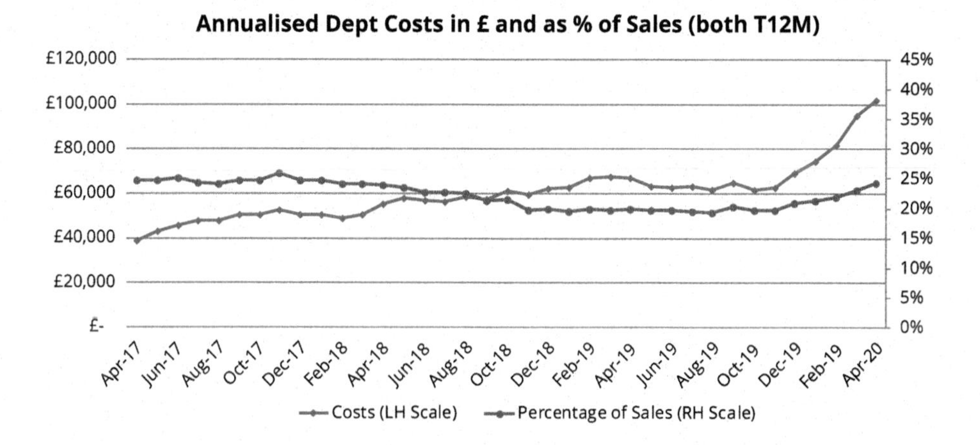

This can feature in the management accounting pack for each department alongside the numbers, or on a separate page of various graphs. Either way, this information is useful for the senior management of the business to track each month.

As an alternative to the above, or, in addition, a target line could be drawn showing where the intended percentage against sales should be. This is another way of tracking the performance against the budget – this time visually.

Dealing with Uneven Seasonality

In the above examples, we have always been looking at a fixed 12-month period, and we have called these T12Ms. But there is no reason why these graphs cannot be for longer, or shorter, periods depending on the individual requirements of the business.

With our greeting card business, the date of Easter moved each year in the calendar. Whilst Easter was not a significant greeting card occasion from a sales viewpoint, Mother's Day most definitely was – and the date of Mother's Day was determined by the date of Easter. Consequently, Mother's Day could be in February some years and March others.

Such a situation would distort a T12M graph, since at certain points one 12-month plot could conceivably contain two Mother's Days. As it was such a significant sales event, this would materially distort the T12M graph.

There are two solutions: the first is to just to live with the distortion, and to recognise when it happens in the data. The second is to change the T12M into a T13M or T14M graph, thus always capturing both years' Mother's Day events regardless of when they occur. The data will therefore always be comparable.

Creating Your Own T12Ms

The easiest way to create your own T12M graphs is to start with our Excel template model, which is available for you to download. This has already been set up to provide the above formats, and can be quickly adapted if it is does not quite match your requirements. Follow the instructions at the start of the spreadsheet.

But be warned – T12M graphs are a little addictive! Identify what really matters to your business and start tracking this data first. *Avoid the temptation to track everything immediately – start small and build from there.* If you introduce too much to your team too quickly, they may become overwhelmed.

Creating Your Own Profitability Map

Profitability mapping is another extremely simple tool that you can employ. It is the process of setting out how the cost structure, and consequently the profitability, should theoretically fit together. If you can achieve the 'map' you can achieve the desired performance.

Profit Map		%
Sales		100
Cost of sales		(40)
Gross profit		**60**
Staff	(12)	
Marketing	(8)	
IT services	(3)	
Finance	(4)	
Premises	(13)	
Total operating expenses		(40)
EBITDA		**20**
Depreciation		(3)
Operating profit		**17**
Interest		(2)
Profit before tax		**15**

In the above example, we have created a theoretical map of how we can get to a 15% profit before tax margin. Instead of just seeing what drops out of the management accounts at the end of the year, we are actively saying:

We expect to achieve a gross margin of 60% on our product sales.
We expect to spend no more that 12% of sales on staff costs.
We expect to spend no more than 8% of sales on marketing.
Etc...

If we achieve all of these we will make a 15% profit before tax margin.

There are limitations to this concept, since if sales expectations are missed in terms of value, all the rest may become potentially meaningless. For example, if our sales are only half our expectation, then we are unlikely to achieve the planned 12% staff costs. But the key benefit is that it provides a framework on which to work, and is a useful tool in the budgeting process. As described earlier, it is helpful to consciously realise we spend 8% of sales on marketing and 4% on finance costs – it allows us to gain some perspective on what is reasonable, particularly in a rapidly scaling business.

Using Profitability Mapping with T12Ms

The profitability map can be used in conjunction with T12M graphs. Below we can see an example where a T12M of operating costs as a percentage of sales has been plotted. The profitability map has been set at 20%, and consequently we can monitor performance against this metric.

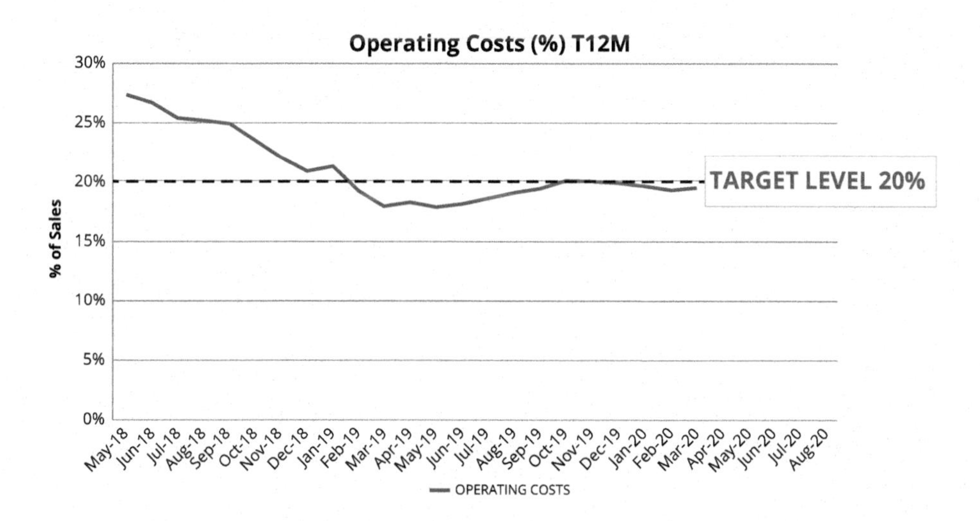

We can easily identify when we are drifting off the planned performance, and it is in a visually clear format for the management team to see. The above graph shows total operating costs, but such graphs can be produced, with appropriate targets, for each and every component of the total, i.e. staff costs, marketing, etc., as well as metrics such as gross margin percentage.

Trailing 12 Month Graphs (T12Ms)

- T12M graphs show 12 months of data for each plot on the graph. The graphs are easy to produce and easy for a management team to understand.
- When used for plotting sales data, they are extremely effective. If the graph dips, the business has just shrunk in size. This is an excellent tool for tracking the sales of a whole company, individual products, or major customers on an individual basis.
- T12M graphs can also be used to track the cost base of the business. Plotting these costs both in value and as a percentage of sales is extremely powerful, as it is a helpful way of keeping a timely track of productivity.
- Mapping out the theoretical profitability of a business is a useful exercise. It gives clarity to how the profitability should come together. It is also helpful when planning budgets by relating the value spend to a percentage of sales.

7.5 LOOKING TO THE FUTURE

All of the processes we have described look at accounting data, either in historical form (i.e. the past management accounts), or in terms of forecasting (i.e. with a 3-year financial model and formal budget).

In doing so, we are looking at the *results* of our performance – either in the past, or as we forecast them into the future. But could we go a little further in our financial intelligence process and try to see whether we can find some data that influences the results we achieve? Something that gives us a forewarning of our future market environment? Would it not be great if we *knew for a fact* what was going to happen in advance to our future performance?

Whilst this may appear at first glance to be a fanciful expectation, in most businesses there are external factors taking place *now* that will change their market's environment, either positively or negatively, *in the future*. We just have to try and find them.

Housing Starts and Completions in the US

The graph below show house starts and completions in the United States going back 50 years.

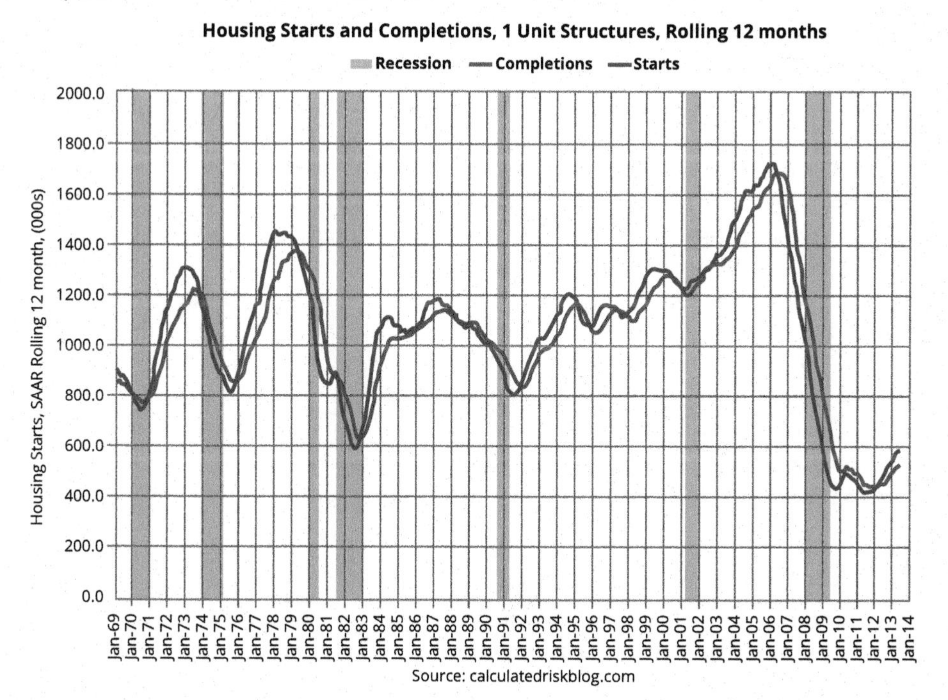

Source: calculatedriskblog.com

Whilst the two lines look like they are on top of each other, they are in fact approximately 9 months apart, reflecting the time it takes to build a house.

Imagine now that we are a roof tile manufacturer, and we tracked house starts closely. We would have a forward indicator as to how busy we were likely to be in around 5 months' time when the roof tiles went on. This could be useful if we were wondering whether now was a good time to start increasing capacity after a slump... we would *know* our market had already turned the corner by the upswing in house starts.

Likewise, we would have an early warning of a potential fall in demand. If house starts were falling rapidly, we would *know* things will get difficult in future months. We could start reducing capacity *now*.

A roof tile manufacturer can get an early indication of future demand by tracking housing starts.

This is just one simple example of a forward-looking key performance indicator (KPI). Such a business could actually also look even further ahead at planning permissions granted. Whilst this is not the same as actual houses being started, it is a long-term indicator of likely future demand.

The business could even track mortgages being granted to consumers. A severe tightening of mortgage credit is likely to lead to a fall in demand for housing, which could *precede* the fall in house starts. So, this may be another forward indicator to track in order to get a feel of what is likely to happen in the coming months or years.

Tracking Your Forward Order Book

The example above relates to *external* macro factors over which the company has no control. *It can only react to the information.* How about a forward-looking indicator that we *can* do something about? A good example might be for a service business such as a firm of management consultants or architects. They could add up the likely value of all the projects they are working on, or are about to start, over the next six months (or whatever period is regarded the most suitable).

Let's imagine this figure comes out at £1.6m and usually runs along at about this sort of level. But one month it suddenly drops to £1.4m, and the following month to £1.2m. We *know for certain*, unless something is done, we are going to see sales fall and be overmanned in the coming months. This information, seen early, is truly valuable – we now have a choice of actions in front of us. We can immediately get our team to focus on generating some new projects, and even if we discover the market is so difficult that a fall in work is unavoidable, at least we are able to start reducing our cost base well in advance.

Five Star Financial Intelligence

We will end this book with a table giving a star rating to the level of financial intelligence a business has reached. It is intended as a discussion tool for a management team and indicates what potential steps could be taken to improve the quality of financial data in the business. From our experience, it takes a while to travel from the early star ratings to a five-star one, but it is a journey worth taking. The rewards are both greater profitability and longer-term financial security.

Star Rating	Typical Level of Financial Intelligence in the Business
*	**Annual accounts produced each year by external accountant** The profit or loss is usually an annual surprise – i.e. no clear expectation of the result: *'It is what it is'.* Trust us, no company should be here!
**	**Basic monthly management accounts** These are frequently in a convoluted format, unhelpful for managing the business. There can also be basic errors – for example, including non-profit & loss items in the statement, such as a monthly loan repayment. **Short-term cash flow planning** This is usually only looking a few weeks ahead, and is frequently associated with 'crisis management' of the cash, i.e. *'Can we pay the wages/suppliers this month?'*
***	**Monthly management accounts with comparison to last year and a budget** This is when some real meaning to the accounts becomes possible. We can start to say performance is good or bad relative to the planned budget, and also relative to last year.
****	**Monthly management accounts as above, plus a rolling forecast of annual outcome and cash flow forecast 12 months ahead** The business is now capable of planning ahead and seeing the potential outcome of decisions in advance. Forward visibility of cash position now allows fund-raising, if required, to take place in a timely fashion. **Basic key performance indicators (KPIs)** These will typically cover gross profit and profit before tax percentage margins, plus a limited number of others.
*****	**Management accounts and forecasts as above, plus extensive KPIs covering entire business** These will analyse gross profit margins across the product ranges as well as covering the entire cost structure of the business. In addition, there will be some financial ratio analysis covering the balance sheet. **Trend analysis** Analysis of trends of the KPIs in the business, using a tool such as Trailing 12 Month graphs. These would cover sales, costs, and margins, with each tracked against target metrics. **Forward visibility of both market and trading performance** Forward looking KPIs monitoring factors in the macro-economic environment, which can impact the performance of the business, as well as any forward order book.

Looking to the Future

- Try and think about what will influence your market in the months ahead. Can you create forward-looking KPIs that will help you *know* – or, at least, make reasonable estimates of – what is going to happen?
- How does your business rate in terms of five-star financial intelligence? Develop a plan with your management team to reach the highest level.

APPENDICES

APPENDIX 1: THE GROSS PROFIT CALCULATION IN A SERVICE BUSINESS

Here are two possible solutions (there will be others):

Solution 1 – Aggregate Revenues and Costs

The first solution is to simply not differentiate between how the employee spent his or her individual hours (i.e. whether on actual contracts or on administration, travel and holidays) and to apply the entire cost to the cost of sales each month.

This method has the advantage of being fairly simple to calculate and if applied to all the employees in aggregate, it should give a consistent and meaningful figure. However, it could mask the productivity of *individual* employees or the true profitability of individual customers.

Solution 2 – Treat Each Job as a Cost Centre

Using this method, the wages would be treated as an operating expense (i.e. below the gross profit line). However, when work was carried out, the specific productive hours would be charged to the jobs (in this case the 20 hours) and would be included in (i.e. debited to) the cost of sales. This amount would then be deducted from (i.e. credited to) the wages below the gross profit line. Hence the wages would appear in two locations in the profit & loss – 'productive' ones in the cost of sales and 'unproductive' ones as an operating expense.

This is more complicated to administer, but highlights the true profitability of each customer. The gross margin percentage for each customer is likely to be more consistent. Unproductive time will also be clearly shown under the expenses and can be monitored separately.

This approach is superior in terms of financial control and would be highly relevant for managing large customers. Should, for example, the cleaning company have large office blocks to service (perhaps at competitive prices) this approach may be critical. They could then ensure each single piece of their business was generating an adequate gross profit. However, if the business was servicing small domestic customers, looking at each customer as an individual cost-centre would probably be overly complicated.

APPENDIX 2: FINANCIAL RATIOS

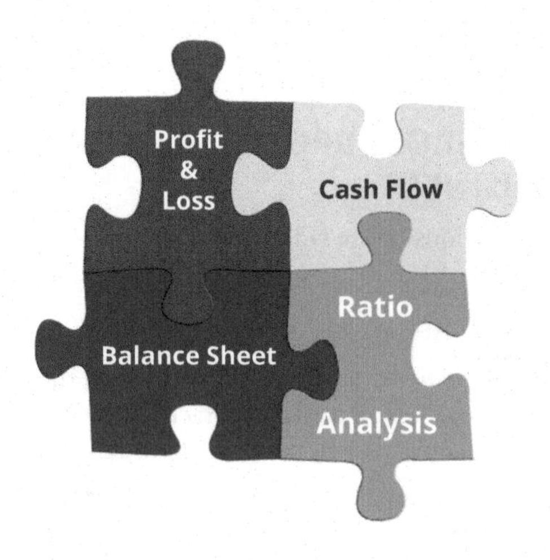

Introduction

Now you have spent time understanding the key statements – the **profit & loss**, **balance sheet**, and **cash flow** – it is time to start using financial ratios. Not only do ratios apply to each statement (e.g. profitability ratios from the profit & loss and liquidity ratios from the balance sheet), they also apply *across* the statements. They put the *absolute* numbers that you will find in the financial statements into a *relative* context. For instance, instead of answering questions such as *'How much profit are we making?'* or *'How much debt are we carrying?'*, ratios can tell you how much profit you are making *relative* to other variables such as sales, or how much debt you are carrying relative to, say, shareholders' equity. As a specific example, **return on capital employed** looks at profitability *relative* to the amount of capital tied up in the business. A business making £1m profit on £2m of capital employed is giving a 50% return. However, a business making a £1m profit on £100m capital employed is just giving a 1% return. They have the same profit figure, but wildly different financial performances.

Ratios are the fourth piece of the puzzle and are useful at illustrating the interconnectivity between the three financial statements. They can provide meaningful insights into the performance of a business and provide clarity on where changes may need to take place.

This appendix is designed to make ratios easy to understand and apply. The tables below will help answer:

- Which ratios should we be using?
- How do we calculate them?
- What does the ratio actually mean?
- What pitfalls may exist when interpreting the ratio?

We have put 'Essential' against the ones that we regard as most vital. In reality, they can all be very important depending on the individual company's situation and market sector. For example, if your business has no debt, you would not need to worry about gearing ratios at all.

If you are running a business, we would recommend you start with a few ratios and track them each month, then, as and when you feel appropriate, add some more to the list.

Five Easy Categories of Ratios

Financial ratios can be divided into five specific categories:

- **Profitability ratios**: How much profit am I making relative to my sales?
- **Gearing ratios** (also known as leverage ratios): How much debt do I have relative to my ability to carry it?
- **Liquidity ratios**: How easily can I pay my debts?
- **Efficiency ratios**: Is my company working efficiently in operational and financial terms?
- **Other ratios**: What are the really important aspects of my business not covered by the ratios above?

The first four categories of ratios are very standard across businesses. However, the fifth category is important because every business has some unique elements to it. Therefore this is your opportunity to invent some ratios that really help you understand what is going on in your business.

Example Financial Statements

The following tables draw upon sample profit & loss and balance sheet statements. These can be found at the end of this appendix, along with a summary of all the ratios.

1. Profitability Ratios		**Profitability ratios are critical. They measure how much profit, at the various different levels, is generated from each £1 of sales. They can also look at how much profit comes back from each £1 the company has tied up in assets. They are best monitored over time.**
Name of ratio & how vital is it?	**How do I calculate it? (£'000)**	**What does it show and why is it important?**
Gross Margin Percentage *Essential*	$Gross\ Margin = \frac{Gross\ Profit}{Sales} = \frac{£4,630}{£6,980} = 66.3\%$	**Shows profit made on a product or service relative to sales.** This is vital to monitor each month. A fall would immediately highlight problems such as wastage, theft or unnoticed supplier price rises. Generally speaking, any gross margin above 50% could be regarded as 'good'. But it is very industry dependent and the best way of benchmarking would be to compare against competitors in the same sector. See Chapters 2.2 and 2.3 for more about gross profit and gross margins.
EBITDA Margin Percentage *Important*	$EBITDA\ Margin = \frac{EBITDA}{Sales} = \frac{£1,070}{£6,980} = 15.3\%$	**Shows profit made from the operation of the business relative to sales.** This is the profit margin of the business without the distortion of Interest charges or depreciation/amortisation. It allows for better comparisons between businesses, which may have significantly different funding situations. Also, depreciation/amortisation can be greatly manipulated. Finally, EBITDA is also the closest profit figure to the actual operating cash flow from the business. But it is far from a perfect measure of profitability, and potentially misleading in capital-intensive businesses. See Chapter 2.1 for more explanation on all the different levels of profit.

Operating Profit (EBIT) Margin Percentage *Important*	*Operating Profit Margin* $= \frac{\text{Operating Profit}}{\text{Sales}} = \frac{£900}{£6,980} = 12.9\%$	**Shows profit made from the operation of the business relative to sales.** An alternative to EBITDA, this is the profit margin of the business without the distortion of interest charges, but it *does* take into account depreciation/amortisation. If depreciation/amortisation is sensibly calculated, operating profit will be a far superior measure of the profit than EBITDA. This ratio, along with **asset turnover**, is a component of **return on capital employed**, and is a measure of the level of profit relative to the sales activity in the business.
Profit Before Tax Margin Percentage *Essential*	*Profit Before Tax Margin* $= \frac{\text{Profit Before Tax}}{\text{Sales}} = \frac{£840}{£6,980} = 12\%$	**Shows the final or 'bottom line' profit relative to sales.** Also known as net margin, this is the final profit figure after taking into account all costs but excluding corporation tax. Generally speaking, any profit before tax margin above 10% could be regarded as 'good'. But, as with gross margin, it is very industry dependent. The profit after tax margin can also be used as an alternative. However, given that the amount of corporation tax paid can vary from year to year according to a variety of factors, including past years' trading losses, a more consistent approach for comparison purposes would be to look at the figures before tax.

1. Profitability Ratios		**Profitability ratios are critical. They measure how much profit, at the various different levels, is generated from each £1 of sales. They can also look at how much profit comes back from each £1 the company has tied up in assets. They are best monitored over time.**
Name of ratio & how vital is it?	**How do I calculate it? (£'000)**	**What does it show and why is it important?**
Return on Equity Percentage *Important*	$Return\ on\ Equity = \frac{Profit\ After\ Tax}{Shareholders'\ Equity}$ $= \frac{£570}{£1,800} = 31.7\%$	**Shows how much profit comes back for each £1 tied up in shareholders' equity (or net assets) in the business.** Profit after tax is the amount of income available from a given period to either distribute to the shareholders or re-invest in the business. This ratio shows the level of return relative to the capital the shareholders have left in the business, i.e. the shareholders' equity, or net assets. It is a key measure of how much wealth is being generated for shareholders. See Chapter 3.3 for more explanation on return on equity.

Return on Capital Employed Percentage *Essential*	*Return on Capital Employed* $= \frac{Operating\ Profit\ (EBIT)}{Shareholders'\ Equity + Debt}$ $= \frac{£900}{£1{,}800 + £250 + £55 + £1{,}080 + £20} = 28.1\%$	**Shows how much profit comes back for each £1 tied up in the total capital used by the business.** This quantifies the operating profitability of a business, and is one of the most important ratios you could ever measure. The greater it is, the more scope there is to expand rapidly without external funding. It is a key measure of the operating efficiency of the business in terms of 'sweating' the assets it employs. It is slightly different than return on equity as it looks at the operating profit relative to the total amount of capital used by the business, which is the shareholders' equity *plus* non-equity capital. Non-equity capital is bank or other interest-bearing debt. Operating profit is used because the profit measure in the numerator must be before payment of interest on any capital included in the denominator. It can in fact be considered in terms of two component ratios, namely **operating profit margin** and **asset turnover**, which when multiplied together will produce the return on capital employed figure. Important notes: • The interest-bearing debt can be in both current liabilities and long-term liabilities. Both must be included if applicable. • Directors' loans made to the business would be included as they are part of the capital employed, even if they were not interest bearing. • Financial, or non-operating, assets are sometimes excluded from the denominator. See Chapter 3.3 for a more detailed explanation of return on capital employed.
	Grow Your Own Cash Just as the best tasting vegetables are those you've grown yourself, so it is that the best source of cash is derived from your own profits. By being fanatical about the *'Essential'* numbers above, and tracking them against budget and last year, it is possible to really drive the profitability of a business forward. In most cases this will lead to a healthy cash flow, and if funding is required, this should be considerably easier to obtain.	

2. Gearing Ratios	**Gearing (or leverage) ratios show how extensively a company is using debt relative to its size and profitability.**	
Name of ratio & how vital is it?	**How do I calculate it? (£'000)**	**What does it show and why is it important?**
Debt to Equity Ratio *Essential*	*Debt to Equity Ratio* $= \frac{Debt}{Shareholders' Equity}$ $= \frac{£250 + £55 + £1,080 + £20}{£1,800} = 0.78$	**Shows how large the company's debt is relative to its net worth. Also known as the gearing ratio.** Note this is not generally expressed as a percentage. Any number greater than one indicates there is more debt than equity – not a healthy situation. Whilst, generally speaking, the lower this number is the better. Other factors are also very relevant. If the industry sector is very volatile (i.e. profits fluctuate wildly), then a low ratio is probably essential. Conversely for a business in a very stable sector it can be higher. Banks will be familiar with what is normal for each industry and therefore acceptable to them. Important notes: • As with the return on capital employed figure, we would include directors' loans, even if these were not interest bearing. • We do not include any trade or other non-financial creditors. See Chapter 3.3 for further explanation on all gearing ratios.
Debt to Capital Ratio *Important*	*Debt to Capital Ratio* $= \frac{Debt}{Capital\ Employed}$ $= \frac{£250 + £55 + £1,080 + £20}{£1,800 + £250 + £55 + £1,080 + £20} = 0.44$	**Shows how large the company's debt is relative to the total capital used.** This is a useful alternative to the debt to equity ratio and shows us what proportion of the total capital employed is made up of debt, rather than equity. This is extremely relevant, and if the industry is volatile (in terms of sensitivity to external factors such as recessions), then this needs to be as low as possible.

Interest Cover *Essential*	$Interest\ Cover = \frac{Operating\ Profit\ (EBIT)}{Annual\ Interest\ Charges}$ $= \frac{£900}{£60} = 15$	**Measures a company's ability to service its interest payment obligations from its operating profits.** Banks are particularly enthusiastic about this number! They want a company to be able to pay interest charges from the profits it is generating. Measuring how many times over it could do this shows how much risk they are facing. In the example, the company could pay it 15 times over so that looks quite safe. However, a sharp rise in interest rates can cause two-way problems for companies, as not only do their interest costs rise but their sales and profits may simultaneously fall due to reduced consumer spending. The ratio may then fall to a point below what the bank requires (this is known a bank covenant). If this happens, the bank can ask for the loan to be repaid, which can then lead to the collapse of the business. See Chapter 5.2 for further explanation on the implications of debt funding.
Debt Service Cover *Essential*	*Debt Service Cover* $= \frac{Operating\ Profit\ (EBIT)}{Annual\ Interest\ Charge + Capital\ Repayments}$ $= \frac{£900}{£60 + £250 + £55} = 2.5$	**Measures a company's ability to service its interest payment and capital repayment obligations from its operating profits.** This ratio is a highly effective way of looking at *both* the interest and capital burdens simultaneously. The denominator includes the interest charge plus the capital repayments due in the next 12 months. It is an indicator as to whether the company has sufficient cash flow to meet these obligations. In our example, operating profit can cover this 2.5 times over, so at present this ratio looks fine. But as stated above, the position could deteriorate rapidly should interest rates rise sharply.
DEBT	**Banks Love These Ratios!** These ratios measure how much of a burden the debt is to a business. This then gives banks a clear indication of the risks they are facing when lending a company money. They want to make certain that their capital is secure, and to ensure that the interest they are due is paid each month. The debt to equity ratio is ideal for the former, whilst the interest or debt service cover ratios work well for the latter.	

3. Liquidity Ratios	Liquidity ratios are critically important. They look at a company's ability to pay its bills. If these ratios are too low, at some point the company will have cash flow difficulties or could even go bust.	
Name of ratio & how vital is it?	**How do I calculate it? (£'000)**	**What does it show and why is it important?**
Current Ratio *Essential*	$Current\ Ratio = \frac{Current\ Assets}{Current\ Liabilities}$ $= \frac{£2,720}{£1,740} = 1.6$	**Shows short term financial strength (or liquidity) of the business.** Note this is not a percentage. 'Current' in accounting terms means less than 1 year. So, current assets are those which can theoretically be turned into cash within a year, and current liabilities are those loans/debts which need to be paid within the next 12 months. If all current assets were turned to cash, could the company easily pay off its debts? If this ratio is less than 1, the answer is no, and is an indicator that the business could face cash flow difficulties in the year ahead. What is the correct ratio? Well if it is >1 the company can pay off its debts, but does it have enough cash to still carry on trading? The ratio, therefore, needs to take this hypothetical scenario into account. It is, however, important to appreciate the ratio is only part of the story. The constitution of a company's current assets is highly relevant. If the value is primarily made up of stock, it is very different to a situation where it is primarily made up of debtors and/or cash. Also, the desirable ratio will be influenced by the stability of the industry – highly predictable profitability performance means a company can safely operate on a lower current ratio than one in a highly volatile and unpredictable market. See Chapter 3.3 for further explanation on both liquidity ratios.

<table>
<tr>
<td>Quick Ratio (also known as the Acid-Test)
Important</td>
<td>Quick Ratio
$= \frac{Current\ Assets - Stock - Prepayments}{Current\ Liabilities}$
$= \frac{£2,720 - £620 - £135}{£1,740} = 1.1$</td>
<td>Shows short term financial strength (or liquidity) of the business. This is similar to the current ratio but removes the value of stock and prepayments. Their removal is for three main reasons:
1. In a crisis situation, such as the business folding, stock may have no practical value (for example if the company no longer existed it could not provide after-sales support). Additionally, prepayments are 'sunk' funds and are unlikely to be turned back into cash.
2. Companies may overinflate the value of their stock by not writing down to zero the value of old or obsolete product (as this would hit their profit before tax figures and make their situation look even worse). This ratio therefore eliminates this risk by removing stock from the calculation.
3. To carry on trading after having theoretically repaid all its debts, a business still needs stock. Hence the correct ratio level still needs to be >1. Basically, the higher the better.
Note you may also see this ratio expressed with prepayments included, and only deducting stock. This is perfectly acceptable but is a less rigorous version of the ratio.</td>
</tr>
<tr>
<td></td>
<td colspan="2">Beware of the Crocodiles!
Over a 10-year period, you can almost guarantee that some nasty thing is going to come along and bite your business. This could be loss of a major customer, your key supplier going bust, a big downturn in consumer spending, or even theft within your company. The list is a long and worrying one. Now here's the point: if the ratios above are very weak (i.e. less than 1 or close to 1) your business may not survive this type of event. On the other hand, if they are very high it is likely that you will be able to sail through the crisis and even come out stronger (e.g. if a competitor of yours did not survive). But what you can be certain of is something is bound to come along to challenge you over a 10-year period, so be ready! This is why these ratios are so vital.</td>
</tr>
</table>

4. Efficiency Ratios	**Efficiency ratios are extremely helpful tools for managing your balance sheet, and hence your cash flow. You could create numerous others to help monitor the efficiency of your business. The ones described below are focusing on financial and trading efficiency.**	
Name of ratio & how vital is it?	**How do I calculate it? (£'000)**	**What does it show and why is it important?**
Stock Days & Stock Turn *Essential*	$Days\ of\ Stock$ $= \frac{Stock}{Cost\ of\ Goods\ Sold\ per\ Day}$ $= \frac{£620}{£2,350/365} = 96.3 = 96\ days$ $Stock\ Turn\ per\ annum = \frac{365}{96} = 3.8\ times$	**Number of days of stock (inventory) holding.** If you carry stock in your business, this is a vital statistic to monitor. If you are holding too much stock, firstly you will have cash tied up unnecessarily, and secondly you will probably have a great deal of stock obsolescence (because of its age it is often no longer saleable). Note that taking the average stock level (over the year) will provide the most meaningful statistic. You can, of course, still work out the ratio based on a single month's figure, or an average of just the start and end of the year. In the example, for simplicity, we have just taken the year-end figure. **Stock turn per annum.** This is another way of looking at stock holding. How many times a year does it turn over? In this example, the company turns their stock over 3.8 times a year. This is equivalent to filling up, then emptying, their warehouse approximately 4 times over in a year. See Chapter 4.2 for more details on stock and other efficiency ratios.

Debtor Days *Essential*	$\text{Debtor Days} = \frac{\text{Trade Debtors}}{\text{Sales per Day}}$ $= \frac{£1{,}530/1.2}{£6{,}980/365} = 66.7 = 67 \text{ days}$	**Shows how quickly a business collects its money from customers.** After you have made a sale, you must collect the money from your customers as soon as possible after the date it is due, otherwise your cash flow will suffer. It is also important to look at this on an aged basis. For example, the average may be 67 days, but if there is a significant amount over 90 days, this would be of concern. Notes: 1. Assuming the company charges VAT, the trade debtors figures will *include* VAT. This needs to be removed in order to be consistent with the denominator, sales per day, which will *exclude* VAT. Otherwise the figures will not be quite comparable. 2. Note that taking the average trade debtors level (over the year) will probably provide the most meaningful statistic. You can, of course, still work out the ratio based on a single month's figure. In the example, it is just taking the year-end figure. But that's not all! In analysing any debtor book, you should also consider the *quality* and *concentration* of the debtors. For example, a debtor book of major companies (Tesco, Sainsburys, BP, Shell, etc.) would be considerably more desirable to a bank than one made up of poor performing SMEs. They would be happier to lend against this portfolio. However, counter to this, what if 90% of the debtor book value was with Tesco? They may be a financially sound customer, but what if they refused to pay their bill as a result of a dispute? Therefore, we also need to consider the concentration of a debtor book around a limited number of customers.

4. Efficiency Ratios	**Efficiency ratios are extremely helpful tools for managing your balance sheet, and hence your cash flow. You could create numerous others to help monitor the efficiency of your business. The ones described below are focusing on financial and trading efficiency.**	
Name of ratio & how vital is it?	**How do I calculate it? (£'000)**	**What does it show and why is it important?**
Creditor Days *Optional*	*Creditor Days* $= \frac{Trade\ Creditors}{Cost\ of\ Sales\ per\ Day}$ $= \frac{£670/1.2}{£2,350/365} = 86.7 = 87\ days$	**Shows how quickly a business pays its suppliers.** Your first thought might be that the longer you take to pay your suppliers the better. The reality is that you need to pay your suppliers on the agreed timescale, which could be 30, 60 or even 90 days. To deliberately go beyond this just causes resentment from suppliers and leads to time spent handling their chasing phone calls, emails, and letters. Also, if a company is already in arrears with its suppliers, it has even less room for manoeuvre in the event of a cash flow crisis. Notes: 1. Assuming the company pays VAT on its purchases from suppliers, the trade creditor figures will *include* VAT. This needs to be removed in order to be consistent with the denominator, cost of sales per day, which will *exclude* VAT. Otherwise the figures will not be quite comparable. 2. Note that taking the average trade creditors level (over the year) will probably provide the most meaningful statistic. You can, of course, still work out the ratio based on a single month's figure. In the example, it is just taking the year-end figure. 3. If there have been large changes in stock levels during the period, it may be necessary to adjust for this to arrive at a more meaningful number. See Chapter 4.3 for ways to improve cash flow.

Cash Conversion Cycle *Important*	*Cash Converstion Cycle* *=Stock Days + Debtor Days − Creditor Days* =96.3 + 66.7 − 86.7 = 76.3 = 76 *days* The 76 days calculated can also be expressed as a value: *76 days × £19k sales per day = £1.4m*	**Measures efficiency of converting company's product (or service) into cash.** A company may have to fund the purchase of raw materials, the manufacturing process, and then the stock holding period. It will also have to fund the debtor period until the customers pays the invoice. This can all be expressed in terms of days. Offsetting this lag is the number of days credit the company receives from its suppliers. So, if the period of credit is deducted it is possible to get the net number of days it takes to convert the investment in product into cash coming in. This can also be expressed as a value by multiplying the number of days by the average sales per day. In this example, the company requires £1.4m of working capital just to fund this process (note this is likely to be *only part* of its required working capital). This will vary greatly from business to business, and a company offering a service may have no stock to finance. See Chapter 4.2 for more details on the Cash Conversion Cycle.
Total Asset Turnover *Important*	$\textit{Total Asset Turnover} = \frac{\textit{Annual Sales}}{\textit{Capital Employed}}$ $= \frac{£6,980}{£1,800 + £250 + £55 + £1,080 + £20}$ *=2.2 times*	**Measures efficiency of use of total assets relative to sales.** This statistic effectively measures how well a company 'sweats' its assets. The recommended formula uses capital employed as the denominator. An alternative would be to use net assets or just non-current assets. But these definitions could be too narrow. A business may not, for example, use many fixed assets but could still have considerable debt capital. This ratio, along with the operating profit margin, is a component of return on capital employed, and is a measure of the level of business activity relative to the assets and capital used in the running of the business.

Efficiency is a Key Driver of Long-Term Profitability

The more efficient you can be in every aspect of your business, the more profit and cash you will generate. Don't be disillusioned if it takes a while to become efficient in all areas of your business. This can understandably take years. However, knowing where you are inefficient is a first vital step in putting things right, which is why these measures are so useful.

5. Other Ratios	Here are some other ratios to look at, all very simple to calculate.	
Name of ratio & how vital is it?	**How do I calculate it? (£'000)**	**What does it show and why is it important?**
Earnings per Share *Optional*	*Earnings per Share* $= \frac{\textit{Profit After Tax}}{\textit{Number of Shares Issued}}$ $= \frac{£570,000}{540,000} = £1.06$ *(In this particular example figures shown are actual numbers, not in £'000).*	**Measures how much wealth each share is generating.** This is vital information when trying to determine a value for the shares. The ratio tells us what each share is generating in terms of profit after tax. A share that is delivering a high income is worth a higher price. This is a key factor that the stock market uses to determine a share price. See Chapter 2.7 for more details on earnings per share and the stock market.
Price/Earnings Ratio *Optional*	$P / E\ Ratio = \frac{\textit{Share Price}}{\textit{Earnings per Share}}$ $= \frac{£17}{£1.06} = 16\ \textit{times}$ *(In this particular example figures shown are actual numbers, not in £'000).*	**Shows how 'expensive' a share is relative to current earnings.** In this example, it is assumed that the share price is £17. If each share generates £1.06 in income each year, then the price is 16 times this amount. In other words, it would take 16 years to get the capital back at this level of earnings (assuming that the share was not sold). This is highly valuable information for the stock market – traders can easily compare two companies in the same sector and use it to help decide which one is better value. A key thing to note is that the P/E ratio will be very influenced by *expectations* of future earnings. A fast-growing company is likely to have a high P/E ratio in anticipation of future earnings growth.

Sustainable Growth Rate *Optional*	*Sustainable Growth Rate* $= \text{Return on Equity} \times (1 - \text{Dividend Payout Rate})$ $= \frac{£570}{£1,800} \times (1 - 0.25) = 24\%$ *(Note, for the purposes of the example, we are assuming that 25% of the Profit After Tax is paid as a Dividend)*	**Measures the ability to grow through internal finance.** This is an interesting ratio to look at, because it indicates how fast your business can grow each year without additional outside finance. It should be noted, though, that this ratio informs of the ability of the business to *finance* its own growth. It says very little about the ability of the business to generate opportunities to *reinvest* that finance profitably. However, it is a useful measure and tells us that, if growing beyond this rate, external funding is likely to be required. It also nicely illustrates how improving your profitability would lift this sustainable growth rate figure. See Section 7 for more details on how to drive profitability in a business.
Sales per Employee *Optional*	*Sales per Employee* $= \frac{\text{Annual Sales}}{\text{Average Number of Employees}}$ $= \frac{£6,980,000}{40} = £174,500$ *(In this particular example figures shown are actual numbers, not in £'000).*	**Measures employee productivity.** This is just one of many measures you could use to track employee productivity. In the example on the left, each employee has, on average, effectively generated £174,500 in sales. This has virtually no meaning in isolation, and it will vary considerably from industry to industry. The power of the measure is when it is looked at for one business over a *period of time*. It should ideally be rising steadily or there is something wrong! It is also powerful when comparing similar *competing* businesses – why does one company achieve such better sales per employee than another? For example, you could compare Tesco and Sainsbury's UK data to identify which company was more productive by this measure. See Chapter 7.4 for details on how to plot this type of data over time.

5. Other Ratios	Here are some other ratios to look at, all very simple to calculate.	
Name of ratio & how vital is it?	**How do I calculate it? (£'000)**	**What does it show and why is it important?**
Net Profit per Employee *Optional*	*Net Profit per Employee* $= \frac{\text{Profit Before Tax}}{\text{Average Number of Employees}}$ $= \frac{£840{,}000}{40} = £21{,}000$ *(In this particular example figures shown are actual numbers, not in £'000).*	**Measures employee productivity.** This is more powerful than sales per employee as it is a more bottom line measure. In the example, on average each employee has effectively generated £21,000 in profit. It *does* have meaning in isolation, but as with the ratio above, it is best compared over time or between competing businesses. As an alternative, you could also use gross profit, EBITDA, operating profit or profit after tax, if felt more applicable.
	It's Your Turn! What aspect of your business do you regard as critically important? Which buttons that you press really generate your sales and profits? Are you measuring this in a key ratio? If not, you should, and if you follow the logic shown above it is easy to set up. Plot these on Trailing 12 Month graphs, as shown in Chapter 7.4. Good luck!	

Tulip Greeting Cards

Profit & Loss Statement	**Year to 31 Dec 2019**
	£ '000
Sales	6,980
Cost of sales	(2,350)
Gross profit	**4,630**
Operating expenses	(3,560)
EBITDA	**1,070**
Depreciation	(170)
Operating profit	**900**
Interest	(60)
Profit before tax	**840**
Corporation tax	(270)
Profit after tax	**570**

Tulip Greeting Cards

Balance Sheet	**As at 31 Dec 2019**
	£ '000
FIXED ASSETS	
Tangible fixed assets	1,920
CURRENT ASSETS	
Stocks	620
Trade debtors	1,530
Accrued income	160
Prepayments	135
Other debtors	25
Cash	250
	2,720
CURRENT LIABILITIES (due < 1 year)	
Bank loans	(250)
Hire purchase finance	(55)
Trade creditors	(670)
Corporation tax	(280)
PAYE & VAT	(165)
Other creditors	(85)
Accruals & deferred income	(235)
	(1,740)
NET CURRENT ASSETS	980
LONG TERM LIABILITIES (due > 1 year)	
Bank loans	(1,080)
Hire purchase finance	(20)
	(1,100)
NET ASSETS	1,800
CAPITAL AND RESERVES	
Called up share capital	240
Share premium	300
Revaluation reserve	510
Retained earnings	750
SHAREHOLDERS' EQUITY	1,800

OTHER INFORMATION	
(actual numbers unless indicated)	
Capital employed (£'000)	3,205
Number of shares in issue	540,000
Assumed share price	£17.00
Market capitalisation (£m)	£9.2
Number of employees	40

RATIOS ANALYSIS SUMMARY

PROFITABILITY	
Gross margin	66.3%
EBITDA	15.3%
Operating profit	12.9%
Profit before tax	12.0%
Return on equity	31.7%
Return on capital employed	28.1%

GEARING	
Debt to equity	0.78
Debt to capital	0.44
Interest cover	15.0

LIQUIDITY	
Current ratio	1.6
Quick ratio (acid test)	1.1

EFFICIENCY	
Stock days	96.3
Stock turn	3.8
Trade debtor days	66.7
Trade creditor days	86.7
Cash conversion cycle	76.3
Total asset turnover	2.2

OTHER	
Earnings per share	£1.06
P/E ratio	16.1
Sustainable growth rate	32%
Sales per employee	£174,500
Profit before tax per employee	£21,000

Important Notes:

- In financial statements numbers that are deducted can be shown in brackets, as above. This does not mean that the number is negative. For example, trade creditors is a positive number – money that is owed by the company to its suppliers. However, in a balance sheet this number is *deducted* from the assets as it is a liability and can therefore be shown in brackets.
- The balance sheet shown above contains more detail than you would usually see in a statement. This detail will normally be found in the notes of the accounts, but is shown here in order to clearly illustrate how the example calculations have been done.
- Most of the figures used throughout are in £'000, but in some cases they are actual numbers, or otherwise stated.

APPENDIX 3: CREATING A CAPITAL INVESTMENT APPRAISAL MODEL IN EXCEL

This is not as difficult as you may think, especially if you use our template as a starting point, which is available for you to download. You can then adapt it as appropriate. Below are some explanations and excerpts from our model explaining the process for both NPV and IRR. Note the third step in each case is slightly different.

Net Present Value (NPV)

NPV Method		**2021**	**2022**	**2023**	**2024**	**2025**	**2026**	**2027**	**2028**
Year	0	1	2	3	4	5	6	7	8
Capital Investment:	£500,000								
Discount Rate:	10.0%								
Free Cash Flows		£100,000	£100,000	£100,000	£100,000	£100,000	£100,000	£100,000	£100,000
Final Value									£25,000
Net Cash Flows	(£500,000)	£100,000	£100,000	£100,000	£100,000	£100,000	£100,000	£100,000	£125,000
Discounted Cash Flows	(£500,000)	£90,909	£82,645	£75,131	£68,301	£62,092	£56,447	£51,316	£58,313
NPV:	**£45,155**	<--- This is calculated using Excel's function.							

To create a model, such as the one shown above, follow these simple steps:

1. Create all the input cells, shown in yellow, for all the relevant criteria, for however many years you wish. These are the 'Capital Investment' (shown in cell C20), the 'Discount Rate' (C21), the 'Free Cash Flows' for each of the years you have created (line 22), and a 'Final Value' for the last year (K23).
2. Create a 'Net Cash Flow' line summing up these flows (line 24). It is this line that is discounted.
3. Note that 'Year Zero' is the initial capital outlay. Also note that the last year adds in the Final Value (K23), as if the capital item had been sold.
4. Note that line 26 is entirely superfluous to the NPV calculation and is just shown for illustrative purposes. If you add up this line it comes to the NPV figure created by the Excel function below.
5. Now create the function for calculating the NPV. From the example above, the formula will look like this:

   =NPV(C21,D24:K24)+C24.

D24:K24 is the 'Net Cash Flow' range *excluding* the 'Year Zero' figure of £500k (C24). This outlay is added separately as above, noting this is a negative figure as it is an outflow.

You can write this formula exactly mimicking the layout above:

=NPV(DiscountRate,NetCashFlowRange)+(YearZeroCapitalOutlay)

You must use the correct spacing and brackets exactly as shown, only adjusting the formula for the appropriate cell numbers.

As an alternative to Step 5, or for additional help in Excel, follow these steps:

1. Select from top menu INSERT, FUNCTION.
2. Type in 'NPV' and then select it.
3. If required, type in NPV into the Help function for more support. This will then provide you with more information, both for the mathematics behind the NPV calculation and for assistance with setting it up. But the simplest way is to copy the formatting and the formula layout, as shown above.

Internal Rate of Return (IRR)

IRR Method		**2021**	**2022**	**2023**	**2024**	**2025**	**2026**	**2027**	**2028**
Year	0	1	2	3	4	5	6	7	8
Capital Investment:	£500,000								
Free Cash Flows		£100,000	£100,000	£100,000	£100,000	£100,000	£100,000	£100,000	£100,000
Final Value									£25,000
Net Cash Flows	(£500,000)	£100,000	£100,000	£100,000	£100,000	£100,000	£100,000	£100,000	£125,000
Discounted Cash Flows	(£500,000)	£88,981	£79,176	£70,452	£62,688	£55,781	£49,634	£44,165	£49,123
IRR:	**12.4%**	<--- If this IRR figure is used as the Discount Rate, the NPV will always be zero!							

To create a model, such as the one shown above, follow the same principles of steps 1 to 4 given for the NPV version, but noting that the cell numbers above are different.

For Step 5, the IRR formula for the example above will be:

=IRR(C38:K38,0.1)

Note C38:K38 is the entire range from 'Year Zero' figure of (£500k) shown in red to the final £125k (line 38).

After the comma, insert the value '0.1', which is 10%. This is a 'guess' as to what the rate will be as a starting point. So enter 0.1 and see if it works! For further explanation on what is happening here, type in IRR into the Help function in Excel where a full explanation is given.

For the Modified Internal Rate of Return (MIRR) follow the same principles as above, using the MIRR function in Excel.

Important Note

As mentioned previously, the Excel functions assume the cash flows arrive at the *end of the year*. In reality, this is likely to be incorrect, as most businesses or investments will yield a return *throughout the year*. The effect is to understate the NPV or IRR.

The way around this is to make an adjustment to the cash flows, effectively averaging them with the following year. An example is shown in the 'Advanced' tab of our Excel spreadsheet.

Bibliography

Books

Berman, K. and Knight, J. with Case, J., (2013). *Financial Intelligence.* 2nd ed. Boston, MA, USA: Harvard Business Review Press.

Feld, B. and Mendelson, J. (2011). *Venture Deals.* Hoboken, N.J., USA: John Wiley & Sons, Inc.

Kramers, K., (2002). *CEO Tools.* Stockbridge, GA, USA: Gandy Dancer Press.

Thomson, D., (2006). *Blueprint To a Billion.* Hoboken, N.J., USA: John Wiley & Sons, Inc.

Reports (in addition to sources already referenced in text):

Gurtu, M., (2018). *The Art of Fundraising.* Cambridge, UK: SyndicateRoom.

Websites (in addition to sources already referenced in text):

Bank of England, https://www.bankofengland.co.uk (accessed 2018-19)

Investopedia, https://www.investopedia.com (accessed 2018-19)

GLOSSARY

Note words shown in **bold** in the Description column are also defined elsewhere in the glossary.

Used Throughout Book	Description
Accelerator programme	A programme by which the sponsoring organisation assists and supports the launch and development of start-up businesses. Specific support might include: premises; seed capital; connections; and education and mentorship. Also known as *start-up* or *seed accelerators*.
Accounting equation	The underlying equation that underpins the double-entry accounting system: **debits** = **credits**, or expressed another way, assets = liabilities + **equity**.
Accounts payable	See **trade creditors**.
Accounts receivable	See **trade debtors**.
Accrual	A provision made on the **balance sheet** for costs incurred, but not yet invoiced or paid.
Accrual accounting	The most widely used system of accounting whereby events and transactions are recorded when they become economically significant to the business, rather than, necessarily, when cash changes hands.
Accrual principle	A fundamental principle of **accrual accounting** whereby either **debit** or **credit** values can accrue without there necessarily being an exchange of money. See also **revenue recognition** and **matching principles**.
Accrued income	A **balance sheet** item which shows the total amount at a given point in time that has been recognised as revenue (i.e. goods or services delivered) but for which no invoice has yet been raised.
Accumulated losses	Historical losses that have accumulated and been brought forward, or will be carried forward, in a company's **balance sheet**.
Articles of association	Document setting out the legal basis on which a company is formed.
Assumptions	A set of assumed numbers and other information forming the inputs to a **financial model**.

Used Throughout Book	Description
Authorised share capital	The **share capital** of a company as authorised by the **articles of association** for issue to new or existing shareholders. Such share capital may or may not be actually in issue.
Balance sheet	One of the three key financial statements, it shows running balances of a company's assets, liabilities and **shareholders' equity** at a defined moment in time. It represents a snapshot of the company's financial affairs at that moment.
Banking covenants	Undertakings made by a borrower as part of the terms and conditions of a loan agreement designed to protect the lender. These might include minimum limits on, say, **interest cover**, requiring profits to exceed interest payable by a specified multiple.
Break-even point	The point at which a company is neither making a profit nor making a loss from its trading activity.
Budget	The financial plan for the business set out for the year ahead, and against which actual performance can be measured.
Burn rate	The rate at which cash resources are being consumed by a start-up or early-stage business prior to the build-up of sales revenues. See also **runway.**
Business angel	An individual who actively invests in the unquoted shares of start-up and early-stage businesses.
Called up share capital	The value of **share capital** that has been issued by a company, but which remains partially or fully unpaid for.
Cash conversion cycle	A measure of the net period of time that a business takes to convert cash outlay from the purchase of **stock** to cash inflow from the sale of goods.
Cash flow statement	One of the three key financial statements, it accounts for how cash has moved through a business over a defined period of time. There are two methods that can be used: **direct** or **indirect.**
Capital allowance	An allowance under UK **corporation tax** law whereby certain amounts and types of **capital expenditure** can be deducted from a company's profits to calculate **taxable profits**.
Capital employed	The capital investment necessary for a business to function. It can be calculated either by reference to the amount of assets required, or, more commonly, the amount of funds necessarily invested in the business: **shareholders' equity** + interest-bearing **debt** – non-trading assets.
Capital expenditure	Amounts that a company spends on acquiring **non-current assets** such as property, plant, vehicles, equipment, etc. Also known as *capex*.

Used Throughout Book	Description
Capital investment appraisal	The planning process whereby a business's proposed capital projects (e.g., purchasing new machinery, buying another business, etc.) are assessed with a view to maximising the efficient use of capital resources. Techniques employed will include **DCF** analysis. See also **NPV** and **IRR**.
Cap table	*Capitalisation table* – a ledger setting out all the shareholders, their shareholdings, types of shares, and the percentage of the total equity they each own. It is updated for each equity fund-raising round.
CEO	*Chief executive officer*. Also known as *managing director*.
CFO	*Chief financial officer*. Also known as *finance director*.
Consistency principle	A fundamental principle of accounting whereby accounting practices should remain consistent across a set of accounts and between different periods of time.
Convertible note	A short-term loan to a company by a would-be shareholder as part of a fund-raising round, which can later be converted to **equity**.
Corporation Tax	A tax paid by companies in the UK as a defined percentage of their annual profits.
Cost of capital	The cost of a company's funding expressed as an annualised percentage rate. Funding may be in the form of **equity**, **debt**, or a combination of both (see **weighted average cost of capital**). See also **hurdle rate** and **discount rate**.
Cost of goods sold	See **cost of sales.**
Cost of sales	Costs arising directly from the purchase, manufacture, processing, delivery and sale of products or services sold. Also known as *cost of goods sold (COGS).*
Credit period	Period of credit allowed by a supplier to its customers between issue and settlement of invoices
Creditor days	A measure of the average number of days' credit provided by **trade creditors**. Calculated by dividing the average balance of trade creditors over a given period by the **cost of sales** per day over that same period,
Creditors	Third parties to whom a company owes money, which can include **trade creditors**, **deferred income**, tax authorities, and lenders. In the context of the balance sheet, the total balance of amounts owing to said third parties at a given point in time. Also known as *payables*.
Credits	One side of the **accounting equation**, denoting *sources* of funds or value. Opposite of **debits**.

Used Throughout Book	Description
Crowdfunding	A process for raising **equity** funding, usually through an online platform, that is generally in the form of small investments by a large number of individuals. More likely to be used by early-stage businesses.
Current assets	Assets held in a company's **balance sheet** that are likely to change, or be transacted in some way, on a daily basis as a result of the company's operating or financing activities. Examples include cash, **stock**, **debtors** and **prepayments**.
Current liabilities	Liabilities held in a company's **balance sheet** that have to be settled *within* the subsequent 12 months.
Current ratio	The ratio of **current assets** to **current liabilities** – an indication of a company's ability to settle short-term liabilities from current assets.
Debenture	A document – in the United Kingdom, formally filed at Companies House – which specifies the security enjoyed by a lender over the assets of a company. If accompanied by a floating charge, the holder will rank ahead of unsecured creditors and shareholders in any distribution of capital from the business.
Debits	One side of the **accounting equation**, denoting the deployment, or use, of funds or value. Opposite of **credits**.
Debt	Capital provided by third parties (e.g. banks, hire purchase companies, private individuals, etc.) as a loan or other form of debt instrument.
Debt service cover	The ratio of **operating profit** to total debt servicing payments in a given period (including interest and capital repayments), indicating the level of comfort that lenders can take from a company's ability to pay its debt service liabilities out of ongoing profits.
Debt to capital	The ratio of all interest-bearing debt to the total capital employed by a company. The latter being the sum of interest-bearing **debt** and **shareholders' funds**.
Debt to equity ratio	The ratio of all interest-bearing debt held by a company to its **shareholders' equity**. A key measure of financial **gearing**.
Debtors	Third parties who owe a company money, which can include **trade debtors**, **prepayments** and **accrued income**. In the context of the **balance sheet**, the total balance of amounts owing by said third parties at a given point in time. Also known as *receivables*.
Debtor days	A measure of the average number of days' credit extended to customers. Calculated by dividing the average balance of **trade debtors** over a given period by **sales** per day (inclusive of VAT) over that same period.

Used Throughout Book	Description
Deferred income	A **balance sheet** item which shows the total amount at a given point in time for which payment has been received but not yet recognised as revenue (i.e. goods or services paid for but yet to be delivered).
Direct method of cash flow	A method of presenting the cash flows of a company during a given period by direct reference to different categories of cash in and cash out.
Directors' loans	Loans made to a company by its directors. These are generally 'soft' loans without complex terms and conditions and usually at a zero rate of interest.
Disclosure letter	A document issued as part of the legal process of selling or issuing shares in a company (including a fund-raising round) in which the directors and/or key shareholders disclose any issues that may constitute a breach of the sale agreement.
Discount rate	The rate used in calculating **NPV** to discount future cash flows back to a **present value**. It is likely to be derived from the **weighted average cost of capital**, and is analogous to the **hurdle rate** (or *required rate of return*).
Discounted cash flow (DCF)	A methodology for evaluating the economic benefit of a business project or investment by converting expected associated future cash flows into an equivalent **present value** based on the concept of the **time value of money**.
Dividends	Payments made by a company to its shareholders – pro rata to the number of shares held – as distributions of current or accumulated past **profits after tax**.
Double entry	A fundamental and widely used system of accounting, whereby every transaction, or significant economic event, is recorded on each side of the **accounting equation**: **debits** indicating uses of funds; and **credits** indicating sources of funds.
Due diligence	In the context of a fund-raising round or sale of shares, the process by which the investor or buyer verifies all aspects of the company being invested in prior to completion of the transaction.
Earnings per share (EPS)	The amount of **profit after tax** a company makes in a given year for each share in issue. Calculated as: **profit after tax** ÷ number of shares in issue.
EBIT	*Earnings before interest and tax* – a measure of a company's profits in a given period before the deduction of interest charges or **corporation tax**. Also known as *profit before interest and tax* (PBIT), or **operating profit**.

Used Throughout Book	Description
EBITDA	*Earnings before interest, tax, depreciation and amortisation* – a measure of a company's profits in a given period before the deduction of interest charges, **corporation tax**, **depreciation** or **amortisation**.
EIS	*Enterprise Investment Scheme* – an investment incentivising scheme run by **HMRC** to encourage investment in early-stage and other unquoted UK companies requiring capital. See also **SEIS**.
Equity	Capital provided by the company's shareholders, whether injected as new funds or reinvested from earlier profits.
Financial model	A mathematical model, usually produced in spreadsheet software such as Excel, by which **profit & loss**, **cash flow** and **balance sheet** forecasts can be made based on a set of assumption inputs.
Financial year	In the context of a company's accounting and financial planning cycle, the year up to its chosen year-end, or '*accounting reference date*'. This may or may not coincide with the calendar year.
First Chicago Method (of NPV)	A business valuation method – widely used in the **venture capital** industry – that is well suited to valuing start-up and early-stage businesses. It combines **DCF** methodology with a projected exit multiple to calculate a probability weighted average valuation from a number (usually three) of different projected scenarios. Also known as the *Venture Capital Method*.
Fixed asset register	A register, in the form of a detailed list or database, of individual **fixed asset** items. Likely to hold information on each item such as: date of purchase, cost, supplier, serial number, depreciation rate, accumulated depreciation and current book value, etc.
Fixed assets	Physical (i.e. tangible) assets that are held and used for the long term, such as property, plant and equipment. They form part (or all) of the **non-current assets** of a company.
Fixed & floating charge	A fixed debenture will have an equitable charge over a specific asset (e.g. a freehold building), whilst a floating **debenture** will cover any of the company's assets (such as the **debtor** book). 'Fixed and floating' covers both.
Fixed costs	See **operating expenses**.
Free cash flow	The surplus cash that the company generates after taking into account all its operational needs. This is after **corporation tax**, any increases in working capital requirements, and any **capital expenditure**.

Used Throughout Book	Description
Future value	The value of money to be received or paid out in the future *before* being discounted by a chosen **discount rate** to determine an equivalent **present value**, based on the concept of the **time value of money**. An essential component of **DCF** analysis.
Gearing	In the context of *financial* gearing, the measure of the extent to which a company has funded its capital requirements by the use of interest-bearing **debt**. Also known as *leverage*. See **debt-to-equity ratio** and **debt to capital ratio**.
General partners	Venture capital or private equity firm which sources and administers **venture capital** investments.
Going concern principle	A fundamental principle of accounting by which all values in a company's set of accounts are based on the assumption that the company will continue to trade as a going concern – for instance, that **stock** can be sold in the normal course of business.
Goodwill	An **intangible asset** that can arise in a company's balance sheet on acquisition of another company, representing the difference between the purchase price and the **net assets** of the acquired company.
Gross margin	**Gross profit** expressed as a percentage of **sales**.
Gross profit	Profit from the sale of products or services in a given period after deduction of the **cost of sales**, but before deduction of any other costs or expenses.
Gross sales	The total value of a company's sales of goods and services to customers in a given period, before deduction of refunds, rebates and product returns. Also known as *gross sales revenue* or *gross turnover*.
HMRC	*Her Majesty's Revenue and Customs* – the UK government agency charged with the collection of tax and excise revenues.
Hurdle rate	The minimum rate of return (e.g. **IRR**) that a business project or investment must be expected to provide before a company considers it to be commercially viable. Also known as the *required rate of return*. See also **discount rate**.
Impairment loss	A loss recognised in a company's accounts arising when an asset's recoverable or market value is deemed to have fallen, for whatever reason, below its net book value.
Indemnity	A guarantee from one contractual party to another, for example by a vendor to compensate a purchaser or investor in the event that a specified problem or issue is not resolved post signing of a contract.

Used Throughout Book	Description
Indirect method of cash flow	A method of presenting the cash flows of a company during a given period by reference to its **profit after tax** and making appropriate adjustments from that.
Intangible assets	Assets held in a company's accounts that are deemed to have real value, but no physical presence. Examples include **goodwill** and **intellectual property**. They form part of the **non-current assets** of a company.
Intellectual property (IP)	An **intangible asset** belonging to a company based on intellectual property rights such as patents, copyrights, trademarks, etc.
Interest cover	The ratio of **operating profit** to interest payable in a given period, indicating the level of comfort that lenders can take from a company's ability to pay its interest liabilities out of ongoing profits.
Internal rate of return (IRR)	A measure of the rate of return of a business, a project or an investment. It is calculated by asking what **discount rate** yields a zero **net present value** when undertaking a **DCF** analysis.
IPO	*Initial public offering* – the initial sale of a company's shares to institutional shareholders and the general public when becoming a public company quoted on a stock exchange.
Inventory	See **stock**.
Investor agreement	See **sale and purchase agreement**.
Key performance indicator (KPI)	A chosen measure of performance that is deemed to be highly significant for the management of a business to monitor on a regular basis.
Leverage	See **Gearing**.
LIBOR	*London Inter-Bank Offered Rate* – a benchmark rate of interest, based on the average rate at which leading London banks borrow from each other at a given moment in time. See also **SONIA**.
Limited partners	The providers of funds to **venture capital** or private equity firms. These will include financial institutions (such as pension funds) as well as high net-worth individuals.
Liquidation	A legal process – often in an insolvency situation and conducted by an appointed liquidator – whereby a company's assets are liquidated (i.e. sold off or realised), and its liabilities are settled as far as is possible from the proceeds. A liquidation can be either voluntary or compulsory. Not to be confused with a **liquidation event**.

Used Throughout Book	Description
Liquidation event	In the language of **equity** fund-raising, an event by which the shareholders in a company liquidate, or realise, their investment. Such events could include: an acquisition; a merger; an IPO; or, in a worst-case scenario, a winding-up such as **liquidation** or **receivership**.
Long-term liabilities	A company's **debts** that are due for repayment *beyond* 12 months from a specified date.
Management accounts	Financial statements produced specifically for the management of the business (as opposed to for statutory purposes).
Margin of safety	In context of break-even analysis, this is the amount **sales** can fall before the company reaches its **break-even point**.
Matching principle	A fundamental principle of accounting which specifies that all costs arising directly from **sales** (i.e. **cost of sales**) must be recorded at the same time as the corresponding sale, and that all other expenses should be recorded in the period in which the goods or services in question are consumed.
Materiality principle	A fundamental principle of accounting whereby items can be ignored if the impact is insignificant, or immaterial, to decision-making.
Modified internal rate of return (MIRR)	A measure of the rate of return of a business, a project or an investment. An alternative to **IRR**, it makes provision for the rate at which cash flows are reinvested.
Non-current assets	The total of a company's **fixed assets** and **intangible assets**.
Net cash flow	The difference between the money coming into a business, and the money going out.
Net current assets	A company's **current assets** after **current liabilities** have been deducted.
Net income/ earnings	See **profit after tax**.
Net present value (NPV)	The inferred value enhancement expected to be derived from an investment or business project, calculated by deducting the initial capital outlay from the sum of all future **net cash flows** discounted to a **present value** by the chosen **discount rate**. It is a key element of **DCF** analysis.
Net profit	See **profit before tax**.
Nominal value of shares	The nominal, or face, value of each class of share that a company may have in issue, as specified in its **articles of association**.

Used Throughout Book	Description
Objectivity principle	A fundamental principle of accounting which states that the financial records and statements of a company should be reliable, verifiable and free of bias.
Operating profit	The pre-tax profit of a company that is derived from its day-to-day trading activities. It is calculated by deducting **operating expenses** (including **depreciation** and **amortisation**) from **gross profit**, but it will exclude items that relate to non-trading activities such as interest received or payable. Also known as **EBIT** (*earnings before interest and tax*) or *PBIT* (*profit before interest and tax*).
Operating expenses	The costs of operating the business which tend to be fixed in their nature (e.g. rent) and do not vary with sales volumes. Also known as *overheads*, *fixed costs*, or *operating costs*. Depending on how defined, can also include **depreciation** and **amortisation**.
Operational gearing	A measure of the degree to which changes in **sales** volume affect changes in **operating profit**. It can be approximated by dividing **gross profit** by the **operating profit**.
Opportunity cost	The sacrifice of alternatives when a particular choice is made from two or more mutually exclusive options (i.e. the choice made rules out the availability of the other options).
Option pool	A proportion of **equity** set aside to allocate to current or future employees.
Ordinary shares	The common **share capital** of a company.
Overdraft facility	A short-term flexible **debt** facility with a bank whereby an account holder can withdraw money from their account such that the balance will go below zero.
Overheads	See **operating expenses**.
Payback method	Simple method of **capital investment appraisal** measuring how long it takes for the investment to be returned.
Post-money valuation	The value placed on a company during a fund-raising round, *after* receipt of capital from the issue of new shares. It can be calculated by adding the value of the new shares to the **pre-money valuation**.
Pre-money valuation	The value placed on a company during a fund-raising round, *before* receipt of capital from the new issue of shares.
Pre-seed investment	The formation or very early-stage funding round of a company, with investment typically from the founding entrepreneurs and, possibly, other small investors. Generally, businesses at concept stage.

Used Throughout Book	Description
Preference shares	**Share capital** of a company which has preferential rights over the **ordinary shares** (e.g. regarding voting, **dividends**, **liquidation**, etc.).
Prepayments	A **current asset** held in a company's **balance sheet** arising from payment of an expense before it is used. A typical example is quarterly payment of rent in advance.
Present value	The value of money to be received or paid out in the future, as discounted by a chosen **discount rate** based on the concept of the **time value of money**. An essential component of **DCF** analysis and **capital investment appraisal.**
Price/ earnings (P/E) ratio	Key metric used for comparing the share price relative to its earnings. The higher the figure, the more apparently expensive the share is relative to the profit being generated.
Private equity	See **venture capital**.
Profit & loss statement	Key financial statement setting out the **sales** revenues and all **operating expenses** or other costs of the business over a defined period of time. The difference is the profit or loss in that period.
Profit after tax	Profit after deduction of all costs, expenses and **corporation tax**. Also known as *PAT*, *net profit after tax*, *net earnings*, or *net income*.
Profit before tax	Profit after deduction of all costs and expenses, but before **corporation tax**. Also known as *PBT*, *net profit*, or *income before taxes.*
Prudence principle	A fundamental principle of accounting which states that, when making a judgement call between two or more otherwise legitimate values or methodologies, the company should choose the more prudent option, such that profit or balance sheet values would be lower as a result.
Quick ratio (acid-test)	The ratio of liquid assets to **current liabilities** in a company's **balance sheet** – an indication of a company's ability to settle short-term liabilities from readily realisable assets. Liquid assets in this context are **current assets,** but excluding **stock** and **prepayments**.
Receivership	Situation where a trustee (the *receiver*) is legally appointed to act as the custodian of a company's assets or business operations. The legal process occurs when a company can no longer service its liabilities. The objective of the process is to return the business to a profitable state, though the existing shareholders are likely to lose their investment.

Used Throughout Book	Description
Reinvestment risk	Uncertainty relating to the rate of return that can be achieved on *reinvesting* cash returns from a project or investment.
Required rate of return (RRR)	See **hurdle rate**.
Retained earnings	**Profits after tax** from previous financial years (though, loosely speaking, could include the current year's profits to date) that have been retained as part of a company's capital, i.e. not distributed to shareholders in the form of dividends or share buy backs, or converted to **share capital** as part of a **scrip issue**. Also can be known as the *profit & loss account* in the **balance sheet**. If there are losses, instead of profits, brought forward from previous years, these would be referred to as **accumulated losses**.
Return on capital employed (ROCE)	Fundamental measure of profitability comparing the **operating profit** of a business to the **capital employed** to generate it.
Revaluation reserve	An item in a company's **balance sheet** created to allow for increases in the value of **fixed assets** (notably property) above the original book cost. It is listed as part of **shareholders' equity**, but is not allowable as a distributable profit unless and until the asset is sold and the profit realised.
Revenue recognition principle	A fundamental principle of accounting which defines when a sale should be recognised and recorded in the accounts at the point when value is delivered to the customer.
Risk premium	The amount of expected return offered in excess of a risk-free return.
Rolling forecast	The expected performance of the business for the remainder of the **financial year** based on any revisions of forecast **sales** or **operating expenses**.
Runway	The amount of time a start-up or early-stage company has remaining before depleting its cash resources at its ongoing **burn rate**. Calculated by dividing current cash balance by current or projected burn rate. Also known as *cash runway*.
SaaS	Software as a Service.
Sale and purchase agreement (SPA)	Legal agreement between parties setting out the terms, conditions and consideration concerning the sale of a business or other assets. In case of an investment in equity, can also be called an **investor agreement**.

Used Throughout Book	Description
Sales	The total value of a company's sales of goods and services to customers in a given period, after deduction of refunds, rebates and product returns. Also known as *sales revenue* or *turnover* (in all cases may also be preceded by *'net'*).
Seed investment	First post-formation funding round, usually at commercial validation stage. Investors could be any of those in the **pre-seed** stage and also more likely to include **accelerator programmes** and **business angels**.
Series A investment	The first major funding round of a company, usually led by a **venture capital** fund. Business is likely to be scaling rapidly at this stage. Letters are added to subsequent major funding rounds (i.e. *Series B, C, etc.*).
Scrip issue	The issue of free shares to shareholders, pro rata to their existing shares, which effectively converts **retained earnings** into **share capital**. Also known as a *bonus issue* or *capitalisation issue.*
SEIS	*Seed Enterprise Investment Scheme* – an investment-incentivising scheme run by **HMRC** to encourage investment in start-up and very early-stage UK companies. See also **EIS**.
Share capital	The capital of a company arising from the issue of shares. It forms part of **shareholders' equity**.
Share premium	Part of a company's **shareholders' equity** arising from and accounting for any difference between the issue price of shares and their **nominal value**.
Shareholders' agreement	A private agreement between the shareholders setting out agreed processes for governance of the company and its **share capital**. Will be in addition to, and usually take precedence over, the **articles of association**.
Shareholders' equity	The part of a company's total capital that belongs to shareholders. It comprises **share capital**, **share premium**, **retained earnings**, and reserves. Also known as *shareholders' funds*.
SME	*Small or Medium-sized Enterprise*, defined by the European Union as having less than 250 employees and less than €50m in sales.
SONIA	*Sterling Overnight Index Average*, an important interest rate benchmark administered by the Bank of England. The index is based on actual transactions and reflects the average of interest rates that banks pay to borrow sterling overnight from other financial institutions. The UK financial industry is planning to move to this benchmark in place of **LIBOR** from 2021.

Used Throughout Book	Description
Statutory accounts	A company's annual accounts legally required for distribution to all shareholders and, in the United Kingdom, for the company's tax return to **HMRC** and filing with Companies House.
Stock	Goods owned by a company – and valued in its **balance sheet** – for the purposes of resale as part of its day-to-day trading activities. Such goods may be raw materials for further assembly or manufacture, work in progress, or finished goods ready for sale. Also known as **inventory**.
Stock days	A measure of the amount of **stock** being carried by a company relative to its **sales**. An indication of the average length of time that goods are held in stock before being sold, it is calculated by dividing average stock value by the average cost of goods sold in a given period. Also known as *inventory days*.
Tax credits	Tax reliefs and benefits available to companies, subject to the **HMRC** regulations.
Tax shield	The amount by which a company's **corporation tax** liability is reduced by claiming a deductible expense, such as interest payable.
Taxable profit	A company's annual profit that is suitably adjusted to comply with corporation tax rules. In broad terms, it is calculated as **profit before tax** plus **depreciation** and any other non-allowable expenses less permitted **capital allowances**.
Term loan	A loan, usually from a bank, which has to be repaid over a set term, usually in regular (often monthly) instalments.
Term sheet	A document setting out the terms and conditions of a business sale or funding round, agreed between investors, company and founders/directors prior to actual legal documents being drafted by the lawyers. Also known as *heads of terms*. This document precedes the production of the **sale and purchase agreement** and will generally not be legally binding.
Time value of money	Concept recognising that funds available at a future time may be of less value than funds today. It is a key element of **DCF** analysis.
Trade creditors	Suppliers to a company who have provided goods or services on **credit**. In a **balance sheet** context, the part of **creditors** specifically relating to money owed to these suppliers. Also known as *accounts payable*.
Trade debtors	Customers of a company to whom goods or services have been provided and invoiced but not yet paid for. In a **balance sheet** context, the part of **debtors** specifically relating to money owed by these customers. Also known as *accounts receivable*.

Used Throughout Book	Description
Variable costs	Costs incurred by a company that are directly linked to the volume or value of business transacted. Closely analogous to **cost of sales**.
VAT (value added tax)	An EU-wide indirect tax, based on set percentages, that businesses are required to add to the value of items sold, and collect from customers (known as *output VAT*). They are also required to pay VAT to their suppliers in an equivalent manner (known as *input VAT*), and they pay the surplus of output over input to **HMRC** on a regular basis (often quarterly). The standard rate in the United Kingdom is currently 20%, though some goods have lower or zero rates.
Venture capital (VC)	A source of private equity funding, particularly for post-seed, but still early-stage, companies that are deemed to have high growth and profit potential. Providers of such capital can be specialist firms, funds, or family offices.
Vesting period	Period of time during which an employee of a company accumulates share options that have been granted to them.
Warrants	Specific rights granted to a shareholder to purchase additional shares (at their discretion) at a later date at a pre-agreed price.
Warranty	A guarantee from one contractual party to another, for example that a particular fact is true in all material respects (such as past profits), or that an event in the future will take place (such as a customer order taking place).
Weighted average cost of capital (WACC)	The overall annual percentage that capital (i.e. funding) costs a company to obtain, taking into account their mix between **equity** and **debt** funding. It is likely to be used in determining appropriate **discount** and **hurdle rates** in **DCF** analysis.
Working capital	The amount of capital deployed by a company in funding its operating liquidity. It is loosely equivalent to **net current assets**.

INDEX

Note: Page numbers followed by 'n' refer to notes

Printed by Printforce, United Kingdom